Here's What You Get on the Two CDs:

On the two CDs included with this book, you'll find valuable materials for preparing for the TCP/IP for NT 4 exam. These include:

The Network Press Edge Test for TCP/IP for NT 4

The first CD (on the following page) includes our exclusive testing program from The Edge Group. Simulate the test-taking experience with challenging questions like those you'll encounter on the actual TCP/IP exam. This improved version comes with a simulated "Adaptive Testing" feature that will give you insight into Microsoft's latest testing format.

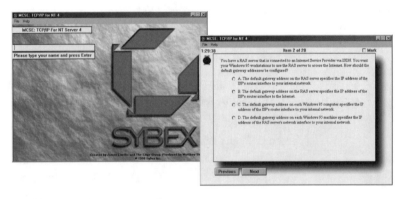

 For additional details, see the following page.

LearnKey's TCP/IP for NT 4 #1 CD-ROM

In the back of the book, you'll find the *TCP/IP #1 CD-ROM* from expert trainers LearnKey, Inc. This $100 product, the first of three CDs in LearnKey's *TCP/IP* course, provides interactive computer-based training covering key TCP/IP topics including the OSI model, IP Addressing, Subnetting, and TCP/IP Utilities. Study with expert video instruction, then use the interactive exercise to test your knowledge.

 For additional details, see the LearnKey pages inside the back cover.

Here's What You Get on the CD:

The CD included with the second edition of the *MCSE: TCP/IP for NT 4* contains invaluable programs and information to help you prepare for your MCSE exams. You can access and install the files on the CD through a user-friendly graphical interface by running the CLICKME.EXE file located in the root directory.

The Sybex CD interface is supported only by Windows 95 and Windows NT. To access the CD contents from Windows 3.x, you must use File Manager.

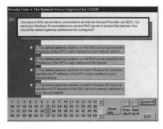

The Sybex MCSE Edge Tests for TCP/IP for NT 4

Test your knowledge with *The Sybex MCSE Edge Test for TCP/IP for NT 4*, a custom version of The Edge Tests, designed exclusively for Sybex by The Edge Group. All of the questions from your Sybex MCSE Study Guide are presented in an advanced testing engine, along with bonus questions to further aid in your studies. To install the Edge Test for Windows 3.1 or 3.11, run the SETUP16.EXE file located in the EDGE\ PLTFRM16 folder on the CD.

Network Press MCSE Study Guide Sampler

Preview chapters from the best-selling line of MCSE study guides from Sybex. We've also included a copy of the Adobe Acrobat Reader, which you'll need to view the various preview chapters. From the core requirements to the most popular electives, you'll see why Sybex MCSE Study Guides have become the self-study method of choice for tens of thousands seeking MCSE certification.

IPCalc 2.0: TCP/IP Address Calculator

Produced by Progression, Inc., *IPCalc 2.0* is a TCP/IP address calculator designed to help you better understand the concepts behind IP addressing. It visually illustrates the bit patterns of an IP address and their behavior as you move from one addressing scheme to another. *IPCalc 2.0* is a 32 bit application and will run on Microsoft Windows 95 or Microsoft Windoes NT. For more product information, visit the Progression Inc. Web site at www.progression-inc.com.

Microsoft Train_Cert Offline Update and Internet Explorer 5

Look to Microsoft's *Train_Cert Offline* Web site, a quarterly snapshot of Microsoft's Education and Certification Web site, for all of the information you need to plot your course for MCSE certification. You'll need to run Internet Explorer 5 to access all of the features of the *Train_Cert Offline* Web site, so we've included a free copy on the CD. To install the *Train_Cert Offline* Web site to your system, run the SETUP file located in the MICROSFT\OFFLINE folder.

Please consult the README file located in the root directory for more detailed information on the CD contents.

MCSE: TCP/IP for NT®
Server 4 Study Guide
THIRD EDITION

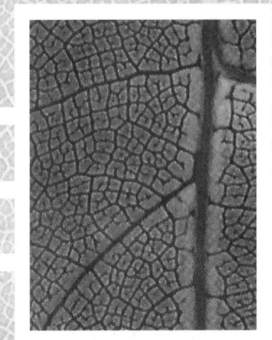

Todd Lammle
with Monica Lammle
and James Chellis

San Francisco • Paris • Düsseldorf • Soest

Associate Publisher: Guy Hart-Davis
Contracts and Licensing Manager: Kristine Plachy
Acquisitions & Developmental Editor: Neil Edde
Editors: Shelby Zimmerman and Brenda Frink
Technical Editor: Jim Cooper
Book Designer: Patrick Dintino
Electronic Publishing Specialist: Kate Kaminski
Production Coordinators: Charles Mathews and Duncan Watson
Indexer: Nancy Guenther
Companion CDs: Molly Sharp and James Chellis
Cover Designer: Archer Design
Cover Photographer: The Image Bank

Library of Congress Card Number: 98-84532
ISBN: 0-7821-2224-8

Manufactured in the United States of America

10 9 8 7 6

November 1, 1997

Dear SYBEX Customer:

Microsoft is pleased to inform you that SYBEX is a participant in the Microsoft®
Independent Courseware Vendor (ICV) program. Microsoft ICVs design, develop,
and market self-paced courseware, books, and other products that support Microsoft
software and the Microsoft Certified Professional (MCP) program.

To be accepted into the Microsoft ICV program, an ICV must meet set criteria. In
addition, Microsoft reviews and approves each ICV training product before
permission is granted to use the Microsoft Certified Professional Approved Study
Guide logo on that product. This logo assures the consumer that the product has
passed the following Microsoft standards:

- The course contains accurate product information.
- The course includes labs and activities during which the student can apply
  knowledge and skills learned from the course.
- The course teaches skills that help prepare the student to take corresponding
  MCP exams.

Microsoft ICVs continually develop and release new MCP Approved Study Guides.
To prepare for a particular Microsoft certification exam, a student may choose one or
more single, self-paced training courses or a series of training courses.

You will be pleased with the quality and effectiveness of the MCP Approved Study
Guides available from SYBEX.

Sincerely,

Holly Heath
ICV Account Manager
Microsoft Training & Certification

MICROSOFT INDEPENDENT COURSEWARE VENDOR PROGRAM

Acknowledgments

The authors would like to recognize with much appreciation their friend and colleague Erik Rozell, whose brilliant technical contribution to several chapters of this book has served to ensure its quality and integrity. Erik is an experienced networking professional certified as a Master CNE, MCSE, and MCT. With a degree in management information systems, Erik directs his own consulting firm, Net Pro Computer Services, in Southern California's San Fernando Valley. This project owes a great debt to Erik's exacting mind and technical expertise. Erik can be reached via e-mail at ERIK@ROCKETMAIL.COM.

We would also like to thank Phil Yee at OnTrak Systems, Inc. who let us test our material in his network lab.

Also crucial to the success of this book were the keen insights and guidance extended generously by Craig Russell, a seasoned Microsoft instructor and integration specialist who owns and operates Craig Russell Connectivity Consulting Inc. Craig's astute eye tirelessly examined and edited our pages, while freely offering important advice throughout this work.

Many thanks are due to Neil Edde. Neil's sharp intellect, wry wit, and positive attitude, combined with his limitless patience, guided the development and evolution of this project. Thanks also to Sybex's Charles Mathews, Duncan Watson, Kate Kaminski, and Brenda Frink, for all their work to make this book a reality.

Contents at a Glance

Table of Contents

Table of Exercises

Introduction

The Microsoft Certified Systems Engineer (MCSE) certification is *the* hottest ticket to career advancement in the computer industry today. Hundreds of thousands of corporations and organizations worldwide are choosing Windows NT for their networks. This means there is a tremendous need for qualified personnel and consultants to help implement NT. The MCSE certification is your way to show these corporations and organizations that you have the professional abilities they need.

This book has been developed in alliance with the Microsoft Corporation to give you the knowledge and skills you need to prepare for the TCP/IP for NT Server 4 exam. Certified by Microsoft, this book presents the information you need to acquire a solid foundation in the field of Microsoft TCP/IP internetworking, to prepare for the Internetworking with Microsoft TCP/IP on Microsoft Windows NT 4.0 exam, and to take a big step toward MCSE certification.

Is This Book for You?

If you want to learn how Microsoft Windows NT TCP/IP works, this book is for you. You'll find clear explanations of the fundamental concepts you need to grasp.

If you want to become certified as a Microsoft Certified Systems Engineer (MCSE), this book is also for you. *Microsoft Certified Professional Magazine* recently completed a survey which revealed that the MCSE certificate adds $11,000 per year to its average holder's salary. If you want to acquire the solid background you need to pass Microsoft's most popular elective exam, take a step closer to your MCSE, and give a big boost to your career efforts, this book is for you.

You can read the entire *Microsoft Certified Professional Magazine* annual salary survey at http://www.mcpmag.com/.

What Does This Book Cover?

Think of this book as your guide to Microsoft Windows NT TCP/IP. It begins by covering the most basic of TCP/IP concepts, such as:

- What is TCP/IP?
- IP addressing
- Subnet addressing
- How do you install TCP/IP?

Next, it covers more advanced topics, including:

- IP routing
- IP address resolution
- NetBIOS name resolution
- Windows Internet Name Service
- Dynamic Host Configuration Protocol
- Internetwork browsing
- Host name resolution
- Connectivity in heterogeneous environments
- Simple Network Management Protocol
- DNS
- Troubleshooting

How Do You Become an MCSE or MCSE+I?

Attaining MCSE or MCSE+I status is a serious challenge. The exams cover a wide range of topics and require dedicated study and expertise. Many people who have achieved other computer industry credentials have had troubles with the MCSE. This challenge is, however, why the MCSE certificates are so valuable. If achieving MCSE or MCSE+I status were easy, the market would be quickly flooded by MCSEs and the certification would quickly become meaningless. Microsoft, keenly aware of this fact, has taken steps to ensure that the certification means its holder is truly knowledgeable and skilled.

Exam Requirements

Successful candidates have to pass a minimum set of exams that measure technical proficiency and expertise:

- Candidates for the MCSE must pass four core requirements and two electives.

- Candidates for the MCSE+Internet must pass seven core and two electives.

Exam #	Title	MCSE	MCSE+ Internet
70-058	Networking Essentials	Required	Required
70-067	Windows NT Server 4.0	Required	Required
70-068	Windows NT Server 4.0 in the Enterprise	Required	Required
70-073 *or* 70-064	Windows NT Workstation 4.0 *or* Windows 95	Required	Required
70-059	**Internetworking with TCP/IP on Windows NT 4.0**	**Elective**	**Required**
70-077 *or* 70-087	Internet Information Server 3.0 and Index Server 1.1 *or* Internet Information Server 4.0	Elective	Required
70-079	Internet Explorer Administration Kit	Elective	Required
70-076 *or* 70-081	Exchange Server 5 *or* Exchange Server 5.5	Elective	Elective
70-026	System Administration for SQL Server 6.5	Elective	Elective
70-088	Proxy Server 2.0	Elective	Elective
70-085	SNA Server 4.0	Elective	Elective
70-018	Systems Management Server 1.2	Elective	Elective

For a more detailed description of the Microsoft certification programs, go to http://www.microsoft.com/train_cert.

This book is a part of a series of Network Press MCSE study guides, published by Sybex, that covers four core requirements as well as the electives you need to complete your MCSE track.

Where Do You Take the Exams?

You may take the exams at any of more than 1000 Authorized Prometric Testing Centers (APTCs) and VUE Testing Center available around the world. For the location of an testing center near you, call 800-755-EXAM (755-3926) or call VUE at 888-837-8616. Outside the United States and Canada, contact your local Sylvan Prometric or VUE registration center.

To register for a Microsoft Certified Professional exam:

1. Determine the number of the exam you want to take.

2. Register with the Sylvan Prometric or VUE registration center that is nearest to you. At this point you will be asked for advance payment for the exam—as of September 1998 the exams are $100 each. Exams must be taken within one year of payment. You can schedule exams up to six weeks in advance or as late as one working day prior to the date of the exam. You can cancel or reschedule your exam if you contact at least two working days prior to the exam. Same-day registration is available in some locations, subject to space availability. Where same-day registration is available, you must register a minimum of two hours before test time.

You may also register for your exams online at http://www.sylvanprometric.com/ or http://www.vue.com/ms/

When you schedule the exam, you'll be provided with instructions regarding appointment and cancellation procedures, ID requirements, and information about the testing center location. In addition, you will receive a registration and payment confirmation letter from Sylvan Prometric or VUE.

Microsoft requires certification candidates to accept the terms of a Non-Disclosure Agreement before taking certification exams.

What is "Adaptive Testing"

Microsoft is in the process of converting all of its exams to a new format, called "adaptive." This format is radically different from the conventional format previously used for Microsoft certification exams. If you have never taken an adaptive test, there are a few things you should know.

Conventional tests and adaptive tests are different in that conventional tests are static, containing a fixed number of questions, while adaptive tests change or "adapt," depending upon your answers to the questions presented. The number of questions presented in your adaptive test will depend on how long it takes the exam to "figure out" what your level of ability is (according to the statistical measurements upon which the exam questions are ranked).

To "figure out" a test-taker's level of ability, the exam will present questions in increasing or decreasing orders of difficulty. By presenting sequences of questions with determined levels of difficulty, the exam is supposedly able to determine your level of understanding.

For example, we have three test-takers, Herman, Sally, and Rashad. Herman doesn't know much about the subject, Sally is moderately informed, while Rashad is an expert. Herman answers his first question incorrectly, so the exam gives him a second, easier question. He misses that, so the exam gives his a few more easy questions, all of which he misses. Shortly thereafter, the exam ends, and he receives his failure report. Sally, meanwhile, answers her first question correctly, so the exam gives her a more difficult question, which she answers correctly. She then receives an even more difficult question, which she answers incorrectly, so the exam gives her a somewhat easier question, as it tries to gauge her level of understanding. After numerous questions, of varying levels of difficulty, Sally's exam ends, perhaps with a passing score, perhaps not. Her exam included far more questions than Herman's included, because her level of understanding needed to be more carefully tested to determine whether or not it was at a passing level. When Rashad takes his exam, he answers his first question correctly, so he's given a more difficult question, which he also answers correctly. He's given an even more difficult question, which he also answers correctly. He then is given a few more very difficult questions, all of which he answers correctly. Shortly thereafter, his exam ends. He passes. His exam was short, about as long as Herman's.

Microsoft is also introducing more simulations into the exams. These simulations require that you complete a task or tasks on an element that looks just like an actual graphical interface from a Microsoft product. If you are familiar with the Microsoft product, you might find these questions to be a bit less abstract, and therefore slightly easier, than similar questions presented in purely text format.

Microsoft moved to adaptive testing for several reasons:

- It saves time, by focusing only on the questions needed to determine a test-taker's abilities. This way an exam which, in the conventional format, took 1 1/2 hours, can be completed in less than half that time. The number of questions presented can far less than the number required by a conventional exam.

- It protects the integrity of the exams. By exposing a fewer number of questions at any one time, it makes it more difficult for individuals to collect the questions in the exam pools with the intent of facilitating exam "cramming."

- It saves Microsoft and/or the test delivery company money by cutting down on the amount of time it takes to deliver a test.

Unlike the previous test format, the adaptive format will NOT allow you to go back to see a question again. The exam only goes forward. Once you enter your answer, that's it; you cannot change it. Be very careful before entering your answer. There is no time limit for each individual question (only for the exam as a whole.) As your exam may be shortened by correct answers (and lengthened by incorrect answers) there is no advantage to rushing through questions.

What the Internetworking with Microsoft TCP/IP on Microsoft Windows NT 4.0 Exam Measures

The Windows NT TCP/IP exam covers concepts and skills required for the support of Windows NT computers running the TCP/IP protocol. It emphasizes the following areas of TCP/IP support:

- Standards and terminology

- Planning

- Implementation

- Troubleshooting

The exam focuses on fundamental concepts relating to Windows NT TCP/IP operation. It can also be quite specific regarding Windows NT requirements and operational settings and particularly about how administrative tasks are performed in the operating system. Careful study of this book, along with hands-on experience with the operating system, will be especially helpful in preparing you for the exam.

Exam objectives are subject to change at any time without prior notice and at Microsoft's sole discretion. Please visit Microsoft's Training and Certification Web site (www.microsoft.com/Train_Cert) for the most current exam objectives listing.

How Microsoft Develops the Exam Questions

Microsoft's exam development process consists of eight mandatory phases. The process takes an average of seven months and contains more than 150 specific steps.

Phase 1: Job Analysis

Phase 1 is an analysis of all the tasks that make up the specific job function based on tasks performed by people who are currently performing the job function. This phase also identifies the knowledge, skills, and abilities that relate specifically to the certification for that performance area.

Phase 2: Objective Domain Definition

The results of the job analysis provide the framework used to develop objectives. The development of objectives involves translating the job function tasks into a comprehensive set of more specific and measurable knowledge, skills, and abilities. The resulting list of objectives, or the objective domain, is the basis for the development of both the certification exams and the training materials.

Phase 3: Blueprint Survey

The final objective domain is transformed into a blueprint survey in which contributors—technology professionals who are performing the applicable job function—are asked to rate each objective. Contributors may be selected from lists of past Certified Professional candidates, from appropriately skilled exam development volunteers, and from within Microsoft. Based on the contributors' input, the objectives are prioritized and weighted. The actual exam items are written according to the prioritized objectives. Contributors are queried about how they spend their time on the job, and if a contributor doesn't spend an adequate amount of time actually performing the specified job function, his or her data is eliminated from the analysis.

The blueprint survey phase helps determine which objectives to measure, as well as the appropriate number and types of items to include on the exam.

Phase 4: Item Development

A pool of items is developed to measure the blueprinted objective domain. The number and types of items to be written are based on the results of the blueprint survey. During this phase, items are reviewed and revised to ensure that they are:

- Technically accurate

- Clear, unambiguous, and plausible

- Not biased toward any population, subgroup, or culture

- Not misleading or tricky

- Testing at the correct level of Bloom's Taxonomy

- Testing for useful knowledge, not obscure or trivial facts

Items that meet these criteria are included in the initial item pool.

Phase 5: Alpha Review and Item Revision

During this phase, a panel of technical and job function experts reviews each item for technical accuracy, then answers each item, reaching consensus on all technical issues. Once the items have been verified as technically accurate, they are edited to ensure that they are expressed in the clearest language possible.

Phase 6: Beta Exam

The reviewed and edited items are collected into a beta exam pool. During the beta exam, each participant has the opportunity to respond to all the items in this beta exam pool. Based on the responses of all beta participants, Microsoft performs a statistical analysis to verify the validity of the exam items and to determine which items will be used in the certification exam. Once the analysis has been completed, the items are distributed into multiple parallel forms, or versions, of the final certification exam.

Phase 7: Item Selection and Cut-Score Setting

The results of the beta exam are analyzed to determine which items should be included in the certification exam based on many factors, including item difficulty and relevance. Generally, the desired items are answered correctly by 25 percent to 90 percent of the beta exam candidates. This helps ensure that the exam consists of a variety of difficulty levels, from somewhat easy to extremely difficult.

Also during this phase, a panel of job function experts determines the cut score (minimum passing score) for the exam. The cut score differs from exam to exam because it is based on an item-by-item determination of the percentage of candidates who would be expected to answer the item correctly. The experts determine the cut score in a group session to increase the reliability.

Phase 8: Exam Live

Once all the other phases are complete, the exam is ready. Microsoft Certified Professional exams are administered by Sylvan Prometric.

Tips for Taking Your Exam

Here are some general tips for taking your exam successfully:

- Arrive early at the exam center so you can relax and review your study materials, particularly tables and lists of exam-related information.

- Read the questions carefully. Don't be tempted to jump to an early conclusion. Make sure you know *exactly* what the question is asking.

- When answering multiple-choice questions you're not sure about, use a process of elimination to get rid of the obviously incorrect answers first. This will improve your odds if you need to make an educated guess.

- This test has many exhibits (pictures). It can be difficult, if not impossible, to view both the questions and the exhibit simulation on 14- and 15-inch screens usually found at the testing centers. Call around to each center and see if they have 17-inch monitors available. If they don't, perhaps you can arrrange to bring in your own. Failing this, some have found it useful to quickly draw the diagram on the scratch paper provided by the testing center and use the monitor to view just the question.

- This is not simply a test of your knowledge of TCP/IP but of how it is implemented in Windows NT. You will need to know about Windows NT, NetBIOS, WINS, DNS, and DHCP.

- You are allowed to use the Windows calculator during your test. However, it may be better to memorize a table of the subnet addresses and to write it down on the scratch paper supplied by the testing center before you start the test.

- On simulations, do not change settings that are not directly related to the question. Also, assume default settings if the question does not specify or imply what they might be.

- A reminder: The adaptive format will NOT allow you to go back to see a question again. Be very careful before entering your answer. Because your exam may be shortened by correct answers (and lengthened by incorrect answers) there is no advantage to rushing through questions.

Once you have completed an exam, you will be given immediate, online notification of your pass or fail status. You will also receive a printed Examination Score Report indicating your pass or fail status and your exam results by section. (The test administrator will give you the printed score report.) Test scores are automatically forwarded to Microsoft within five working days after you take the test. You do not need to send your score to Microsoft. If you pass the exam, you will receive confirmation from Microsoft, typically within two to four weeks.

How to Use This Book

This book can provide a solid foundation for the serious effort of preparing for the TCP/IP for NT Server 4 exam. To best benefit from this book, you might want to use the following study method:

1. Study a chapter carefully, making sure you fully understand the information.

2. Complete all hands-on exercises in the chapter, referring to the chapter so that you understand each step you take.

3. Answer the exercise questions related to that chapter. (You will find the answers to these questions in Appendix A.)

4. Note which questions you did not understand and study those sections of the book again.

5. Study each chapter in the same manner.

6. Before taking the exam try Sybex MCSE Edge Test included on the CD that comes with this book.

If you prefer to use this book in conjunction with classroom or online training, you have many options. Both Microsoft-authorized training and independent training are widely available. CyberState University offers excellent online MCSE programs across the Internet, using the SYBEX materials. Their program also includes an online NT lab where you can practice many of the exercises in this book, as well as videos, exam preparation software, chat forums, and lectures, all centered around the SYBEX MCSE Study Guide series. You can reach CyberState at 1-888-GET-EDUCated (888-438-3382) or www.cyberstateu.com.

To learn all the material covered in this book, you will need to study regularly and with discipline. Try to set aside the same time every day to study, and select a comfortable and quiet place in which to do it. If you work hard, you will be surprised at how quickly you learn this material. Good luck.

What's on the CDs?

The CDs contain several valuable tools to help you study for your MCSE exams:

- Multimedia TCP/IP for Windows NT training from LearnKey
- The Sybex MCSE Edge Test for TCP/IP for NT 4
- Microsoft's Train_Cert Offline
- Microsoft's Internet Explorer 4

Contact Information

To find out more about Microsoft Education and Certification materials and programs, to register with Sylvan Prometric, or to get other useful information, check the following resources. Outside the United States or Canada, contact your local Microsoft office or Sylvan Prometric testing center.

Microsoft Certified Professional Program (800) 636-7544   Call the MCPP number to get information about the Microsoft Certified Professional program and exams and to order the latest Microsoft Roadmap to Education and Certification.

Sylvan Prometric Testing Centers (800) 755-EXAM   To register to take a Microsoft Certified Professional exam at any of more than 800 Sylvan Prometric testing centers around the world, or to order this Exam Study Guide, call the Sylvan Prometric testing center.

VUE testing centers — (888) 837-8616   To register to take a Microsoft Certified Professional exam at a VUE testing centers call the VUE registration center.

Microsoft Certification Development Team http://www.microsoft.com/Train_Cert/mcp/examinfo/certsd.htm   Contact the Microsoft Certification Development Team through their Web site to volunteer for participation in one or more exam development phases or to report a problem with an exam. Address written correspondence to: Certification Development Team; Microsoft Education and Certification; One Microsoft Way; Redmond, WA 98052.

Microsoft TechNet Technical Information Network (800) 344-2121
The is an excellent resource for support professionals and system administrators. Outside the United States and Canada, call your local Microsoft subsidiary for information.

EdgeTest's Free Resume Center   If you are seeking employment, or are looking for career advancement, e-mail a copy of your resume to resume@edgetest.com. EdgeTest offers free job placement services throughout the United States.

The Authors   You can e-mail Todd and Monica at Globalnet System Solutions, their training and consulting company in Colorado:

    globalnetsys@earthlink.net

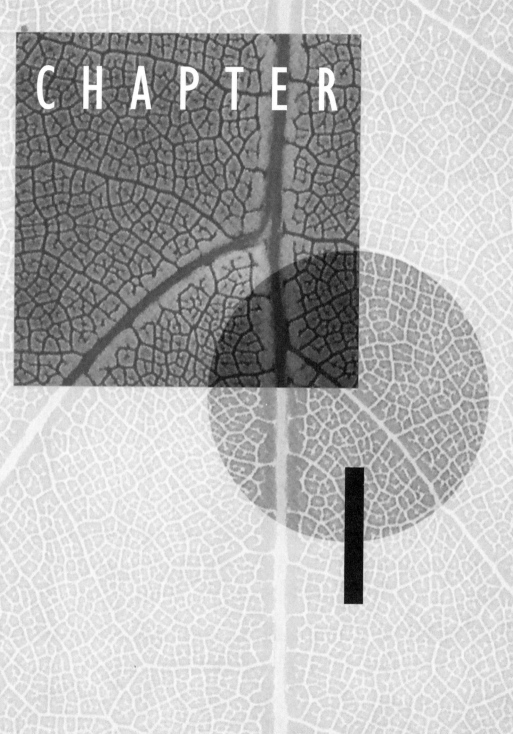

CHAPTER

1

An Introduction to TCP/IP

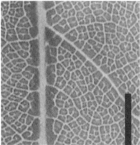

n this chapter, we'll cover the basics of this popular pair of protocols, opening with a definition of TCP/IP, its beginnings, and why
it's so important today. We'll progress to discover how TCP/IP fits
into the Department of Defense (DOD) networking archetype, and move on
to explore both the DOD and the Open Systems Interconnection (OSI) reference models. We'll then zoom in for a close-up of the TCP/IP protocol suite,
closing the chapter with an in-depth look at the individual protocols and utilities, including their special functions.

If you are unfamiliar with TCP/IP, or are planning to take the certification
test, keep the following points in mind as you work through this chapter.
They are target issues of the chapter, and it's your goal to be thoroughly
familiar with them when you've completed it. The exercise and review section
at the end of the chapter will also help you achieve these goals. You should be
able to:

- Define TCP/IP

- Describe its advantages on Windows NT

- Explain the Request for Comments (RFCs) document

- Describe how the TCP/IP protocol suite maps to a four-layer model

- Identify and describe the protocols and utilities in the Microsoft TCP/IP
  protocol suite

What Is TCP/IP?

T CP/IP stands for *Transmission Control Protocol/Internet Protocol*.
Essentially, it is a set of two communication protocols that an application can

use to package its information for sending across a network or networks. For readers familiar with traditional NetWare protocols, TCP is roughly comparable to SPX (Sequenced Packet Exchange), and IP approximates IPX (Internetwork Packet Exchange).

TCP/IP also refers to an entire collection of protocols, called a *protocol suite*. This collection includes application protocols for performing tasks such as e-mail, file transfers, and terminal emulation. Additional supporting protocols take an application's data and package it for transmission. Two examples of this sort would be the TCP and IP protocols. Still others exist for the physical transmission of data, such as Ethernet and Token Ring. All of these are related and part of the TCP/IP protocol suite.

As another example, whether we realize it or not, many of us use the *SMTP—Simple Mail Transport Protocol*. SMTP is an application protocol that enables us to communicate by e-mail. E-mail programs running on personal computers, minicomputers, UNIX workstations, and even mainframes can use the SMTP protocol to exchange e-mail between applications.

A Brief History of TCP/IP

The period of computer history spanning the 1950s and 1960s was not a good time for networking. During this Dark Age of Computerdom, almost all computer systems were "technocentric," operating autonomously—they weren't designed to connect to other systems. In that politically incorrect period of computer prejudice, hardware, operating systems, file formats, program interfaces, and other components were all designed to work only with a particular type of computer system, excluding all others.

The Interest in Packet-Switched WANs

In the late 1960s, the United States Department of Defense (DOD) became interested in some academic research concerning a *packet-switched wide-area network,* or *WAN.* The basic idea was to connect multiple, geographically dispersed networks, and allow for data, in the form of *packets*, to be sent to the various locations within the WAN.

The concept of packets can be explained like this: Imagine you have a really long letter to send—so long, it's impossible to fit it into one measly little #10 envelope. You've been given explicit instructions—you must use the #10s. So, you begin to break up the letter into smaller sections, fitting each into an individual envelope. As you address each envelope, you number them sequentially so the recipient at its destination can successfully reassemble your letter. The letter we're talking about is analogous to data that a user has created within an application and wishes to send to another user. The envelopes represent packets. In WANs, information is transported by electronically putting it into packets, which are addressed, sequenced, and then sent on their way.

The *switched* part of a packet-switched network refers to the routing of the packets to a destination. Because packets are addressed individually, they can be transmitted along different physical routes to their ultimate destination. This flexible transmission method is referred to as *packet-switching*. The original reason the DOD was interested in this research was because they wanted to create a fault-tolerant WAN that could carry, command, and control information in the event of a nuclear war. Because a network of this type would have multiple, geographically dispersed sites, and data would be sent in a packet-switched manner, there would be no single point of failure in the system.

The Initial Research Issues behind the Internet

The research arm of the DOD was an agency called the Advanced Research Projects Agency (ARPA), now called the Defense Advanced Research Projects Agency (DARPA). The mission of this group was to fund basic research that could possibly contribute to the defense effort. It was this agency that funded and managed the project to create a packet-switched WAN. The scientists and engineers that were recruited for this project came from major universities and the private firm of Bolt, Beranek, and Newman (BBN) in Cambridge, Massachusetts. The challenge they faced related to two main areas: *interconnectivity* and *interoperability*.

Interconnectivity deals with transporting information. A software protocol was needed that could package and route information between multiple sites. Out of the concept of the packet-switched WAN evolved the protocol that eventually rose to meet this need: the *Internet Protocol (IP)*.

With the problem of transmission resolved, the team moved on to tackle the next issue—communication. What good was transporting information from an application on a computer *here* if the system's applications on the receiving end *there* couldn't understand it? This would be about as effective as arguing with Bavarian airport staff about your shredded luggage in Swahili—you'd be hearing each other loud and clear, but failing to communicate because you spoke different languages. As you're sure to be guessing, interoperability has to do with application-to-application communication—the interpreter rushed to the scene. Achieving interoperability was a real challenge.

Applications would be running on vastly disparate hardware platforms with equally different operating systems, file formats, terminal types, and so on. For interoperability to be a reality, a way to bridge all these differences was required.

The solution was to develop a series of standard application protocols that would enable application-to-application communication and be independent of the extensive array of computer platforms. For instance, if a mainframe-based e-mail program and a PC-based e-mail program were both using the same standard e-mail protocol, they could exchange e-mail. This would be possible despite the use of two totally different systems. This same principle was used to create standard protocols for file transfers, terminal emulation, printing, network management, and other applications.

From the ARPANET to the Internet

When the original team of researchers decided to conduct their first test of these ideas, they chose four universities for sites: the University of California at Los Angeles (UCLA), the Stanford Research Institute (SRI), the University of California at Santa Barbara (UCSB), and the University of Utah. In September of 1969, these four sites were connected using 50Kbps (kilobits per second) leased voice lines, and the resulting network was called the *Advanced Research Projects Agency Network*, or *ARPANET*.

Although the original aim of this research was military, it was soon used for other purposes. Researchers at the different sites utilized the ARPANET to log into distant sites and communicate with each other by sending files and electronic mail.

Because the funding for this research was obtained from the U.S. government, and therefore from U.S. taxpayers, the subsequent technology was considered owned by the U.S. public. And since the government hadn't classified the technology as top secret, it was considered to be in the public domain. This meant that any individual, organization, or company could receive documentation of the protocols and write programs based on them. That's exactly what happened. Other universities and research and commercial organizations soon began to use this technology to create their own networks. Some of these networks were then connected to the ARPANET.

Another factor in the rapid growth of this technology was the inclusion of the TCP/IP protocols in the Berkeley version of UNIX. The DOD folks funded two projects that lead to this. First, they had Bolt, Beranek, and Newman modify the TCP/IP protocols to work with the UNIX operating system. Then they had the University of California at Berkeley include them in their version of UNIX, called Berkeley UNIX or Berkeley Software Distribution UNIX (BSD UNIX). Things from Berkeley get around. Because 90 percent of all university science departments were using this version of UNIX, the TCP/IP protocols quickly gained wide usage, and more and more networks were created with them.

Mainframes, minicomputers, and microcomputers all became hardware platforms for TCP/IP protocols. Likewise, software environments from Digital Equipment Corporation (DEC), International Business Machines (IBM), Microsoft, and many others developed products that supported them. Over time, these networks began to connect to each other. Where there was originally only one, the ARPANET, soon there were many separate networks. Eventually, all these individual, interconnected TCP/IP networks were collectively referred to as the Internet, or more simply, the Net.

The Internet Today

Though the numbers increase with each day, the Internet connects about 40 million users worldwide. The following is a very short list of some of the networks on the Internet:

- NSFNet (National Science Foundation Network)

- SPAN (Space Physics Analysis Network)

- CARL (Colorado Alliance of Research Libraries)

- LawNet: Columbia Law School Public Information Service

- The WELL (Whole Earth 'Lectronic Link)

- E.T. Net: The National Library of Medicine

- USEnet: A very large bulletin board system made up of thousands of different conferences

We commonly use the Internet for sending e-mail. The TCP/IP protocol that relates to this function is SMTP. As mentioned earlier, this protocol allows people from all over the world, using disparate hardware and software platforms, to communicate with one another.

Another common application of the Internet is to transfer files. Someone on a Macintosh computer in Iowa can download a file from a minicomputer in Norway. This type of file transfer is accomplished, in part, by the File Transfer Protocol (FTP) running on both machines.

A third frequently used application is *terminal emulation*, sometimes called *remote login*. TCP/IP's *Telnet* protocol allows a user to log in to a remote computer. The computer logging in acts as, or emulates, a terminal off the remote system; hence, the term terminal emulation.

Locating Information on the Internet

Surfing the Net has become so popular that, like snowboarding, it may soon be added to the Olympics. The reason for its popularity is that whether you garden to Mozart, or bungee-jump to Pearl Jam, there's something for you there. Yes, a great feature of the Internet is its astounding amount of information and other resources, like shareware and freeware. However, as answers often lead to more questions, this enormous expanse of information does often raise a few concerns for you and me staring into the screen.

Let's explore this a bit. Imagine this: There you are—just you and your computer and your mind racing with all the amazing stuff you've heard can be found on the Net. You fire up Ol' Bessie—your computer may, of course, have a different name—and the screen crackles to life. With heady anticipation, you click the Internet icon, listen for that squeal/collision, modem noise, and...there it is! THE INTERNET. The Information superhighway that, full of promise, can lead nowhere fast, like a bad relationship, if you don't know what to do with it.

Has this been you? You know the information you are looking for. You know it's out there...but where? And what's the easiest way to get there? Fortunately, TCP/IP has application protocols that address these issues. The following are four methods of finding information on the Internet, known as *information retrieval services*.

- WAIS
- Archie
- Gopher
- World Wide Web (WWW)   HTTP

WAIS

Wide Area Information Server (WAIS) allows you to search for a specific document inside a database. WAIS is a distributed information service that offers natural language input as well as indexed searching that lets the results of initial searches influence future searches. You can Telnet to DS.INTERNIC.NET to access a WAIS client. Log in as **wais**, without a password. WAIS searches may also be done in the World Wide Web.

Archie

A program called *Archie* was created to help users find files. Archie is essentially an indexing and search tool that works by indexing a large number of files. Periodically, participating Internet host computers will download a listing of their files to a few specified computers called *Archie servers*. The Archie server then indexes all these files.

When you are looking for a specific file, you can run the Archie client software and *query* (search through) the Archie server. The Archie server will examine its indexes and send back a description and location of the files that match your query. You can then use FTP to transfer the file or files.

Gopher

Another great Internet tool is *Gopher*. Created at the University of Minnesota, where the school mascot is a gopher, it organizes topics into a menu system and allows you to access the information on each topic listed. Through its menu system, you can see at a glance what information is available there. This system includes many levels of submenus, allowing you to burrow down to the exact type of information you're looking for. When you choose an item, Gopher transparently transfers you to another system on the Internet where your choice resides.

Gopher actually uses the Telnet protocol to log you into the other system. This action is hidden from users, who just see the Gopher menu interface. This means that Gopher doesn't merely tell you where your information is located, as Archie does, but also transparently takes you to it. Gopher could be characterized as a menuing tool, a search tool, and a navigation tool that sends you places.

World Wide Web

The *World Wide Web (WWW)* is a type of data service running on many computers on the Internet. These computers utilize a type of software that allows for text and graphics to have cross-links to other information. You can access a WWW server, and a particular Web page, to see a great—depending on its creator's talent—graphic display of text, pictures, icons, colors, and other elements.

To access the Web server, you use client software called a *browser program*. With a browser, you can choose an element on the Web page, which can then cross-link you to a computer animation, or play sounds, or display another Web page. Browsers can even contact another Web server located across the world. All the Web servers on the Internet are collectively referred to as the World Wide Web (WWW) and can be thought of as Jungian consciousness for computers.

The most popular World Wide Web browsers are Netscape's Navigator and Microsoft's Internet Explorer.

Request for Comments (RFCs)

In Life, if it's there long enough, politics will find it. Sometimes this is good. Sometimes its absolutely necessary, as is the case when the goal is setting *standards* for TCP/IP. These standards are published in a series of documents called *Request for Comments*, or *RFCs*, and they describe the internal workings of the Internet.

RFCs and standards are not one and the same. Though many are actual standards, some RFCs are there for informational purposes or to describe a work in progress. Still others exist as a sort of forum, providing a place for industry input relevant to the process of updating IP standards.

The Internet's standardization process resembles that of a bill becoming a law. Similarities include the fact that there exists more than one governing body and interested parties watching closely and making decisions about it. Another resemblance is that an RFC document goes through several stages, each subjecting it to examination, analysis, debate, critique, and testing on its way to becoming a standard.

First, an individual, company, or organization proposing a new protocol, improvement to an existing protocol, or even simply making comments on the state of the Internet, creates an RFC. If it deems it worthy, after at least a six-month wait, the *IESG (Internet Engineering Steering Group)* promotes the RFC to the status of *Draft Standard*, where it reenters the arena of review before finally becoming a bonafide *Internet Standard*. It is then published and assigned a permanent RFC number.

If the standard is changed or updated in any way, it gets a whole new number, so rest assured—you've got the latest model. Also handy to note: If what you're looking at *is* a revised edition, the dated version or versions are referenced on its title page. Also noteworthy, a letter that follows an RFC's number indicates the status of that RFC (for example, RFC 1390H). The following is a list of status designations for Internet protocols:

Historic Protocols that have either been outmoded or are no longer undergoing consideration for standardization

Experimental Protocols being experimented with

Informational Exactly what you might think

Proposed Standard Being analyzed for future standardization

Draft Standard In home stretch—the final review period prior to becoming a standard

Standard An Internet protocol which has arrived, and is fully official

There are also instructions for the treatment of Internet protocols. They are:

Limited Of possible use to some computer systems. Highly specialized or experimental protocols are sometimes given this designation. Historic protocols can be given this status as well.

Elective These protocols may possibly be implemented.

Recommended These should be implemented.

Required Protocols considered a "must." They are required to be implemented on the Internet.

Important to note is the fact that not every protocol enjoying wide usage on the Net is an Internet standard. TCP/IP's *NFS (Network File System)* is a stellar example. Developed by Sun Microsystems, the NFS is a critical TCP/IP protocol, and is therefore inextricably entwined with the Internet. This protocol, though indispensable, has not received approval from the IAG, and so cannot be given the status of Standard.

Internet Activities Board (IAB)

The *IAB* is a committee responsible for setting Internet standards and for managing the process of publishing RFCs. The IAB is in charge of two task forces: the *Internet Research Task Force (IRTF)* and the *Internet Engineering Task Force (IETF)*. The IRTF is responsible for coordinating all TCP/IP-related research projects. The IETF focuses on problems on the Internet.

For more information on the Internet, try (you guessed it) the Internet. There's a memo called Internet Official Protocol Standards, and the last time I checked, its publishing number was RFC 1800. It describes the above process much more thoroughly than space allows us here. InterNIC Directory and Database Services

InterNIC Directory and Database Services

The *InterNIC Directory and Database*, provided by AT&T, is a service that furnishes us with sources of information about the Internet, including RFCs. A WHOIS server provides a white page directory of Internet users and a Gopher database provides access to Internet documents. InterNIC is a primary depository that offers many options for retrieval. Have fun!

Previously, the best way to check out RFCs, and to get up-to-date information about their sources, was to send an e-mail to rfc-info@isi.edu, including the message **help: ways_to_get_rfcs**. If you weren't looking for a specific RFC, you downloaded a file named RFC—INDEX.TXT, which offered the complete banquet of all the RFCs in the world. Today, the easiest way to go RFC hunting is to point a Web browser at www.internic.net, which will lavish you with a nice searchable interface. Still, RFCs may be obtained via FTP from these servers:

- DS.INTERNIC.NET (InterNIC Directory and Database Services)

- NIS.NSF.NET

- NISC.JVNC.NET

- FTP.ISI.EDU

- WUARCHIVE.WUSTL.EDU

- SRC.DOC.IC.AC.UK

- FTP.NCREN.NET

- FTP.SESQUI.NET

- NIS.GARR.IT

The TCP/IP Protocol Suite and the DOD Networking Model

Computers, like people, become confused and offended when protocols for proper communication aren't followed. Give one an offending command once too often and the screen just might go dark on you—complete rejection! Try that on a person, and lo an' behold...same thing happens. The TCP/IP protocol suite is essentially an integration of various communications functions governed by strict, required, and agreed-upon rules for how they are performed, implemented, and so on. The required, agreed-upon rules part refers to the standard class of protocols we talked about in our discussion of RFCs. The DOD's networking model conforms to the *International Standards Organization's (ISO)* model, which is similar in concept to the *Open Systems Interconnection (OSI)* reference model. Before we see how they all compare, let's take a look at the general concept of reference models.

Reference Models: An Overview

A *reference model* is a conceptual blueprint of how communications should take place. It addresses all the processes that are required for effective communication. These processes are divided into logical groupings called *layers*. When a communication system is designed in this manner, it's known as *layered architecture.*

Think of it like this: Imagine you and some friends want to start a company. One of the first things you'd do is sit down and think through the things that must be done, who will do them, in what order, and how they relate to each other. Ultimately, you might group these tasks into departments. Let's say you decide on having an order-taking department, an inventory department, and a shipping department. Each of your departments have their own unique tasks keeping them very busy, requiring them to focus on only their own duties.

In this scenario, departments are a metaphor for the layers in a communication system. For things to run smoothly, each department will have to trust and rely heavily on the others to do their jobs and handle their special responsibilities. In your planning sessions, you'll probably take notes to document the meeting. The entire process will then be recorded for you to discuss later, agreeing upon standards of operation that will serve as your business blueprint, or reference model, if you will.

Once your business is launched, your department heads, armed with the part of the blueprint relating to their department, will need to develop practical methods to implement the tasks assigned to them. These practical methods, or protocols, will need to be classified into a Standard Operating Procedures manual, and followed closely. The various procedures in your manual will have different reasons for having been included, as well as varying degrees of importance and implementation. If you form a partnership, or acquire another company, it will be imperative for their business protocols—their business blueprint—to match yours.

Software developers can use a reference model to understand computer communication processes, and to see what types of functions need to be accomplished on any one layer. If they are developing a protocol for a certain layer, all they need to concern themselves with is their chosen layer's functions, not those of any other layer. The other functions will be handled by some other layer and protocol. The technical term for this idea is *binding*. The communication processes that are related to each other are bound, or grouped together, at a particular layer.

Advantages of Reference Models

The advantages of using a model are many. Remember, because developers know that functions they're not currently working on will be handled by another layer, they can confidently focus on just one layer's functions. This promotes specialization. Another benefit is that if changes are made to one layer, it doesn't necessarily change anything with the other layers.

Suppose an executive in your company, who's in the management layer, sends a letter. This person doesn't necessarily care if his or her company's shipping department, a different layer, changes from UPS to Federal Express, or vice-versa. All they're concerned with is the letter, and the recipient of the letter. It is someone else's job to see to its delivery. The technical phrase for this idea is *loose coupling*. You've probably heard phrases like this: "It's not *my* fault—it's not my department!" or, "So-'n-So's group always messes up stuff like this—we never do!" Loose coupling provides for a *stable* protocol suite. Passing the buck doesn't.

Another big advantage is *compatibility*. If software developers adhere to the specifications outlined in the reference model, all the protocols written to conform to that model will work together. This is very good. Compatibility creates the potential for a large number of protocols to be written and used.

Physical and Logical Data Movement

The two additional concepts that need to be addressed in a reference model are the *physical movement of data* and the *logical movement of data*.

As illustrated in Figure 1.1, the physical movement of data begins by going down the model. For example, an application creates some information. It passes it down to a communication protocol that packages it and hands it down to a transmission protocol for its actual physical transmission. The data then moves across the model, which signifies it moving across some type of physical channel—like cable, fiber, or radio frequencies and microwaves.

FIGURE 1.1

Physical data flow through a model

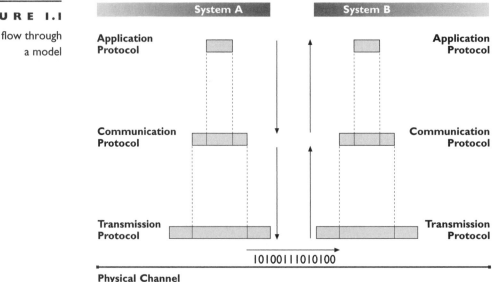

When the data reaches the destination computer, it moves up the model. Each layer at the destination only sees and deals with the data that was packaged by its counterpart on the sending side. Referring back to our analogy about the executive and the letter, the shipping department at the destination only sees the shipping packaging and the information provided by the sending side's shipping department. The destination's shipping department does not see the actual letter because peeking into mail addressed to someone else is a federal offense. The destination company's executive is the party who will open and process the letter.

The logical movement of data is another concept addressed in a reference model. From this perspective, each layer is only communicating with its counterpart layer on the other side (see Figure 1.2). Communication in the realm of humans flows best when it happens between peers—between people on the same level, or layer in life. The more we have in common, the more similarities in our personalities, experiences, and occupations, the easier it is for us to relate to one another—for us to connect. Again, its the same with computers. This type of logical communication is called *peer-to-peer communication*. When more than one protocol is needed to successfully complete a communication process, they are grouped into a team we call a *protocol stack*. Layers in a system's protocol stack only communicate with the corresponding layers in another system's protocol stack.

F I G U R E 1.2

Logical data flow between peer layers

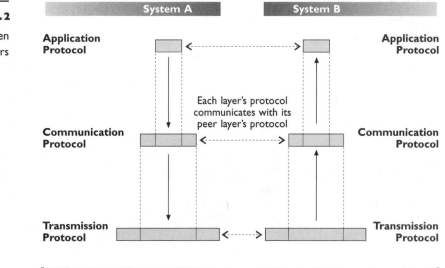

The OSI Reference Model

The International Standards Organization (ISO) is the Emily Post of the protocol world. Just like Ms. Post, who wrote the book setting the standards—or protocols—for human social interaction, the OSI developed the OSI reference model as the guide and precedent for an open protocol set. Defining the etiquette of communication models, it remains today the most popular means of comparison for protocol suites. The OSI reference model has seven layers:

- Application

- Presentation

- Session

- Transport

- Network

- Data Link

- Physical

Figure 1.3 shows the way these "macro-layers" fit together.

FIGURE 1.3

The macro-layers of the OSI reference model

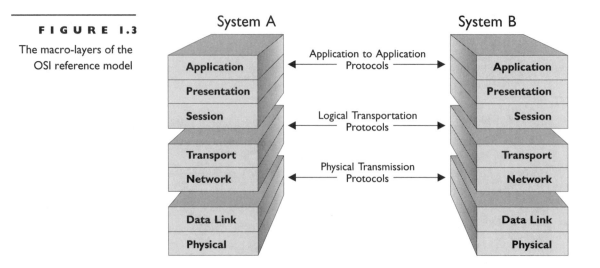

The ISO model's top three layers—Application, Presentation, and Session—deal with functions that aid applications in communicating with other applications. They specifically deal with tasks like filename formats, code sets, user interfaces, compression, encryption, and other functions relating to the exchange occurring between applications.

The Application Layer

The Application layer of the ISO model supports the components that deal with the communicating aspects of an application. Although computer applications sometimes require only desktop resources, applications may unite communicating components from more than one network application: for example, things like file transfers, e-mail, remote access, network management activities, client/server processes, and information location. Many network applications provide services for communication over enterprise networks, but for present and future internetworking, the need is fast developing to reach beyond their limits. For the '90s and beyond, transactions and information exchanges between organizations are broadening to require internetworking applications like the following:

Handwritten annotation in left margin:
Protocol
HTTP 1.0 →
    1.1
(uses TCP port 80)

send
→ SMTP → TCP port 25
→ POP 3 → TCP port 110
obtain

The World Wide Web (WWW) Connects countless servers (the number seems to grow with each passing day) presenting diverse formats. Most are multimedia, and include some or all of the following: graphics, text, video, and even sound. Netscape Navigator, Internet Explorer, and other browsers like Mosaic simplify both accessing and viewing Web sites.

E-mail Gateways E-mail gateways are versatile, and can use Simple Mail Transfer Protocol (SMTP) or the X.400 standard to deliver messages between different e-mail applications.

Electronic Data Interchange (EDI) This is a composite of specialized standards and processes that facilitates the flow of tasks like accounting, shipping/receiving, and order and inventory tracking between businesses.

Special Interest Bulletin Boards These include the many chat rooms on the Internet where people can connect and communicate with each other either by posting messages, or typing a live conversation. They can also share public domain software.

Internet Navigation Utilities Applications like Gopher and WAIS, as well as search engines like Yahoo, Excite, and Alta Vista, help users locate the resources and information they need on the Internet.

HTTPS
(TCP port 443)

Financial Transaction Services These are services that target the financial community. They gather and sell information pertaining to investments, market trading, commodities, currency exchange rates, and credit data to their subscribers.

An important thing to mention here is an *application program interface (API)*. Used jointly with application layer services, developer of protocols and programs often include APIs in the package with their products. APIs are important because they make it possible for programmers to customize applications and reap the benefits of their wares. An API is essentially a set of guidelines for user-written applications to follow when accessing the services of a software system. It's a channel into the harbor. BSD UNIX has an API called Berkeley Sockets. Microsoft changed it slightly and renamed it Windows Sockets. Indeed, things from Berkeley *do* get around!

The Presentation Layer

The Presentation layer gets its name from its purpose: It presents data to the Application layer. It's essentially a translator. A successful data transfer technique is to adapt the data into a standard format before transmission. Computers are configured to receive this generically-formatted data and then convert the data back into its native format for reading. The OSI has protocol standards that define how standard data should be formatted. Tasks like data compression, decompression, encryption, and decryption are associated with this layer.

The Abstract Syntax Representation, Revision #1 (ASN.1) is the standard data syntax used by the Presentation layer. This kind of standardization is necessary when transmitting numerical data that is represented very differently by various computer systems' architectures.

Some Presentation layer standards are involved in multimedia operations. The following serve to direct graphic and visual image presentation:

PICT A picture format used by Macintosh or PowerPC programs for transferring QuickDraw graphics.

TIFF The Tagged Image File Format is a standard graphics format for high-resolution, bitmapped images.

JPEG These standards are brought to us by the Joint Photographic Experts Group.

Others guide movies and sound:

MIDI The Musical Instrument Digital Interface is used for digitized music.

MPEG The Motion Picture Experts Group's standard for the compression and coding of motion video for CDs is increasingly popular. It provides digital storage and bit rates up to 1.5Mbps.

QuickTime This is for use with Macintosh or PowerPC programs; it manages these computer's audio and video applications.

The Session Layer

The Session layer's job can be likened to that of a mediator or referee. Its central concern is *dialog* control between devices, or *nodes*. It serves to organize their communication by offering three different modes—*simplex, half-duplex,* and *full-duplex*—and by splitting up a communication session into three different phases. These phases are: *connection establishment, data transfer,* and *connection release.* In simplex mode, communication is actually a monologue with one device transmitting and another receiving. To get a picture of this, think of the telegraph machine's form of communication: .....--..----...---..-...

When in half-duplex mode, nodes take turns transmitting and receiving—the computer equivalent of talking on a speaker phone. Some of us have experienced proper conversation etiquette being forced upon us by the unique speaker phone phenomenon of forbidden interruption. The speakerphone's mechanism dictates that you may indeed speak your mind, but you'll have to wait until the other end stops chattering first. This is how nodes communicate when in half-duplex mode.

Full-duplex's only conversational proviso is *flow control.* This mitigates the problem of possible differences in the operating speed of two nodes, where one may be transmitting faster than the other can receive. Other than that, communication between the two flows unregulated, with both sides transmitting and receiving simultaneously.

Formal communication sessions occur in three phases. In the first, the connection-establishment phase, contact is secured and devices agree upon communication parameters and the protocols they will use. Next, in the data transfer phase, these nodes engage in conversation, or dialog, and exchange information. Finally, when they're through communicating, nodes participate in a systematic release of their session.

A formal communications session is connection-oriented. In a situation where a large quantity of information is to be transmitted, rules are agreed upon by the involved nodes for the creation of checkpoints along their transfer process. These are highly necessary in the case of an error occurring along the way. Among other things, they afford us humans the luxury of preserving our dignity in the face of our closely watching computers. Let me explain. In the 44th minute of a 45-minute download, a loathsome error occurs...again! This is the third try, and the file-to-be-had is needed more than sunshine. Without your trusty checkpoints in place you'd have to start all over again. Potentially, this could cause the coolest of cucumbers to tantrum like a two-year-old, resulting in an extremely high degree of satisfaction on the part of his or her computer. Can't have that! Instead, we have checkpoints secured—something we call activity management—ensuring that the transmitting node only has to retransmit the data sent since the last checkpoint. Humans: 1; Computers: 0...And the crowd goes crazy!

It's important to note that in networking situations, devices send out simple, one-frame status reports that aren't sent in a formal session format. If they were, it would unnecessarily burden the network and result in lost economy. Instead, in these events, a *connectionless* approach is used, where the transmitting node simply sends off its data without establishing availability, and without acknowledgment from its intended receiver. Connectionless communication can be thought of like a message in a bottle—they're short and sweet, they go where the current takes them, and they arrive at an unsecured destination.

The following are some examples of session-layer protocols and interfaces:

Network File System (NFS) Developed by Sun Microsystems and used with TCP/IP and UNIX workstations to allow transparent access to remote resources.

SQL The Structured Query Language developed by IBM provides users with a simpler way to define their information requirements on both local and remote systems.

RPC The Remote Procedure Call is a broad client/server redirection tool used for disparate service environments. Its procedures are created on clients and performed on servers.

X Window This is widely used by intelligent terminals for communicating with remote UNIX computers. It allows them to operate as though they were locally-attached monitors.

ASP Another client/server mechanism, the AppleTalk Session Protocol both establishes and maintains sessions amid AppleTalk client and server machines.

DNA SCP The Digital Network Architecture Session Control Protocol is a DECnet session layer protocol.

The Transport Layer   *TCP or UDP*

Uses TCP - connection protocol.

Services located in the Transport layer both segment and reassemble data from upper-layer applications, and unite it onto the same data stream. They provide end-to-end data transport services, and establish a logical connection between the sending host and destination host on an internetwork. Data integrity is ensured at this layer by maintaining flow control, and also by allowing users the option of requesting reliable data transport between systems. Flow control prevents the problem of a sending host on one side of the connection overflowing the buffers in the receiving host—an event which can result in lost data. Reliable data transport employs a connection-oriented communications session between systems, and the protocols involved ensure that the following will be achieved:

- The segments delivered are acknowledged back to the sender upon their reception.

- Any segments not acknowledged are retransmitted.

- Segments are sequenced back into their proper order upon arrival at their destination.

- A manageable data flow is maintained in order to avoid congestion, overloading, and loss of any data.

An important reason for different layers to coexist within the OSI reference model is to allow for the sharing of a transport connection by more than one application. This sharing is available because the transport layer's functioning happens segment by segment, and each segment is independent of the others. This allows different applications to send consecutive segments, processed on a first-come, first-served basis, that can be intended either for the same destination host or for multiple hosts.

Figure 1.4 shows how the transport layer sends the data of several applications originating from a source host to communicate with parallel applications on one or many destination host(s). The specific port number for each software application is set by software within the source machine before transmission. When it transmits a message, the source computer includes extra bits that encode the type of message, the program with which it was created, and which protocols were used. Each software application transmitting a data stream segment uses the same preordained port number. When it receives the data stream, the destination computers are empowered to sort and reunite each application's segments, providing the Transport layer with all it needs to pass the data up to its upper-layer peer application.

FIGURE 1.4

Transport layer data segments sharing a traffic stream

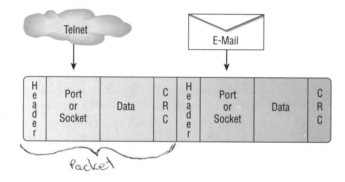

In reliable transport operation, one user first establishes a connection-oriented session with its peer system. Figure 1.5 portrays a typical connection-oriented session taking place between sending and receiving systems. In it, both hosts' application programs begin by notifying their individual operating systems that a connection is about to be initiated. The two operating systems communicate by sending messages over the network confirming that the transfer is approved and that both sides are ready for it to take place. Once the required synchronization is complete, a connection is fully established and the data transfer begins. While the information is being transferred between hosts, the two machines periodically check in with each other, communicating through their protocol software, to ensure that all is going well and the data is being received properly. The following summarize the steps in a connection-oriented session pictured in Figure 1.5:

- The first "connection agreement" segment is a request for synchronization.

- The second and third segments acknowledge the request and establish connection parameters between hosts.

- The final segment is also an acknowledgment. It notifies the destination host that the connection agreement is accepted and that the actual connection has been established. Data transfer can now begin.

FIGURE 1.5

Establishing a connection-oriented session

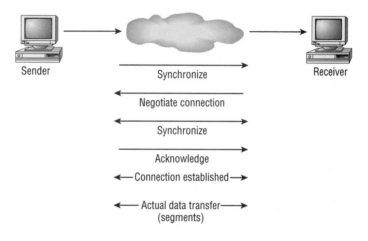

During a transfer, congestion can occur because either a chatty, high-speed computer is generating data traffic faster than the network can transfer it, or because many computers are simultaneously sending datagrams through a single gateway or destination. In the latter case, a gateway or destination can become congested even though no single source caused the problem. In either case, the problem is basically akin to a freeway bottleneck—too much traffic for too small a capacity. Usually, no one car is the problem, it's that there are simply too many cars on that freeway.

When a machine receives a flood of datagrams too quickly for it to process, it stores them in memory. This buffering action solves the problem only if the datagrams are part of a small burst. However, if the datagram deluge continues, a device's memory will eventually be exhausted. Its flood capacity will be exceeded, and it will discard any additional datagrams that arrive. But, no worries—because of transport function, network flood control systems work quite well. Instead of dumping resources and allowing data to be lost, the transport can issue a "not ready" indicator, as shown in Figure 1.6, to the overzealous sender. This mechanism works kind of like a stoplight, signaling the sending device to stop transmitting segment traffic to its overwhelmed peer. When the peer receiver has processed the segments already in its memory reservoir, it sends out a "ready" transport indicator. When the machine waiting to transmit the rest of its datagrams receives this "go" indictor, it can then resume its transmission.

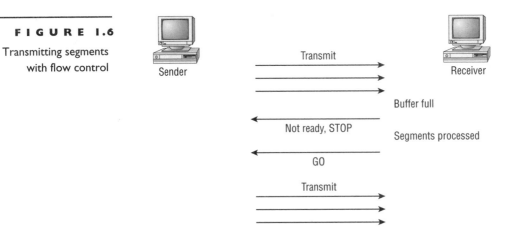

FIGURE 1.6

Transmitting segments with flow control

In fundamental, reliable, connection-oriented data transfer, datagrams are delivered to the receiving host in exactly the same sequence they're transmitted, and the transmission fails if this order is breached. Other things that will cause a failure to transmit are any data segments being lost, duplicated, or damaged along the way. The answer to the problem is to have the receiving host acknowledge receiving each and every data segment.

Data throughput would be low if the transmitting machine had to wait for an acknowledgment after sending each segment, so because there's time available after the sender transmits the data segment and before it finishes processing acknowledgments from the receiving machine, the sender uses the break to transmit more data. How many data segments the transmitting machine is allowed to send without receiving an acknowledgment for them is called a *window*.

Windowing controls how much information is transferred from one end to the other. While some protocols quantify information by observing the number of packets, TCP/IP measures it by counting the number of bytes. In Figure 1.7, we show a window size of 1 and a window size of 3. When a window size of 1 is configured, the sending machine waits for an acknowledgment for each data segment it transmits before transmitting another. Configured to a window size of 3, it's allowed to transmit three data segments before an acknowledgment is received. In our simplified example, both the sending and receiving machines are workstations. Reality is rarely that simple, and most often acknowledgments and packets will commingle as they travel over the network and pass through routers. Routing complicates things, but not to worry, we'll be covering applied routing later in the book.

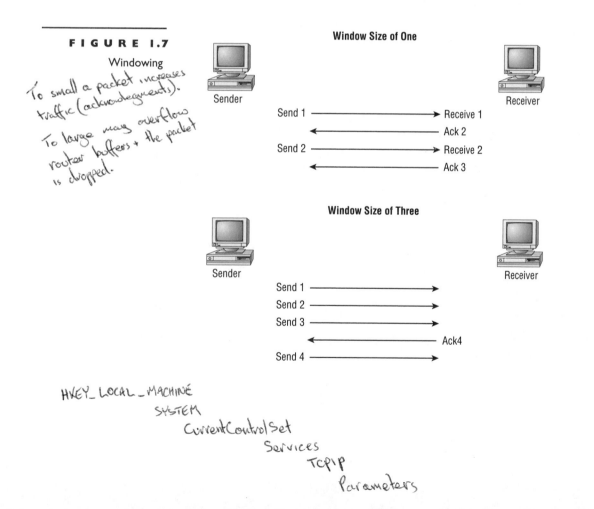

FIGURE 1.7

Windowing

To small a packet increases traffic (acknowledgments).

To large may overflow router buffers + the packet is dropped.

Window Size of One

Sender

Receiver

Send 1 ⟶ Receive 1

⟵ Ack 2

Send 2 ⟶ Receive 2

⟵ Ack 3

Window Size of Three

Sender

Receiver

Send 1 ⟶

Send 2 ⟶

Send 3 ⟶

⟵ Ack4

Send 4 ⟶

HKEY_LOCAL_MACHINE

SYSTEM

CurrentControlSet

Services

TCPIP

Parameters

Reliable data delivery ensures the integrity of a stream of data sent from one machine to the other through a fully functional data link. It guarantees the data won't be duplicated or lost. The method that achieves this is known as *positive acknowledgment with retransmission*. This technique requires a receiving machine to communicate with the transmitting source by sending an acknowledgment message back to the sender when it receives data. The sender documents each segment it sends and waits for this acknowledgment before sending the next segment. When it sends a segment, the transmitting machine starts a timer and retransmits if it expires before an acknowledgment for the segment is returned from the receiving end.

In Figure 1.8, the sending machine transmits segments 1, 2, and 3. The receiving node acknowledges it has received them by requesting segment 4. When it receives the acknowledgment, the sender then transmits segments 4, 5, and 6. If segment 5 doesn't make it through to the destination, the receiving node acknowledges that event with a request for the segment to be resent. The sending machine will then resend the lost segment and wait for an acknowledgment, which it must receive in order to move on to the transmission of segment 7.

F I G U R E 1.8

Transport layer reliable delivery

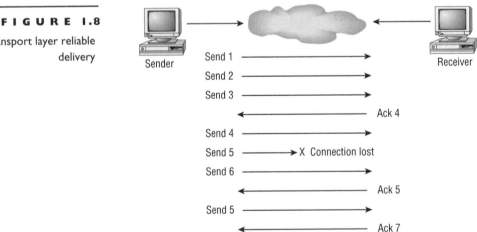

The Network Layer IP or IPX

Contains routing information protocols.

In life, there are lots of roads leading to Rome. The same holds true with the complicated cloud of networks, and the proper path through them is determined by protocols residing in layer number three—the Network layer. Path determination makes it possible for a router to appraise all available paths to a given destination and decide on the best one. Routers use network topology information when orienting themselves to the network and evaluating the different possible paths through it. These network "maps" can be configured by the network's administrator or obtained through dynamic processes running on the network. The Network layer's interface is connected to networks, and it's employed by the Transport layer to provide the best end-to-end packet delivery services. The job of sending packets from the source network to the destination network is the Network layer's primary function. After the router decides on the best path from point A to point B, it proceeds with switching the packet onto it—something known as *packet switching*. This is essentially forwarding the packet received by the router on one network interface, or *port*, to the port that connects to the best path through the network cloud. This will then send the packet to that particular packet's destination. We'll cover packet switching more thoroughly later on.

An internetwork must continually designate all paths of its media connections. In Figure 1.9 each line connecting routers is numbered, and those numbers are used by routers as network addresses. These addresses possess and convey important information about the path of media connections. They're used by a routing protocols to pass packets from a source onward to its destination. The Network layer creates a composite "network map"—a communication strategy system—by combining information about the sets of links into an internetwork with path determination, path switching, and route processing functions. It can also use these addresses to provide relay capability and interconnect independent networks. Consistent across the entire internetwork, layer three addresses also streamline the network's performance by preventing unnecessary broadcasts that gobble up precious bandwidth. Unnecessary broadcasts increase the network's overhead and waste capacity on any links and machines that don't need to receive them. Using consistent end-to-end addressing that accurately describes the path of media connections enables the Network layer to determine the best path to a destination without encumbering the device or links on the internetwork with unnecessary broadcasts.

FIGURE 1.9

Communicating through
an internetwork

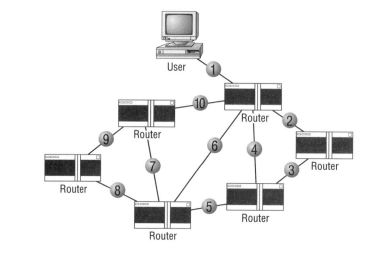

When an application on a host wants to send a packet to a destination device located on a different network, a data-link frame is received on one of the router's network interfaces. The router proceeds to decapsulate, then examine, the frame to establish what kind of network-layer data is in tow. After this is determined, the data is sent on to the appropriate network-layer process, but the frame's mission is fulfilled, and it's simply discarded.

Detailed in Figure 1.10 is the Network layer process examining the packet's header to discover which network it's destined for. It then refers to the routing table to find the connections the current network has to foreign network interfaces. After one is selected, the packet is re-encapsulated in its data link frame with the selected interface's information and queued for delivery off to the next hop in the path toward its destination. This process is repeated every time the packet switches to another router. When it finally reaches the router connected to the network that the destination host is located on, the packet is encapsulated in the destination LAN's data link frame type. It is now properly packaged and ready for delivery to the protocol stack on the destination host.

The Data Link Layer

The Data Link layer ensures that messages are delivered to the proper device and translates messages from up above into bits for the Physical layer to transmit. It formats the message into *data frames* and adds a customized header containing the hardware destination and source address. This added

FIGURE 1.10

The Network layer
process

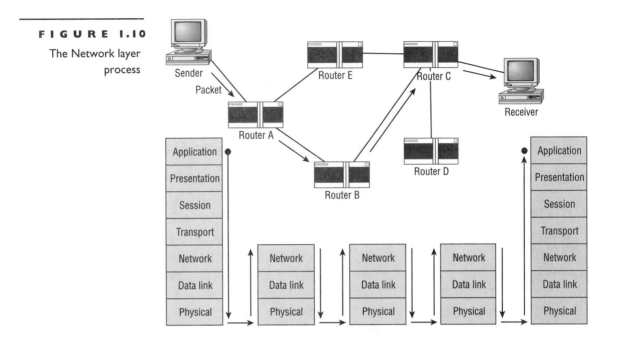

information forms a sort of capsule that surrounds the original message much like when engines, navigational devices, and other tools were attached to the lunar modules of the Apollo project. These various pieces of equipment were only useful during certain stages of space flight, and were stripped off the module and discarded when their designated stage was complete. Data traveling through networks is much the same. A data frame that's all packaged up and ready to go follows the format outlined in Figure 1.11. Its various elements are described here:

- The *Preamble* or *start indicator* is made up of a special bit pattern that alerts devices to the beginning of a data frame.

- The destination address (DA) is there for obvious reasons. The Data Link layer of every device on the network examines this to see if it matches its own address.

- The source address (SA) is the address of the sending device; it exists to facilitate replies to the messages.

- In Ethernet_II frames, the two-byte field following the source address is a type field. This field specifies the upper-layer protocol that will receive the data after data link processing is complete.

- In 802.3 frames, the two-byte field following the source address is a length field, which indicates the number of bytes of data that follow this field and precede the Frame Check Sequence (FCS) field. Following the length field could be an 808.2 header for Logical Link Control (LLC) information. This information is needed to specify the upper layer process, because 802.3 does not have a type field.

- The *data* is the actual message, plus all the information sent down to the sending device's Data Link layer from the layers above it.

- Finally, there's the Frame Check Sequence (FCS) field. Its purpose corresponds to its name, and it houses the Cyclic Redundancy Checksum (CRC). An IP packet contains a bit of data called a *checksum header*, which checks whether the header information was damaged on the way from sender to receiver. CRCs work like this: The device sending the data determines a value summary for the CRC and stashes it within the frame. The device on the receiving end performs the same procedure, then checks to see if its value matches the total, or sum, of the sending node, hence the term *checksum*.

FIGURE 1.11

Ethernet_II and 802.3 frames

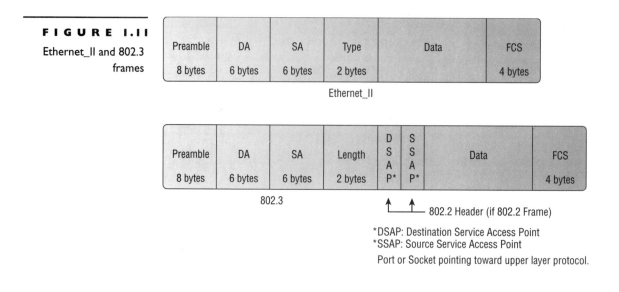

Checksum works a bit like counting all of the jellybeans in your bag, then passing the bag to someone else to give to your friend. To make sure none of the jellybeans get pilfered along the way, you send along a message stating the total number of jellybeans in the bag, and asking your friend to recount them. If your friend arrives at the same total, you both can safely assume none were snagged en route—that your jellybeans were successfully transmitted without error.

WAN Protocols at the Data Link Layer The typical encapsulations for synchronous serial lines at the Data Link layer are:

High Level Data Link Control (HDLC) The ISO created the HDLC standard to support both point-to-point and multi-point configurations. Unfortunately, most vendors implement HDLC in different manners, so HDLC is often not compatible between vendors.

Synchronous Data Link Control (SDLC) A protocol created by IBM to aid their mainframes in connecting remote offices. Created for use in WANs, it became extremely popular in the 1980s, as many companies were installing 327x controllers in their remote offices to communicate with the mainframe in the corporate office. SDLC defines and uses a polling media access, which means the *Primary* (front-end) asks, or polls, the *Secondaries* (327x controllers) to find out if they need to communicate with it. Secondaries cannot speak unless spoken to, nor can two Secondaries speak to each other. (Master\Slave terminology was used until it was deemed distasteful and not politically correct.)

Link Access Procedure, Balanced (LAPB) Created for use with X.25, it defines and is capable of detecting out-of-sequence or missing frames and retransmitting, exchanging, and acknowledging frames.

X.25 The first packet switching network. This defines the specifications between a DTE and a DCE.

Data link Frame *

Serial Line IP (SLIP) An industry standard developed in 1984 to support TCP/IP networking over low-speed serial interfaces in Berkeley UNIX. With the Windows NT RAS service, Windows NT computers can use TCP/IP and SLIP to communicate with remote hosts.

Data link frame → **Point-to-Point Protocol (PPP)** SLIP's big brother. It takes the specifications of SLIP and adds login, password, and error correction. See RFC 1661 for more information, as described by the IETF.

Integrated Services Digital Network (ISDN) Analog phone lines converted to use digital signaling. They can transmit both voice and data.

Frame Relay This is an upgrade from X.25 to be used where LAPB is no longer used. It's the fastest of the WAN protocols listed because of its simplified framing, which has no error correction. It must use the high-quality digital facilities of the phone company and therefore is not available everywhere.

High Speed Ethernet at the Data Link Layer Users need bandwidth, and 10Mbps isn't good enough; they need 100Mbps—switched! A 100Mbps Ethernet rises to this call well. Some of the new technologies are:

100BaseFX Ethernet over fiber at 100Mbps using 802.3 specs.

100Base4 Using 802.3 specs, 100Mbps over category 3, 4, or 5 cabling.

100BaseTX Fast Ethernet over category 5 cabling. It's compatible to the 802.3 specifications.

100BaseVG AnyLan IEEE movement into fast Ethernet and Token Ring, which seems to be going nowhere fast, mostly because it is *not* compatible with the 802.3 standards.

The Physical Layer

The Physical layer focuses on two responsibilities: It sends bits and receives bits. Bits only come in values of 1 or 0—a Morse code with numerical value. The Physical layer communicates directly with the various types of actual communication media. Different kinds of media represent these bit values in different ways. Some use audio tones, while others employ *state transitions*—changes in voltage from high to low and low to high. Specific protocols are needed for each type of media that describes the proper bit patterns to be used, how data is encoded into media signals, and the various qualities of the physical media's attachment interface.

At the Physical layer, the interface between the Data Terminal Equipment, or DTE, and the Data Circuit-terminating Equipment, or DCE, is identified. The DCE is usually the service provider, while the DTE is the attached device.

The services available to the DTE are most often accessed via a modem or Channel Service Unit/Data Service Unit (CSU/DSU).

The following Physical layer standards define this interface:

- EIA/TAI-232

- EIA/TIA-449

- V.24

- V.35

- X.21

- G.703

- EIA-530

- High-Speed Serial Interface (HSSI)

The DOD Reference Model

The DOD model is a condensed version of the OSI model. It is comprised of four instead of seven layers:

- Process/Application

- Host-to-Host

- Internet

- Network Access

Figure 1.12 shows a comparison of the four-layer DOD model and the seven-layer OSI reference model. As you can see, the two are similar in concept, but have a different number of layers with different names.

The DOD model's corresponding layer to the OSI's top three is known as the *Process/Application layer*. A whole lot of work gets done at this layer, and in it is found a vast array of protocols that combine to integrate the various activities and duties spanning the focus of the OSI's Session, Presentation, and Application layers. We'll be looking closely at those protocols in the next part of this lesson. The Process/Application layer defines protocols for host-to-host application communication. It also controls user interface specifications.

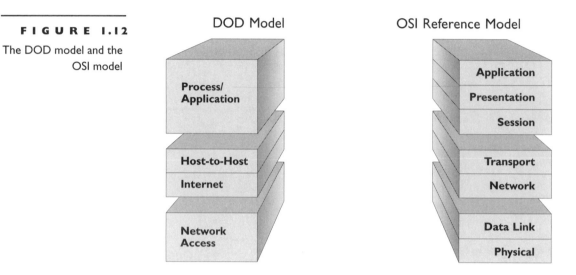

FIGURE 1.12

The DOD model and the OSI model

The *Host-to-Host layer* parallels the functions of OSI's Transport layer, defining protocols for setting up the level of transmission service for applications. It tackles issues like creating reliable end-to-end communication and ensuring the error-free delivery of data. It handles packet sequencing, and maintains data integrity.

The *Internet layer* corresponds to the Network layer, designating the protocols relating to the logical transmission of packets over the entire network. It takes care of the addressing of hosts by giving them an *IP address,* and handles the routing of packets among multiple networks. It also controls the communication flow between two applications.

At the bottom, the *Network Access layer* monitors the data exchange between the host and the network. The equivalent of the data link and physical layers of the OSI model, it oversees hardware addressing and defines protocols for the physical transmission of data.

The DOD Protocols

While the DOD model and the OSI model are truly alike in design and concept, with similar things happening in similar places, the specifications on *how* those things happen are different. This leads to a much different suite of protocols for the DOD model than those existing for the OSI model. Figure 1.13 shows the TCP/IP protocol suite, and how its protocols relate to the DOD model layers.

FIGURE 1.13

The TCP/IP protocol suite

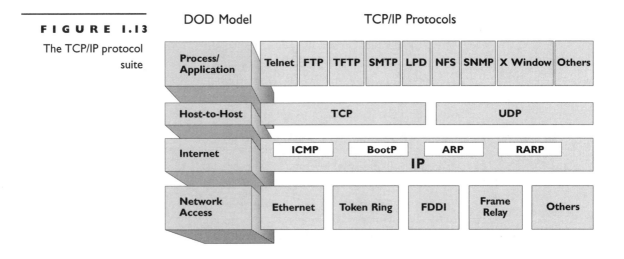

Process/Application Layer Protocols

As we explored earlier, one of the design goals of the original creators of the Internet was to have applications that could run on different computer platforms and yet, somehow, still communicate. The cavalry arrived in the form of Process/Application layer protocols, which address the ability of one application to communicate with another, regardless of hardware platform, operating system, and other features of the two hosts.

Most applications written with TCP/IP protocols can be characterized as *client/server* applications. This means that there are two major parts to the software involved, and that it's probably running on two different machines.

The server part of this software duo usually runs on the machine where the data is actually residing. This machine is the Big Dog. It tends to be powerful because much of the data processing, as well as storage, is done on it. It works like this: The client software sends requests to the server software for it to fulfill. Some typical requests include searches for information, printing, e-mail stuff, application services, and file transfers.

In addition to communicating with the server, another function of client software is to provide an interface for the user. It also allows you to tinker with the data you've managed to coax from the server.

These matters in hand, we'll move along and investigate just what sort of protocols populate the DOD model's Process/Application layer.

Telnet

The chameleon of protocols, *Telnet*'s specialty is terminal emulation. It allows a user on a remote client machine, called the *Telnet client,* to access the resources of another machine, the *Telnet server.* Telnet achieves this by pulling a fast one on the Telnet server, dressing up the client machine to appear like a terminal directly attached to the local network. This projection is actually a software image, a virtual terminal that can interact with the chosen remote host. These emulated terminals are of the text-mode type and can execute refined procedures like displaying menus that give users the opportunity to choose options from them, accessing the applications on the duped server. Users begin a Telnet session by running the Telnet client software, then logging on to the Telnet server.

Telnet's capabilities are limited to running applications or peeking into what's on the server. It's a "just looking" protocol. It can't be used for file sharing functions like downloading stuff. For the actual snatching of goodies, one must employ the next protocol on the list: FTP.

FTP (File Transfer Protocol)

This is the "grab it—give it" protocol that affords us the luxury of transferring files. *FTP* can facilitate this between any two machines that are using it. But FTP is not just a protocol—it's also a program. Operating as a protocol, FTP is used by applications. As a program, it's employed by users to perform file tasks by hand. FTP also allows for access to both directories and files, and can also accomplish certain types of directory operations, like relocating into different ones. FTP teams up with Telnet to transparently log you in to the FTP server, and then provides for the transfer of files.

Wow! Obviously, a tool this powerful would need to be secure—and FTP is! Accessing a host through FTP is only the first step. Users must then be subjected to an authentication login that's probably secured with passwords and usernames placed there by system administrators to restrict access. (And you thought this was going to be easy!) Not to fear, you can still get in by adopting the username "anonymous," but what you'll gain access to once you are in there will be limited.

Even when being employed by users manually as a program, FTP's functions are limited to listing and manipulating directories, typing file contents, and copying files between hosts. It can't execute remote files as programs.

TFTP (Trivial File Transfer Protocol)

Not supported by NT

TFTP is the stripped-down, stock version of FTP, though it's the protocol of choice if you know exactly what you want, and where it is to be found. It doesn't spoil you with the luxury of functions that FTP does. TFTP has no directory browsing abilities; it can do nothing but give and receive files. This austere little protocol also skimps in the data department, sending much smaller blocks of data than FTP. Also noteworthy is that TFTP will only open boring, public files, thereby depriving you of both the rush of having gotten away with something *and* the feeling of being special and privileged. There's no authentication as there is with FTP, so it's insecure; and few sites actually support it due to the inherent security risks.

NFS (Network File System)

Not supported by NT

Introducing...*NFS*! This is a jewel of a protocol specializing in file sharing. It allows two different types of file systems to interoperate. It's like this: Suppose the NFS server software is running on an NT server, and the NFS client software is running on a UNIX host. NFS allows for a portion of the RAM on the NT server to transparently store UNIX files, which can, in turn, be used by UNIX users. Even though the NT file system and the UNIX file system are unlike—they have different case sensitivity, filename lengths, security, and so on—both the UNIX users and the NT users can access that same file with their normal file systems, in their normal way.

Imagine yourself as an African back at the airport in Bavaria, heading toward the baggage claim area. With NFS in tow, you're equipped to actually retrieve your luggage, in a non-annihilated state, and get it through customs—all whilst chatting glibly in Swahili as you normally would! Additionally, the good news doesn't end there. Where Telnet, FTP, and TFTP are limited, NFS goes the extra mile. Remember that FTP cannot execute remote files as programs? NFS can! It can open a graphics application on your computer at work, and update the work you did on the one at home last night on the same program. NFS has the ability to import and export material—to manipulate applications remotely.

SMTP (Simple Mail Transfer Protocol)

Out of baggage-claim, and into the mail room.... *SMTP*, answering our ubiquitous call to e-mail, uses a *spooled, or queued*, method of mail delivery. Once a message has been sent to a destination, the message is spooled to a device—usually a disk. The server software at the destination posts a vigil, regularly checking this spool for messages, which upon finding, proceeds to deliver to their destination.

✷ LPD (Line Printer Daemon)

This protocol is designed for printer sharing. The *LPD* daemon, along with the *LPR (Line Printer)* program, allows print jobs to be spooled and sent to the network's printers.

X Window**S**

Designed for client-server operations, *X Windows*defines a protocol for the writing of graphical user interface-based client/server applications. The idea is to allow a program, called a client, to run on one computer and allow it to display on another computer that is running a special program called a window server.

✷ SNMP (Simple Network Management Protocol)

Just as doctors are better equipped to maintain the health of their patients when they have the patient's history in hand, network managers are at an advantage if they possess performance histories of the network in their care. These case histories contain valuable information that enables the manager to anticipate future needs and analyze trends. By comparing the network's present condition to its past functioning patterns, managers can more easily isolate and troubleshoot problems.

SNMP is the protocol that provides for the collection and manipulation of this valuable network information. It gathers data by *polling* the devices on the network from a management station at fixed intervals, requiring them to disclose certain information. When all is well, SNMP receives something called a *baseline*—a report delimiting the operational traits of a healthy network. This handy protocol can also stand as a watchman over the network, quickly notifying managers of any sudden turn of events. These network watch-men are called *agents*, and when aberrations occur, agents send an alert called a *trap* to the management station.

The sensitivity of the agent, or threshold, can be increased or decreased by the network manager. An agent's threshold is like a pain threshold; the more sensitive it is set to be, the sooner it screams an alert. Managers use baseline reports to aid them in deciding on agent threshold settings for their networks. The more sophisticated the management station's equipment is, the clearer the picture it can provide of the network's functioning. More powerful consoles have better record-keeping ability, as well as the added benefit of being able to provide enhanced graphic interfaces that can form logical portraits of network structure.

Host-to-Host Layer Protocols

As you learned earlier, the broad goal of the Host-to-Host layer is to shield the upper layer applications from the complexities of the network. This layer says to the upper layer, "Just give me your data, with any instructions, and I'll begin the process of getting your information ready for sending." The following sections describe the two main protocols at this layer.

TCP (Transmission Control Protocol)

TCP has been around since networking's early years when WANs weren't very reliable. It was created to mitigate that problem, and reliability is TCP's strong point. It tests for errors, resends data if necessary, and reports the occurrence of errors to the upper layers if it can't manage to solve the problem itself.

This protocol takes large blocks of information from an application and breaks them down into *segments*. It numbers and sequences each segment so that the destination's TCP protocol can put the segments back into the large block the application intended. After these segments have been sent, TCP waits for acknowledgment for each one from the receiving end's TCP, retransmitting the ones not acknowledged.

Before it starts to send segments down the model, the sender's TCP protocol contacts the destination's TCP protocol in order to establish a connection. What is created is known as a *virtual circuit*. This type of communication is called *connection-oriented*. During this initial handshake, the two TCP layers also agree on the amount of information that is to be sent before the recipient TCP sends back an acknowledgment. With everything agreed upon in advance, the stage is set for reliable Application layer communication to take place.

TCP is a full-duplex connection, reliable, accurate, jellybean-counting protocol, and establishing all these terms and conditions, in addition to following through on them to check for error, is no small task. It's very complicated, and very costly in terms of network overhead. Using TCP should be reserved for use only in situations when reliability is of utmost importance. For one thing, today's networks are much more reliable than those of yore, and therefore the added security is often a wasted effort. We'll discuss an alternative to TCP's high overhead method of transmission next.

UDP (User Datagram Protocol)

This protocol is used in place of TCP. *UDP* is the scaled down economy model, and is considered a *thin protocol*. Like a thin person on a park bench, it doesn't take up a lot of room—in this case, on a network. It also doesn't offer all the bells and whistles of TCP, but it does do a fabulous job of transporting stuff that doesn't require reliable delivery—and it does it using far fewer network resources.

There are some situations where it would definitely be wise to opt for UDP rather than TCP. Remember that watchdog SNMP up there at the Process/Application layer? SNMP monitors the network sending intermittent messages and a fairly steady flow of status updates and alerts, especially when running on a large network. The cost in overhead necessary to establish, maintain, and close a TCP connection for each one of those little messages would reduce a normally healthy, efficient network to a sticky, sluggish bog in no time. Another circumstance calling for the deployment of UDP over TCP is when the matter of reliability is seen to at the Process/Application layer. NFS handles its own reliability issues, making the use of TCP both impractical and redundant.

UDP receives upper-layer blocks of information, instead of streams of data like its big brother TCP, and breaks them into segments. Also like TCP, each segment is given a number for reassembly into the intended block at the destination. However, UDP does *not* sequence the segments, and does not care in which order the segments arrive at the destination. At least it numbers them. But after that, UDP sends them off and forgets about them. It doesn't follow through, check up on, or even allow for an acknowledgment of safe arrival—complete abandonment. Because of this, it's referred to as an *unreliable* protocol. This does not mean that UDP is ineffective—only that it doesn't handle issues of reliability.

There are more things UDP doesn't do. It doesn't create a virtual circuit, and it doesn't contact the destination before delivering stuff to it. It is therefore considered a *connectionless* protocol.

Key Concepts of Host-to-Host Protocols

The following list highlights some of the key concepts that you should keep in mind regarding these two protocols.

TCP	UDP
Virtual circuit	Unsequenced
Sequenced	Unreliable
Acknowledgments	Connectionless
Reliable	Low overhead

Instructors commonly use a telephone analogy to help people understand how TCP works. Most of us understand that before you talk with someone on a phone, you must first establish a connection with that other person—wherever they may be. This is like a virtual circuit with the TCP protocol. If you were giving someone important information during your conversation, you might say, "Did you get that?" A query like that is like a TCP acknowledgment. From time to time, for various reasons, people also say, "Are you still there?" They end their conversations with a "goodbye" of some sort, putting closure on the phone call. These types of functions are done by TCP.

On the other hand, using UDP is like sending a postcard. To do that, you don't need to contact the other party first. You simply write your message, address it, and mail it. This is analogous to UDP's connectionless orientation. Since the message on the postcard is probably not a matter of life or death, you don't need an acknowledgment of its receipt. Similarly, UDP does not involve acknowledgments.

Internet Layer Protocols

There are two main reasons for the Internet layer: routing, and providing a single network interface to the upper layers. None of the upper-layer protocols, and none of the ones on the lower layer, have any functions relating to routing. Routing is complex and important, and it's the job of the Internet layer to carry it out. The protocol *IP* is so integral to this layer, the very name of it is the name of the layer itself. So far, in discussing the upper layers, we've begun with a brief introduction, and left any specific treatise on their resident protocols to supporting sections. However here, IP, though only a protocol, is essentially the Internet layer. We've therefore included it in our introductory talk on the layer. The other protocols found here merely exist to support it. IP contains the Big Picture, and could be said to "see all," in that it is aware of all the interconnected networks. It can do this because all the machines on the network have a software address called an IP address, which we will cover more thoroughly later, in Chapter 3.

IP looks at each packet's IP address. Then, using a routing protocol, it decides where this packet is to be sent next, choosing the best path. The Network Access layer protocols at the bottom of the model don't possess IP's enlightened scope of the entire network; they deal only with point-to-point physical links.

A second main reason for the Internet layer is to provide a single network interface to the upper-layer protocols. Without this layer, application programmers would need to write "hooks" into every one of their applications for each different Network Access protocol. This would not only be a pain in the neck, it would lead to different versions of each application—one for Ethernet, another one for Token Ring, and so on. To prevent this, IP, lord of the Internet layer, provides one single network interface for the upper-layer protocols. That accomplished, it's then the job of IP and the various Network Access protocols to get along and work together.

All network roads don't lead to Rome—they lead to IP, and all the other protocols at this layer, as well as all the upper-layer protocols, use it. Never forget that. All paths through the model go through IP. The following sections describe the protocols at the Internet layer.

✳ IP (Internet Protocol)

Identifying devices on networks requires having the answers to these two questions: Which network is it on, and what is its ID on that network? The first is the *software address* (the right street); the second, the *hardware address* (the right mailbox). All hosts on a network have a logical ID called an IP address. This is the software address, and it contains valuable encoded information greatly simplifying the complex task of routing.

IP takes segments from the Host-to-Host layer and fragments them into *datagrams* (packets). IP also reassembles datagrams back into segments on the receiving side. Each datagram is assigned the IP address of the sender and the IP address of the recipient. Each machine that receives a datagram makes routing decisions based upon the packet's destination IP address.

✳ ARP (Address Resolution Protocol)

When IP has a datagram to send, it has already been informed by upper-layer protocols of the destination's IP address. However, IP must also inform a Network Access protocol, such as Ethernet, of the destination's hardware address. If IP does not know the hardware address, it uses the *ARP* protocol to find this information. As IP's detective, ARP interrogates the network by sending out a broadcast asking the machine with the specified IP address to reply with its hardware address. ARP is able to translate a software address, the IP address, into a hardware address—for example, the destination machine's Ethernet board address—thereby deducing its whereabouts. This hardware address is technically referred to as the *media access control (MAC) address*.

✳ RARP (Reverse Address Resolution Protocol)

When an IP machine happens to be a diskless machine, it has no way of initially knowing its IP address. But it does know its MAC address. The *RARP* protocol is the psychoanalyst for these lost souls. It sends out a packet that includes its MAC address, and a request to be informed of what IP address is assigned to its MAC address. A designated machine, called a *RARP server*, responds with the answer, and the identity crisis is over. Like a good analyst, RARP uses the information it does know about the machine's MAC address, to learn its IP address and complete the machine's ID portrait.

✳ BootP

BootP stands for *Boot Program*. When a diskless workstation is powered on, it broadcasts a BootP request on the network. A BootP server hears the request, and looks up the client's MAC address in its BootP file. If it finds an appropriate entry, it responds by telling the machine its IP address, and the file— usually via the TFTP protocol—that it should boot from.

BootP is used by a diskless machine to learn the following:

- Its IP address

- The IP address of a server machine

- The name of a file that is to be loaded into memory and executed at boot up

✳ ICMP (Internet Control Message Protocol)

ICMP is a management protocol and messaging service provider for IP. Its messages are carried as IP datagrams. *RFC 1256, ICMP Router Discovery Messages* is an annex to ICMP, which affords hosts extended capability in discovering routes to gateways. Periodically, router advertisements are announced over the network reporting IP addresses for its network interfaces. Hosts listen for these network infomercials to acquire route information. A *router solicitation* is a request for immediate advertisements, and may be sent by a host when it starts up. The following are some common events and messages that ICMP relates to:

Destination unreachable If a router cannot send an IP datagram any further, it uses ICMP to send a message back to the sender advising it of the situation.

Buffer full If a router's memory buffer for receiving incoming datagrams is full, it will use ICMP to send out this message.

Hops Each IP datagram is allotted a certain number of routers that it may go through, called *hops*. If it reaches its limit of hops before arriving at its destination, the last router to receive that datagram throws it away. The executioner router then uses ICMP to send an obituary message informing the sending machine of the demise of its datagram. This is network population control.

Network Access Layer Protocols

Programmers for the DOD model didn't define protocols for this layer; instead, their focus began at the Internet layer. In fact, this is exactly the quality that makes this model able to be implemented on almost any hardware platform. Obviously, this is one of the reasons why the Internet protocol suite is so popular. Every protocol listed here relates to the physical transmission of data. The following are the Network Access layer's main duties:

- Receiving an IP datagram and *framing* it into a stream of bits—ones and zeros—for physical transmission. (The information at this layer is called a *frame*.) An example of a protocol that works at this level is *CSMA/CD*, or *Carrier Sense, Multiple Access with Collision Detect*. Again, purpose equals name. It checks the cable to see if there's already another PC transmitting (Carrier Sense), allows all computers to share the same bandwidth (Multiple Access), and detects and retransmits collisions. Essentially, it is the highway patrol of the Network Access layer.

- Specifying the *MAC address*. Even though the Internet layer determines the destination MAC address (the hardware address), the Network Access protocols actually place that MAC address in the MAC frame.

- Ensuring that the stream of bits making up the frame have been accurately received by calculating a CRC (Cyclic Redundancy Checksum) jellybean count.

- Specifying the access methods to the physical network, such as *Contention-based for Ethernet* (first come, first served), *Token-passing* (wait for token before transmitting) for Token Ring, *FDDI*, and *Polling* (wait to be asked) for IBM mainframes.

- Specifying the physical media, the connectors, electrical signaling, and timing rules.

Some of the technologies used to implement the Network Access layer are:

- LAN-oriented protocols:

  - Ethernet (thick coaxial cable, thin coaxial cable, twisted-pair cable)

  - Token Ring

  - ARCnet

- WAN-oriented protocols:

  - Point-to-Point Protocol (PPP)

  - X.25

  - Frame Relay

Summary

In this chapter we covered the basics of TCP/IP, opening with a definition of this popular pair of protocols, its beginnings, and why it's so important today. We discovered how TCP/IP fits into the Department of Defense

(DOD) networking archetype, and moved on to explore both the DOD and the Open Systems Interconnection (OSI) reference models. We then zoomed in for a close-up of the TCP/IP protocol suite, closing the chapter with an in-depth look at the individual protocols and utilities, including their special functions.

Not to worry, the test does not cover too many of the objectives in this first chapter. However, go through the exercises below to make sure you have a good understanding of what TCP/IP is and the protocols associated with it.

Review Questions

To make sure you're getting all of this, take a moment to both read and work with the multiple choice and scenario-based questions offered below.

1. What is TCP/IP?

   A. A collection of packets sent through the Internet

   B. A collection of packages for use on the Internet

   C. A suite of protocols that provide routing and addressing in wide-area networks, and connectivity to a variety of hosts

   D. A freeware program

2. What are the layers in the DOD four-layer model used by TCP/IP?

   A. Process/Application

   B. Session

   C. Network Access

   D. Internet

   E. Host-to-Host

   F. Transport

3. What core TCP/IP protocols are provided with Microsoft TCP/IP?

   A. TCP

   B. UDP

   C. DUP

   D. ICMP

   E. PI

   F. IP

   G. PAR

   H. ARP

   I. CTP

4. What parameters are required for a TCP/IP host to communicate in a wide-area network?

   A. IP Address

   B. Subnet Mask

   C. Zip Code

   D. Default Gateway

   E. Login Name

5. It's Monday morning. Just as you arrive at your desk, your boss calls you into his office and says he read about TCP/IP in a Microsoft magazine over the weekend. Because he now believes that all Microsoft products are fabulous, he's set on having someone implement MS TCP/IP at all twelve branch office sites. He says that because of your quality work over the past few months, you're his first choice. However, before he names you the project's leader, he wants you to give him a complete explanation of TCP/IP and how it will meet his networking needs. Can you? Try it.

6. To get a jump on the competition, you need to find some information on a new, highly efficient protocol being developed. Where would you find this information? How would you access it and through which server? If you have access to the Internet, try this as an exercise on your computer.

7. Your boss tells you she spent lunch at the gym, where she overheard a great way to look up information on the Internet. She tells you that it organizes subjects into a menu system and allows you to access the information on each topic listed. She's frustrated because she can't remember what it's called—can you?

8. You are the senior communication technician for a small computer store. The sales staff is complaining that they cannot deliver or receive mail on their TCP/IP computers. All other applications on the network seem to work properly. The location of the problem is likely to be on *which layer* of the DOD model?

9. The IS department is planning to implement TCP/IP. Your manager, who knows and understands the OSI reference model, asks you, "What are the layers in the four-layer model used by the DOD for TCP/IP, and how does each layer relate to the OSI reference model?" What do you tell him?

10. You are the network administrator for a large accounting office. They have seven offices, all connected. You get a call from a remote office complaining that their workstations cannot connect to the network. After talking with them for a few minutes, you discover that network connectivity is down at all seven offices. What layer of the DOD model is likely at fault?

11. The accounting department calls you about two workstations in their department, complaining that "they're taking turns like twins, with only one being able to log in to the network at a time." All the other workstations in the department are fine. What's the problem, and how do you fix it?

12. You're the network manager for a large aircraft company. The reservationists have been griping for two weeks about the slow response of their computers. You've narrowed the problem down to noise on the thin-net coax cabling. Which layer of the DOD model is responsible?

13. Your co-worker calls you because she is confused about the differences between the OSI reference model and the DOD model. She can't figure out where packets are framed with the hardware address and a cyclic redundancy check. What do you tell her?

14. You're in an interview for an important position at a good company. You've studied hard and know your TCP/IP. The interviewer asks you, "What is the connectionless protocol at the Internet layer of the DOD model, and what is its function?" Do you stare back blankly, mouth agape, or answer confidently with...?

15. After you breeze through that last question in the interview, the interviewer then asks you, "At what layer are messages segmented and what protocol is used for segmenting them?" What's your answer?

16. Your pal just landed a job as a Help Desk operator and is brushing up on her TCP/IP protocols to prepare for her first day. She calls you with this question: "Ones and zeros are extracted from the cable and formed into logical groups called frames. The hardware destination is then checked, and a cyclic redundancy checksum is performed. If the hardware address is correct, and the CRC matches its original mathematical algorithm, then the packet is sent to which protocol at which layer?" What do you tell her?

17. You're a software developer who enjoys writing video games to play on the Internet with TCP/IP. You want to use the fastest protocol at the Transport layer of the OSI model to ensure no delay when blowing up all the Morphofreaks. What protocol do you use? Also, at what corresponding layer of the DOD model would this protocol run?

18. Your UNIX diskless workstations cannot logon to the host. After troubleshooting, you notice that when they boot up, the hardware address is sent to the host, but the host rejects them. Which protocol is asleep on the job?

19. You need to install network management to keep track of network errors and to baseline for future growth. Which protocol do you use, and which layer of the DOD does it operate on?

CHAPTER

2

Identifying Machines with IP Addressing

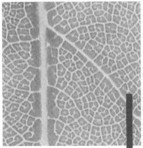

n this chapter, we'll probe further into the basics of TCP/IP and examine the supremely important subject of how accurate communication is achieved between specific networks and host systems through proper IP addressing. We'll discuss how and why that communication happens, why it doesn't when it fails, and how to configure devices on both LANs and WANs to ensure solid performance for your network.

The following items are central to this chapter. As you look over the list, make a mental note of them to keep in mind as you read on. You should be able to define and/or perform them when you're finished with this section.

- Define an IP address.

- Know the different classes of IP addresses.

- Identify both the network and host IDs in class A, B, and C addresses.

- Identify both valid and invalid class A, B, and C addresses.

- Assign appropriate host and network IDs.

- Understand which network components require IP addresses.

- Understand common IP addressing problems.

- Know what a subnet is.

- Know what a subnet mask is, and how it works.

- Know what a default subnet mask is, and how it works.

- Outline a range of valid host IDs for multiple subnets.

- Create an effective subnet mask for a WAN comprised of many subnets.

What Is IP Addressing?

One of the most important topics in any discussion of TCP/IP is *IP addressing*. An IP address is a numeric identifier assigned to each machine on an IP network. It designates the location of the device it is assigned to on the network. As mentioned earlier, this type of address is a software address, not a hardware address, which is hard-coded in the machine or network interface card.

The Hierarchical IP Addressing Scheme

An IP address is made up of 32 bits of information. These bits are divided into four sections containing one byte (8 bits) each. These sections are referred to as *octets*. There are three methods for depicting an IP address:

- Dotted-decimal, as in 130.57.30.56

- Binary, as in 10000010.00111001.00011110.00111000

- Hexidecimal, as in 82 39 1E 38

All of these examples represent the same IP address.

The 32-bit IP address is a structured or hierarchical address, as opposed to a flat or nonhierarchical one. Although either type of addressing scheme could have been used, the hierarchical variety was chosen, and, as will be explained in this section, for a very good reason.

A good example of a flat addressing scheme is a social security number. There's no partitioning to it, meaning that each segment isn't allocated to numerically represent a certain area or characteristic of the individual it's assigned to. If this method had been used for IP addressing, every machine on the Internet would have needed a totally unique address, just as each social security number is unique. The good news about this scheme is that it can handle a large number of addresses, namely 4.2 billion (a 32-bit address space with two possible values for each position—either zero or one—giving you 2^{32}, which equals 4.2 billion). The bad news, and the reason for it being passed over, relates to routing. With every address totally unique, all routers on the Internet would need to store the address of each and every machine on the Internet. It would be fair to say that this would make efficient routing impossible even if a fraction of the possible addresses were used.

The solution to this dilemma is to use a two-level, hierarchical addressing scheme that is structured by class, rank, grade, and so on. An example of this type is a telephone number. The first section of a telephone number, the area code, designates a very large area, followed by the prefix, narrowing the scope to a local calling area. The final segment, the customer number, zooms in on the specific connection. It's similar with IP addresses. Rather than the entire 32 bits being treated as a unique identifier as in flat addressing, a part of the address is designated as the *network address*, and the other part as a *node address*, giving it a layered, hierarchical structure.

The network address uniquely identifies each network. Every machine on the same network shares that network address as part of its IP address. In the IP address 130.57.30.56, for example, the 130.57 is the network address.

The node address is assigned to, and uniquely identifies, each machine on a network. This part of the address must be unique because it identifies a particular machine—an individual, as opposed to a network, which is a group. This number can also be referred to as a *host address*. In the sample IP address 130.57.30.56, the .30.56 is the node address.

The designers of the Internet decided to create classes of networks based on network size. For the small number of networks possessing a very large number of nodes, they created the rank *Class A network*. At the other extreme is the *Class C network*, reserved for the numerous networks with a small number of nodes. The class distinction for networks in between very large and very small is predictably called a *Class B network*. How one would subdivide an IP address into a network and node address is determined by the class designation of one's network. Table 2.1 provides us with a summary on the three classes of networks, which will be described in more detail in the following sections.

To ensure efficient routing, Internet designers defined a mandate for the leading bits section of the address for each different network class. For example, since a router knows that a Class A network address always starts with a zero, the router might be able to speed a packet on its way after reading only the first bit of its address. Figure 2.1 illustrates how the leading bits of a network address are defined.

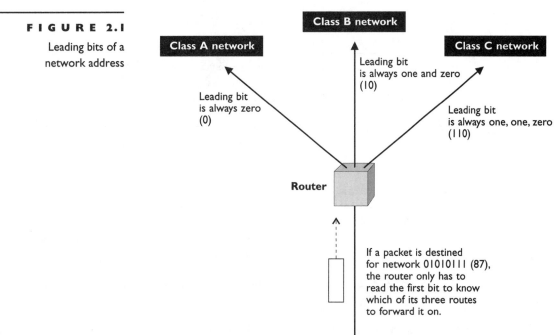

FIGURE 2.1

Leading bits of a
network address

Some IP addresses are reserved for special purposes, and shouldn't be assigned to nodes by network administrators. Table 2.2 lists the members of this exclusive little club, along with their reason for being included in it.

TABLE 2.1

Summary of the Three
Classes of Networks

Class	Format	Leading Bit Pattern	Decimal Range of First Byte of Network Address	Maximum Networks	Maximum Nodes per Network
A	Node	0	1—127	127	16,777,214
B	Node	10	128—191	16,384	65,534
C	Node	110	192—223	2,097,152	254

Subnet masks

A = 255.0.0.0

B = 255.255.0.0

C = 255.255.255.0

	Address	Function
TABLE 2.2 Reserved IP Addresses	Network address of all zeros	Interpreted to mean "this network"
	Network address of all ones	Interpreted to mean "all networks"
	Network 127	Reserved for loopback tests. Designates the local node and allows that node to send a test packet to itself without generating network traffic.
	Node address of all zeros	Interpreted to mean "this node"
	Node address of all ones	Interpreted to mean "all nodes" on the specified network; for example, 128.2.255.255 means "all nodes" on network 128.2 (Class B address)
	Entire IP address set to all zeros	Used by the RIP protocol to designate the default route
	Entire IP address set to all ones (same as 255.255.255.255)	Broadcast to all nodes on the current network; sometimes called an "all ones broadcast"

Class A Networks

In a Class A network, the first byte is assigned to the network address, and the three remaining bytes are used for the node addresses. The Class A format is:

Network.Node.Node.Node.

For example, in the IP address 49.22.102.70, 49 is the network address, and 22.102.70 is the node address. Every machine on this particular network would have the distinctive network address of 49.

With the length of a Class A network address being a byte, and with the first bit of that byte reserved, seven bits in the first byte remain for manipulation. That means that the maximum number of Class A networks that could be created would be 128. Why? Because each of the seven bit positions can either be a zero or a one, thus 2^7 or 128. To complicate things further, it was also decided that the network address of all zeros (0000 0000) would be reserved (see Table 2.2). This means the actual number of usable Class A network addresses is 128 minus 1, or 127.

Take a peek and see this for yourself in the decimal-to-binary chart shown in Table 2.3. Start at binary 0 and view the first bit (the leftmost bit). Continue down through the chart until the first bit turns into the digit 1. See that? Sure enough, the decimal range of a Class A network is 0 through 127. Since the Much Ado About Nothing Address (all zeros) is one of those special, reserved-club members, the range of network addresses for a Class A network is 1 through 127. Eventually, we'll see that another Class A number is in that club—number 127. This little revelation technically brings the total down to 126.

T A B L E 2.3	**Decimal**	**Binary**	**Decimal**	**Binary**	**Decimal**	**Binary**

T A B L E 2.3

Decimal-to-binary chart

Decimal	Binary	Decimal	Binary	Decimal	Binary
0	0000 0000	13	0000 1101	26	0001 1010
1	0000 0001	14	0000 1110	27	0001 1011
2	0000 0010	15	0000 1111	28	0001 1100
3	0000 0011	16	0001 0000	29	0001 1101
4	0000 0100	17	0001 0001	30	0001 1110
5	0000 0101	18	0001 0010	31	0001 1111
6	0000 0110	19	0001 0011	32	0010 0000
7	0000 0111	20	0001 0100	33	0010 0001
8	0000 1000	21	0001 0101	34	0010 0010
9	0000 1001	22	0001 0110	35	0010 0011
10	0000 1010	23	0001 0111	36	0010 0100
11	0000 1011	24	0001 1000	37	0010 0101
12	0000 1100	25	0001 1001	38	0010 0110

TABLE 2.3 (cont.)	Decimal	Binary	Decimal	Binary	Decimal	Binary
Decimal-to-binary chart	39	0010 0111	60	0011 1100	81	0101 0001
	40	0010 1000	61	0011 1101	82	0101 0010
	41	0010 1001	62	0011 1110	83	0101 0011
	42	0010 1010	63	0011 1111	84	0101 0100
	43	0010 1011	64	0100 0000	85	0101 0101
	44	0010 1100	65	0100 0001	86	0101 0110
	45	0010 1101	66	0100 0010	87	0101 0111
	46	0010 1110	67	0100 0011	88	0101 1000
	47	0010 1111	68	0100 0100	89	0101 1001
	48	0011 0000	69	0100 0101	90	0101 1010
	49	0011 0001	70	0100 0110	91	0101 1011
	50	0011 0010	71	0100 0111	92	0101 1100
	51	0011 0011	72	0100 1000	93	0101 1101
	52	0011 0100	73	0100 1001	94	0101 1110
	53	0011 0101	74	0100 1010	95	0101 1111
	54	0011 0110	75	0100 1011	96	0110 0000
	55	0011 0111	76	0100 1100	97	0110 0001
	56	0011 1000	77	0100 1101	98	0110 0010
	57	0011 1001	78	0100 1110	99	0110 0011
	58	0011 1010	79	0100 1111	100	0110 0100
	59	0011 1011	80	0101 0000	101	0110 0101

TABLE 2.3 (cont.)	Decimal	Binary	Decimal	Binary	Decimal	Binary
Decimal-to-binary chart	102	0110 0110	124	0111 1100	146	1001 0010
	103	0110 0111	125	0111 1101	147	1001 0011
	104	0110 1000	126	0111 1110	148	1001 0100
	105	0110 1001	127	0111 1111	149	1001 0101
	106	0110 1010	128	1000 0000	150	1001 0110
	107	0110 1011	129	1000 0001	151	1001 0111
	108	0110 1100	130	1000 0010	152	1001 1000
	109	0110 1101	131	1000 0011	153	1001 1001
	110	0110 1110	132	1000 0100	154	1001 1010
	111	0110 1111	133	1000 0101	155	1001 1011
	112	0111 0000	134	1000 0110	156	1001 1100
	113	0111 0001	135	1000 0111	157	1001 1101
	114	0111 0010	136	1000 1000	158	1001 1110
	115	0111 0011	137	1000 1001	159	1001 1111
	116	0111 0100	138	1000 1010	160	1010 0000
	117	0111 0101	139	1000 1011	161	1010 0001
	118	0111 0110	140	1000 1100	162	1010 0010
	119	0111 0111	141	1000 1101	163	1010 0011
	120	0111 1000	142	1000 1110	164	1010 0100
	121	0111 1001	143	1000 1111	165	1010 0101
	122	0111 1010	144	1001 0000	166	1010 0110
	123	0111 1011	145	1001 0001	167	1010 0111

	Decimal	Binary	Decimal	Binary	Decimal	Binary
T A B L E 2.3 *(cont.)* Decimal-to-binary chart	168	1010 1000	189	1011 1101	210	1101 0010
	169	1010 1001	190	1011 1110	211	1101 0011
	170	1010 1010	191	1011 1111	212	1101 0100
	171	1010 1011	192	1100 0000	213	1101 0101
	172	1010 1100	193	1100 0001	214	1101 0110
	173	1010 1101	194	1100 0010	215	1101 0111
	174	1010 1110	195	1100 0011	216	1101 1000
	175	1010 1111	196	1100 0100	217	1101 1001
	176	1011 0000	197	1100 0101	218	1101 1010
	177	1011 0001	198	1100 0110	219	1101 1011
	178	1011 0010	199	1100 0111	220	1101 1100
	179	1011 0011	200	1100 1000	221	1101 1101
	180	1011 0100	201	1100 1001	222	1101 1110
	181	1011 0101	202	1100 1010	223	1101 1111
	182	1011 0110	203	1100 1011	224	1110 0000
	183	1011 0111	204	1100 1100	225	1110 0001
	184	1011 1000	205	1100 1101	226	1110 0010
	185	1011 1001	206	1100 1110	227	1110 0011
	186	1011 1010	207	1100 1111	228	1110 0100
	187	1011 1011	208	1101 0000	229	1110 0101
	188	1011 1100	209	1101 0001	230	1110 0110

	Decimal	Binary	Decimal	Binary	Decimal	Binary
TABLE 2.3 *(cont.)* Decimal-to-binary chart	231	1110 0111	240	1111 0000	249	1111 1001
	232	1110 1000	241	1111 0001	250	1111 1010
	233	1110 1001	242	1111 0010	251	1111 1011
	234	1110 1010	243	1111 0011	252	1111 1100
	235	1110 1011	244	1111 0100	253	1111 1101
	236	1110 1100	245	1111 0101	254	1111 1110
	237	1110 1101	246	1111 0110	255	1111 1111
	238	1110 1110	247	1111 0111		
	239	1110 1111	248	1111 1000		

Each Class A network has three bytes (24 bit positions) for the node address of a machine. That means there are 2^{24}—or 16,777,216—unique combinations, and therefore precisely that many possible unique node addresses for each Class A network. Because addresses with the two patterns of all zeros and all ones are reserved, the actual maximum usable number of nodes for a Class A network is 2^{24} minus 2, which equals 16,777,214.

Class B Networks

In a Class B network, the first two bytes are assigned to the network address, and the remaining two bytes are used for node addresses. The format is:

Network.Network.Node.Node

For example, in the IP address 130.57.30.56, the network address is 130.57, and the node address is 30.56.

With the network address being two bytes, there would be 2^{16} unique combinations. But the Internet designers decided that all Class B networks should start with the binary digits 1 and 0. This leaves 14 bit positions to manipulate, and therefore 16,384 unique Class B networks.

If you take another peek at the decimal-to-binary chart in Table 2.3, you will see that the first two bits of the first byte are 1 0 from decimal 128 up to 191. Therefore, if you're still confused, remember that you can always easily recognize a Class B network by looking at its first byte—even though there are 16,384 different Class B networks! All you have to do is look at that address. If the first byte is in the range of decimal 128 to 191, it is a Class B network.

A Class B network has two bytes to use for node addresses. This is 2^{16} minus the two patterns in the reserved-exclusive club (all zeros and all ones), for a total of 65,534 possible node addresses for each Class B network.

Class C Networks

The first three bytes of a Class C network are dedicated to the network portion of the address, with only one measly byte remaining for the node address. The format is:

Network.Network.Network.Node

In the example IP address 198.21.74.102, the network address is 198.21.74, and the node address is 102.

In a Class C network, the first *three* bit positions are always the binary 110. The calculation is such: Three bytes, or 24 bits, minus three reserved positions, leaves 21 positions. There are therefore 2^{21} or 2,097,152 possible Class C networks.

Referring again to that decimal-to-binary chart in Table 2.3, you will see that the lead bit pattern of 110 starts at decimal 192 and runs through 223. Remembering our handy, non-calculatory, easy-recognition method, this means that although there are a total of 2,097,152 Class C networks possible, you can always spot a Class C address if the first byte is between 192 and 223.

Each unique Class C network has one byte to use for node addresses. This leads to 2^8 or 256, minus the two special club patterns of all zeros and all ones, for a total of 254 node addresses for each Class C network.

Additional Classes of Networks

Another class of network is Class D. This range of addresses is used for *multicast packets*. The range of numbers is from 224.0.0.0 to 239.255.255.255.

A *multicast transmission* is used when a host wants to broadcast to multiple destinations. Hosts do this when attempting to learn of all the routers on its network. Using the ICMP protocol, it sends out a *router discovery packet*. This packet is addressed to 224.0.0.2, fingering it as a multicast packet to all the routers on its network.

There is also a Class E range of numbers starting at 240.0.0.0 and running to 255.255.255.255. These numbers are reserved for future use.

Unless you revel in chaos, and desire to add stress to your life, both Class D and E addresses should not be assigned to nodes on your network.

Who Assigns Network Addresses?

If your network will be connected to the Internet, you must be proper and petition the official Internet authorities for the assignment of a network address. An official Internet organization called the Network Information Center (NIC) can assist you in this process. For further information, contact:

Network Solutions InterNIC Registration Services
505 Huntmar Park Drive
Herndon, VA 22070

You may also obtain help by sending e-mail to:

hostmaster@internic.net

If your network will not be connected to the Internet, you are free to assign any network address you wish.

For the most part, you are now able to obtain valid IP addresses from your Internet Service Provider (ISP). The NIC would prefer for you to do it that way, as it cuts down on the work they need to do.

Subnetting a Network

If an organization is large and has a whole bunch of computers, or if its computers are geographically dispersed, it makes good sense to divide its colossal network into smaller ones connected together by routers. The benefits to doings things this way include:

Reduced network traffic We all appreciate less traffic of any kind! So do networks. Without trusty routers, packet traffic could grind the entire network down to near standstill. With them, most traffic will stay on the local network—only packets destined for other networks will pass through the router.

Optimized network performance This is a bonus of reduced network traffic.

Simplified management It's easier to identify and isolate network problems in a group of smaller networks connected together than within one gigantic one.

Facilitates spanning large geographical distances Because WAN links are considerably slower and more expensive than LAN links, having a single large network spanning long distances can create problems in every arena listed above. Connecting multiple smaller networks makes the system more efficient.

All this is well and good, but if an organization with multiple networks has been assigned only one network address by the NIC, that organization has a problem. As the saying goes, "Where there is no vision, the people perish." The original designers of the IP protocol envisioned a teensy Internet with only mere tens of networks and hundreds of hosts. Their addressing scheme used a network address for each physical network.

As you can imagine, this scheme and the unforeseen growth of the Internet created a few problems. To name one, a single network address can be used to refer to multiple physical networks. An organization can request individual network addresses for each one of its physical networks. If these were granted, there wouldn't be enough to go around for everyone.

Another problem relates to routers. If each router on the Internet needed to know about each existing physical network, routing tables would be impossibly huge. There would be an overwhelming amount of administrative overhead to maintain those tables, and the resulting physical overhead on the routers would be massive (CPU cycles, memory, disk space, and so on).

An additional consequence is that because routers exchange routing information with each other, there would result a terrific overabundance of network traffic. Figure 2.2 illustrates some of these problems.

Although there's more than one way to approach this tangle, the principal solution is the one that we'll be covering in this book... subnetting.

What is subnetting? Subnetting is a dandy TCP/IP software feature that allows for dividing a single IP network into smaller, logical subnetworks. This trick is achieved by using the host portion of an IP address to create something called a subnet address.

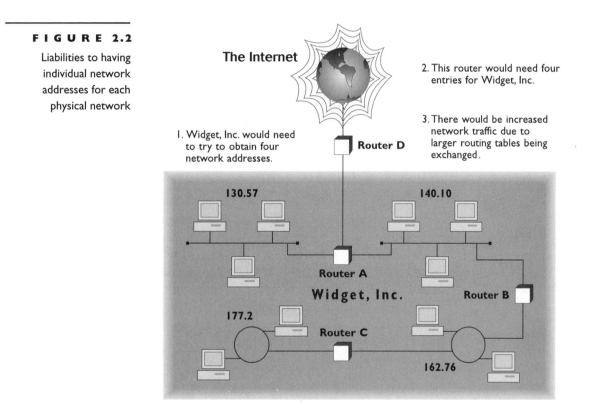

Implementing Subnetting

As you know, the IP addressing scheme used for subnets is referred to as sub-netting. Before you implement subnetting, you need to determine your current requirements and plan for future requirements. Follow these guidelines:

Microsoft ✓ *Exam* *Objective*	**Given a scenario, identify valid network configurations.**

1. Determine the number of required network IDs.

   ■ One for each subnet

   ■ One for each wide area network connection

2. Determine the number of required host IDs per subnet.

- One for each TCP/IP host

- One for each router interface

3. Based on the above requirement create:

- One subnet mask for your entire network

- A unique subnet ID for each physical segment

- A range of host IDs for each subnet

Subnetting is network procreation. It is the act of creating little subnetworks from a single, large parent network. An organization with a single network address can have a subnet address for each individual physical network. Each subnet is still part of the shared network address, but it also has an additional identifier denoting its individual subnetwork number. This identifier is called a subnet address. Take a parent who has two kids. The children inherit the same last name as their parent. People make further distinctions when referring to someone's individual children like, "Kelly, the Jones's oldest, who moved into their guest house, and Jamie, the Jones's youngest, who now has Kelly's old room." (They may make other kinds of distinctions too, but we won't talk about those here.) Those further distinctions are like subnet addresses for people.

This practice solves several addressing problems. First, if an organization has several physical networks but only one IP network address, it can handle the situation by creating subnets. Next, because subnetting allows many physical networks to be grouped together, fewer entries in a routing table are required, notably reducing network overhead. Finally, these things combine to collectively yield greatly enhanced network efficiency.

Information Hiding

As an example, suppose that the Internet refers to Widget, Inc. only by its single network address, 130.57. Suppose as well that Widget Inc. has several divisions, each dealing with something different. Since Widget's network administrators have implemented subnetting, when packets come into its network, the Widget routers use the subnet addresses to route the packets to the correct internal subnet. Thus, the complexity of Widget, Inc.'s network can be hidden from the rest of the Internet. This is called *information hiding*.

Information hiding also benefits the routers inside the Widget network. Without subnets, each Widget router would need to know the address of each machine on the entire Widget network—a bleak situation creating additional overhead and poor routing performance. Because of the subnet scheme, which alleviates the need for each router to know about every machine on the entire Widget network, their routers need only two types of information:

- The addresses of each machine on subnets to which it is attached

- The other subnet addresses

How to Implement Subnetting

Subnetting is implemented by assigning a subnet address to each machine on a given physical network. For example, in Figure 2.3, each machine on Subnet 1 has a subnet address of 1.

Microsoft ✓ *Exam* *Objective*	**Configure subnet masks.**

Next, we'll take a look at how a subnet address is incorporated into the rest of the IP address.

The network portion of an IP address can't be altered. Every machine on a particular network must share the same network address. In Figure 2.4, you can see that all of Widget, Inc.'s machines have a network address of 130.57. That principle is constant. In subnetting, it's the host address that's manipulated. The subnet address scheme takes a part of the host address and redesignates it as a subnet address. Bit positions are stolen from the host address to be used for the subnet identifier. Figure 2.4 shows how an IP address can be given a subnet address.

Since the Widget, Inc. network is the Class B variety, the first two bytes refer to the network address, and are shared by all machines on the network—regardless of their particular subnet. Here, every machine's address on the subnet must have its third byte read 0000 0001. The fourth byte, the host address, is the unique number that identifies the actual host. Figure 2.5 illustrates how a network address and a subnet address can be used. The same concepts and practices apply to each subnet created in the network.

FIGURE 2.3

The use of subnets

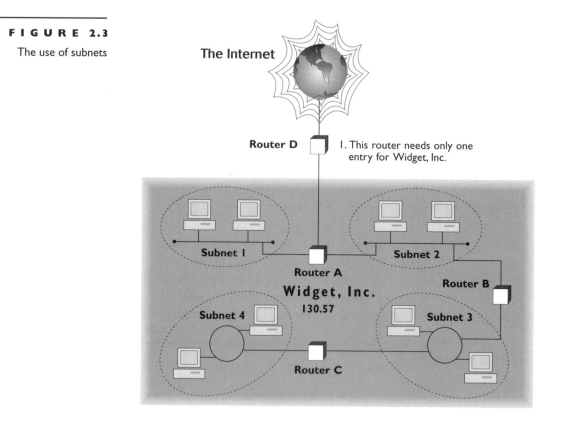

FIGURE 2.4

An IP address can be given a subnet address by manipulating the host address.

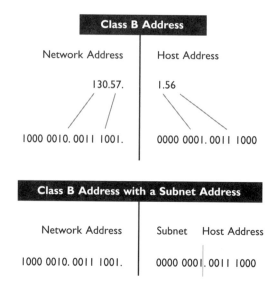

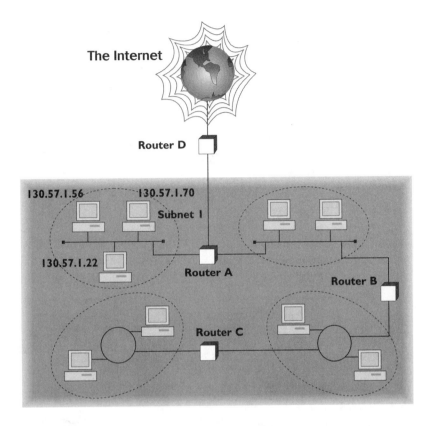

FIGURE 2.5

A network address and a subnet address

Subnet Masks

For the subnet address scheme to work, every machine on the network must know which part of the host address will be used as the subnet address. This is accomplished by assigning each machine a *subnet mask*.

The network administrator creates a 32-bit subnet mask comprised of ones and zeros. The ones in the subnet mask represent the positions that refer to the network or subnet addresses. The zeros represent the positions that refer to the host part of the address. These concepts are illustrated in Figure 2.6.

In our Widget, Inc. example, the first two bytes of the subnet mask are ones because Widget's network address is a Class B address formatted Net.Net.Node.Node. The third byte, normally assigned as part of the host address, is now used to represent the subnet address. Hence, those bit positions are represented with ones in the subnet mask. The fourth byte is the only part in our example that represents the unique host address.

FIGURE 2.6

A subnet mask

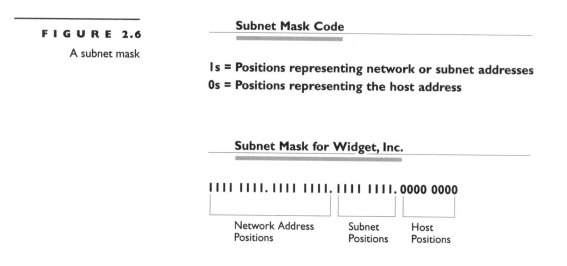

FIGURE 2.6

A subnet mask

The subnet mask can also be denoted using the decimal equivalents of the binary patterns. The binary pattern of 1111 1111 is the same as decimal 255 (see the decimal-to-binary chart in Table 2.3). Consequently, the subnet mask in our example can be denoted in two ways, as shown in Figure 2.7.

FIGURE 2.7

Subnet mask depiction

Subnet Mask in Binary: IIII IIII. IIII IIII. IIII IIII. 0000 0000

Subnet Mask in Decimal: 255 .   255 .   255 .   0

(The spaces in the above example are only for illustrative purposes. The subnet mask in decimal would actually appear as 255.255.255.0.)

All networks don't need to have subnets, and therefore don't need to use subnet masks. In this event, they are said to have a default subnet mask. This is basically the same as saying they don't have a subnet address. The default subnet masks for the different classes of networks are shown in Table 2.4.

TABLE 2.4

Default subnet masks

Class	Format	Default Subnet Mask
A	Net.Node.Node.Node	255.0.0.0
B	Net.Net.Node.Node	255.255.0.0
C	Net.Net.Net.Node	255.255.255.0

Once the network administrator has created the subnet mask and assigned it to each machine, the IP software views its IP address through the subnet mask to determine its subnet address. The word *mask* carries the implied meaning of a lens because the IP software looks at its IP address through the lens of its subnet mask to see its subnet address. An illustration of an IP address being viewed through a subnet mask is shown in Figure 2.8.

FIGURE 2.8

An IP address viewed through a subnet mask

Subnet Mask Code

1s = Positions representing network or subnet addresses

0s = Positions representing the host address

Positions relating to the subnet address.

Subnet Mask: 1111 1111. 1111 1111. 1111 1111. 0000 0000

IP address of a machine on subnet 1:   1000 0010. 0011 1001. 0000 0001. 0011 1000
(Decimal: 130.57.1.56)

Bits relating to the subnet address.

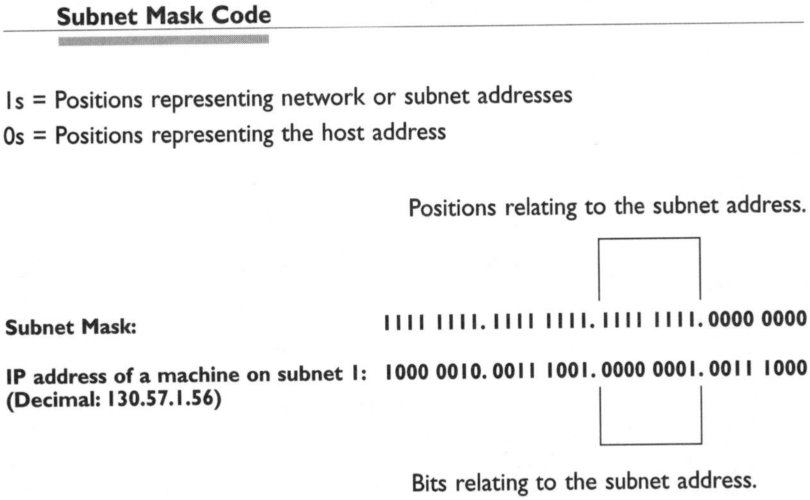

In this example, the IP software learns through the subnet mask that, instead of being part of the host address, the third byte of its IP address is now going to be used as a subnet address. The IP software then looks at the bit positions in its IP address that correspond to the mask, which are 0000 0001.

The final step is for the subnet bit values to be matched up with the binary numbering convention and converted to decimal. The binary numbering convention is shown in Figure 2.9.

In the Widget, Inc. example, the binary-to-decimal conversion is simple, as illustrated in Figure 2.10.

By using the entire third byte of a Class B address as the subnet address, it is easy to set and determine the subnet address. For example, if Widget, Inc. wants to have a Subnet 6, the third byte of all machines on that subnet will be 0000 0110. The binary-to-decimal conversion for this subnet mask is shown in Figure 2.11.

FIGURE 2.9

Binary numbering
convention

Binary Numbering Convention

Position / Value: ← (continued) 128 64 32 16 8 4 2 1

Binary Example: 0   0   0   1 0 0 1 0

Decimal Equivalent: 16 + 2 = 18

FIGURE 2.10

Binary-to-decimal
conversion

Binary Numbering Convention

Position / Value: ← (continued) 128 64 32 16 8 4 2 1

Widget third byte: 0   0   0   0 0 0 0 1

Decimal Equivalent: 0 + 1 = 1

Subnet Address: 1

Using the entire third byte of a Class B network address for the subnet allows for a fair number of available subnet addresses. One byte dedicated to the subnet provides eight bit positions. Each position can be either a one or a zero, so the calculation is 2^8, or 256. But because you cannot use the two patterns of all zeros and all ones, you must subtract two, for a total of 254. Thus, our Widget, Inc. company can have up to 254 total subnetworks, each with 254 hosts.

Although the official IP specification (RFC's) limits the use of zero as a subnet address, some products do permit this usage. Microsoft's NT TCP/IP implementation and the Novell MultiProtocol Router (MPR) software are

FIGURE 2.11

Setting a subnet

Binary Numbering Convention

Position / Value:	← (continued)	128	64	32	16	8	4	2	1

Binary Example: 0   0   0   0 0 1 1 0

Decimal Equivalent: 4 + 2 = 6

Subnet Address: 6

examples of products that do permit using a zero as a subnet address. Also, adding special commands into your Cisco routers, will allow you to use an all zero subnet mask. Doing so will avail one additional subnet number. For example, if the subnet mask is 8 bits, then rather than 254 (because $2^8-2=254$), the amount of subnets available would instead be 255 (because 256–1=255).

WARNING   Allowing a subnet address of zero increases the number of subnet numbers by one. However, you should not use a subnet of zero (all zeros) unless all of the software on your network recognizes this convention.

The formulas for calculating the maximum number of subnets and the maximum number of hosts per subnet are:

$2^{number\ of\ masked\ bits\ in\ subnet\ mask}-2=$*maximum number of subnets*

$2^{number\ of\ unmasked\ bits\ in\ subnet\ mask}-2=$*maximum number of hosts per subnet*

In the formulas, *masked* refers to bit positions of 1, and unmasked refers to positions of 0. Figure 2.12 shows an example of how these formulas can be applied.

The down side to using an entire byte of a node address as your subnet address is that you reduce the possible number of node addresses on each subnet. As explained earlier, without a subnet, a Class B address has 65,534 unique combinations of ones and zeros that can be used for node addresses.

Network Address: 161.11 (class B)

	Network	Subnet	
		Masked	*Unmasked*
Subnet Mask:	1111 1111. 1111 1111.	1110 0000.	0000 0000
Decimal:	255 . 255	. 224	. 0

If you use an entire byte of the node address for a subnet, you then have only one byte for the host addresses, leaving only 254 possible host addresses. If any of your subnets will be populated with more than 254 machines, you have a problem on your hands. To solve it, you would then need to shorten the subnet mask, thereby lengthening the host address, which benefits you with more potential host addresses. A side effect of this solution is that it causes the reduction of the number of possible subnets. Time to prioritize!

Figure 2.13 shows an example of using a smaller subnet address. A company called Acme, Inc. expects to need a maximum of 14 subnets. In this case, Acme does not need to take an entire byte from the host address for the subnet address. To get its 14 different subnet addresses, it only needs to snatch four bits from the host address ($2^4-2=14$). The host portion of the address has 12 usable bits remaining ($2^{12}-2=4094$). Each of Acme's 14 subnets could then potentially have a total of 4094 host addresses, or 4094 machines on each subnet.

Wait a minute, this is confusing! All those numbers—how can you ever remember them? We'll, let's step back a minute and take a look at the different classes of networks and how to subnet each one. We'll start with class C because it only uses 8 bits and so it's the easiest to calculate.

Class C

As you know, a class C network uses the first three bytes (24 bits) to define the network address. This leaves us one byte (8 bits) with which to address hosts. So, if we want to create subnets, our options are limited because of the small number of bits left available.

FIGURE 2.13

Using four bits of the host address for a subnet address

Acme, Inc.

Network Address:	**132.8 (Class B; net.net.host.host)**
Example IP Address:	**1000 0100. 0000 1000. 0001 0010. 0011 1100**
Decimal:	**132 . 8 . 18 . 60**

Subnet Mask Code

1s = Positions representing network or subnet addresses
0s = Positions representing the host address

Subnet Mask:

Binary:	**1111 1111. 1111 1111. 1111 0000. 0000 0000**
Decimal:	**255 . 255 . 240 . 0**

(The decimal '240' is equal to the binary '1111 0000.'
Refer to Table 3.3: Decimal to Binary Chart.)

Positions relating to the subnet address.

Subnet Mask: **1111 1111. 1111 1111. 1111 0000. 0000 0000**

IP address of a Acme machine:
(Decimal: 132.8.18.60) **1000 0100. 0000 1000. 0001 0010. 0011 1100**

Bits relating to the subnet address.

Binary to Decimal Conversion for Subnet Address

Subnet Mask Positions:	1	1	1	1	0	0	0	0
Position / Value: ◄── (continue)	128	64	32	16	8	4	2	1
Third Byte of IP address:	0	0	0	1	0	0	1	0
Decimal Equivalent:				0 + 16 = 16				
Subnet Address for this IP address:				16				

If you break down your subnets smaller than the default class C, then fig-uring out the subnet mask, network number, broadcast address, and router address can be kind of confusing. Table 2.5 summarizes how you can break a class C network down into one, two, four, or eight smaller subnets, with the subnet masks, network numbers, broadcast addresses, and router addresses. The first three bytes have simply been designated *x.y.z.*

T A B L E 2.5 Breaking a class C network into subnets	**Number of Desired Subnets**	**Subnet Mask**	**Network Number**	**Router Address**	**Broadcast Address**	**Remaining Number of IP Addresses**
	1	255.255.255.0	x.y.z.0	x.y.z.1	x.y.z.255	253
	2	255.255.255.128	x.y.z.0	x.y.z.1	x.y.z.127	125
		255.255.255	x.y.z.128	x.y.z.129	x.y.z.255	125
	4	255.255.255.192	x.y.z.0	x.y.z.1	x.y.z.63	61
		255.255.255	x.y.z.64	x.y.z.65	x.y.z.127	61
		255.255.255	x.y.z.128	x.y.z.129	x.y.z.191	61
		255.255.255	x.y.z.192	x.y.z.193	x.y.z.255	61
	8	255.255.255.224	x.y.z.0	x.y.z.1	x.y.z.31	29
		255.255.255	x.y.z.32	x.y.z.33	x.y.z.63	29
		255.255.255	x.y.z.64	x.y.z.65	x.y.z.95	29
		255.255.255	x.y.z.96	x.y.z.97	x.y.z.127	29
		255.255.255	x.y.z.128	x.y.z.129	x.y.z.159	29
		255.255.255	x.y.z.160	x.y.z.161	x.y.z.191	29
		255.255.255	x.y.z.192	x.y.z.193	x.y.z.223	29
		255.255.255	x.y.z.224	x.y.z.225	x.y.z.255	29

For example, suppose you want to chop up a class C network, 200.211.192.*x*, into two subnets. As you can see in the table, you'd use a subnet mask of 255.255.255.128 for each subnet. The first subnet would have network number 200.211.192.0, router address 200.211.192.1, and broadcast address 200.211.192.127. You could assign IP addresses 200.211.192.2 through 200.211.192.126—that's125 different IP addresses. (Notice that heavily subnetting a network results in the loss of a progressively greater percentage of addresses to the network number, broadcast address, and router address.) The second subnet would have network number 200.211.192.128, router address 200.211.192.129, and broadcast address 200.211.192.255.

Now, I know what you're thinking. How can you subnet a class C network like I talked about in the table above? If you use the 2^x–2 calculation, the subnet 128 in the table doesn't make sense!

Well, glad you noticed! Follow the steps below to find out where that subnet came from:

1. Remember that using subnet zero is a No-No according to the RFC's, but, by using it, you can subnet your class C network with a subnet mask of 128. This only uses one bit, and according to my trusty calculator, 2^1–2=0. Zero subnets.

2. By using an NT router, or putting in the IP subnet zero command into your Cisco routers, you can assign 1–127 for hosts, and 129–254 as stated in the table. This saves a bunch of addresses! If you were to stick to the method defined by RFC standards, the best you could gain is a subnet mask of 192, (two bits), that allows you only two subnets (2^2–2=2).

3. To figure out how many valid subnets exist, subtract the subnet mask from 256. Our example yields the following equation: 256–192=64. So sixty-four is your first subnet.

4. To determine a second subnet number, add the first subnet number to itself. To determine a third subnet number, add the first subnet number to the second subnet number. To determine a fourth subnet number, add the first subnet number to the third subnet number. Keep adding the first subnet number in this fashion until you reach the actual subnet number. For example, 64 plus 64 equals 128, so your second subnet is 128. 128 plus 64 is 192. Because 192 is the subnet mask, you cannot use it as an actual subnet. This means your valid subnets are 64 and 128.

5. The numbers between the subnets are your valid hosts. For example, the valid hosts in a class C network with a subnet mask of 192 are:

Subnet 64 65–126 which gives you 62 hosts per subnet (using 127 as a host would mean your host bits would be all ones). That's not allowed because the all ones format is reserved as the broadcast address for that subnet.

Subnet 128 129–190. Huh? What happened to 191–254? The subnet mask is 192, which you cannot use, and 191 would be all ones and used as the broadcast address for this subnet. Anything above 192 is also invalid for this subnet because these are automatically lost through the subnetting process.

As you can see, this solution wastes a lot of precious addresses: 130 to be exact! In a class C network, this would certainly be hard to justify—the 128 subnet is a much better solution if you only need two subnets.

Okay…So what happens if you need four subnets in your class C network? Well, by using the calculation of $2^{number\ of\ masked\ bits}-2$, you would need three bits to get six subnets ($2^3-2=6$). What are the valid subnets and what are the valid hosts of each subnet? Let's figure it out.

1. 11100000 is 224 in binary, and would be our subnet mask. This must be the same on all workstations.

Note for test takers: If a workstation has an incorrect mask, the router could "think" the workstation is on a different subnet than it actually is. When that happens, the misguided router won't forward packets to the workstation in question. Similarly, if the mask is incorrectly specified in the workstation's configuration, that workstation will observe the mask and send packets to the default gateway when it shouldn't. Keep in mind that the test has many questions on it where the answer *can be* an invalid subnet mask.

2. To figure out the valid subnets, subtract the subnet mask from 256. 256–224=32, so 32 is your first subnet. The other subnets would be 64, 96, 128, 160, and 192. The valid hosts are the numbers between the subnet numbers except the numbers that equal all ones. These numbers would be 63, 95, 127, 159, 191 and 223. Remember, all ones is reserved as the broadcast address for each subnet.

Subnet	Hosts
32	33–62
64	65–94
96	97–126
128	129–158
160	161–190
192	193–222

Are you getting all this? Let's add one more bit to the subnet mask just for fun.

1. We were using 3 bits, which gave us 224. By adding the next bit, the mask now becomes 240 (11110000).

2. By using 4 bits for the subnet mask we get 14 subnets because $2^4-2=14$. This subnet mask also gives us only 4 bits for the host addresses or 14 hosts per subnet. As you can see, the amount of hosts per subnet gets reduced rather quickly when subnetting a class C network.

3. The first valid subnet for subnet 240 is 16 (256–240=16). Our subnets are then 16, 32, 48, 64, 80, 96, 112, 128, 144, 160, 176, 192, 208, and 224. Remember, you cannot use the actual subnet number as a valid subnet, so 240 is invalid as a subnet number. The valid hosts are the numbers between the subnets, except for the numbers that are all ones— the broadcast address for the subnet.

So our valid subnets and hosts are:

Subnet	Hosts
16	17–30
32	33–46
48	49–62
64	65–78
80	81–94

96	97–110
112	113–126
128	129–142
144	145–158
160	161–174
176	177–190
192	193–206
208	209–222
224	225–238

Now that you've made it through that, we'll do it all again for a class B network.

Class B

Because a class B network has 16 bits for host addresses, we have plenty of available bits to play with when figuring out a subnet mask. Remember, you have to start with the leftmost bit and work towards the right. For example, a class B network would look like X.Y.0.0, with the default mask of 255.255.0.0. Using the default mask would give you one network, with 16,384 hosts.

The default mask in binary is 11111111.11111111.00000000.00000000. The ones represent the network, and the zeros represent the hosts. So when creating a subnet mask, the leftmost bit(s) will be borrowed from the hosts bits (zeros, not ones) to become the subnet mask. Let's play with the 16 bits available for hosts.

If we use only one bit, we have a mask of 255.255.128.0. This mask will be a bit more complicated to subnet than the class C 128 subnet mask. With 16 bits, we typically don't need to worry about a shortage of host IDs, so using 128 just isn't worth the trouble. The first mask you should use is 255.255.192.0, or 11111111.11111111.11000000.00000000.

We now have three parts of the IP address: the network address, the subnet address, and the host address. A 192 mask is figured out the same way a class C address 192 address is, but this time, we'll end up with a lot more hosts.

There are two subnets because $2^2-2=2$. The valid subnets are 64 and 128 (256–192=64, and 64+64=128). However, there are 14 bits (zeros) leftover for host addressing. This gives us 16,382 hosts per subnet ($2^{14}-2=16382$).

Subnet	Hosts
64	X.Y.64.1 through X.Y.127.254
128	X.Y.128.1 through X.Y. 191.254

Let's add another bit to our subnet mask, making it 11111111.11111111. 11100000.00000000 or 255.255.224.0. There are six subnets ($2^3-2=6$). The valid subnets are 32, 64, 96, 128,160 and 192 (256–224=32). The valid hosts are listed below:

Subnet	Hosts
32	X.Y.32.1 through 63.254
64	X.Y.64.1 through 95.254
96	X.Y.96.1 through 127.254
128	X.Y.128.1 through 159.254
160	X.Y.160.1 through 191.254
192	X.Y.192.1 through 223.254

So, if we use a 255.255.224.0 subnet mask, we can create six subnets, each with 8192 hosts.

Let's add a few more bits to the subnet mask and see what happens. If we use nine bits for the mask, it gives us 510 subnets ($2^9-2=510$). With only seven bits for hosts we have 126 hosts per subnet ($2^7-2=126$). The mask looks like this:

11111111.11111111.11111111.10000000 or 255.255.255.128

Let's add even more bits and see what we get. If we use 14 bits for the subnet mask, we get 16,382 subnets ($2^{14}-2=16382$), but this gives us only two hosts per subnet ($2^2-2=2$). The subnet mask looks like this:

11111111.11111111.11111111.11111100 or 255.255.255.252

Why would you ever use a 14 bit subnet mask with a class B address? Well, believe it or not, this approach is actually very common. Think about having a class B network and using a subnet mask of 255.255.255.0. You'd have 254 subnets and 254 hosts per subnet, right? Imagine also that you have a network with many WAN links. Typically, you'd have a direct connection between each site. Each of these links must be on their own subnet or network. There will be two hosts on these subnets—one address for each router port. If you used the mask as described above (255.255.255.0), you would waste 252 host addresses per subnet. By using the 255.255.255.252 subnet mask, you have many, many subnets available, each with only two hosts.

You can use this approach only if you are running a routing algorithm like EIGRP or OSPF. These routing protocols allow what is called variable length subnet masks (VLSM). VLSM allows you to run the 255.255.255.252 subnet mask on your interface to the WANs, and run 255.255.255.0 on your router interfaces in your LAN. It works because the routing protocols like EIGRP and OSPF transmit the subnet mask information in the update packets that it sends to other routers. RIP and IGRP do not support this feature.

Is this getting any clearer? Don't stop now, we still have class A networks to subnet!

Class A

Class A networks have a ton of bits available we can use to create subnets. A default class A network subnet mask is only 8 bits or 255.0.0.0, giving us a whopping 24 bits to play with.

If you use a mask of 11111111.**1111111**.00000000.00000000, or 255.255.0.0, you'll have eight bits for subnets or 254 subnets ($2^8-2=254$). This leaves 16 bits for hosts, or 65,536 hosts per subnet ($2^{16}-2=65536$). The valid hosts are as follows:

Subnet	Hosts
1	X.1.0.1 through X.1.255.254
2	X.2.0.1 through X.2.255.254
3	X.3.0.1 through X.3.255.254
This will continue until...	
254	X.254.0.1 through X.254.255.254

How about if we split the subnets down the middle with 12 bits for the subnets and 12 bits for hosts? Sound good? It does to me! The mask would

look like this: 11111111.**11111111.1111**0000.00000000 or 255.255.240.0.
Please take the time to figure out your valid subnets and hosts. I'll wait....

Okay, enough time?

The answer is 4094 subnets each with 4094 hosts ($2^{12}-2=4094$). Sounds pretty good for a class A network don't you think? Did you figure out the valid hosts and subnets yet? It's a little more complicated then our class C examples. Well, okay, a lot more complicated.

The second octet will be somewhere between 1 and 254. However, the third octet you need to figure out. Because the third octet has a 240 mask you'll get 16 (256–240=16) as your base subnet number. The third octet must start with 16 and will be the first subnet, the second subnet will be 32, and so on. This means that your valid subnets are:

X.1-254.16.1 through X.1-254.31.254.
X.1-254.32.1 through X.1-254.47.254
X.1-254.48.1 through X.1-254.63.254
Etc, etc, etc.

This is a lot of work! Using DHCP to assign the hosts for this one is a really good idea!

The IPCONFIG Utility

The IPCONFIG utility can be used to verify the TCP/IP configuration parameters on a host, including the IP address, subnet mask, and default gateway. This is useful in determining whether the configuration is initialized or if a duplicate IP address is configured.

If a configuration has been initialized, the configured IP address, subnet mask, and default gateway appear. If a duplicate address is configured, the IP address appears configured, but the subnet mask appears as 0.0.0.0.

If you're using Windows 95, use the WINIPCFG utility.

Let's move on to installing, configuring, and testing TCP/IP on your NT 4.0 workstation or server.

In Exercises 2.1 through 2.5 you'll install, configure, and test the TCP/IP transport.

EXERCISE 2.1

Installing TCP/IP

1. From the Start menu, point to Settings, and then click Control Panel. The Control Panel appears.

2. Double-click Network. The Network dialog box appears.

3. Click the Protocols tab.

4. Click Add. The Select Network Protocol dialog box appears.

5. Select TCP/IP Protocol, and then click OK.

6. Type the path to the distribution files.

7. Click Continue.

8. The needed files will be copied to your hard drive.

9. Click Close. The Microsoft TCP/IP Properties dialog box appears.

10. Click OK.

11. Click OK in the Network dialog box. A Network Settings Change box will appear, prompting you to restart your computer.

12. Click Yes.

13. The computer will now restart.

To complete these exercises, you'll need at least one computer with Microsoft Windows NT Workstation or Microsoft Windows NT Server installed.

EXERCISE 2.2

Configuring TCP/IP

1. Click Start ➤ Settings ➤ Control Panel. Then double-click Network.

2. Click the Protocol tab.

3. Double-click TCP/IP Protocol. The Microsoft TCP/IP Properties dialog box appears.

> **Microsoft TCP/IP Properties**   ? ✕
>
> | IP Address | DNS | WINS Address | DHCP Relay | Routing |
>
> An IP address can be automatically assigned to this network card by a DHCP server. If your network does not have a DHCP server, ask your network administrator for an address, and then type it in the space below.
>
> Adapter:
>
> [1] Novell NE2000 Adapter
>
> ○ Obtain an IP address from a DHCP server
>
> ● Specify an IP address
>
> IP Address: 100 . 100 . 110 . 100
>
> Subnet Mask: 255 . 255 . 0 . 0
>
> Default Gateway: 111 . 111 . 111 . 11
>
> Advanced...
>
> OK   Cancel   Apply

4. Type your IP Address, Subnet Mask, and Default Gateway; and click OK. A Network Settings Change dialog box appears, indicating the computer needs to be restarted to initialize the new configuration.

5. Click No.

If you click Yes, the following exercise will not work.

EXERCISE 2.3

Testing the TCP/IP Configuration

1. At a command prompt, type **ipconfig**, and then press Enter. Notice the response is an empty table.

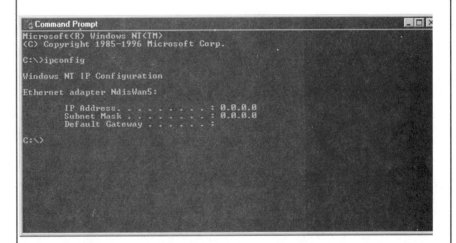

2. IRestart your computer.

3. After rebooting and logging on as an administrator, open a command prompt.

4. Type **ipconfig**. Notice that the IP Address, Subnet Mask, and Default Gateway Configuration values are displayed.

5. Ping the loopback address by typing **ping 127.0.0.1**. You should receive four replies.

6. Ping the IP address of your workstation to verify that it was config-ured correctly. Type **ping ip_address** (where *ip_address* is the ip_address of your workstation); then press Enter. You should receive four replies.

7. Ping the address of your default gateway. You should receive four replies.

EXERCISE 2.4

Determining the Effects of Duplicate IP Addresses

1. Configure a duplicate IP address by going to the Microsoft TCP/IP Properties box.

2. In the IP Address box, type the IP address of someone else on your network.

3. Click OK at the TCP/IP Properties box. The Network Dialog box appears.

4. Click OK at the Network dialog box.

5. Go to Event Viewer to see the error.

6. Click Start ➤ Programs ➤ Administrative Tools; and then click Event Viewer.

7. After noticing the address conflict, close the Event Viewer.

8. Access the Microsoft TCP/IP Properties box.

9. Type your original IP address, and click OK.

10. Open a command prompt and type ipconfig.

11. Verify that your address is correct.

EXERCISE 2.5

Determining the Effects of an Invalid Subnet Mask

1. Modify the subnet mask by going to the Microsoft TCP/IP Properties box.

2. In the Subnet Mask box, type an incorrect subnet mask for your network.

3. Click OK.

4. Click OK at the Network dialog box.

EXERCISE 2.5 (CONTINUED FROM PREVIOUS PAGE)

5. Open a command prompt, and type **ipconfig**.

6. Ping your default gateway and notice the error.

7. Ping a host on your network. (This may or may not work, depending on your IP address and the IP address of the destination host.)

8. Convert your computer's IP address and the IP address of your default gateway to binary format, and then AND them to the subnet mask to determine why the subnet mask is invalid.

9. Restore your subnet mask to its correct value.

Microsoft Network Monitor

The *Microsoft Network Monitor* simplifies the task of troubleshooting complex network problems by monitoring and capturing network traffic for analysis. Network Monitor configures the network adapter card to capture all incoming and outgoing packets. Exercise 2.6 explains how to install the Network Monitor on your server.

EXERCISE 2.6

Installing the Network Monitor on Your Server

1. Go to the Control Panel and double-click Network.

2. Click the Services tab.

3. Click Add.

4. Click Network Monitor Tools and Agents, then click OK.

5. Type the path to the distribution files.

6. Click Close, then Yes to reboot your computer.

You can define the capture filters so that only specific frames are saved for analysis. Filters can be defined based on source and destination MAC addresses, source and destination protocol addresses, and pattern matches.

Once a packet has been captured, *display filtering* can be used to further analyze the problem. Once a packet has been captured and filtered, Network Monitor interprets the binary trace data into readable terms.

The default version that comes with NT Server can only capture data whose source or destination is the server. No other computers or servers on your segment can be monitored. However, the full version of Network Monitor is available with Microsoft Systems Management System (SMS).

Starting the Capture Process

Network Monitor uses many windows for displaying different data. One of the primary windows is the Capture window. When this window has the focus, the toolbar will show you options to start, pause, stop, and view captured data. On the Capture menu, click Start to start a capture. While the capture process is running, the statistical information will be displayed in the capture window.

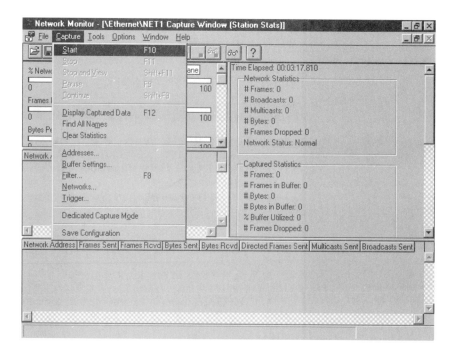

Stopping the Capture

After you have generated the network traffic you are analyzing, click Stop in the Capture menu to stop the capture. You can then create another capture or display the current capture data. You can also click Stop and View from the Capture menu to stop a capture and immediately open it for viewing.

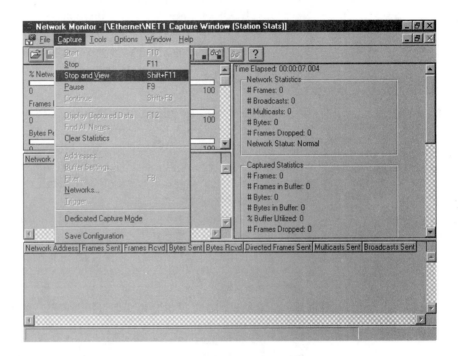

Viewing the Data

When opening a capture to view, a Summary window appears showing each frame capture. The Summary window contains a frame number, time of frame reception, source and destination addresses, highest protocol layer used in the frame, and a description of the frame.

For more detailed information on a specific frame, on the Window menu, click Zoom. In Zoom view you get two additional windows, the Detail frame and Hexadecimal frame. The Detail frame shows the protocol information in detail. The Hexadecimal frame shows the raw bytes in the frame.

Shooting Trouble

At this stage of the game, we thought it would be a great idea to introduce you to some of the realities of networking in the real world. Since this is, as we said, the real world, and not the sweet by-and-by, that reality necessarily involves a look into what can and does go wrong. The following section will give you a start in becoming prepared to deal with some commonly encountered network nightmares survived by many a network professional.

Bug Collections

Networks have special capabilities. One of them is turning molehills into mountains. Often, small network problems can turn into large network-outage catastrophes, but if a few prudent little precautions are taken, you can actually be found eating dinner with your family once in awhile instead of hunched over some console, working 36 hours straight chasing the cockroaches out of your system!

Here's an example. Because we humans are involved in the deed of sending electronic mail, error detection is built into the transmission process. This only serves to fabricate for us an exquisitely false sense of security. Why? Well, because even a horribly misconfigured server can present a terrifically realistic facade of working beautifully fine for weeks—even *months*. A positively heinous, but true fact. One morning you innocently walk into your office and your voice mail is already and unbelievably full by the wee hour of 8:00 AM. This could most certainly mean that something significant has completely collapsed—something everyone depends on and wants—now! You check your messages, and find that, sure enough, no one can send or receive e-mail, and they are, of course, freaking out, and sending their stress your way. After checking out the network and finding everything in top form, you check the server. After two hours of sweaty investigation, you find the misconfigured setting, and reset it. The nightmare is finally over, and everyone now thinks you're Gandhi. Could this cataclysm have been prevented? Let's explore it a bit....

Pest Control

Employing that indispensable human faculty of hindsight, you remember that e-mail had been going more than a bit slow for weeks now, but, well, you had other problems. Since it was working—kind of—you ignored the phenomenon, hoping it would just go away, forgetting that this only happens with the good things in life that you ignore.

When planning a strategy to diagnose internetwork-related problems, it's important to reconsider the focus of the Internet layer we discussed in Chapter 1. Remember that its principal province is routing, with the desired result being successful connectivity between two hosts. Enlightened, we now know that the issues of addressing, subnet assignments, and masks are inextricably associated with routing. Because addresses are not always known, protocols such as ARP (Address Resolution Protocol), RARP (Reverse Address Resolution Protocol), and BootP may be used. As we learned, the DNS (Domain Name System) can be employed to this end. These things in mind, you are equipped with an ability to make an educated guess at where your network troubles originate.

For instance, if a problem occurs in the Internet, and the Network Interface layer is happy and healthy, look for diagnostic clues at the Internet layer. The Internet Protocol works at this layer, which you've now learned relates to datagram delivery, address assignment, and communication between routers. Also, notification of router errors by ICMP, which gives messages to IP, may prove to be a fabulous source of information into why a problem has arisen in delivering datagrams.

Intelligent, CPU-operational devices known as *routers* use addresses to guide the datagram through the Internet. These routers communicate with each other using *RIP (Routing Information Protocol)* or *OSPF (Open Shortest Path First)* protocols. These protocols fall into a group known as *IGP's (Interior Gateway Protocols)*. ICMP (Internet Control Message Protocol), as you may recall, can help hosts determine if the packets weren't delivered correctly, and assist in discerning other malfunctions.

Ping, an ICMP Echo message, is used to verify connectivity between Internet devices. The Ping message can be used in a sequential manner to isolate a problem. For an exercise, first ping a device on your own subnet by going to a command prompt and typing ping, followed by the proper host name you desire to locate. If a response is received, existence is verified. Having this verification will further your cause, because you are now certain the host name is there. Certainty is all-important in Networkland. By starting from a verified location and moving to the other side of the router, pinging each step of the way progressively until your ping-beckon is not returned, the source of your faulty connection trouble can be triumphantly isolated.

The following case studies will show examples of how the knowledge of these clues and what they mean will empower you in your role of network exterminator, physician, and sleuth.

The Trouble with Clones

Or…double trouble. In our previous sections, we looked at the difference between physical hardware addresses and the logical software addresses related to Internet nodes. A chip on the network interface card, called a ROM (Read Only Memory), normally contains a six-byte physical address. Half of it (three bytes) is assigned by the IEEE, and the other three bytes by the manufacturer. The network administrator assigns the logical address. What would happen if two IP (Logical) addresses are assigned with the same number? Let's find out.

This is the story of two administrators, Jane and Bob, who wish to TELNET to a router in order to manage, or configure it. Jane TELNETs successfully, establishing a connection to the router. Her session appears to be first class until Bob starts to transmit. Then, poor Jane's connection fails. What happened?

When Jane connected to the router, she claimed that her source address was 131.195.116.42. The router responded with the following sequence number in the TCP header: seq=265153482.

Then, Bob began to transmit. When he did, his hosts sent an ARP broadcast looking for the hardware address of the router so he could TELNET. The router readily responded to the ARP request from Bob's workstation in the TCP header with a different sequence number then Jane's—let's say, seq=73138176. It was different because the router received the ARP request asking for a new connection.

Jane was communicating to the router using the IP source address 131.195.116.42, which is the same as Bob's. Things began to sour when the router responded with a sequence number different from Jane's. That is why Jane's Telnet connection failed. Bob established a connection with the router using the same IP source address as Jane's, only Bob wasn't doing so from the same source. This happened because they had the same IP destination address but different sequence numbers related to the same source address.

Routers examine the IP source address, not the hardware address. As a result, it was unable to differentiate between the duplicate IP addresses with different sequence numbers.

The Moral of the Story   In Networkland, twins do not co-exist harmoniously, chatting happily in their own private languages. Give each item its own private identity—or else! No duplicate IP addresses allowed!

Hide and Seek

Introducing Scot, a network manager whose current desire is to check the status of a particular host on a different segment of his Class B network. The address of the host he has in mind is 132.163.129 .15, and it's connected to his segment via a router. Scot hasn't implemented subnetting on his network, which means that only the datagrams meant for the local network will be delivered directly. All those destined for other networks should make a little trip through that router. Since Scot's network is the Class B variety without any subnetting, he'll be using a default subnet mask of 255.255.0.0, which corresponds with a network ID of 16 bits, and a host ID of 16 bits.

Introducing Kim, a network specialist whose workstation's software stores a number of parameters, including the above subnet mask. Kim happily logs on and uses the ICMP echo (Ping) command to check the status of her host. She experiences quite a delay in receiving the ICMP echo reply—and with some concern, wonders what's going on. After all, she knows that if all systems are functioning properly, an ICMP echo reply should follow the ICMP echo immediately.

Back to ol' Scot. Scot's workstation first broadcasts an ARP message, looking for a router because it thinks the host Scot's after is not on the same segment as the source host. This is unexpected, since a router is not required for this transaction. Next, it attempts an ICMP echo request, and gets the ICMP redirect message in reply. This message indicates that datagrams are being redirected for the host, and gives the address of the correct router, 132.163.132.12, for the operation. Scott's workstation then sends another ARP request looking for the hardware address of 132.163.132.12, and the router responds. All this traffic is what caused the delay Kim experienced on her end. The question remains, why did Scot's workstation access the router, causing the ICMP redirect message?

Scott's workstation and the router are both on the same network (132.163). Since this is a Class B network without subnetting, the subnet mask should be 255.255.0.0. When Scot examined the subnet mask in his workstation's parameters, he found that it had been set for a Class B network with an 8-bit subnet mask (255.255.255.0).

Because the workstation found the source and destination devices had different subnet addresses, it incorrectly concluded that the two devices were on different subnets, requiring the assistance of the router. When Scott reconfigured his workstation's subnet address to 255.255.0.0, the ICMP Echo request proceeded without jumbling things up with a router-assisted search for a different segment it didn't actually need.

The Moral of the Story   In Networkland, looks are everything. Make sure your subnet masks fit properly before you go to the broadcast party.

Do I Hear an Echo?

As we began to see in Case Study 2.2, using ICMP messages can answer many a question regarding the health of your network. The ICMP Echo and reply messages, commonly know as Ping , are some of the most frequently used.

You can invoke Ping from your local workstation to test the path to a particular host. If all is well, a message will return, verifying the existence of the path to the host or network. One caution is in order, however: Unpredictable results can occur if you ping an improper destination address. For example, pinging address 255.255.255.255 (broadcast) may cause excessive internetwork traffic. Let's take a look at an example.

At 3:30 AM, one long night, Corrie, a network administrator, decides to test the paths to some of the hosts on the Internet. She can do this two ways: by sending an ICMP Echo message to each separately, or by sending a directed broadcast to all the hosts on her network and subnetwork. Corrie's tired, so she decides on the latter and enters the destination address 129.99.23.255. This will ping all of the hosts on Class B network 129.99, subnet 23.

Corrie's workstation receives an ICMP echo reply from all the hosts on her segment. The routers, however, did not respond to the ping because their design protects against such a transmission. Other hosts may be designed in a similar fashion. The originator's destination address is set for broadcast, causing echo replies to come back to the originating workstation. The first response is followed by 123 other host responses. The ICMP header contains an identifier that correlates echo and echo reply messages—in this case, pings

> to and from different hosts, which occur simultaneously. One needs only to pause fleetingly to imagine the epicly-proportioned, network-jamming Ping-Pong tournament Corrie caused from this well-intentioned, and normally appropriate, little action.
>
> **The Moral of the Story**   Look both ways before you ping. The ICMP Echo message can be a very valuable troubleshooting tool, but check your destination address before you initiate the command! A ping broadcast could have a great or a terrible impact on the internetwork traffic.

Summary

In this chapter, we probed further into the basics of TCP/IP and examined the supremely important subject of how accurate communication is achieved between specific networks and host systems through proper IP addressing. We then discussed how and why that communication happens, why it doesn't when it fails, and how to configure devices on both LANs and WANs to ensure solid performance for your network.

The test emphasizes the objectives in this chapter. You need to understand IP addresses and subnetting very well. Go through the exercise questions below and make sure you understand the answer to every question.

Review Questions

1. You want to collect the TCP/IP frames that are received by your Windows NT Server computer, and then save the data in a file to analyze later. Which utility should you use?

   A. NETSTAT.EXE

   B. Performance Monitor

   C. NBTSTAT.EXE

   D. Network Monitor

2. You need to determine whether the TCP/IP configuration is initialized or if a duplicate IP address is configured on your NT Workstation. Which utility should you use?

   A. RP.EXE

   B. NBSTST.EXE

   C. NETSTAT.EXE

   D. IPCONFIG.EXE

   E. PING.EXE

3. You have four NT Server computers, and you want to find out which computers send the most traffic to each server. What should you do to find out?

   A. Use Performance Monitor on each server.

   B. Use Network Monitor on each server.

   C. Use NETSTAT.EXE on each server.

   D. Use NBTSTAT.EXE on each server.

   E. Use ROUTE.EXE on each server that is functioning as a router.

4. You have a network ID of 150.150.0.0 and you need to divide it into multiple subnets. You need 600 host IDs for each subnet, with the largest amount of subnets available. Which subnet mask should you assign?

   A. 255.255.224.0

   B. 255.255.240.0

   C. 255.255.248.0

   D. 255.255.252.0

5. You have a network ID of 150.150.0.0 with eight subnets. You need to allow the largest possible number of host IDs per subnet. Which subnet mask should you assign?

   A. 255.255.224.0

   B. 255.255.240.0

C. 255.255.248.0

D. 255.255.252.0

6. You have a network ID of 206.17.45.0 and you need to divide it into multiple subnets. You need 25 host IDs for each subnet, with the largest amount of subnets available. Which subnet mask should you assign?

   A. 255.255.255.192

   B. 255.255.255.224

   C. 255.255.255.240

   D. 255.255.255.248

7. You have a Class A network address with 60 subnets. You need to add 40 new subnets in the next two years and still allow for the largest possible number of host IDs per subnet. Which subnet mask should you assign?

   A. 255.240.0

   B. 255.248.0

   C. 255.252.0

   D. 255.254.0

8. You want to capture and view packets that are received by your Windows NT computer. Which utility should you use?

   A. NETSTAT.EXE

   B. Performance Monitor

   C. IPCONFIG.EXE

   D. Network Monitor

9. You have a Class B network, and you plan break it up into seven subnets. One subnet will be connected to the Internet, but you want all computers to have access to the Internet. How should you assign the subnet mask for the networks?

   A. By using a default subnet mask

   B. By creating a custom subnet mask

C. By assigning a subnet mask of 0.0.0.0

D. By assigning a subnet mask that has the IP address of the router

10. You need to come up with a TCP/IP addressing scheme for your company. How many host IDs must you allow for when you define the subnet mask for the network? (Choose all the correct answers.)

A. One for each subnet

B. One for each router interface

C. One for each WAN connection

D. One for each network adapter installed on each host

11. You have a Class B network address divided into 30 subnets. You will add 25 new subnets within the next two years. You need 600 host IDs for each subnet. Which subnet mask should you assign?

A. 255.192.0

B. 255.254.0

C. 255.255.248.0

D. 255.255.252.0

12. You have a network ID of 206.17.250.0 and you need to divide it into nine subnets. You need to provide for the largest possible number of host IDs per subnet. Which subnet mask should you assign?

A. 255.255.255.192

B. 255.255.255.224

C. 255.255.255.240

D. 255.255.255.248

13. You have a Class C network address divided into three subnets. You will need to add two subnets in the next two years. Each subnet will have 25 hosts. Which subnet mask should you assign?

A. 255.255.255.0

B. 255.255.255.192

C. 255.255.255.224

D. 255.255.255.248

14. You need to come up with a TCP/IP addressing scheme for your company. How many network IDs must you allow for when you define the subnet mask for the network? (Choose all the correct answers.)

   A. One for each subnet

   B. One for each host ID

   C. One for each router interface

   D. One for each WAN connection

   E. One for each network adapter installed on each host

15. You need to come up with a TCP/IP addressing scheme for your company. Which two factors must you consider when you define the subnet mask for the network? (Choose two.)

   A. The number of subnets on the network

   B. The number of host IDs on each subnet

   C. The volume of network traffic on each subnet

   D. The location of DNS servers

   E. The location of default gateways

16. You have a Class C network address of 206.17.19.0 with four subnets. You need the largest possible number of host IDs per subnet. Which subnet mask should you assign?

   A. 255.255.255.192

   B. 255.255.255.224

   C. 255.255.255.240

   D. 255.255.255.248

17. You have a Class C network address of 206.17.88.0 and you need the largest amount of subnets, with up to 12 hosts per subnet. Which subnet mask should you assign?

   A. 255.255.255.192

   B. 255.255.255.224

   C. 255.255.255.240

   D. 255.255.255.248

18. A user can ping the IP address of her workstation, but she cannot ping the IP address of any other computer. This user also cannot connect to any workstation through NT Explorer. What is most likely the problem?

    A. The workstation is configured with an invalid default gateway address.

    B. The workstation is configured with an invalid subnet mask.

    C. The workstation is configured with a duplicate IP address.

    D. The workstation is not configured to use WINS.

19. You need to check connectivity with TCP/IP to an NT Server on a remote subnet. Which utility should you use?

    A. ARP.EXE

    B. NETSTAT.EXE

    C. NBTSTAT.EXE

    D. PING.EXE

    E. ROUTE.EXE

20. You need to perform network capacity planning for various types of IP traffic, and you want to analyze and decode TCP/IP packets. Which utility should you use?

    A. NETSTAT.EXE

    B. Performance Monitor

    C. NBTSTAT.EXE

    D. Network Monitor

21. You need to get an IP address assigned so you can broadcast your company on the Internet. Who do you contact?

22. You need to send a broadcast message on the network informing users that the server is going down. When you send the multicast transmission, which address will IP use to broadcast the message to all users?

23. The NIC assigns you a Class B address for your company's network. How many octets define the network portion of the address?

24. The NIC has assigned a Class C address for your new Internet Web server. How many bits can you use for the host address?

25. You look in your workstation configuration and notice there's an IP address of 127.0.0.1. What does this mean?

26. You decide you want to subnet your Class B network with a mask of 255.240.0.0. When implemented it does not work. Why?

27. Your boss read in a Microsoft magazine that creating subnets will help her network run more efficiently. She's decided to implement this and wants you to lead the project. She wants you to outline what the advantages of subnetting the network are so she can justify the project to her superiors in a meeting this afternoon. What will you equip her with? Take a minute to create a list of the benefits of subnetting for her.

28. You have four offices and 25 nodes at each office. Which subnet mask would you assign to your Class C network address of 201.201.201.0?

29. You have a Class B network address of 187.32.0.0. Which subnet address would give you at least 200 subnets?

30. Your network is not assigned an address by the NIC and you do not need to be on the Internet. You create a Class A address of 36.0.0.0 with a subnet mask of 255.255.0.0. How many subnets can you use, and how many hosts can be on each subnet?

31. Your IS manager asks you if there is some kind of computer that will map host names to IP addresses for groups of computers called domains. What do you tell him?

32. You're called upon to help train a new network Help Desk employee who is confused about the Domain Name System. How do you explain it to her?

33. The CIO of your company is assessing the knowledge level of his network operating system staff. He calls to ask you the difference between NIS and DNS. What do you say?

CHAPTER

3

Implementing IP Routing

ith TCP/IP basics covered and conquered in Chapters 1 and 2, our focus is going to both sharpen and shift. Our attention will now be concentrated on Microsoft-specific issues and intricacies. We will begin Chapter 3 with a crisp discussion on IP routing.

Our topic scope will encompass several important topics. By the end of this chapter, you should be able to do the following:

- Explain the difference between static and dynamic IP routing.

- Explain the host configuration requirements to communicate with a static or dynamic IP router.

- Configure a computer running Windows NT to function as an IP router.

- Build a static routing table.

- Use the TRACERT utility to isolate route or network link problems.

What Is IP Routing?

IP routing is the process of sending data from a host on one network to a *remote host* on another network through a *router*, or routers. A router is either a specifically assigned computer or a workstation that's been configured to perform routing tasks. In IP terminology, routers are referred to as *gateways*. Gateways are basically TCP/IP hosts that have been rigged with two or more network connection *interfaces*. Outfitted in this manner, they're known as *multihomed hosts,* which we'll discuss more thoroughly later in the chapter.

The path that a router uses to deliver a packet is defined in its *routing table.* A routing table contains the IP addresses of router interfaces that connect to the other networks the router can communicate with. The routing table is consulted for a path to the network that is indicated by the packet's destination address. If a path isn't found, the packet is sent to the router's *default gateway* address—if one is configured. By default, a router can send packets to any network for which it has a configured interface. When one host attempts communication with another host on a different network, IP uses the host's default gateway address to deliver the packet to the corresponding router. When a route is found, the packet is sent to the proper network, then onward to the destination host. If a route is not found, an error message is sent to the source host.

The IP Routing Process

The IP routing process is fairly direct when a datagram's destination is located on a neighboring network. In this kind of situation, a router would follow a simple procedure, as shown in Figure 3.1.

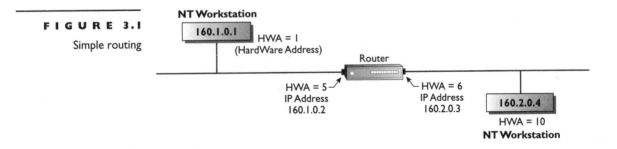

FIGURE 3.1

Simple routing

First, when a workstation wants to send a packet to a destination host, in this instance 160.1.0.1 transmitting to 160.2.0.4, host 160.1.0.1 checks the destination IP address. If it determines the address isn't on the local network, it must then be routed. Next, 160.1.0.1 calls on ARP to obtain the hardware address of its default gateway. The IP address of the default gateway is configured in machine 160.1.0.1's internal configuration, but 160.1.0.1 still needs to find the hardware address of the default gateway, and sends out an ARP request to get it. IP then proceeds to address the packet with the newly obtained destination hardware address of its default router. The information utilized for addressing the packet includes:

- Source hardware address 1
- Source IP address 160.1.0.1
- Destination hardware address 5
- Destination IP address 160.2.0.4

IP, on the receiving router with the hardware address of 5, establishes that it is not the final, intended recipient by inspecting the packet's destination IP address, which indicates it must be forwarded to network 160.2. Then, IP uses ARP to determine the hardware address for 160.2.0.4. The router then puts the newly identified hardware address into it's ARP cache for easy reference the next time it's called upon to route a packet to that destination.

This accomplished, the router sends the packet out to network 160.2 with a header that includes:

- Source hardware address 5
- Source IP address 160.1.0.1
- Destination hardware address 10
- Destination IP address 160.2.0.4

As the packet travels along network 160.2, it looks for hardware address 10, with the IP address of 160.2.0.4. When an NIC card recognizes its hardware address, it grabs the packet.

It's important to note here that the source IP address is that of the host that created the packet originally, but that the hardware address is now that of the router's connection interface to network 160.1. It's also significant that although both source and destination software IP addresses remain constant, both source and destination hardware addresses necessarily change at each hop the packet makes.

Sounds simple right? Well, it is in a situation like the one we just presented. However, those of you who possess some firsthand experience with this sort of thing may now be finding yourselves just a little distracted with thoughts of a genuinely sarcastic variety. Before turning your nose up and slamming this book shut, let it be known that we, too, are fully aware that this isn't a perfect world, and that if things were that straightforward, there wouldn't be a market for books about them! On the other hand, to those readers becoming uncomfortable with the now present implications of potential chaos, we say, relax, make some tea, sit down, and read on.

Start by considering this foul and ugly possibility: What if the destination network is in the dark because it's not directly attached to a router on the delivery path for that nice little datagram? Things come a tumblin' down, that's what! Remember hearing somewhere that there's a reason for everything? Well, we're not sure about that, but the heinous, confusion-producing scenario we just posited is one most excellent reason for the existence of routing tables. With a handy-dandy routing table, the fog clears, clouds part, and destinations sing! Routers, and those dependent on them, again become happy, efficient things. Routing tables are maintained on IP routers. IP consults these to determine where the mystery network is, so that it can send its mystery packet there. Some internetworks are very complex. If this is the case, routing tables should designate all available routes to a destination network, as well as provide an estimate advising the efficiency of each potential route. Routing tables maintain entries of where networks are located, not hosts.

Dynamic versus Static IP Routing

There are two breeds of routing tables. There are static tables, and there are dynamic tables. Static types are laboriously maintained by a network manager, while the dynamic variety is sustained automatically by a routing protocol. Here's a list spotlighting some specific routing table characteristics:

Dynamic Routing	Static Routing
Function of inter-routing protocols	Function of IP
Routers share routing information automatically	Routers do not share routing information
Routing tables are built dynamically	Routing tables are built manually
Requires a routing protocol, such as RIP or OSPF	Microsoft supports multihomed systems as routers
Microsoft supports RIP for IP and IPX/SPX	

Windows NT Server 4.0 provides the ability to function as an IP router using both static and dynamic routing. A Windows NT-based computer can be configured with multiple network adapters and can route between them. This type of system, which is ideal for small, private internetworks, is referred to as a multihomed computer.

Windows NT Server 4.0 has the ability to function as a Routing Information Protocol (RIP) router that supports dynamic management of Internet Protocol (IP) routing tables. RIP eliminates the need to establish static IP routing tables.

Dynamic IP Routing

On large internetworks, dynamic routing is typically employed. This is because manually maintaining a static routing table would be overwhelmingly tedious, if not impossible. With dynamic routing, minimal configuration is required by a network administrator. Figure 3.2 shows an example of dynamic routing.

FIGURE 3.2

An example of dynamic routing

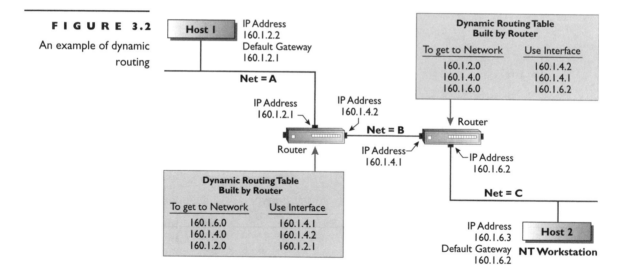

For a host to communicate with other hosts on the internetwork, its default gateway address must be configured to match the IP address of the local router's interface.

In Figure 3.2, Host 1 requires a default gateway address in order to be able to send packets to any network other than Network A. Host 1's default gateway address is configured for the router port attached to Network A. If Host 1 sends a packet that's not destined for the local network, it will be sent to the default gateway address. If no gateway is defined, the packet will be discarded. Host 2 works the same way; however, it's default gateway is the router port attached to Network C. When the router receives a packet either from Host 1 or 2, it will observe the destination's IP address and forward it according to the information in its routing table, which is built and maintained through inter-routing protocols.

Dynamic routing is a function of inter-routing, network gossip protocols such as the Routing Information Protocol (RIP) and Open Shortest Path First (OSPF). These routing protocols periodically exchange routes to known networks among dynamic routers. If a given route changes, they automatically update the router's routing table and inform other routers on the internetwork of the change.

Routing Information Protocol (RIP)

RIP is a type of protocol known as a *distance vector routing protocol*. RIP is used to discover the cost of a given route in terms of hops, and store that information in the routing table, which IP uses in selecting the most efficient, low-cost route to a destination. It works by watching for routing table broadcasts by other routers and updating its own routing table in the event a change occurs. RIP routing tables provide, at a minimum, the following information:

- IP destination address

- A metric (numbered from 1 to 15) indicative of the total cost in hops of a certain route to a destination

- The IP address of the router a datagram would reach next on the path to its destination

- A marker signaling recent changes to a route

- Timers

Some drawbacks to RIP include a problem known as "counting to infinity," as illustrated in Figure 3.3. In certain internetwork configurations, an endless loop between routers can occur if one of the networks becomes unavailable. RIP keeps counting hops each time the broadcast reaches a router, in hopes of finding a new route to the formerly available network. To prevent this, a hop-limit count between 1 and 15 is configured to represent infinity, which necessarily imposes size restrictions on networks. RIP can't be utilized on a network with an area consisting of more than 15 hops. In Figure 3.3, Network 6's location was lost between Routers B and D. Router B then looks for a new route to Network 6. Router B already knows that Router C can get to Network 6 with four hops because Router C advertised this information in a broadcast, and all routers save this broadcasted information in their routing tables. Since Router B is looking for a new route to Network 6, Router B references its routing table and finds that Router C can reach Network 6 in four hops. Router B determines it can reach Network 6 in five hops because Router C can make it in four hops. This is because Router B must add an extra hop for itself—four from Router C plus one for Router B. Router B then broadcasts the new route information back out onto the network. Router C receives this information, and enters into its route table that Network 6 is now six hops away—five from Router B, plus one for itself. This process continues until the 15-hop limit is reached. At this point, the route to Network 6 is finally dubbed an unreachable destination, and all related route information regarding it is removed from both Router B's and Router C's routing tables.

FIGURE 3.3

"Counting to infinity"

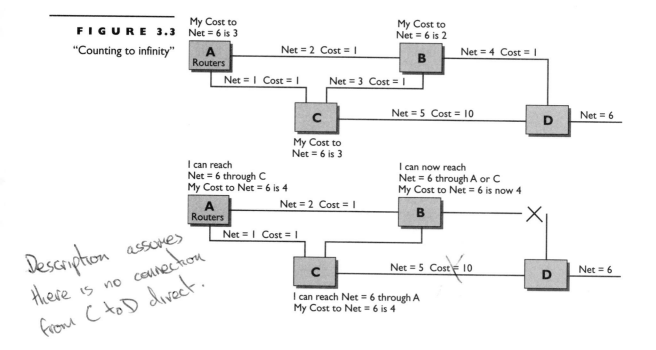

Another problem with large internetworks centers around the fact that RIP routers broadcast routing table advertisements every 30 seconds. On today's gargantuan networks, populated with an abundance of routers, momentous amounts of bandwidth can get gobbled up simply accommodating all the RIP response packet noise.

Open Shortest Path First (OSPF)

Because of these potentially network-hostile characteristics, OSPF is quickly gaining popularity within the Internet community. OSPF is based on *link-state algorithms*, and is therefore known as a *link-state routing protocol*. It's deployed within an *autonomous system*, which is a group of routers that share a certain routing protocol. When that protocol happens to be OSPF, each router retains its own database describing the topology of the autonomous system on which it's located. This kind of system is much more flexible, and has the following advantages as well:

- Network administrators can assign costs to a particular link.

- The total cost for a given path doesn't necessarily have to have a limit.

- Its upper metric limit being 65,535, it has the ability to accommodate vast networks.

- Each node creates a link-state database tree representing the network and places itself as that tree's root, where it can choose the most direct path to a given destination.

- Related to the above benefit, in the event that more than one route of equal cost exists, OSPF routers can balance the load of network traffic between all available and equally cost-effective routes.

- Link-state routing advertisements are broadcasted much less often—only when a change is detected, thereby reducing network overhead.

- Link-state routing update packets can efficiently carry information for more than one router.

- This type of packet is only sent to *adjacencies,* or neighboring routers selected to swap routing information—a "tell a friend" arrangement that again contributes to network efficiency.

Static IP Routing

Static routing is a function of IP. Static routers require that routing tables be built and updated manually. If a route changes, static routers are secretive and do not share this information to inform each other of the event. They're also very cliquey, and do not exchange routes with dynamic routers.

Windows NT can function as an IP router using static routing. NT network administrators must maintain their tables or acquire a commercial router. A Windows NT-based computer can be configured with multiple network adapters and routes between them. This type of system, which is ideal for small, private internetworks, is referred to as a *multihomed computer.*

Routing tables inventory known networks and the IP addresses used to access them. Windows NT static routing tables are maintained by a route utility, and are comprised of five columns of data, reading left to right. In the list below, the first entry represents the left-most column, the second represents the next one, and so on.

Network Address: A roster of addresses for known networks. Included here is an entry both for the local network (0.0.0.0) and for broadcasts (255.255.255.255).

Netmask: This column lists all subnet masks in use for each network.

Gateway Address: This is a list of the IP addresses employed as the primary datagram receivers for each network.

Interface: Each network card installed in a computer is assigned an interface number.

Metric: This is a list providing an estimate of the number of hops the route would cost. A hop is each pass a datagram makes through a router.

Here are the key things to remember about static routers:

- A static router can only communicate with networks with which it has a configured interface.

- A Windows NT computer can be configured as a multihomed computer.

- A static route can be configured as either a default gateway address or an entry in a routing table.

- A static router, such as a Windows NT multihomed computer, can only communicate with networks to which it has a configured interface. This limits communications to local networks.

Figure 3.4 illustrates static routing.

As shown in Figure 3.4, Host 1 has local connections to Networks A and B. This means that hosts on Network A can communicate with hosts on Network B, and vice versa, because Host 1 knows about both networks and will pass packets destined for either one. Hosts on Network A will not be able to communicate with hosts on Network C.

F I G U R E   3.4

Static routers

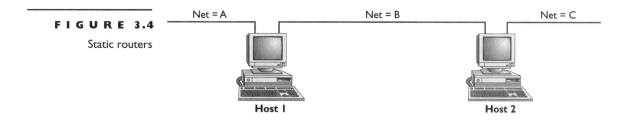

Host 2 has local connections to Networks B and C and will be able to pass packets destined for either network. However, Network C will not be able to send packets to Network A.

After taking all this in, you may have been left with the impression that dynamic routing is the method of choice for everyone's routing needs. While that's certainly true when the network in question is large and complex, providing a multiplicity of paths to destinations and/or growing rapidly, static routing is wonderfully suited for small to moderately sized networks that rarely change. An important consideration is, as is so often the case, cost. All that fabulous intelligence and flexibility, and all those bells and whistles that dynamic routers offer cost a lot—up to around $50k or more apiece! They're one of the most expensive pieces of equipment one can hook up to a network! Windows NT comes out of the box equipped with static routing built right in—in other words...it's free! It's also free of charge in terms of overhead costs on your network, and it creates the environment for a much closer, more involved relationship between you and your beloved network.

IP Routing Applied

Now that you have a clear picture of exactly what IP routing is, and what it involves, you're ready to learn how it's done. In this section, we'll give you the skinny on configuration and integration issues, and the procedures required for implementation.

Using the Default Gateway Address on a Static Router

Gateways are most often dedicated computers, or routers. The *default gateway* is like a network mediator with connections. It's the node on the local network that knows the network IDs of other networks linked to the greater internetwork. Since it has access to this privileged information, when a given workstation sends out some data that reaches the default gateway, it can forward it along to other gateways as required to reach its proper destination..

Microsoft
Exam
Objective

Configure a Windows NT Server computer to function as an IP router.

• Install and configure the DHCP Relay Agent.

One method of configuring a static route without manually adding routes to a routing table is to configure each multihomed computer's default gateway address as the local interface to the other multihomed computer on the common network. It's a type of circular reasoning for computers.

A multihomed computer (a computer with more than one NIC card) can send IP packets to destinations other than those they are locally attached to by setting the internal configuration of the default gateway to the other multihomed computer's network interface. For example, in Figure 3.4, Host 2 would set its default gateway to the network interface on Host 1. Network C then would be able to pass packets to Network A. Host 1 would set its default gateway to the network interface on Host 2, enabling Network A to communicate with Network C.

Whenever Host 1 receives a packet destined for a host on Network C, it'll check its local routing table. If it doesn't find a route to Network C, it forwards the packet to its default gateway, which is a local interface on Host 2. Host 2 will then route the packet to the appropriate interface for delivery on Network C.

Using the default gateway address as a static route only works well with two routers. If more than two are used, you must manually add an entry in the routing table.

Using Additional Default Gateways

Although more than one default gateway can be configured, only the first one will be used for routing purposes. The others will be used only as backups should the primary one become unavailable for some reason. This means you can't use multiple gateways to nab more network bandwidth. However, better fault tolerance is still a definite plus. As I'm sure you are well aware, this backup stuff is by no means unimportant.

Let's say Router A in Figure 3.5 goes on the blink and is out of commission when the client boots up. The client wants to connect to the server, but the default gateway that the client is defined for is currently unavailable, so it's out of luck. The client has no other default gateway defined, so the client will not be redirected to Router C to connect to the server. However, if the client was to define a second default gateway for Router C, the client would then be directed on towards the server.

FIGURE 3.5

A hypothetical routing dilemma

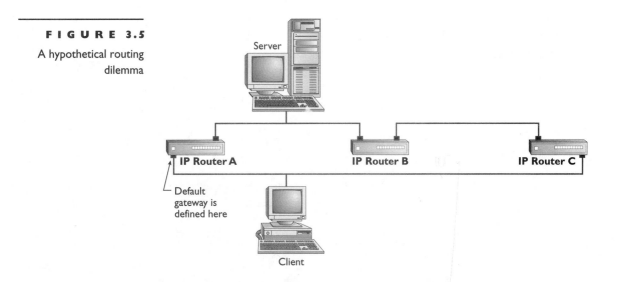

The client is going to have to sit on the other side of the abyss dreaming of multiple default gateways, wishing he or she had a more thorough network administrator who took these kind of precautions. Would that be you?

When one configures one's Windows NT system in this way, retransmission problems at the TCP layer will cause the IP routing software to try the routers listed in the Additional Gateways value. This is again a great backup plan. Why? Well...what if Client and Server were in the middle of an established session, and that troublesome Router A went down again? TCP would send a message to IP to try one of the additional routers in the registry. IP would then try Router C, use a double hop route, and continue exchanging data at no cost to the session. When Router A again breathes a breath of life, the inter-routing protocol will force Router C to redirect the session's traffic back through the more optimal, one-hop route provided by the now living Router A.

In order for any host to be able to communicate with other hosts located somewhere out there on the internetwork, its default gateway address positively must be configured to match the IP address of the router's interface on the local segment.

Default Routing Table Entries

Windows NT 4.0, NT 3.51, and Windows for Workgroups 3.11 routing tables maintain the default entries shown in Table 3.1.

T A B L E 3.1	**Address Examples**	**Description**
Default routing tables for Windows NT 4.0, 3.51, and Windows for Workgroups 3.11	0	The address used as a default route for any network not specified in the route table
	Subnet broadcast	The address used for broadcasting on the local subnet
	Network broadcast	The address used for broadcasting throughout the internetwork
	Local loopback 127.0.0.1	The address used for testing IP configurations and connections
	Local network	The address used to direct packets to hosts on the local network
	Local host	The address of the local computer; references the local loopback address

Adding Static Entries

The route command is used, as detailed in Table 3.2, to add static entries to a routing table.

TABLE 3.2	To Add or Modify a Static Route	Function
Commands Used for Adding Static Entries	route add [network address] mask [gateway address]	Adds a route
	route delete [network address] [gateway address]	Deletes a route
	route change [network address] [gateway address]	Modifies a route
	route print [network address] [gateway address]	Prints a route
	route -s [gateway address]	Adds a route to a smart gateway
	route -f	Clears all routes

It works like this: To add a static route, enabling communications between a host on network 160.1.89.0 from a host on network 160.1.66.0, you would run the following command:

```
route add 160.1.89.0 mask 255.255.255.0 160.1.66.1
```

NOTE Static routes are stored in memory unless the -p parameter is used. No, it doesn't stand for permanent; it stands for persistent. Persistent routes are stored in the registry. If you restart your NT Server or workstation, you will have to re-create all nonpersistent routes if you're using a static routing table.

If your internetwork has more than two routers, at least one of which is a static router, you'll need to configure static routing table entries to all known networks on a table at each multihomed computer, as shown in Figure 3.6.

A static routing table for Network C, IP address 160.1.43.0, is created on multihomed Host 1, directing the router to send the packets to interface 160.1.89.1. This will permit packets to move from Network A to Network C.

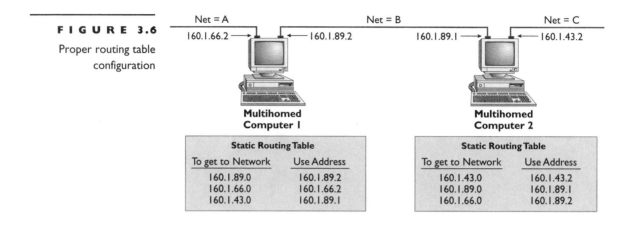

FIGURE 3.6

Proper routing table
configuration

Also, a static route is configured on Host 2 to allow Network C to send packets to Network A. This is accomplished by referencing the network address 160.1.66.0, directing the router to send packets on to IP address 160.1.89.2, which can directly deliver packets destined for Network A.

The static routing table is always checked before a packet is routed. If there is no static route to a particular host, the packet is sent to the configured default gateway. For a host to communicate with other hosts on the internetwork, its default gateway address must be configured to match the IP address of the local router's interface.

Integrating Static and Dynamic Routing

As mentioned above, breeds of routers stick to their own and do not speak with those of a different feather. Static routers do not trade routing information with dynamic routers unless they're forced to. As they say, where there's a will, there's a way! To route from a static router through a dynamic router, such as a RIP or OSPF-enabled IP router, one must first add a static route to the routing tables located on both the static and dynamic routers, as shown in Figure 3.7.

In order to route packets from Network A to the Internet, Host 2 requires that a route be added to its routing table. This addition includes the IP address of the closest interface (in this case, 160.1.66.2) that can access the dedicated IP router to the Internet.

To route packets from Networks B and C to the Internet, a static entry must be added to Computer B's routing table. This entry includes the IP address of the nearest interface (160.1.89.2) on the dedicated IP router to the Internet.

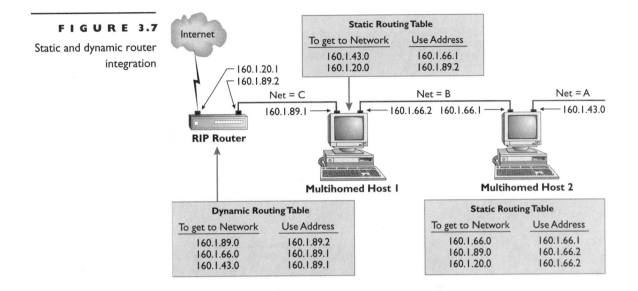

FIGURE 3.7

Static and dynamic router integration

To allow computers on the Internet to communicate with hosts on Networks 1 and 2, one must statically configure the dedicated IP router with the IP address of the interface to Host 1. Host 1 then acts as a gateway to other subnets.

It's important to mention here that some implementations of RIP do not propagate static routing tables. Should you find yourself beset with this dilemma, you'd have to statically configure the remote routers in the Internet cloud to achieve your routing goals. Also important to note here is that the exact method for configuring a static route on a RIP router varies with each kind of router. It is therefore very wise to refer to your particular router's vendor documentation for more information.

In Exercise 3.1, you'll view and configure the routing table.

Implementing a Windows NT Router

Windows NT originally shipped with the ability to act as a static IP router. The static IP router was enabled by creating a multihomed system and enabling routing either through the registry or through a checkbox in the Advanced TCP/IP Configuration dialog box.

On a Windows **NT Server** computer, configure Microsoft **TCP/IP** to support multiple network adapters.

EXERCISE 3.1

Viewing and Configuring the Routing Table

1. From a command prompt, type **route print**, and then press Enter to view the route table.

```
                         Command Prompt
Microsoft(R) Windows NT(TM)
(C) Copyright 1985-1995 Microsoft Corp.

C:\users\default>route print

Active Routes:

  Network Address          Netmask  Gateway Address        Interface  Metric
        0.0.0.0          0.0.0.0     100.1.1.100      100.1.1.100       1
      100.0.0.0        255.0.0.0     100.1.1.100      100.1.1.100       1
    100.1.1.100  255.255.255.255       127.0.0.1        127.0.0.1       1
100.255.255.255  255.255.255.255     100.1.1.100      100.1.1.100       1
      127.0.0.0        255.0.0.0       127.0.0.1        127.0.0.1       1
      224.0.0.0        224.0.0.0     100.1.1.100      100.1.1.100       1
255.255.255.255  255.255.255.255     100.1.1.100      100.1.1.100       1

C:\users\default>
```

2. Under Gateway Address, you should find your default gateway address—the router interface address attached to your local network interface.

3. Remove your default gateway address from your computer. This will prevent any packets being sent to the default gateway for routing and require all routing to be done from existing route entries.

4. Access the Microsoft TCP/IP Properties dialog box.

---

5. Delete the Default Gateway address.

6. Click OK in the Microsoft TCP/IP Properties box.

7. Click OK.

8. Switch to a command prompt, and use the route print command. The default gateway should not be listed.

Next, attempt communication with both local and remote hosts.

1. Ping the IP address of a local host. This should be successful.

2. Ping the IP address of a host on a remote address. This should fail, with a "Destination host unreachable" error.

3. Add a route entry to your computer.

4. Type the following command: **route add** *remote_network_id* **mask** *subnet_mask your_default_gateway*. (For example, if your workstation is on network 150.150.28.0 and the remote network is 150.150.40.0, the command would look like this: **route add 150.150.40.0 mask 255.255.252.0 150.150.28.200**. This means that to get to network 150.150.40.0, you would use address 150.150.28.200, which should be the default gateway.)

5. View the route table.

6. Ping a remote host. This should be successful.

7. Restore your default gateway.

8. Test communication by pinging your default gateway.

Static routing can work well for small networks and remote sites, but for large internetworks, the overhead of manually maintaining routing tables is significant. By enabling the RIP for IP routing protocol, Windows NT Server 4.0 can be a dynamic IP router. Windows NT 4.0 RIP for IP eliminates the manual configuration of routing tables. RIP for IP is suitable for medium-size internetworks, but it is not suitable for large IP internetworks because of the significant amount of broadcast traffic it generates.

To implement a Windows NT Router:

1. Install multiple adapter cards and appropriate drivers, or configure multiple IP addresses on a single card.

2. Configure the adapter card(s) with a valid IP address and subnet mask.

3. On the Routing tab of the Microsoft TCP/IP Properties dialog box, select the Enable IP Forwarding checkbox.

4. Depending on which version of Windows NT you are running:

   ■ On the Services tab of the Control Panel Network tool, add the RIP for Internet Protocol service.

   ■ Add static routes to the static routers routing table for all networks to which the computer has no configured interface.

The TRACERT Utility

The *TRACERT utility* is essentially a verification tool. It's used to substantiate the route that's been taken to a destination host. TRACERT is also highly useful in isolating routers and identifying WAN Links that are not functioning and/or are operating too slowly. Here's the relevant command syntax for deploying TRACERT:

```
tracert 160.1.89.100
```

where 160.1.89.100 is the remote computer.

```
                          Command Prompt

C:\users\default>
C:\users\default>tracert 160.1.89.100

Tracing route to TCPIP [160.1.89.100]
over a maximum of 30 hops:

  1   <10 ms   <10 ms   <10 ms  TCPIP [160.1.89.100]

Trace complete.

C:\users\default>_
```

Below is an example of the output that would result from entering the command if the computer was on the network:

```
Tracing route to 160.1.89.100 over 2 hops1 <10 ms <10 ms <10 ms¬
160.1.89.22 <10 ms <10 ms <10 ms 160.1.89.100
```

TRACERT can aid in determining if a router has failed by the degree of success the command enjoys. For example, if the command is unsuccessful, it is possible to assess router or WAN link problems and identify the point at which routing failed. The response time for the command is returned in the output. The information contained in the output can be readily compared to that recorded for another route to the same destination. This greatly facilitates identifying a slow or ineffective router or WAN link.

For example, the command tracert 160.1.66.11 would display the path taken from the local host to the destination host: 160.1.66.11. The output from the preceding command would confirm that the router address 160.1.66.1 was the route taken from the local host to the destination host. Here's what that output would look like:

```
Tracing route to 160.1.66.11 over a maximum of 30 hops1 <10 ms¬
<10 ms <10 ms 160.1.66.12 <10 ms <10 ms <10 ms 160.1.66.11
```

Let's go to the Internet and do a tracert to the White House. This is the output we receive:

```
C:\WINDOWS>tracert www.whitehouse.gov

Tracing route to www.whitehouse.gov [198.137.240.92]

over a maximum of 30 hops:

 1 191 ms 136 ms 138 ms 38.1.1.1

 2 142 ms 132 ms 137 ms 38.17.3.1

 3 157 ms 151 ms 152 ms 38.1.42.3

 4 152 ms 149 ms 147 ms 38.1.42.3

 5 206 ms 285 ms 338 ms se.sc.psi.net [38.1.3.5]

 6 286 ms 290 ms 265 ms rc5.southeast.us.psi.net [38.1.25.5]

 7 278 ms 317 ms 268 ms ip2.ci3.herndon.va.us.psi.net
[38.25.11.2]

 8 268 ms 264 ms 313 ms 198.137.240.33
```

```
9 288 ms 279 ms 346 ms www.whitehouse.gov [198.137.240.92]
```

Trace complete.

C:\WINDOWS>

IPv6 (IPng)

This protocol used to be referred to as "IP Next Generation" or "IPng." IP version 6 (IPv6) is a new version of the Internet Protocol designed as a successor to IP version 4 (Ipv4, RFC-791). The current header in IPv4 hasn't been changed or upgraded since the 1970s! The initial design, of course, failed to anticipate the growth of the Internet, and the eventual exhaustion of the IPv4 address space. IPv6 is an entirely new packet structure, which is incompatible with IPv4 systems.

Expanded Addressing Capabilities

IPv6 has a128-bit source and destination IP addresses. With approximately five billion people in the world using 128-bit addresses, there are 2^{128} addresses, or almost 296 addresses per person! An IPv6 valid IP address will look something like this:

```
3F3A:AE67:F240:56C4:3409:AE52:220E:3112
```

IPv6 uses 16 octets; when written, it is divided into eight octet pairs, separated by colons and represented in hexadecimal format.

Header Format Simplification

The IPv6 headers are designed to keep the IP header overhead to a minimum by moving nonessential fields and option fields to extension headers after the IP header. Anything not included in the base IPv6 header can be added through IP extension headers placed after the base IPv6 header.

Improved Support for Extensions and Options

IPv6 can easily be extended for unforeseen features by adding extension headers and option fields after the IPv6 base header. Support for new hardware or application technologies is built in.

Flow Labeling Capability

A new field in the IPv6 header allows the pre-allocation of network resources along a path, so time-dependent services such as voice and video are guaranteed a requested bandwidth with a fixed delay.

Not to worry, they don't ask you to subnet IPv6 on the NT 4.0 TCP/IP test.

Supernetting

The Internet is running out of IP addresses. To prevent the complete depletion of network IDs, the Internet authorities have come up with a scheme called *supernetting*. The main difference between subnetting and supernetting is that supernetting borrows bits from the network ID and masks them as the host ID for more efficient routing. For example, rather then allocate a Class B network ID to a company that has 1800 hosts, the InterNIC allocates a range of eight Class C network IDs. Each Class C network ID gives 254 available hosts for a total of 2,032 host IDs.

However, this means that the routers on the Internet now must have an additional eight entries in their routing tables to route IP packets to the company. To prevent this problem, a technique called *Classless Inter-Domain Routing (CIDR)* is used to collapse the eight entries used in the above example to a single entry corresponding to all of the Class C network IDs used by that company.

Let's take a look at how this would work with eight Class C networks IDs starting with the network ID 220.78.168.0 through the network ID 220.78.175.0. In the routing table the entry then would be:

Network ID	Subnet Mask	Subnet Mask Binary
220.78.168.0	255.255.248.0	11111111.11111111.11111000.00000000

A typical Class C network would have a subnet mask of 255.255.255.0. Only the fourth octet would be available for subnetting and hosts. However, in supernetting, we can use bits in the usually reserved third octet to combine networks. With a 255.255.248.0 subnet, counting the zeros, we have three bits to work with. Each bit can be either a 1 or a 0. So, for each bit we get two choices. With three bits, it then becomes $2^3=8$ subnets (don't subtract 2 in supernetting like you would in subnetting). Because the first network ID is 220.78.168.0, the router know to count up eight networks starting with 220.78.168.0 and going to 220.78.175.0.

Summary

Well, we hope you've found all of this helpful and enlightening. To make sure none of it got lost in the shuffle, let's take a moment to recap things.

We explained the difference between static and dynamic IP routing, and also the host configuration requirements to communicate with a static or dynamic IP router. We configured a computer running Windows NT to function as an IP router. We also talked about building a static routing table and the use of the TRACERT utility, which allows us to isolate route or network link problems.

In regards to the NT TCP/IP 4.0 test, we hope you were paying attention in this chapter. Microsoft seems to want you to understand how routing works. So, to make sure you were paying attention, go through the exercises below.

Review Questions

1. You have four Class C network addresses: 203.200.5.0, 203.200.6.0, 203.200.7.0, and 203.200.8.0. You want to combine these addresses into one logical network to increase the host IDs that you can have on one subnet. Which subnet mask should you assign?

   A. 255.255.252.0

   B. 255.255.254.0

   C. 255.255.255.252

   D. 255.255.255.254

2. You can ping all the computers on your subnet and your default gateway, but you cannot ping any of the computers on a remote subnet. Other users on your subnet can ping computers on the remote subnet. What could be the problem?

   A. The subnet mask on the router is invalid.

B. The subnet mask on your computer is invalid.

C. The default gateway address on your computer is invalid.

D. The computers on the remote subnet are not configured for TCP/IP.

E. The route to the remote subnet has not been established on the router.

3. Using Windows NT Explorer, your Windows NT Workstation can connect to a remote server, but not to a server on your local subnet. What is most likely the cause of the problem?

A. Invalid default gateway address on your workstation

B. Invalid default gateway address on the local server

C. Invalid subnet mask on your workstation

D. Invalid subnet mask on the remote server

4. Using Windows NT Explorer, your Windows NT Workstation cannot connect to a local server, but all other users can. When you run Network Monitor, you notice that each time the workstation attempts to connect to the server, it broadcasts an ARP request for the default gateway. What is most likely the cause of the problem?

A. Invalid default gateway address on the workstation

B. Invalid subnet mask on the workstation

C. The workstation has a duplicate IP address.

D. The workstation is not configured to use WINS.

5. Your NT Workstation cannot connect to a remote server, but all other workstations can. The network is configured as follows: two subnets, one router. The router has two interfaces: Network A with 167.191.32.1 and Network B with 167.191.64.1. All computers use a subnet mask of 255.255.240.0. You are located on Network B. When

you run IPCONFIG on your workstation, you receive the following output:

IP Address	167.191.82.17
Subnet Mask	255.255.240.0
Default Gateway	167.191.64.1

What is most likely the cause of the problem?

A. IP address on workstation is invalid.

B. Subnet mask on workstation is invalid.

C. Default gateway on workstation is invalid.

D. IP address on server is invalid.

E. Default gateway on server is invalid.

6. You are troubleshooting a Windows NT Server computer on a TCP/IP network. The server is located on a subnet with a network ID of 167.170.2.0. The default gateway address is 167.170.2.1. Users on a remote subnet cannot access the server. You run ipconfig /all at the server and receive the following output:

Host Name	pdctest
DNS Servers	
Node Type	Hybrid
NetBIOS scope ID	
IP Routing Enabled	no
WINS Proxy Enabled	no
NetBIOS Resolution Uses DNS	no
Physical Address	00-20-AF-CA-E5-27
DHCP Enabled	no
IP Address	167.170.2.223
Subnet Mask	255.255.0.0
Default Gateway	167.170.2.1
Primary WINS Server	167.170.2.46

What is most likely the cause of the problem?

A. Subnet mask is incorrect.

B. NetBIOS scope ID is incorrect.

C. NetBIOS node type is incorrect.

D. IP address is out of range for this subnet.

7. You have five Windows NT Server computers all configured as static routers. Which utility should you use to identify the path that a packet takes as it passes through the routers?

   A. Network Monitor

   B. ROUTE.EXE

   C. TRACERT.EXE

   D. IPCONFIG.EXE

   E. NETSTAT.EXE

8. You have an NT Server on a remote subnet. You cannot ping this server by its IP address, but you can ping your default gateway and all other computers on the remote subnet. What could the problem be? (Choose two.)

   A. The server is not WINS enabled.

   B. The server has an invalid subnet mask.

   C. The server has an invalid default gateway address.

   D. Your workstation is configured with an invalid subnet mask.

   E. Your workstation is configured with an invalid default gateway address.

9. You can connect through NT Explorer to all workstations on your local subnet, but cannot connect to any workstations or servers on a remote subnet. Which IP address should you ping first to diagnose the problem?

   A. The local server

   B. The default gateway

  C. The remote server

  D. None, TCP/IP isn't loaded

  E. None, reboot the router

10. Your Windows NT Workstation cannot connect to a remote Windows NT Server using NT Explorer. All other computers can connect to the remote NT Server. You run Network Monitor and notice that each time the workstation attempts to connect to the server, the workstation broadcasts an ARP request for the remote server's IP address. What is most likely the cause of the problem?

  A. The workstation is configured with an invalid default gateway address.

  B. The workstation is configured with an invalid subnet mask.

  C. The workstation is configured with a duplicate IP address.

  D. The workstation is not configured to use WINS.

11. You have a RAS server that is connected to an Internet Service Provider via ISDN. You want your Windows 95 workstations to use the RAS server to access the Internet. How should the default gateway addresses be configured?

  A. The default gateway address on the RAS server specifies the IP address of the ISP's router interface to your internal network.

  B. The default gateway address on the RAS server specifies the IP address of the ISP's router interface to the Internet.

  C. The default gateway address on each Windows 95 computer specifies the IP address of the ISP's router interface to your internal network.

  D. The default gateway address on each Windows 95 machine specifies the IP address of the RAS server's network interface to your internal network.

12. Your NT Server has three network adapters. You configure the server to route TCP/IP packets, and you want it to be able to automatically update its routing tables by using routing information from other routers on the network. Which service must you install on the Windows NT Server computer?

A. RIP for IP

B. RIP for NWLink IPX/SPX Compatible Transport

C. The DHCP Relay Agent

D. The DHCP Service

13. You have five multihomed Windows NT Server computers running TCP/IP and routing TCP/IP packets. You want to configure the routing tables on these servers with a minimum of administrative effort. What should you do?

A. Use NETSTAT.EXE to configure the routing tables.

B. Use ROUTE.EXE to configure the routing tables.

C. Install the DHCP Relay Agent.

D. Install RIP for IP.

14. You have a multihomed Windows NT Server that you want to configure as a TCP/IP static router. What two steps must you complete?

A. Enable IP forwarding.

B. Configure each network adapter with a unique subnet mask.

C. Configure each network adapter with an IP address, and ensure that each IP address is from a different subnet.

D. Configure each network adapter with an IP address, and ensure that each IP address is from a different address class.

15. You have installed two routers on one subnet to provide redundancy. When one router fails, users start complaining that they cannot access remote subnets, even though you have a second router on the network. What should you do to prevent this problem from occurring the next time a router fails?

A. Configure each workstation with multiple default gateway addresses.

B. Configure each workstation with multiple IP addresses.

    C. Install a WINS server on each subnet.

    D. Install the DHCP Relay Agent on both routers.

16. The network is configured as follows: two subnets, one router. The router has two interfaces: Network A with 167.191.32.1 and Network B with 167.191.64.1. All computers use a subnet mask of 255.255.224.0. Your NT Workstation cannot connect to a remote server on Network A, but all other workstations on Network B can. You are located on network B. When you run IPCONFIG on your workstation, you receive the following output:

IP Address	167.191.82.17
Subnet Mask	255.255.224.0
Default Gateway	167.191.32.1

What is most likely the cause of the problem?

    A. IP address on workstation is invalid.

    B. Subnet mask on workstation is invalid.

    C. Default gateway on workstation is invalid.

    D. IP address on server is invalid.

    E. Default gateway on server is invalid.

17. The network is configured as follows: two subnets, one router. The router has two interfaces: Network A with 167.191.32.1 and Network B with 167.191.64.1. All computers use a subnet mask of 255.255.224.0. Your NT Workstation cannot connect to a remote server on Network A, but all other workstations on Network B can. You are located on Network B. When you run IPCONFIG on your workstation, you receive the following output:

IP Address	167.191.96.17
Subnet Mask	255.255.224.0
Default Gateway	167.191.64.1

What is most likely the cause of the problem?

A. IP address on workstation is invalid.

B. Subnet mask on workstation is invalid.

C. Default gateway on workstation is invalid.

D. IP address on server is invalid.

E. Default gateway on server is invalid.

18. **Situation:** You are installing an NT TCP/IP server with three network adapters. You also plan to use this server as a router.

Required results:

- The new server must be configured to route TCP/IP.

Optional desired results:

- The server must dynamically update its routing tables.

- The server must provide IP addresses to all clients located on all subnets.

- The server must be able to send trap messages across the network to a Windows NT workstation computer.

Proposed solution:

- Install TCP/IP and configure one IP address for each of the server's network adapters.

- Install PPTP on the server.

- Install DHCP on the server and configure one scope for each subnet.

- Install SNMP on the server and configure SNMP to forward traps messages to the workstation.

Which results does the proposed solution produce?

A. The proposed solution produces the required result and produces all of the optional desired results.

B. The proposed solution produces the required result and produces only two of the optional desired results.

C. The proposed solution produces the required result but does not produce any of the optional desired results.

D. The proposed solution does not produce the required result.

19. **Situation:** You are installing an NT TCP/IP server with three network adapters. You also plan to use this server as a router.

Required result:

- The new server must be configured to route TCP/IP.

Optional desired results:

- The server must dynamically update its routing tables.

- The server must provide IP addresses to all clients located on all subnets.

- The server must be able to send trap messages across the network to a Windows NT workstation computer.

Proposed solution:

- Install TCP/IP and configure one IP address for each server's network adapters.

- Enable IP forwarding on the server.

- Install PPTP on the server.

- Install the DHCP Relay Agent on the server.

Which results does the proposed solution produce?

A. The proposed solution produces the required result and produces all of the optional desired results.

B. The proposed solution produces the required result and produces only two of the optional desired results.

C. The proposed solution produces the required result but does not produce any of the optional desired results.

D. The proposed solution does not produce the required results.

20. Situation: You are installing an NT TCP/IP server with three network adapters. You also plan to use this server as a router.

Required result:

- The new server must be configured to route TCP/IP.

Optional desired results:

- The server must dynamically update its routing tables.

- The server must provide IP addresses to all clients located on all subnets.

- The server must be able to send trap messages across the network to a Windows NT workstation computer.

Proposed solution:

- Install TCP/IP and configure one IP address for each server's network adapters.

- Enable IP forwarding on the server.

- Install RIP for IP on the server.

- Install DHCP with scopes for all subnets.

Which results does the proposed solution produce?

A. The proposed solution produces the required result and produces all of the optional desired results.

B. The proposed solution produces the required result and produces only two of the optional desired results.

C. The proposed solution produces the required result but does not produce any of the optional desired results.

D. The proposed solution does not produce the required results.

21. Situation: You are installing an NT TCP/IP server with three network adapters. You also plan to use this server as a router.

Required result:

- The new server must be configured to route TCP/IP.

Optional desired results:

- The server must dynamically update its routing tables.

- The server must provide IP addresses to all clients located on all subnets.

- The server must be able to send trap messages across the network to a Windows NT workstation computer.

Proposed solution:

- Install TCP/IP and configure one IP address for each server's network adapters.

- Enable IP forwarding on the server.

- Install DHCP with scopes for all subnets.

- Install SNMP on the server and configure SNMP to forward trap messages to the workstation.

- Install a third-party SNMP manager on the server.

Which results does the proposed solution produce?

A. The proposed solution produces the required result and produces all of the optional desired results.

B. The proposed solution produces the required result and produces only two of the optional desired results.

C. The proposed solution produces the required result but does not produce any of the optional desired results.

D. The proposed solution does not produce the required results.

22. Assign the missing IP and subnet mask values for each customer below:

Beginning IP address	192.24.0.1
Ending IP address	192.24.7.8
Subnet Mask	
Beginning IP address	192.34.16.1
Ending IP address	
Subnet Mask	255.255.240.0

Beginning IP address

Ending IP address   192.24.11.254

Subnet Mask   255.255.252.0

Beginning IP address   192.24.14.1

Ending IP address

Subnet Mask   255.255.254.0

CHAPTER

4

IP Address Resolution

Great news...Of all the chapters in this book, this is one of the teensiest. It's not to be underestimated though—lots of small things are seriously important and valuable. Things like viruses, diamonds, atomic particles, and pebbles in your shoes while summiting a granite peak. This chapter is like that—small, but special.

You can't do much before IP address resolution has occurred. It's a primary, fundamental thing. The other types of resolution, host name and NetBIOS, discussed in the next two chapters, can only work for you if the IP address is known first. These operations require the knowledge of IP addresses for the messages they send via TCP/IP to reach their destinations. In short, if communication is to occur, IP addresses must first be resolved. This chapter will focus on how a number assigned to a host system is resolved to find its MAC, or hardware address.

After you've made short work of this chapter, you should find yourself in possession of sage wisdom about:

- IP address resolution

- How IP address resolution is achieved locally

- How IP address resolution is achieved remotely

- The ins and outs of IP address resolution and ARP caching

- How to deal effectively with some common IP address resolution hang-ups

- The reasons why these hang-ups happened in the first place—and how to prevent them from happening again

IP Address Resolution Defined

The process of resolution involves asking a question and receiving an answer to it. In the case of IP address resolution, the question posed resembles, "Which device is the owner of IP address 192.57.8.8?" The resolution, or answer, to that question would include the MAC address of the NIC (network interface card), as encoded by the manufacturer. In essence, IP address resolution is the linking of an IP, or software, address to a hardware, or MAC, address.

Getting to a specific place first requires knowing where that place is located. Similarly, resolving an IP address is to network managers what locating a certain parcel of land on a planner's grid map is to a city planner or industrial engineer. Suppose your neighbor desired an additional room for their flourishing family, and an expansion was planned. Before the first contractor's hammer fell, a permit for the remodeling would have to be obtained from the city. Those responsible for awarding that permit would then have to "resolve" your neighbor's home address to its physical coordinates—its individual place on their grid. Knowing its "map address," they would then have access to the information they need to proceed with issuing a permit.

The protocol that answers these questions regarding IP address ownership is called ARP. You may recall some discussion about ARP from Chapter 2. In case you don't, ARP stands for "Address Resolution Protocol," and is described thoroughly in RFC 826. ARP is the IP address resolution engine. Regardless of where the ultimate destination is located, ARP always uses a local broadcast to determine where data should be sent. If the destination happens to be on a remote network, the local default gateway's hardware address will be used to hop over to it. Once the mystery address has been resolved, it is recorded in a table called the ARP cache. If additional messages are sent to the same destination, the ARP cache will be checked first so as to prevent unnecessary network traffic generated by a broadcast. This keeps the local network running efficiently as it's examined and logged.

You might also remember our discussion of RARP (Reverse Address Resolution Protocol) in Chapter 2. Like inductive vs. deductive reasoning, it's the inverse operation of ARP—it's used to get an IP address from a Mac Address.

Local Resolution

Each subnet of the network can be thought of as an island that contains a city—say, Maui. So long as you never have to leave that island, you've remained local—or as is the case with computers, on the local network. If you require a service or permit concerning your property on the island, you could contact Maui's local city planning office, and give them your address. They would respond by assigning a permit according to your mapped coordinates. Likewise, whenever a request is made that requires IP address resolution, ARP, IP's city employee, is deployed to the task of confirming your identity and whereabouts.

The process of resolving the IP address of a machine existing on the local network is shown in Figure 4.1, and outlined below. While reading through these steps, notice how ARP works in a way that minimizes network overhead.

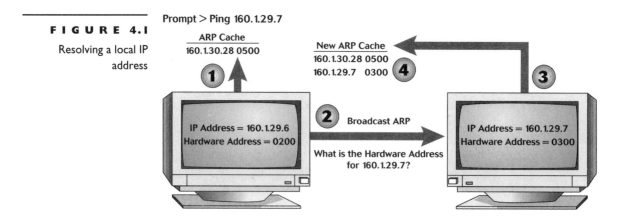

FIGURE 4.1

Resolving a local IP address

Step One The destination machine's IP address is checked to see if it's on the local network. If so, the host system will then check its ARP cache for the machine's hardware address.

Step Two Provided that the ARP address didn't find 0300 in the host system's ARP cache, ARP will attempt to enter it by sending a message requesting the owner of that IP address to send back its hardware address. Because the hardware address is still unknown, the ARP message is sent out as a broadcast that's read by each and every system on the local network. Like a self-addressed envelope that's sent inscribed with all the information necessary to get it back to its sender, both the IP address and the hardware address of the requesting system are included in the broadcast message.

Step Three The reply message is sent directly to the hardware address of the requesting system. Only the owner of the requested IP address will respond. All other systems will disregard the request.

Step Four Upon receiving the reply, the requesting machine will append the address into its ARP cache. At this point, communication has been established.

Remote Resolution

When it comes to computer operations, communications are usually much simpler if they involve devices within the local network. These processes can't always be simple though. Complex internetworks with subnets have bridges or routers set up between them that connect them together. These devices are filters that serve to sort data according to its destination—they don't allow all data to cross indiscriminately. To distinguish which data gets to pass through, routers look at the IP address destination located in the packet's header, whereas bridges look at a frame's header for the destination hardware address. Going back to our subnet island of Maui, let's say you find it necessary to contact someone or something that doesn't reside there, but exists on another island—Molokai. Since those who populate Molokai aren't Maui locals, by attempting to make contact with them, you are attempting remote communication. Let's pretend that to reach them, you must cross a draw bridge. Unless you arrive at the draw bridge with a specific, remote Molokai address, the bridge operator will keep the bridge drawn, and you won't be allowed to cross.

Figure 4.2 and the steps immediately following it illustrate the process of resolving the IP address of a machine located on a remote network. These steps are repeated at every router the data encounters en route to its final destination.

Step One The destination IP address is checked to see if it is on the local network. Once determined otherwise, the system will check its local route table for a path to the remote network. If a path is found, the ARP cache is checked for the hardware address of the default gateway specified in the routing path. Note: In general, the most efficient path to a remote network will be established by a router utilizing OSPF (Open Shortest Path First). This reduces network traffic overhead.

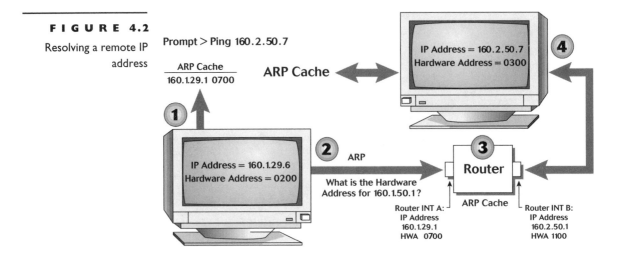

FIGURE 4.2

Resolving a remote IP
address

Step Two When a path is not found, an ARP request is generated to determine the hardware address of the default gateway or router (see Figure 4.2). Since the only thing that is known about the destination is that it is on a remote network, the router will have to be used as the medium to reach the remote destination.

Step Three The router will reply with its hardware address to the requesting host. The source host will then use ICMP to issue an echo request back to the router, which will then deliver the echo request to the remote network that will eventually reach the destination host. The router will then repeat step one (that is, check if it's local or remote, and then take the correct action. Generally, unless a routing path is found at the server, steps one through three are repeated until the client is on a local network. Note that the router can use either a broadcast or its cache in determining the hardware address of the destination system.

Step Four The destination machine will also respond to the ARP request with an ICMP echo reply. Since the requesting system is on a remote network, the reply will be sent to the router. As with previous resolutions, if the router (default gateway) is not in the ARP cache, a local IP address resolution scenario will take place to determine the router's address. In turn, the router will then set the route accordingly.

What's more confusing is that there are often multiple bridges to the same location. Finding the shortest path is usually handled by the router, and will remain an issue until the data finds its way to the router directly connected to the destination address's local subnet.

The ARP Cache

The ARP cache is a table used to store both IP addresses and MAC addresses. Each time communication is initiated with another machine, it checks its ARP cache for an entry. If it doesn't find one, an ARP request is broadcasted, the address is resolved, and it is then entered into its ARP cache. The address is now handy, much like an entry in your home address book would be, for the next time communication with that device is necessary. Additionally, the ARP cache maintains the hardware broadcast address (FFFFFFFF) for the local subnet as a permanent entry. Though it doesn't appear when the cache is viewed, this entry allows a host to accept ARP broadcasts.

ARP Entry Lifetimes and the ARP.EXE Utility

Entries in the ARP table include an IP address, a hardware address, and a time stamp. Each entry in the ARP cache has a potential lifetime of no more than 10 minutes. If an entry isn't used within two minutes, it'll be removed from the cache. With some implementations of TCP/IP, the 10 minute maximum lifetime is automatically extended each time the entry is used. This isn't the case with Windows NT, which simply deletes entries from the cache, starting with the oldest, to make room for new ones as the capacity limits of its ARP table are reached. It will do this to an old entry even if its lifetime hasn't yet expired.

The ARP.EXE utility allows you to view, add, and delete entries in the ARP cache (see Exercise 4.1). Entries are added by typing the command format -s (*ip address*)(*mac address*). An example would be ARP -s 134.57.8.8 05-20-4a-29-95. These entries are permanently stored in the ARP cache table. Since these entries don't change, they're also referred to as static entries. The only time that these entries will be removed is if the computer is restarted, or if a broadcast is received, indicating that the hardware address has changed. In the latter case, the updated entry becomes dynamic instead of static. Entries can be deleted by typing **ARP -d 135.57.8.8**.

All entries in the ARP cache can be displayed by typing **ARP -a or ARP -g**(-g isn't supported by Windows for Workgroups). These case-sensitive commands can be highly useful when questing for the hardware address of a destination system. For example, if you needed to know the hardware address of a particular workstation, you could use ping to open a communications path to it, and then review the ARP cache to determine the hardware address associated with the pinged IP entry.

The ARP system is kind of like jail. Like all ARP entries—IP addresses having both a hardware address and a time stamp—every jail inmate has a number and exit date. In both cases, depending on the inmate/entry's behavior, the time spent "inside" will vary. Though lifetimes aren't definite for inmates, both ARP entries and inmates have them, along with maximum time periods for their duration. Depending on the jail's capacity, older inmates may be released early, just as old ARP entries are when the ARP cache is full. Occasionally, a judge assigns the death penalty or consecutive lifetime sentences to an individual inmate—like making a manual entry into the ARP table. The only time these special inmates are released is when they're dead (deleted from the ARP cache), a pardon is given, allowing the inmate to begin a new life (restarting the computer), or if the system discovers it has the wrong person (a broadcast notifying ARP of a new, corrected hardware address).

Follow the steps outlined in Exercise 4.1 to view the ARP cache.

EXERCISE 4.1

Viewing the ARP Cache

1. Logon as Administrator.

2. Go to a DOS prompt and type **ARP -g**.

3. Record your results.

4. Ping a local host. This will add an entry into the cache.

5. Check to see if the entry was added. It should show up as a dynamic entry.

6. Now, ping a remote host. This will also add an entry into the cache.

7. Check to see if the entry was added. The entry should be that of your default gateway.

Exercise 4.2 will detail how to add entries to and delete entries from the ARP cache.

EXERCISE 4.2

Adding and Deleting Entries in the ARP Cache

To add an entry to the ARP cache:

1. At a DOS prompt, type **ARP -s 160.1.8.18 05-20-4a-29-95-92**.

2. To view your new entry, type **ARP -a** (arp -a and arp -g are the same command).

3. The entry should show up as a static entry.

To delete an entry from the ARP cache:

1. At a DOS prompt, type **ARP -d 160.1.8.18**.

2. View your ARP cache to make sure the entry was deleted.

3. Type **ARP -a**.

In Exercise 4.3, you will use Network Monitor to capture and display packets.

EXERCISE 4.3

Examining an ICMP Packet

To start Network Monitor:

1. On the Start menu, point to Programs ➢ Administrative Tools ➢ Network Monitor. The Network Monitor window appears.

2. Maximize the Network Monitor window.

3. Maximize the Capture window.

4. To capture the network data: Click Start on the Capture menu. This starts the data capture process. Network Monitor allocates buffer space for network data and begins capturing frames.

5. To generate network traffic: Open a command prompt and type **ping** *default_gateway*.

EXERCISE 4.3 (CONTINUED FROM PREVIOUS PAGE)

6. To stop the network data capture: Switch back to Network Monitor and then, on the Capture menu in Network Monitor, click Stop. Network Monitor stops capturing frames and displays four panes: Graph, Total Stats, Session Stats, and Station Stats.

7. To view captured data: Click Display Captured Data on the Capture menu. The Network Monitor Capture Summary window appears, displaying the summary record of all frames captured.

8. To highlight captured data: Click Colors on the Display menu. The Protocol Colors dialog box appears. Under Name, select ICMP (Internet Control Message Protocol). Under Colors, set Foreground to Red, and then click OK. The Network Monitor Capture Summary window appears, displaying all ICMP frames in red.

To View frame details:

1. Under Description, double-click an ICMP frame that has an entry of Echo in the description column. This frame shows an ICMP echo request from the client. Three separate windows are displayed. The top window displays the frame summary, the middle window displays the selected frame details, and the bottom window displays the selected frame details in hexadecimal notation.

2. In the Detail window, click ICMP with a plus sign (+) preceding it. The plus sign indicates that the information can be expanded by clicking it.

3. Expand the ICMP details. The ICMP properties expand to show more detail. The contents of the ICMP packet are highlighted and displayed in hexadecimal notation in the bottom window.

4. In the Detail window, click ICMP: Packet Type = Echo. What hexadecimal number corresponds with ICMP: Packet Type = Echo?

5. In the Detail window, click ICMP: Packet Type = Echo, and then click Find Next Instance. The Find Frame Expression dialog box appears, displaying information about the packet type.

6. Click Cancel.

7. In the Detail window, click Checksum. What is the Checksum number?

8. In the Detail window, click Identifier. What is the Identifier number?

9. In the Detail window, click Sequence Number. What is the Sequence Number?

10. In the Detail window, click Data. The data received in the echo message must be resumed in the echo reply message.

11. Repeat steps 1 through 9 for the Echo Reply packet that follows the echo packet that is currently displayed. You should have found the following changes: Packet Type changed from Echo to Echo Reply; Checksum changed (numbers will vary); Identifier was the same for all ICMP packets; Sequence Numbers remained the same for all echo packet pairs.

Finally, to save the capture for later analysis:

1. On the File menu, click Save As.

2. Under File Name, type **test1.lab**, and then click OK.

3. On the File menu, click Close. The Network Monitor Capture window appears, still displaying the statistics from the last capture.

4. Exit Network Monitor.

Exercise 4.4 outlines the procedures for examining an ARP packet.

Examining an ARP Packet

To capture network data:

1. Start Network Monitor.

2. On the Capture menu, click Start.

3. Open a command prompt, and type **ping *remote_host***.

4. On the Capture menu in Network Monitor, click Stop and View. The Network Monitor Capture Summary window appears, displaying the summary record of all frames captured.

EXERCISE 4.4 (CONTINUED FROM PREVIOUS PAGE)

5. Maximize the Capture window.

To highlight captured data:

1. On the Display menu, click Colors. The Protocol Colors dialog box appears.

2. Under Name, select ARP_RARP.

3. Under Colors, set Foreground to Red, and then click OK. The Network Monitor Capture Summary window appears, displaying all ARP frames in red.

To view the ARP request frame details:

1. Under Description, double-click ARP: Request.

2. In the Detail window, click Frame with a plus sign (+) preceding it.

3. Expand the Frame details. The frame size should be 42 bytes.

4. Collapse the base frame properties.

5. In the Detail window, expand ETHERNET. The ETHERNET frame properties are displayed. The destination address should be FFFFFFFF.

Common Problems

Many communications problems are in some way related to resolution. The two most common ones are redundant IP addresses and incorrect subnet masks.

A redundant IP address can cause a variety of networking ills. Under Windows NT, it is very obvious indeed when you have duplicate addresses because the host system will simply refuse to initialize TCP/IP. However, not all systems make this problem so deliciously apparent. For example, if a server or gateway were to have their addresses used in more than one place, the wrong system may receive or respond to requests, or even just hang there in suspended animation. Imagine the confusion caused by two people using the same social security number!

The existence of incorrect subnet masks can also make for a gloomy day in Networkland. For example, when a host is attempting to determine if an address is local or remote, it will look to the subnet mask to determine which portions of the address are network-based, and which are node-based. If the system discovers a remote machine on the local network, lots of unnecessary traffic will be created from broadcasts while it attempts to resolve the addresses. Depending on the level at which the broadcast is generated, something called a *broadcast storm* may take place. These are as sinister as they sound—their "storm surges" being capable of destroying network performance by causing systems caught in the deluge to "time-out," and hang there as if frozen.

Summary

Well...quick as a desert thundershower, this chapter's over—but hopefully, not before you know it! The IP address resolution process was likened to the human process of asking a question and receiving its answer...the communications equivalent of asking, "What device is the owner of a certain IP address?" and receiving the answer "the MAC address of the NIC card as encoded by the manufacturer." IP address resolution was resolved (pun intended) to be the linking of an IP, or software, address to a hardware, or MAC, address.

You learned, by means of a four-step process, how to resolve IP addresses locally. You also noticed how ARP works in a way that minimizes network overhead. Remote resolution, also a four-step process, is a bit more complicated because of the involvement of routers, or "bridges."

We also took a look at the arp command and viewed ICMP and ARP packets through Network Monitor.

The test does not focus on this chapter too heavily. However, there are some good troubleshooting exercises throughout this chapter that will help you in your job. Make sure and understand the exercises and go through the questions below to help you remember the information presented in this chapter.

Review Questions

1. What is IP address resolution?

    A. Resolving duplicate IP addresses

    B. The successful mapping of an IP address to its hardware address

    C. Resolving invalid subnet masks

    D. Resolving errors when IP tries to resolve an IP address to a hardware address

2. How do you resolve IP addresses locally?

    A. By typing Resolve IP address ip-address

    B. By typing ARP -s ip-address

    C. With an ARP request and an ARP reply

    D. With an RARP request and an RARP reply

3. How does your computer resolve IP addresses remotely?

    A. It sends an ARP to the destination machine.

    B. It sends an RARP to the destination machine.

    C. It sends an RARP to the default gateway.

    D. It sends an ARP to the default gateway.

4. Which is true about the ARP cache?

    A. It's cleared out every time the computer is rebooted.

    B. The ARP cache stores only dynamic IP and hardware addresses.

    C. The ARP cache stores only static IP and hardware addresses.

    D. It's permanent.

5. What's the maximum lifetime of an entry in the ARP cache?

    A. Two minutes

    B. As specified by the system administrator

C. Ten minutes

D. ARP entries are permanent and can only be removed by typing **ARP -d.**

6. Aside from the initial entry into the cache, if the destination system isn't contacted again, how long will the entry remain in the cache?

   A. Ten minutes

   B. Two minutes

   C. Five minutes

   D. Until deleted

7. Under Windows NT, if the cache fills up, what happens to old and new entries?

   A. If their lifetime expires, old entries are deleted, and new ones added.

   B. Regardless of whether or not an old entry's lifetime has expired, it is deleted in favor of adding the new one.

   C. Old entries are cached for future use, and new ones added to the ARP table.

   D. Nothing.

8. You're a computer science professor at a major university. One of your students wants to know why an IP address needs to be resolved. She asks "Why is it necessary to know both the software and hardware addresses— why isn't knowing the hardware address enough?" What do you tell her?

9. You're being interviewed for a network specialist position. Your potential employer asks, "In what way could an incorrect subnet mask cause a problem? When would this problem occur, and who, if anyone, would notice?" How would you answer?

10. When you go to a DOS prompt and type **ARP –g,** what do you see? (Choose all that apply.)

    A. IP to NetBIOS names that have been resolved.

    B. The IP Cache

    C. The entries in the ARP cache

    D. IP to MAC addresses that have been resolved

CHAPTER

5

Host Name Resolution

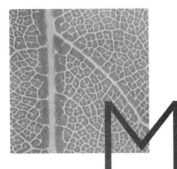

ost people have more than a little trouble remembering a bunch of 32-bit, binary numbers. The IP address is most commonly represented by four 8-bit numbers instead; but even then, remembering a throng of cryptic number sequences is, at best, a hassle. TCP/IP allows language-loving humans to use host names for their machines instead. Though TCP/IP hosts do require an IP address to communicate with each other, hosts can be referenced by a handy host name for easy identification by their significant human or humans.

Read the chapter again should you find yourself on the other side of it without total recall regarding the following:

- The definition of host naming

- Host name resolution on both local and remote networks

- Host name resolution and configuration via a DNS

- Host name resolution and configuration via a HOSTS file

- The Microsoft way of achieving host name resolution

- Commonly experienced problems with the above

Host Names Defined

An obviously critical first thing to get straight is what, exactly, a host name is. A *host name* is an assigned identifier called an "alias" that's used to designate a specific TCP/IP host in a logical way. This alias can be any string of up to 256 characters of any type. A single host can have many host names that may be the same, or different, from that system's NetBIOS name (we'll discuss this in Chapter 6). The alias allows a given machine to be referenced by name, function, or anything else that makes the light of recognition burn brightly in the mind of the human who needs to remember which one it is.

Host names are much like NetBIOS names in that their functional uses are the same. For example, a host name such as "Hal" may be resolved to the IP address 160.1.92.26. As we already know, IP addresses can then be resolved to a hardware address, fully identifying the device. This is the same with Net-BIOS. Highly noteworthy is the fact that UNIX machines, as well as some others, don't use NetBIOS names. The main difference in referencing the two types of hosts is that with NetBIOS, you must always communicate using the name with Microsoft network commands—not just the IP address. Using TCP/IP utilities to reference a UNIX host will allow you to access the host using the IP address. UNIX has always been TCP/IP-based, and TCP/IP has been specifically tailored to fit the needs of this operating system. However, Microsoft has been backward fitting their operating systems to function with TCP/IP, and with much success. The NetBIOS names used by Microsoft are intended to function under the guidance of different protocols which use a different naming convention, both for user and program-oriented communication.

To a UNIX-based machine, the naming function for both user and program communication may be referenced by anything that is an equivalent to what it's used to seeing. For instance, a UNIX utility like FTP will allow you to contact a host by its host name, domain name, or IP address. To demonstrate this, suppose that you were on the Internet with a UNIX workstation. If you desired to retrieve files from Microsoft's FTP site, you could open FTP.MICROSOFT .COM, or access it by entering its IP address—whichever you prefer.

In the example above, FTP.MICROSOFT.COM is called the FQDN, or Fully Qualified Domain Name. When working with TCP/IP, systems are addressed in a hierarchy that can logically locate a system based on its domain identifier. This system works using host but not NetBIOS names.

The Host Naming Hierarchy

TCP/IP has full support for host naming, which is organized into a hierarchical structure. Each host belongs to a domain, and each domain is classified further into domain types, much like the scientific naming-scheme convention of class, order, phylum, genus, family, and species. Microsoft.com is a commercial organization—the "com" standing for "commercial." (See Figure 5.1.)

FIGURE 5.1

Domain name hierarchy

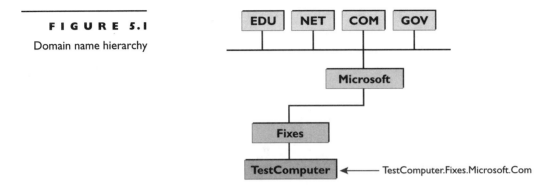

You can tell immediately what type of group you are dealing with by the suffix following the organization name. The following chart lists the various types of organizations suffixed in this manner, which you may come across as you explore TCP/IP through the Internet. Some common ones are shown in Figure 5.2.

FIGURE 5.2

Internet top-level
domain names

Domain Name	Meaning
COM	Commercial Organization
EDU	Educational Institution
GOV	Government Institution
MIL	Military Group
NET	Major Network Support Center
ORG	Organization other than those above
INT	International Organization

Your computer will refer to a DNS server to resolve names listed in the hierarchy. Domain names require a Domain Name Service—a computing service, such as UNIX, that requires a *server daemon*, which is a program for UNIX that runs in the background, just like a TSR does for DOS. A Domain Name Service provides a centralized online database for resolving domain names to their corresponding IP addresses. The base-names, like "Microsoft" in "Microsoft.com," are registered by the *Stanford Research Institute Network Information Center,* or *SRI International/SRI NIC*, so they're kept unique on the Internet.

Resolving Host Names

The name resolution methods are similar to those used in NetBIOS over TCP/IP resolution processes, as you'll see in Chapter 6. Microsoft TCP/IP can use any of six methods to resolve host names. The first three resolution methods—WINS, Local Broadcast, and the LMHOSTS file—will be discussed in greater detail in the next chapter on NetBIOS. The local host name, and the use of DNS and the HOSTS file are the remaining three. We'll be discussing the last two, the DNS and the HOSTS file methods, as they're applied in the UNIX world. We'll also explore how they translate into the Microsoft environment. The methods that Windows NT can use to resolve a host name are configurable.

Standard Resolution

Local host name This is the name of the local configured machine as it relates to the destination host. It's typically used for loopback, or recursive connections.

HOSTS file This is a table stored in a local file and used to resolve host names to IP addresses. It conforms to Berkeley Software Distribution's version 4.3 UNIX's HOSTS file. This file is most commonly used with TCP/IP utilities such as FTP, TELNET, and PING, to resolve a host's name. It may be used to address a computer by an alias, and in many cases, be placed on multiple computers of varying platforms for host resolution purposes.

Domain Name Service (DNS) This service is a cornerstone in the UNIX world, and is found on systems running the DNS service daemon. It's commonly employed for the resolution of host name to IP addresses. This file can be thought of as a networked HOSTS file.

Specific Resolution

Local broadcast An announcement made on a local network requesting the IP address for the system assigned to a specific NetBIOS or host name. It is commonly referred to as a b-node broadcast.

Windows Internet Name Service This is commonly implemented as a WINS, or Windows Internet Name Server. This type of name resolution service corresponds to RFC 1001/1002, and delivers NetBIOS or host name resolution from a server that's running it.

LMHOSTS file   This is also a table that's stored in a local file and used to resolve NetBIOS or host names to IP addresses on remote networks. It's similar to the HOSTS file discussed in detail next, but offers some functions we'll discuss more in the next chapter on NetBIOS.

Resolution via the HOSTS File

Before getting down to the nitty-gritty on the host name resolution process, it's important to examine in more detail a few particulars regarding the HOSTS file.

Microsoft ✓ *Exam* *Objective*   **Configure HOSTS and LMHOSTS files.**

The HOSTS File

The HOSTS file is an ordinary text document that can be created or modified using any text editor. It's used by ping and other TCP/IP utilities to resolve a host name to an IP address on both local and remote networks. Each line with a host name or alias can only correspond to one IP address. Because the file is read from top to bottom, duplicate names will be ignored, and commonly used names should be placed nearer the top for speedier access. Older implementations of TCP/IP with Windows NT maintained the case-sensitivity associated with UNIX, but this is no longer the case (pun intended). An entry can be any valid string of up to 256 characters, with comments placed to the right of a pound (#) sign. By default, Microsoft installs a HOSTS file in \%*SYSTEMROOT*%\SYSTEM32\DRIVERS\ETC, with 127.0.0.1 localhost as a loopback entry.

```
#Sample Host file
#
127.0.0.1     loopback      localhost    #Entries used for
                                         loopback diagnostics
#
160.1.27.3    My_Computer    #Entries to describe my System
160.1.4.87    UnixMaster     #The UNIX system that I talk to
160.1.98.89   Router12       # My Subnet's Router
```

The HOSTS File Resolution Process

The HOSTS file has long been used for name resolution purposes as implemented with TCP/IP on most UNIX hosts. Because a host can have multiple names, the HOSTS file will commonly contain listings of the local host 127.0.0.1, as well as other names, called *aliases*, by which the machine may be known when it's referenced by other systems. The HOSTS file will be checked for all host name resolutions, including itself.

Resolution begins when a command is issued requesting resolution. This command can be either machine or user generated. The system will initially check the destination name against its own. If a match is found, it's a done deal—the name's been resolved. However, in some cases, like when the required destination turns out to be on a remote system, or if the request is actually an alias for itself, the system will proceed to check the HOSTS file for a match. If no match is found, and the HOSTS file is the only configured method for resolution, an error will be spawned and sent back. If a match is achieved, the IP address is then used to resolve the destination's IP address to a hardware address with ARP, and the destination host is found. If the destination host is on a remote network, ARP obtains the hardware address of the proper router (default gateway), and the request is then forwarded to the destination host. In Figure 5.3, a user types Ping Alta from the host named Aspen, IP address 160.1.24.3. Aspen first looks into its HOSTS file, and finds an entry for "Alta" of 160.1.29.7. If the name wasn't found in the HOSTS file, an error would be generated reading, "no such host." If Aspen has talked with Alta before, the hardware address would be in Aspen's ARP cache. If not, host Aspen would then ARP for the hardware address for the workstation Alta.

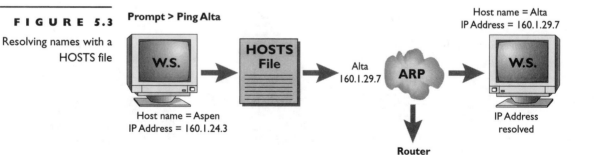

FIGURE 5.3

Resolving names with a HOSTS file

At this point, the process is identical to NetBIOS resolution. We keep comparing the two resolution methods because it's very important for you to understand their similarities and differences. A local machine will resolve to its hardware address, while a remote machine will resolve to the hardware address of the proper default gateway. No local cache is used with host name resolution. You will configure the HOSTS file in Exercise 5.1.

Resolution via DNS

A DNS Server can be thought of as a networked version of the HOSTS file. In computing environments such as UNIX, the DNS provides a central reservoir used to resolve fully qualified domain names (FQDNs) to IP addresses. Windows NT 4.0 can use a DNS Server and provides DNS server services.

As shown in Figure 5.4, resolution begins with the issuing of a command requiring resolution. Again, the command can originate from either a machine or a user. In our example, we show a user originated command: Ping Alta .Fixes.Microsoft.Com. The DNS receives a request for the IP address of the host system "Alta." If found, the DNS will reply with the matched address. If no match is found, or the DNS server does not respond to requests made at 5, 10, 20, 40, 5, 10, and 20 second intervals progressively, an error will be generated, assuming that DNS is the only configured host name service. If a match is achieved, the IP address is then used to resolve the destination's IP address to a hardware address with ARP. Remember...a local machine—a destination host located on the same subnet as the sending host—will resolve to its hardware address, while a destination for a remote host will resolve to the hardware address of the default gateway.

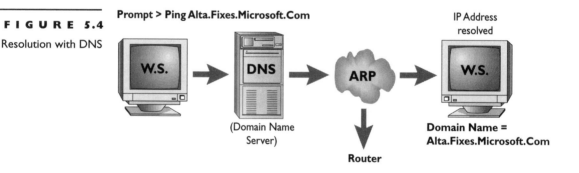

FIGURE 5.4

Resolution with DNS

Exercise 5.1 will take you through the steps for configuring the HOSTS file.

EXERCISE 5.1

Configuring the HOSTS File

In this exercise, you will add host name/IP address mappings to your HOSTS file, and then use the file to resolve host names.

To determine the local host name:

1. Open a command prompt.

2. Clear the NetBIOS name cache. We wouldn't want any unwelcome resolutions happening during our exercise.

3. Type **hostname** and then press Enter. The local host name is displayed.

To ping local host names:

1. Type **ping *hostname*** (where *hostname is* the name of your computer), and then press Enter. You should receive four successful "Reply from IP address" messages.

2. Type **ping *hostname*** (where *hostname is* the name of another computer on your subnet), and then press Enter. You should receive four successful "Reply from IP address" messages.

To attempt to ping a remote computer name:

1. Type **ping remote_host**, and then press Enter.

2. You should receive the following response: "Bad IP address *remote_host*." (You were able to ping local computer names but not remote computer names because the Microsoft TCP/IP protocol uses broadcasts to resolve the computer name to an IP address.)

To add an entry to the HOSTS file:

1. Change to the following directory by typing: **cd *%systemroot%*\ system32\drivers\etc.**

2. You will now use a text editor to modify a file called HOSTS. Type **edit HOSTS**.

EXERCISE 5.1 (CONTINUED FROM PREVIOUS PAGE)

3. Add the following entry to the HOSTS file: *ip_address* **Remote Host**.

4. Save the file, and then exit Edit.

5. Type **ping** *remote_ip_address*, and then press Enter. You should receive four successful "Reply from IP address" messages.

Exercise 5.2 shows you how to identify Domain Name Server resolution problems.

EXERCISE 5.2

Identifying Domain Name Server Resolution Problems

In this exercise, you will configure your computer to use a Domain Name Server (DNS), and you will identify problems in the host name resolution process. In this case, the DNS will fail because it doesn't exist.

To configure DNS support on Windows NT Server:

1. Access the Microsoft TCP/IP Properties dialog box.

2. Click the DNS tab. The DNS properties sheet appears.

3. Under DNS Service Search Order, click Add. The TCP/IP DNS Server dialog box appears.

4. In the TCP/IP DNS Server dialog box, type **remote_host_ip_address**, and then click Add. The IP address of the remote_host appears in the DNS Service Search Order box.

5. Click OK. The Network dialog box appears.

6. Click OK.

EXERCISE 5.2 (CONTINUED FROM PREVIOUS PAGE)

In the following procedure, you will determine the effects of trying to resolve a host name using a DNS, when the DNS is not available.

1. Open a command prompt.

2. Type **ping remote_host**, and then press Enter. After a long delay (approximately one minute), a "Bad IP address remote_host" message appears.

3. Modify the HOSTS file to include the following entry: *ip_address* **remote_host**.

4. Type **ping** *remote_host*, and then press Enter. You should receive four successful "Reply from remote_host" messages. In the following procedure, you will remove the DNS IP Address so TCP/IP will not attempt to use a DNS for name resolution.

5. Access the Microsoft TCP/IP Properties dialog box.

6. Click the DNS tab. The DNS properties sheet appears.

7. Under DNS Service Search Order, click Remove. The IP address is removed from the DNS Service Search Order box.

8. Click OK. The Network dialog box appears.

9. Click OK.

The Microsoft Method

Windows NT can be configured to resolve host names using either the HOSTS file or a DNS. If one of them fails, the other is there to provide backup. Microsoft's implementation of TCP/IP under Windows NT supports all forms of resolution mentioned earlier: WINS, b-node broadcasts, and LMHOSTS. In Figure 5.5, we show a system configured to support all forms of name resolution.

Microsoft
✓ ***Exam***
Objective

Configure and support browsing in a multiple-domain routed network.

FIGURE 5.5

Microsoft's method of resolving host names

Prompt > Ping Alta

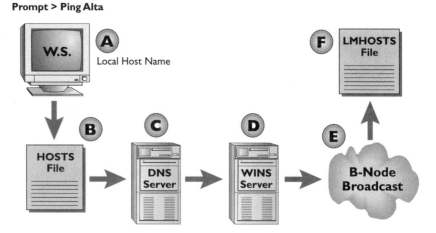

Such a system would have the following search order:

Step A Beginning with a command requiring host name resolution (i. e., Ping, TELNET, FTP, etc.), the local machine's host name will be checked for a match. In the example in Figure 5.5, this would be Ping Alta. If a match is found, no further action is required, and no network traffic is created.

Step B If the name isn't found, the next step would be to review the HOSTS file on the local machine. Again, if a match is found, no further action is required, and no network traffic is created.

Step C If the name isn't found, the next strategy will be to attempt resolution through the DNS. If no response is received from the DNS machine, repeat requests will be sent in intervals of 5, 10, 20, 40, 5, 10 and 20 seconds, progressively. If your system is configured for DNS, and the unit is offline or down, all other systems using DNS in some form will experience a considerable slow down—so much so that they may appear to have crashed while attempting to resolve the name.

Step D If the DNS server was offline, or is unable to resolve the name for some reason, a check is run on the NetBIOS name cache, followed by three attempts to get the WINS server to resolve the name.

Step E If none of the attempts in Step D successfully resolve the host name, three b-node broadcasts are then sent out.

Step F If this is also unsuccessful, the final step is to search the LMHOSTS file. This action is very similar to, and corresponds to, the behavior of a Microsoft enhanced b-node system.

If all of these resolution attempts fail, an error will be returned. Since the name can't be resolved, the only remaining way to communicate with the unresolved machine will be to use its specific IP address.

The action path of host name resolution closely resembles that of NetBIOS name resolution. The key difference between them is that NetBIOS name resolution methods generate less network traffic, whereas host names are resolved by standard UNIX methods.

Some Common Problems

There are several problems associated with host name resolution. Commonly, ping is used to verify entries. This works extremely well unless a different client has the IP address, resulting in the dismal fact that you are actually checking the wrong machine. There is a great degree of similarity between the following list of headaches plaguing host name resolution, and those experienced with NetBIOS name resolution.

HOSTS/DNS Does Not Contain a Name

Like the search for Atlantis, you just can't find something if it isn't there. If the name doesn't exist, the system can't find it. Quite often, companies will implement DNS as a solution. It's important to remember that if your system is configured for the wrong DNS server, you won't be successful in resolving the filename, and therefore will also fail to resolve the host name to an address. This same predicament occurs when backup copies of the HOSTS file are created, but the wrong one is modified.

HOSTS Contains a Misspelled Entry

People who tell you not to let little things bug you have never spent the night in the same room with a thirsty mosquito. Little things are capable of great destruction, and host name resolution can fail because of something as simple as a spelling error in a command or an entry in the HOSTS file. Be sure to back up the HOSTS file before making changes. HOSTS files can become large, containing a multitude of entries—a very daunting, confusing thing to encounter late at night when it's easy to make mistakes like typing in the wrong IP addresses or host names. These entries just won't work if the host names are spelled incorrectly.

HOSTS Entry Has the Wrong IP Address

Most often, it's not that the IP address is wrong in the HOSTS file or DNS, so much as the host's IP address has changed. If this is the case, then you are trying to reach a host at an IP address that either no longer exists, or has been reassigned elsewhere. When you come across this problem, be sure to verify that you really do have the right IP address. Commonly, in our busy world, when systems are moved and IP addresses are changed, small things like the HOSTS file are overlooked. Sure, the DNS was changed and a memo was sent to management, but if the numbers don't match, your memo was a lie. If you change a machine's IP address, pay close attention to these numbers—sometimes the only way to know for sure is to check the host itself. This applies to a wrong IP address attached to a DNS server.

HOSTS File or DNS Contains Repeat NetBIOS Name Entries

Once the host name has been found with an IP address, there is no further need to search any further. The systems involved consider the name to be resolved. Unfortunately, if the IP address recorded in the file is an old one, and the correct entry located below it contains the right one, the proper system will never be reached. Make sure you have only one up-to-date entry for each host name entered in the file.

Summary

A host name is defined as an assigned identifier, called an *alias*, that is used to designate a specific TCP/IP host in a logical way. This alias can be any string of up to 256 characters of any type. It allows a given machine to be referenced by a name, function, etc. that's more easily recalled by the user than an abstract number.

TCP/IP host naming is organized into a hierarchical structure. Each host belongs to a domain, and each domain is classified further into domain types. For example, Microsoft.com is a commercial organization—the "com" stands for "commercial."

Microsoft TCP/IP can use any of six configurable methods to resolve host names, some used for standard resolution, and others for specific resolution. Standard resolution is accomplished through:

- Local host name

- HOSTS file

- Domain Name Service (DNS)

Specific resolution is achieved through:

- Local broadcasts

- Windows Internet Name Service (WINS)

- LMHOSTS file

In regard to the NT 4.0 TCP/IP test, the questions are not based so much on your understanding of resolution explained in this chapter, but how to configure the HOSTS file and DNS.

Review Questions

1. You're trying to connect to workstations by using their host name, and you receive errors. You check the HOSTS file on the workstation, and it contains the following entries:

127.0.0.1	#localhost loopback diagnostic	
150.170.16.200	#AtLibrary atLibrary &	# Lib Server
150.170.3.2	#router2 Router2	# Engr $ router
150.170.3	#net3 Net3	# Engineering Dept

What must you do to the HOSTS file on the workstation?

A. Remove all the $ characters.

B. Remove all the & characters.

C. Remove the first # character from each line.

D. Change the IP address in the last line to 142.170.3.0.

2. What is a domain name?

A. The Microsoft implementation of a NetBIOS name server

B. A text file in the same format as the 4.3 BSD UNIX file

C. A hierarchical name that is implemented using a Domain Name Server (DNS)

D. A flat name that is implemented using a Domain Name Server (DNS)

3. What is host name resolution?

A. A B-node broadcast on the local network for the IP address of the destination NetBIOS name

B. The process of mapping a host name to an IP address

C. A hierarchical name that is implemented using a Domain Name Server (DNS)

D. A local text file that maps IP addresses to the NetBIOS computer names

4. What is true of a host name?

A. The NAMEHOST utility will display the host name assigned to your system.

B. It is an alias assigned to a computer by an administrator to identify a TCP/IP host.

C. A host name never corresponds to an IP address that is stored in a HOSTS file or in a database on a DNS or WINS server.

D. Host names are not used in Windows NT commands.

E. A host name cannot be used in place of an IP address when using PING or other TCP/IP utilities.

5. Which are common problems associated with host name resolution? (Choose all correct answers.)

   A. Multiple entries for the same host on different lines

   B. Host name is misspelled

   C. Case-sensitivity

   D. IP address is invalid

6. You have enabled all Windows NT name resolving techniques: WINS, b-node broadcast, and LMHOSTS, in addition to the HOSTS file and DNS. But none of these methods resolves a host name. What is the only way to communicate with this host?

7. When resolving names with a HOSTS file, the local names are being resolved while none of the remote host names are being resolved. What would stop the remote host names from being resolved?

8. When resolving names with a HOSTS file, you notice that a host name is being resolved incorrectly. When checking the HOSTS file, you don't see a problem, as the name is spelled correctly and the IP address is correct. What else could be wrong?

9. Your company needs to resolve names on the Internet for its customers trying to look up information on the state of the company. What service will you use to resolve names?

10. On Windows NT, the HOSTS file is stored where?

   A. In the %SYSTEMROOT% directory

   B. In the %SYSTEMROOT% \SYSTEM32 directory

   C. In the %SYSTEMROOT% \SYSTEM32\DRIVERS\ETC directory

   D. In the %SYSTEMROOT% \SYSTEM32\ETC directory

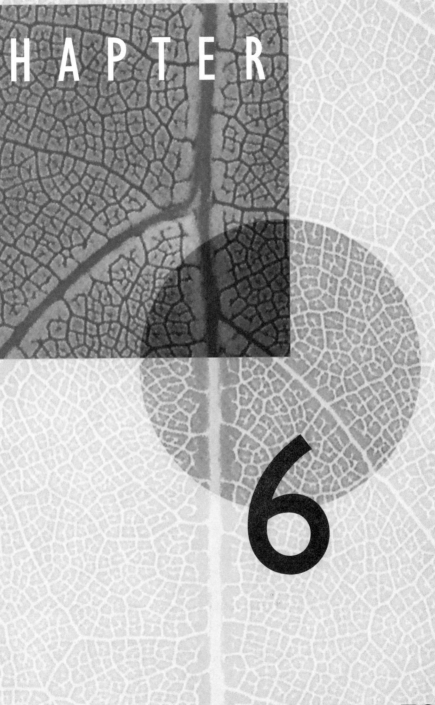

CHAPTER

6

NetBIOS over TCP/IP

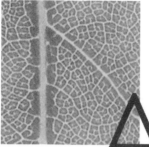

After Chapter 4's initiation into the realm of address resolution, followed by Chapter 5's introduction into exploration of the next layer—host name-to-IP addressing—you're probably beginning to get a pretty clear picture of how naming and the resolution of those names works. This chapter will delve deeper into this theme, offering you another view of resolution as achieved through NetBIOS.

By the time you're finished reading this chapter, the items listed below should be as easy to recall as your best friend's phone number. You should have a working knowledge of:

- NetBIOS naming

- The various NetBIOS over TCP/IP node types

- NetBIOS name resolution via broadcasts

- NetBIOS name resolution via LMHOSTS

- NetBIOS name resolution via NetBIOS Name Server

- NetBIOS name resolution configuration on both local or networked LMHOSTS files

- Common problems concerning NetBIOS names, and their likely causes

NetBIOS Naming

When people refer to the place where the U.S. President lives in everyday conversation, most would simply call it "the White House" rather than refer to his actual address of 1600 Pennsylvania Avenue. Furthermore, it would indeed be a rare bird who would reference the White House by noting its lot number as defined in a city planning grid for Washington, DC.

It's the same with computer programs, especially those that human beings interact with. That's because for us, it's just easier to recall and keep track of a name, as opposed to an impersonal and nondescript number. This given, a logical name is referred to as a *NetBIOS name*. A NetBIOS name may be up to 15 characters in length, with an additional 16th character which internally represents the service or application that was utilized to enter the name.

When communicating with each other, systems such as Windows NT, Windows 95, Windows for Workgroups, LAN Manager, and LAN Manager for UNIX use NetBIOS names rather than IP addresses. NetBIOS names are generally registered when a service or application requiring use of NetBIOS is started up. A good example is Windows NT, in which the NetBIOS name is registered during the initialization phase of the server or workstation that's running it.

NetBIOS naming is widely employed in Microsoft's suite of operating systems. In Windows NT, the NetBIOS name can be viewed by typing **nbtstat -n** or by clicking the Network icon in Control Panel. It can also be accessed in the registry under

`\CurrentControlSet\Control\ComputerName`

Another common use for NetBIOS names in Windows NT is in command line entries, which enable connections through File Manager by using the *UNC (Universal Naming Convention)* with the NET command. This naming scheme serves to make connectivity management more simple and efficient. Let's say you wanted to see exactly which shared directories were available on a certain NetBIOS computer named "Bill." On a Windows NT computer, you'd begin by entering the command prompt: **NET VIEW \\BILL**. If all goes well, from there you'd see that there's also a shared directory appropriately named "Share." To connect to this directory, you would type **NET USE Z: \\BILL \Share**. You'd then find yourself privy to all directories located therein.

The Name Resolution Process

Again, looking to the White House analogy, suppose you'd like to send a letter to the U.S. President. In order to make it possible for your note to reach him, you'd need to resolve the name "White House" to its actual, physical location of 1600 Pennsylvania Ave., Washington, DC, plus the zip code. To find the proper address information, you could look in a telephone book, ask a buddy, or call a government office. NetBIOS names are resolved much the same way, and just as in the above scenario, there are several ways to accomplish that goal. These possible resolution avenues can be sorted into two categories: *standard resolution* and *specific resolution*. Under Windows NT, all methods by which resolution may be achieved are configurable.

Standard NetBIOS Resolution

Standard NetBIOS Name Resolution, which is the process of mapping a NetBIOS name to an IP address, is done dynamically by Windows NT. Standard resolution comes in three forms:

Local Broadcast A request sent out on a local network announcing a specific device's NetBIOS name with the goal of discovering its IP address. Commonly referred to as a b-node broadcast.

NetBIOS Name Cache A listing comprised of both locally resolved names and names, other than local ones, that have been recently resolved.

NBNS, or NetBIOS Name Server Commonly implemented as a *WINS (Windows Internet Name Service)*, this type of name resolution conforms to RFC 1001/1002, performing NetBIOS naming resolution from a server that's running it.

NBTSTAT Utility

This utility checks the state of current NetBIOS over TCP/IP connections, updates the LMHOSTS cache, and determines your registered name and scope ID. This program is also useful for troubleshooting and pre-loading the NETBIOS name cache. Here is the command syntax:

nbtstat -n Lists the NetBIOS names registered by the client

nbtstat -c Displays the NetBIOS name cache

nbtstat - Manually reloads the NetBIOS name cache using entries in the LMHOSTS file with a #PRE parameter

Specific NetBIOS Resolution

On the other hand, specific resolution is a manual process. It is the Microsoft-specific NetBIOS Name Resolution method of building a set of tables, and referring to them for resolution. As with standard resolution, specific resolution also comes in three different varieties: .

Microsoft
✓ *Exam*
Objective

Configure and support browsing in a multiple-domain routed network.

LMHOSTS file A table stored in a local file used in resolving NetBIOS names to IP addresses on remote networks. Though similar to the HOSTS file listed below, it offers further functionality that will be explained more thoroughly later in the chapter.

HOSTS file Remember our discussion in Chapter 2 about the table stored in a local file used to resolve host names to IP addresses? A fact we didn't mention there is that this file conforms to BSD UNIX Version 4.3's HOSTS file. Because of its versatility—it's at home on many a different platform—this is the file most commonly used with the TCP/IP utilities FTP, Telnet, and Ping for host name resolution. It may additionally be used to address a computer by an alias.

Domain Name Service (DNS) Here's another one we discussed earlier. It's also common in the UNIX world and used for resolving a host name to an IP address. This file can be functionally thought of as a networked HOSTS file.

NetBIOS over TCP/IP Node Types

As is certainly apparent by now, there exist different modes and means by which NetBIOS names can be resolved. Just as in other forms of problem resolution, the process chosen implies, and sometimes determines, the tools that must be used. For example, when faced with a numbingly boring TV show, we may (A) turn off the tube or (B) fall asleep. If we opt for choice A, we'll either employ hands, fingers, and a remote control; or legs and feet or a wheelchair, etc., to personally deactivate it. Option B would require mentally tuning it out and closing our eyes. Similarly, the modes by which a client resolves a host address are also different and named accordingly. Collectively, there are five modes for resolving names, of which four are defined by RFC 1001/1002, and one by LMHOSTS as specified by Microsoft. They are as follows:

- B-node (broadcast)

- P-node, or peer-to-peer

- M-node (mixed)

- H-node (hybrid)

Uses LMHOSTS file ⟹ ■ Microsoft enhanced B-node

B-Node (Broadcast)

Operating in this mode resolves and registers names via the broadcast of UDP datagrams. On small networks, this works well. However, as the networking environment grows, UDP data broadcasting both increases traffic and falls short of achieving its goal when routing is introduced. Typically, routers won't pass broadcasts, creating the undesirable consequence of only local systems receiving messages. One way around this is to configure the router to pass B-node broadcasts. Unfortunately, the vast amount of traffic generated by doing so quickly defeats the whole purpose of having a functional network in the first place, and is therefore not recommended.

P-Node, or Peer-to-Peer

This method of operation provides an effective and efficient means for resolving names directly from a NetBIOS Name Server (NBNS) such as WINS—with only one major draw back: The WINS IP address must be specified at each client, leading to major issues if the IP address is ever changed or the server goes offline. Microsoft does provide for a secondary server, but this causes a performance reduction while waiting for the primary server to time-out. Also, since broadcasts aren't used, local communication isn't possible in the event a WINS server is unavailable as specified in the TCP/IP configuration at each host.

M-Node (Mixed)

NetBIOS over TCP/IP Name Resolution *M-mode* (*Mixed*) is a composite mode wherein a client behaves as both a B-node and a P-node system. In the event the system is unable to find the IP address of a given destination machine via the broadcast mode, it'll switch to using the NBNS P-mode method to directly resolve the name.

H-Node (Hybrid)

NetBIOS over TCP/IP Name Resolution *H-node (Hybrid)* is a combination of B-node and P-node. Here, we see the inverse operation of the M-node mode, and by default, an H-node functions as a P-node. Employing H-node, a system will first query the NBNS, only sending a broadcast as a secondary name-resolution strategy.

Microsoft Enhanced B-Node

When Microsoft TCP/IP is initialized, it will load the #PRE portion of the LMHOSTS static map file into the address cache. During operation, a Microsoft enhanced B-node system first attempts to resolve names by checking the address cache before a broadcast is sent out. The system will only issue a broadcast if the name isn't found in the cache. If these efforts are unsuccessful, as a last resort the system will examine the LMHOSTS file directly to achieve resolution.

Common NetBIOS Names

Viewing the registered names can be helpful in determining which services are running on a computer. The following names describe common NetBIOS names that you will see in the WINS database:

\\computer_name[00h] The name registered for the Workstation service on the WINS client

\\computer_name[03h] The name registered for the Messenger service on the WINS client

\\computer_name[20h The name registered for the Server service on the WINS client

\\username[03h The name of the user currently logged on to the computer. The username is registered by the Messenger service so that the user can receive NET SEND commands sent to their username. If more than one user is logged on with the same username (such as Administrator), only the first computer from which a user logged on will register the name.

\\domain_name[lBh] The domain name registered by the Windows NT Server Primary Domain Controller (PDC) that is functioning as the Domain Master Browser. This name is used for remote domain browsing. When a WINS server is queried for this name, it returns the IP address of the computer that registered this name.

NetBIOS Name Registration, Detection, and Discharge

We have the option to have our names listed in the telephone book, to look to see if we're listed in it, and if desired, to remove our names from it. NetBIOS naming is similar in this respect. All modes of NetBIOS over TCP/IP use a form of registration and duplicate detection, and all discharge obsolete or otherwise unwanted names. Operations such as these are commonly resolved through broadcasts, or by contacting a NetBIOS name service. There are three ways NetBIOS names are registered, released, and discovered as part of the NetBIOS Name Resolution process. They are as follows:

Name registration As a NetBIOS over TCP/IP host starts up, it registers its name through a NetBIOS name registration request. If the designated name is found to be a duplicate, the host, or NetBIOS Name Server to which the client is registering, will counter with a negative name registration response. An initialization error will result.

Name detection When communicating between NetBIOS hosts, a name query request is issued for resolution. Depending on how the request was issued, either the host that possesses that name or the NetBIOS Name Server will reply with a positive name query response.

Name discharge At the conclusion of a NetBIOS over TCP/IP host-assisted session, the NetBIOS name that the system has used is discharged. This prevents the system from issuing negative name regis-tration responses resulting from duplicates when later attempts are made to register that same name by a different system. This catharsis takes place when the unit is either taken offline or workstation service ends.

B-Node: Resolving NetBIOS Names Locally

The steps listed below are crucial in understanding NetBIOS Name Resolution, and why it functions the way it does. A solid grasp of how NetBIOS names are resolved when the destination host is on the local network will equip you with much more than answers to basic questions—it provides a foundation for understanding later topics that evolve from it. The process for achieving the resolution of NetBIOS names on the local network is shown in Figure 6.1 and described below:

Step A Systems operating in B-node mode initiate a command with a NetBIOS requirement like NET USE K: \\Alpine\public (see Figure 6.1). To prevent costly name-resolution transactions, the system will first check the local address cache. If the name is found there, adding traffic to the network and thereby reducing its speed and efficiency can be successfully avoided. If no match is found, the system moves on to Step B.

FIGURE 6.1

A local NetBIOS name is resolved to an IP address using a b-node broadcast.

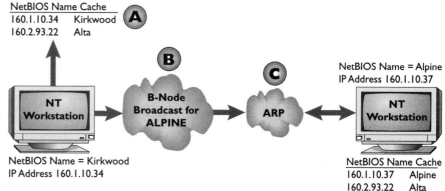

DOS Prompt > NET USE K: \\Alpine\public

NetBIOS Name Cache
160.1.10.34   Kirkwood Ⓐ
160.2.93.22   Alta

Ⓑ

Ⓒ

NT Workstation

B-Node Broadcast for ALPINE

ARP

NT Workstation

NetBIOS Name = Alpine
IP Address 160.1.10.37

NetBIOS Name = Kirkwood
IP Address 160.1.10.34

NetBIOS Name Cache
160.1.10.37   Alpine
160.2.93.22   Alta

Step B At this stage, name query broadcasts are sent out on the local network carrying the request for the destination's NetBIOS name.

Step C The broadcast is received by all systems on the local network. They will all begin to check to see if their name matches the one broadcasted. If the owner is found, that device will prepare a name query response. This response is sent out as soon as ARP resolves the hardware address of the system that initiated the name query. As the requesting system receives the positive response, a NetBIOS connection is established.

Recall that, typically, routers won't pass broadcasts, resulting in only the local systems getting the message. Broadcasts that are passed increase network traffic, thereby decreasing performance. Because of this, even though many routers can support broadcasts, the function is usually disabled.

Enhanced B-Node: Resolving Remote NetBIOS Names

When a host resides on a remote system, a local broadcast will still be issued in an attempt to resolve the name. If the broadcast is passed by the router, the request will be answered and processed in the same manner as a local b-node resolution request. If this effort fails, the LMHOSTS file is examined in a further attempt to locate the specific address (see Figure 6.2).

FIGURE 6.2

Resolving remote
NetBIOS names
(enhanced n-node)

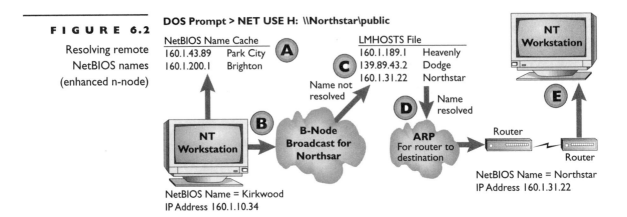

Step A Systems operating in enhanced B-node mode initiate a command with a NetBIOS requirement—again, as an example: **NET USE H: \\North-Star\ public** (see Figure 6.2). As in regular B-node mode, the system checks the local address cache, looks no further if found, and moves on to the next step if this endeavor is unsuccessful.

Step B Again, as in non-enhanced B-node mode, at this stage the system broadcasts a name query request on the local network, looking for \\North-Star. Assuming the destination system resides on another network, and the mediating router won't pass B-node broadcasts, the resolution request will again fail, requiring things to proceed to Step C.

Step C Here, the LMHOSTS file is searched and the corresponding entry is found: NorthStar, IP address 160.1.31.22. The address is resolved.

Step D Once the IP address is revealed to the requesting remote system, the local routing table is consulted for the most efficient path to it. If one isn't found, an ARP request is made to obtain the hardware address of the default gateway. Whenever a remote address is identified, it will be sent to the gateway for delivery. Because the gateway is used frequently, its hardware address is usually acquired from the local cache. Alternately, if it's not present in the cache, it can be located via broadcast.

Step E A response is sent out as soon as ARP resolves the hardware address of the router. When the response is received by the requesting system, a NetBIOS connection is established.

Resolving NetBIOS Names with a NetBIOS Name Server

In this section, we'll look at how name resolution works when using a NetBIOS Name Server (NBNS). A common implementation of an NBNS is a WINS (Windows Internet Name Service) server. An NBNS is highly flexible, so these servers enjoy wide usage. They'll function in P-node, M-node, and H-node modes of NetBIOS over TCP/IP. Another reason for their popularity is that using an NBNS extends better performance than does traditional broadcast resolution. Figure 6.3 illustrates how NetBIOS names are resolved to an IP address using a NetBIOS Name Server.

FIGURE 6.3

Resolving names with a Net BIOS Name Server

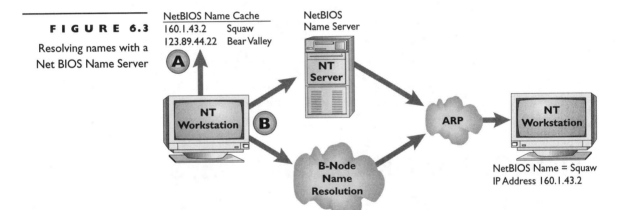

As in prior examples, the process of resolving a NetBIOS name begins with entering a command that triggers its initiation (e.g., NET USE, NET VIEW, etc.). It also parallels previous methods in the following ways:

Step A NET USE L: \\SquawValley\public. The system will explore the local address cache to try to resolve the name.

- If found, resolution is achieved, and the ARP process will commence for the additional resolution of the hardware address.

- The object of things functioning in this manner is to avoid creating any additional traffic on the network.

- In this mode of operation, no matter what's done, the local cache will always be checked before any further resolution efforts are begun.

Step B Depending on the mode by which TCP/IP is configured, the step that comes next varies. Following is a list organizing these special circumstances for you.

P-Node (Peer to Peer) After Step A collectively fails to resolve the name, a request is sent directly to the NetBIOS Name Server. If found, the identified name is returned in a response to the requesting system.

M-Node (Mixed) If Step A fails to resolve the name, the steps outlined for B-node broadcasts are followed. If this strategy also misfires, the host will then attempt to resolve the NetBIOS name as if it were configured as a P-node.

H-Node (Hybrid) Again, as with M-Node, should Step A attempts prove unsuccessful, the steps detailed earlier in the section for P-nodes are then followed. If these also flop, the host will then attempt to resolve the NetBIOS name as if it were a B-node—by using a broadcast.

Step C As soon as the host name is resolved, as in steps A or B, ARP is used to determine the hardware address.

NetBIOS Name Resolution in Action

Microsoft's implementation of TCP/IP under Windows NT supports all forms of resolution mentioned earlier. If your system has been configured in this fashion, you will find that Microsoft has designated that name searches follow the sequence shown in Figure 6.4 and outlined below.

Step A The process begins by entering a command initiating NetBIOS Name Resolution, such as **NET USE W: \\Aspen\public** (see Figure 6.4). At this point, the local address cache will be checked for the destination host.

Step B Assuming the name wasn't found, the next step is to contact the WINS server, following the process outlined under P-node in this chapter.

Step C If the WINS server was unable to locate the name, or if it did and identified it as unavailable, Microsoft's TCP/IP would then issue a B-node type broadcast.

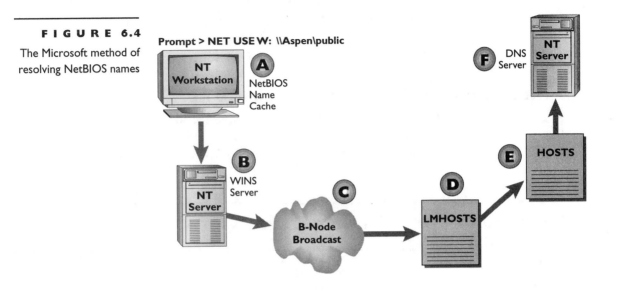

FIGURE 6.4

The Microsoft method of resolving NetBIOS names

Step D If the broadcast fails to hit paydirt, the next step is to search the LMHOSTS file. The action taken corresponds to that of a Microsoft enhanced B-node system.

Step E At this point, the HOSTS file, which resides on the local hard drive, will be examined.

Step F The last-gasp efforts that will be made are done though DNS. If the DNS machine is ignoring you and not responding, a repeat request will be sent to it at intervals of 5, 10, 20, 40, 5, 10, and 20 seconds. If your system's configured for DNS, and the unit has crashed or is offline, all systems on the network that are using DNS in some form or another will experience a considerable operational slowdown. The delay can be so pronounced that systems can appear to have crashed while resolving the name. This sinister effect is most commonly seen with Windows for Workgroups, and isn't nearly as nasty with Windows NT. NT's process managing is much more efficient.

If all attempts at resolution fall short of the target, an error message will be sent in reply. However, it should be pointed out here that Microsoft's implementation provision for name resolution is not only tenacious, it's efficient. Its system's sequence of resolution strategies prioritize in such a way that it first chooses the quickest method, requiring the minimum cost in network overhead. Also important to note is that once resolution is achieved, no further steps are taken—it does not simply complete a predetermined process, it monitors that process, only doing that which is required to achieve success, and no more.

Local NetBIOS Resolution via LMHOSTS

LMHOSTS is a static table that's stored in a local file used to resolve NetBIOS names to IP addresses on remote networks. Just like any other table, LMHOSTS has a specific format and supports special functions based on the commands entered therein.

Microsoft ✓ *Exam* *Objective* **Configure HOSTS and LMHOSTS files.**

```
Notepad - LMHOSTS
File   Edit   Search   Help

160.1.84.97      Heavenly     #net group's DC
160.1.12.102     Alpine       #special app server
160.1.74.123     Squaw        #PRE      #source server
160.1.32.117     NorthStar    #PRE      #needed for the include
```

Functionally, LMHOSTS offers the following:

- Name resolution, when called upon

- A single entry for names-to-IP addresses. All other following entries will be ignored if the same NetBIOS name is used in combination with a different IP address.

To avoid constant reboots for changes in the LMHOSTS file, entries can be manually loaded by typing **NBTSTAT -R**. Note that the -R is case-sensitive.

- You can load the IP addresses of frequently accessed host machines into memory by using the #PRE remark after the entry. This is a handy little feature for reducing network traffic, since it warrants that no broadcasts need to be made to access the host. The information intended for the lines with the #PRE remark is loaded when NetBIOS over TCP/IP is initialized.

- The LMHOSTS file can support domain validation, account synchronization, and browsing by adding #DOM to an entry line.

All statements in Microsoft TCP/IP32 that begin with a # sign are treated as comments.

- Supports old LMHOSTS files originating from older implementations of Microsoft TCP/IP, such as LAN Manager.

- On Windows NT systems, LMHOSTS is maintained in \%*SYSTEM-ROOT*%\SYSTEM32\DRIVERS\ETC, where %SYSTEMROOT% is the directory in which Windows NT has been installed. The default directory is WINNT. If it is installed from an upgrade, it will be in the previous versions of the Windows directory.

Networked NetBIOS Resolution via LMHOSTS File

As mentioned earlier, Microsoft has created enhanced flexibility with their implementation of TCP/IP. Conforming to this standard is the expanded functionality of LMHOSTS. Microsoft has added features to LMHOSTS, like the unprecedented ability to use it within a networked, or centralized, configuration. This not only makes the file readily accessible, and easily amended and expanded, but facilitates and simplifies the entire TCP/IP management process.

A networked LMHOSTS file can be added to a local LMHOSTS file by adding #INCLUDE to the beginning of the line that precedes the file you desire to add.

The graphic demonstrates how to use a networked LMHOSTS file.

```
                        Notepad - LMHOSTS
File   Edit   Search   Help

  160.1.84.97      Heavenly       #net group's DC
  160.1.12.102     Alpine         #special app server
  160.1.74.123     Squaw          #PRE     #source server
  160.1.32.117     NorthStar      #PRE     #needed for the include

  #INCLUDE \\localsrv\public\lmhosts
  #INCLUDE \\rhino\public\lmhosts

  160.1.55.23      Dodge          #Worthless server
```

Windows NT 4.0 automatically examines the LMHOSTS file prior to users logging on. Because the NetBIOS Helper service starts at boot-up, when it doesn't yet have a username to retrieve the LMHOSTS file from a remote system, a null username is substituted.

Shared LMHOSTS files should be accessible by all users. To make a share accessible by a null user, use REGEDT32 to modify:

\HKEY_LOCAL_MACHINE\SYSTEM\CurrentControlSet\Services\
LanmanServer\Parameters\NullSessionShares

On a new line in NullSessionShares, type the name of the share for which you want NULL session support, such as Public. This complete, you can now activate it by either rebooting, or stopping and then starting, the server service.

This process sounds rather long; however, in practice these steps go by rather quickly.

An alternative to modifying the registry is to manually run the NBTSTAT -R command to include the remote LMHOSTS files. Depending on your requirements, you could place this command in a batch file such as a LOGIN script, if used, or place an icon in the startup group to automate a manual process. If you opt for the latter, keep in mind that the startup group is kept on a per-user basis, and is not a COMMON group. You will therefore have to add the icon for each user who works on that particular machine. This can get more than a tad tedious if that group of users numbers many! Consequently, the best approach is to either modify the Registry or place the file in a Login Script. Here's your chance to get your hands dirty and experience for yourself the stuff of NetBIOS name resolution. In Exercises 6.1 and 6.2, you'll practice configuring LMHOSTS, as well as gain some insight into the workings of both local and remote name resolution.

Block Inclusion

The LMHOSTS file has one final feature that we haven't yet discussed—block inclusion. This is a special, last resort, reconnaissance-type feature that enables you to spy into another system's LMHOSTS file and look up unresolved names. The only time block inclusion is used is after all other LMHOSTS search path possibilities have been exhausted. If the system is unable to find the name you desire resolved in the local cache, and additionally fails through use of any #PRE tags and preexisting file entries to the block inclusion, only then should you use block inclusion.

A block inclusion is designated by placing #BEGIN_ALTERNATE and #END_ALTERNATE at the beginning and end of the block, respectively. During a search, the first system listed in the inclusion block is checked for a match to a requested name. Whether that name is successfully resolved or not, no additional systems will be searched in the block unless that first system is unreachable, and perhaps offline. Only then would the next entry in the inclusion block be read. Lines that are typically found in the block inclusion are usually started with #INCLUDE, which designates a remote system. When deciding whether or not to search LMHOSTS files recorded in a block inclusion, keep in mind that this feature exists more for purposes of fault tolerance than it does for facilitating group searches. Doing multiple recursive searches may progressively lead to longer and longer resolution times as your list grows.

Speaking of performance, when initially designing the LMHOSTS file, it's very important to keep in mind that the names of the most commonly used systems should be placed at the top of the file, and all #PRE entries at the bottom. Since the LMHOSTS file is read top to bottom, doing this will help you to find your more commonly accessed machines more quickly. The #PRE entries can be ignored after TCP/IP initializes.

The following graphic is an example of an LMHOSTS file with block inclusion.

```
┌──────────────────────────────────────────────────────────────────────┐
│ ─                       Notepad - LMHOSTS                         ▼ ▲ │
│ File   Edit   Search   Help                                          │
├──────────────────────────────────────────────────────────────────────┤
│                                                                    ▲ │
│    160.1.84.97      Heavenly        #net group's DC                  │
│    160.1.12.102     Alpine          #special app server             │
│    160.1.74.123     Squaw           #PRE      #source server        │
│    160.1.32.117     NorthStar       #PRE      #needed for the include│
│                                                                      │
│    #INCLUDE \\localsrv\public\lmhosts                                │
│    #INCLUDE \\Boreal\public\lmhosts                                  │
│                                                                      │
│                                                                      │
│    160.1.55.23      Dodge           #Worthless server               │
│                                                                      │
│  # BEGIN_ALTERNATE                                                   │
│    #INCLUDE \\ASPEN\public\lmhosts #backup Server                   │
│    #INCLUDE \\Vail\public\lmhosts  #backup Server                   │
│  # END_ALTERNATE                                                     │
│                                                                    ▼ │
├──────────────────────────────────────────────────────────────────────┤
│ ◄ ►                                                              → │
└──────────────────────────────────────────────────────────────────────┘
```

Predefined Keywords

Here is a summary of the key words that can be included in your LMHOSTS file:

#PRE Defines which entries should be initially preloaded as permanent entries in the name cache. Preloaded entries reduce network broadcasts, because names are resolved from cache rather than from broadcast or by parsing the LMHOSTS file. Entries with a #PRE tag are loaded automatically at initialization or manually by typing **NBTSTAT -R** at a command prompt.

#DOM [domain_name] Facilitates domain activity, such as logon valida-tion over a router, account synchronization, and browsing

#NOFNR Avoids using NetBIOS-directed name queries for older LAN Manager UNIX systems

#BEGIN_ALTERNATE and #END_ALTERNATE Defines a redundant list of alternate locations for LMHOSTS files. The recommended way to #INCLUDE remote files is using a UNC path to ensure access to the file. Of course, the UNC names must exist in the LMHOSTS file with a proper IP address-to-NetBIOS name translation.

#INCLUDE Loads and searches NetBIOS entries in a separate file from the default LMHOSTS file. Typically, a #INCLUDE file is a centrally-located, shared LMHOST file.

#MH Adds multiple entries for a multihomed computer

The NetBIOS name cache and file are always read sequentially. Add the most frequently accessed computers to the top of the list. Add the #PRE-tagged entries near the bottom, because they will not be accessed again once TCP/IP initializes.

Exercise 6.1 will take you through the steps of configuring an LMHOSTS file.

EXERCISE 6.1

Configuring the LMHOSTS File

In this exercise, you will configure the LMHOSTS file to resolve NetBIOS names to IP addresses.

Attempt to resolve a remote computer name using just a local broadcast.

1. Start Windows NT Explorer.

2. On the Tools menu, click Map Network Drive. The Map Network Drive dialog box appears.

3. In the Path box, type *remote_comuter_host_name* and then click OK. The network name cannot be found.

4. Click OK.

5. Click Cancel.

6. Close Windows NT Explorer.

In this procedure, you will see what happens when you attempt to resolve a remote NetBIOS computer name with a properly configured LMHOSTS file.

1. Open a command prompt.

2. Using edit, open the LMHOSTS file:
   %*SYSTEMROOT*%\SYSTEM32\DRIVERS\ETC\LMHOSTS.SAM

EXERCISE 6.1 (CONTINUED FROM PREVIOUS PAGE)

3. At the beginning of the LMHOSTS file, read the instructions for adding entries.

4. Go to the end of the file, and add the following entry:
   ip_address_of_remote_host host name

5. Save the file as LMHOSTS.

6. Start Windows NT Explorer.

7. On the Tools menu, click Map Network Drive. The Map Network Drive dialog box appears.

8. In the Path box, type ***host_ name_ of_ remote_ host*** and then click OK. A list of shared resources for \\remote_host appears.

9. Edit the LMHOSTS file, and add the NetBIOS name/IP address mappings of other computers located on a remote network.

10. Save and exit the file.

11. Using Windows NT Explorer, verify that each entry is correct by viewing the shared resources of the computer. Success is indicated by a list of shared resources or an empty list. If you receive an error message, compare the command syntax to the spelling of the LMHOSTS file entry.

NetBIOS Name Resolution Headaches

Just as it is with so many things (too many?) in this ol' world, you have to follow certain guidelines in order for things to operate smoothly. For example, if, like so many people, you fail to change your car's oil every 3500 miles, you spend far too much time with your mechanic, and bring about premature death to your car. It's much the same with the LMHOSTS file, as it is with TCP/IP in general. Not understanding or following guidelines and proper procedure, and failing to maintain things well, causes problems. Here are a few common ones:

Words to the Wise

Debugging problems in TCP/IP is easy if you have a clear understanding of each part's function. While each element and its role is pretty straightforward stuff, trying to put it all together to grasp the big picture can be difficult and confusing. Small, simple details can grow to become really big problems if overlooked, or are otherwise hidden from you. For instance, if a certain host was moved, and another device was put in its place using the same IP address, when pinging diagnostically, you'd get the impression that the server was up and running. However, what's really happening is that the address no longer represents the server you think it does—you're not talking to the server, you're talking to some mysterious other machine! All in all, understanding how all the pieces of the TCP/IP puzzle fit together, paying attention to details, and considering an action's consequences will make you better able to prevent problems before they occur, and equip you with solutions to solve them when they do.

Case Study 6.1: A Horse with No Name—When NetBIOS Names Cannot Be Resolved

We know you'll be absolutely stunned to hear that when a NetBIOS name can't be resolved, it's usually because a user has forgotten that a specific entry is required for each device that needs to be resolved by the system that's been asked to resolve it. For instance, a company that uses both a WINS server and an LMHOSTS file may find that they can only access some of their computers when their WINS server is taken offline. Why? Because the WINS server was nicely up-to-date, but the LMHOSTS file wasn't.

The Moral of the Story   Ignore it, and it will go away—maintain it, and it's here to stay.

Case Study 6.2: Spell Check

Or the case of mistaken identity. It's amazing how many times people will add a host name containing a 1, and replace it with a lower case L, or the roman numeral one (I). The way a NetBIOS name is spelled in the system is exactly the way it must be entered when trying to resolve it.

The Moral of the Story   Don't get creative with host names—keep 'em the same.

Case Study 6.3: Return to Sender—No Longer at This Address

Usually it's not that the IP address is entered incorrectly in the LMHOSTS file, but that the host's IP address has changed. If it has, then you are trying to reach a host at an IP address that either no longer exists, or has now been reassigned. It's important to be sure—verify that you really do have the right IP address. During a big undertaking, such as the movement of an entire network system, or when IP addresses on hosts are changed, small things like LMHOSTS files are commonly overlooked. Sure, the DNS was changed, memos were e-mailed to management, etc., but even the most efficient folks can make mistakes. Pay close attention to the numbers—sometimes the only way to know is to check the host itself.

The Moral of the Story   Make your list and check it twice.

Case Study 6.4: Sorry—I Thought You Were Someone Else

As we've pounded into your brain, once the name has been found, accompanied by its corresponding IP address, there's no need to search any further. Resolution has been achieved. Unfortunately, if the name listed in the file is

> associated with the wrong, or more commonly, obsolete IP address, the correct entry below it will never be reached. Just as you're sometimes judged by the company you keep, so are computers!
>
> **The Moral of the Story** Don't procrastinate—stay up to date. Make sure that you have only one, *current* entry for each NetBIOS name.

Summary

Now that you are finished reading this chapter, the items listed below should be as easy to recall as your best friend's phone number. You should have a working knowledge of:

- NetBIOS naming

- The various NetBIOS over TCP/IP node types

- NetBIOS name resolution via broadcasts

- NetBIOS name resolution via LMHOSTS

- NetBIOS name resolution via NetBIOS Name Server

- NetBIOS name resolution configuration on both local or networked LMHOSTS files

- Common problems concerning NetBIOS names, and their likely causes

For the NT 4.0 TCP/IP test, you must have a working knowledge of the LMHOSTS file and how the predefined key words work. Go through the review questions below to check your understanding.

Review Questions

1. What are some of the key words that can be included in your LMHOSTS file? (Choose all that apply.)

   A. #PRE

   B. #LAST

   C. #INCLUDE

   D. #MH

2. What is a P-Node? (Choose all that apply.)

   A. A broadcast to resolve names

   B. A method to resolve names from a NBNS

   C. A method to resolve names from a DNS server

   D. A method to resolve names from a WINS server

3. What is the function of the LMHOSTS file?

   A. To resolve DNS names of remote hosts

   B. To resolve UNIX names of remote hosts

   C. To resolve NetBIOS names of remote hosts

   D. To resolve a MAC address to a NetBIOS name

4. Which methods are used to resolve NetBIOS names? (Choose all that apply.)

   A. Local Broadcast

   B. LMHOSTS file

   C. NBNS

   D. HOSTS file

   E. DNS

5. On Windows NT systems, LMHOSTS is maintained in

  A. %SYSTEMROOT%\SYSTEM\DRIVERS\ETC

  B. %SYSTEMROOT%\SYSTEM32\DRIVERS\HOSTS

  C. %SYSTEMROOT%\SYSTEM32\DRIVERS\ETC

  D. %SYSTEMROOT%\SYSTEM\UNIX\ETC

6. What does the NBTSTAT utility do?

  A. Checks the state of current NetBIOS over TCP/IP connections

  B. Checks the state of current WinSOCK over TCP/IP connections

  C. Checks the state of current TCP/IP packet throughput

  D. Checks the status of your network

7. You are trying to connect to a 3.51 NT Server with the net use *server_name* command. That works OK, but when you try net use \\IP _address, it gets a bad command or filename. You checked the IP address and it is correct. What could the problem be?

8. You get calls from users complaining that NetBIOS names are not being resolved all the time. "It's flaky," says one user. You open the LMHOSTS file and find some errors: a misspelled name, some old IP addresses, and a couple of misplaced comments. What effect can these erroneous entries have on the LMHOSTS file?

9. While cleaning out the LMHOSTS file, you found entries that started with #PRE. Where should you locate the LMHOSTS entries with the #PRE identifier? Why?

10. You have been promoted to network manager. Your first job is to make sure you are using all of the company's bandwidth properly. Which node modes should you use? Which mode will be the most efficient for your network?

11. Someone in your office deleted the # signs in the LMHOSTS file because they thought they were comments. After you replaced the # signs and the phones stopped ringing (two hours later!), this staff member wants to know what the # identifiers that are used in the LMHOSTS file are used for. What do you tell her?

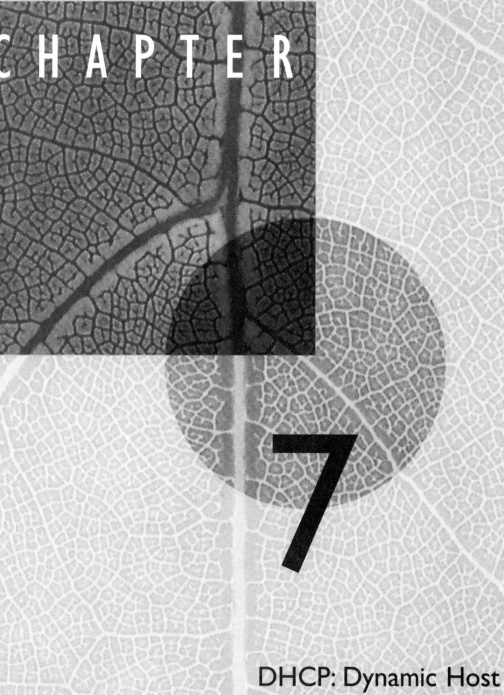

CHAPTER

7

DHCP: Dynamic Host
Configuration Protocol

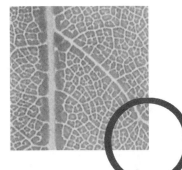

ur goal for this chapter is to instill in you a thorough understanding of DHCP—how it works, and how to work successfully with it. We'll present you with the evidence in favor of implementing DHCP, and point out the drawbacks related to doing so. We'll also give you practical tips for dealing with the complexities of installing and configuring DHCP on both clients and servers. After you've completed this chapter, you'll have considerable insight into making TCP/IP a trouble-free, low-maintenance partner in networking.

Upon completion of this section, you should have the following items indelibly written into your memory:

- The definition of DHCP

- How to install DHCP

- DHCP in action

- DHCP requests and leasing

- How DHCP is configured for multiple subnets

- DHCP clients

- DHCP and the IPCONFIG utility

- DHCP database backup and recovery issues

- The DHCP database JETPACK compression utility

DHCP Defined

DHCP's purpose is to centrally control IP-related information and eliminate the need to manually keep track of where individual IP addresses are allocated. Choosing whether or not to use DHCP is like choosing whether or not to use a database. For example, imagine that you're the local telephone company busily assigning telephone numbers to your customers. Suppose that for some strange reason you choose to keep track of your assignments on paper—without the aid of a computer. As customers come and go, voids develop in your list where numbers that have been assigned, and then dropped, are no longer anywhere to be found. Still others begin to be assigned duplicate numbers—further confusing matters. Clearly, storing your customer information in a central database would prevent this chaos, automatically enabling you to keep abreast of all these changes. DHCP can also help in a situation where a network is running out of IP addresses. For example, if an administrator assigns static IP addresses for network hosts on a class C network, that leaves the administrator only 254 addresses to assign hosts—even less if the administrator subnets. If the amount of hosts numbers nears 300, the administrator can use DHCP to assign hosts and lease IP addresses for a short period of time. This is a terrific, serviceable benefit of DHCP—the ability to actually have fewer IP addresses than hosts.

> ### Microsoft ✓ Exam Objective
>
> **Given a scenario, select the appropriate services to install when using Microsoft TCP/IP on a Microsoft Windows NT Server computer.**

> **NOTE** This only works on a network whose hosts can function well when using IP addresses periodically.

DHCP has a history. Originally, it was called BootP protocol and was designed to provide IP addresses to diskless workstations. Today, DHCP is built onto the BootP protocol (RFC 951) in an effort to simplify and centralize IP addressing. DHCP is formalized and defined by RFCs 1533, 1534, 1541, and 1542.

When TCP/IP starts up on a DHCP-enabled host, a special message is sent out requesting an IP address and a subnet mask from a DHCP server. The contacted server checks its internal database, then replies with a message offer comprised of the information the client requested. DHCP can also respond with a default gateway address, DNS address(es), or a NetBIOS Name Server, such as WINS. When the client accepts the IP offer, it is then extended to the client for a specified period of time, called a lease. If the DHCP server is out of IP addresses, no IP addressing information can be offered to the clients, causing TCP/IP initialization to fail.

The lease procedure can be likened to that of leasing a car. After negotiating acceptable terms with an automobile dealer, a lease is secured, permitting you use of a certain car for a specific period of time. If the car dealership doesn't have the terms or vehicle you want, you don't drive off the lot with one.

DHCP—the Good, the Bad, and the Ugly

If we were to pause here and ask you whether or not you should opt to utilize DHCP, based on the telephone company example given earlier, you might think it's a no-brainer and answer with a resounding "Yes!" Recall, though, that we mentioned there were some drawbacks to doing so. If so, you're probably getting pretty curious about what exactly those drawbacks might be.

To Use or Not to Use DHCP?

To help you understand the potential drawbacks to DHCP, as well as why you would choose to use DHCP, here's a list of both the pros and cons associated with using it.

The Good   No additional services are required by the computer to assign numbers.

- No additional computer is needed when assigning addresses.

- It's inexpensive!

- IP configuration information is entered electronically by another system, eliminating the human-error factor. No more typing in the wrong addresses, subnet masks, gateways, DNS addresses, and NetBIOS Name Server addresses—Yippee!

- Configuration problems are minimized, clearing up a labyrinth of possible situations that lead to big messes and obscure, hard-to-find problems.

- IP becomes a "plug and play operation." We, the members of the world-wide Now Society, collectively concur that getting things up and running sooner is certainly better. Most often, when running DHCP, new or moved systems can be plugged into a network segment instantly with no additional configuration requirements—no strings attached!

The Bad   Users with a new machine may randomly select an IP address to gain immediate access to the network. Later, that number may be assigned to a different user and show up as a duplicate. This will not be fun for the network's caretaker to find.

- Because input for the IP addresses, subnet masks, gateways, DNS addresses, and NetBIOS Name Server address is done by a human on a PC, it can easily be entered incorrectly. There are quite a number of required entries allowing little or no margin for error. As if that weren't bad enough, these erroneous numbers appear to work initially, schmoozing you in for the kill with friendly, false effectiveness. Later, you may find that you have someone else's IP address, are incapable of resolving NetBIOS names, or find yourself marooned—unable to get to another subnet.

- Having all one's eggs in one basket is never a good idea. Exclusive reliance on the DHCP server during the TCP/IP initialization phase could potentially result in an initialization failure if that server is down, or otherwise unavailable.

- Certain applications of TCP/IP, like logging in to a remote network through a firewall, require the use of a specific IP address. DHCP allows for exclusions and holes that prevent certain IP address ranges from being used. If your needed address happens to be found in a specified exclusive range, you're in trouble.

The Ugly   There's an extensive amount of incredibly tedious work involved in maintaining an accurate roster of both used and free IP addresses. To those detail-oriented individuals in the audience whose greatest joy is to stay up all night keeping records, this may not sound too appalling—until you find out that once the information goes into error, it's almost impossible to fix it. What does this vile fact translate to in reality? Well, it means that you may find yourself forever in the dark regarding the status of a given computer. Whether it's on, off, or otherwise engaged, will be an eternal mystery to you. It could, therefore, easily cause you not to register a certain IP address (the mystery node's). After all, how could you register something you didn't know existed?

Of course, it could also simply be that the wrong one was entered in the first place, but knowing this still wouldn't help you. Your only option at this point would be to go host-to-host, one at a time, checking IP addresses.

Final Analysis   All things considered, that which is gained when using DHCP does outweigh that which is lost. However, it should be noted that it's ultimately up to you—the network professional—whether or not DHCP is the best choice for your particular networking environment. Generally, unless your network is very tiny, or is running applications that are incompatible with DHCP (e.g., routers that can't handle the BootP/DHCP protocol), you should opt to utilize this feature.

Further Considerations About Implementing DHCP

As stated, DHCP's purpose is to make IP address management a breeze. However, as we just established, it's not for everyone, or every situation. Here are a few more points to ponder before you dive right into implementing DHCP:

- What kind of IP information will the DHCP server deliver? Is it possible to deliver IP addresses for all the different scenarios that are required?

- Are all machines on the network, regardless of operating system or function, going to utilize DHCP? If, for application purposes, some will not, are you well aware of the static addresses for each of those devices?

- Will the DHCP server support subnets other than its own? If so, it will obviously operate via a router. Does that router support the BootP protocol? If not, it won't pass BootP broadcasts, and a DHCP server will have to be placed on every segment.

- Regarding the dual, pivotal issues of performance and reliability: How many DHCP servers would your network require? DHCP servers are selfish, secretive, and possessive devices that do not share their information with other machines.

If you find that yours is a situation that will require multiple DHCP servers, consider the following as an implementation forethought: For reasons of performance and fault tolerance, every DHCP server should have 75% of the available IP addresses on it own subnet, and 25% of those from a remote subnet. This arrangement is highly beneficial, and provides for a backup in the event that any one DHCP server becomes unavailable.

DHCP in Action

DHCP is a simple process by which a host system obtains an IP address. This address is a necessary prerequisite to performing any communications with the rest of the network and depends on the number of *NICs (network interface cards)* that are configured with the TCP/IP and DHCP protocol. The number of NIC cards necessarily equals the number of instances that the DHCP process runs and, additionally, determines the number of IP addresses received. Each card has its own IP address. In order for DHCP to operate on remote networks, the router must support the forwarding of DHCP broadcasts (RFC 1542). To fully understand the operation of DHCP, it's necessary to assess the steps by which it operates. These steps can be organized into four operational stages, as follows:

Stage One: IP Lease Request

This is the first step for a system seeking to acquire an IP address under DHCP. It's triggered whenever TCP/IP, configured with DHCP, is started for the first time. It also occurs when a specific IP address is requested but unavailable, or an IP address was used and then released. Because the requesting client isn't aware of its own IP address or that it belongs to the DHCP server, it will use 0.0.0.0 and 255.255.255.255, respectively. This is known as a *DHCP discover message*. The broadcast is created in a scaled down TCP/IP with UDP ports 67 (BootP client) and 68 (BootP server). This message contains the hardware address and NetBIOS name for the client system to be used in the next phase of sending a lease offer. The client waits one second for an offer, and if no DHCP server responds to the initial broadcast, then the request is repeated three more times at 9-, 13-, and 16-second intervals, plus a random event occurring in the period between 0 and 1000 milliseconds. If still no response is received, a broadcast message will be made every five minutes until it is finally answered. If no DHCP server ever becomes available, no TCP/IP communications will be possible.

Stage Two: IP Lease Offer

The second phase of DHCP involves the actual information given by all DHCP servers that have valid addressing information to offer. Their offers consist of an IP address, subnet mask, lease period (in hours), and the IP address of the proposing DHCP server. These offers are sent to the requesting client's hardware address. The pending IP address offer is reserved temporarily to prevent it from being taken simultaneously by another machine, creating horrid address-clone duplicates and interminable chaos. Since multiple DHCP servers can be configured, it also adds a degree of fault tolerance should one of the DHCP servers go down.

Stage Three: IP Lease Selection

During this phase, the client machine will select the first IP addressing offer it receives. Clients reply by broadcasting an acceptance message, requesting to lease IP information. Just as in Stage One, this message is broadcast as a DHCP request, but this time, it also includes the IP address of the DHCP server whose offer was accepted. All other DHCP servers will then revoke their offers.

Stage Four: IP Lease Acknowledgment

The accepted DHCP server proceeds to assign an IP address to the client, then sends an acknowledgment message, called a *DHCPACK,* back to the client. Occasionally, a negative acknowledgment, called a *DHCPNACK,* is returned. This type of message is most often generated if the client is attempting to lease its old IP address which has since been reassigned elsewhere. Negative acceptance messages can also mean that the requesting client has an inaccurate IP address, resulting from physically changing locations to an alternate subnet.

After this final phase has been successfully completed, the client machine integrates the new IP information. It endows it with a fully functional TCP/IP configuration, usable with all utilities, as if the newly acquired information had been in its possession prior to using DHCP. In Windows for Workgroups, DHCP information is stored in an encrypted format inside the Windows directory in a file called *DHCP.BIN.* In Windows NT, this DHCP information can be found in:

HKEY_LOCAL_MACHINE\SYSTEM\CurrentControlSet\Services\
adapter\Parameters\Tcpip

The different steps undergone in this process of sending and receiving offers are not just formalities. They're quite necessary. Following them ensures that only one offer is accepted—preventing duplicate addressing pandemonium, as well as producing a good measure of fault tolerance. Additionally, if every machine that sent out an offer immediately assigned it to a requesting workstation, there would soon be no numbers left to assign. Furthermore, if the acceptance response to these offers was controlled by the client instead of the server, there would be a much greater risk of creating duplicate IP addresses. The server could misinterpret a slow response from the engaged client, caused by the network, and propose the offer information to another client. Two or more clients would then be receiving the same offer from the same server simultaneously—Networkland bigamy, resulting in Networkland polygamy, causing ultimate chaos for Networkland officers (you)! With these logistical conditions in mind, it's clear that DHCP is an honorable pragmatist, and it's above outlined method of operation is indeed sensible and functionally sound.

DHCP Lease Renewal

Recalling the fact that with DHCP, IP addresses are leased for a period of time—not indefinitely—would necessarily bring up questions about what happens when the lease ends or needs to be renewed. Regardless of the length of time an IP address is leased, the leasing client will send a *DHCPREQUEST* to the DHCP server when its lease period has elapsed by 50%. If the DHCP server is available, and there are no reasons for rejecting the request, a DHCP acknowledge message is sent to the client, updating the configuration and resetting the lease time. If the server is unavailable, the client will receive an "eviction" notice stating that they had not been renewed. In this event, that client would still have a remaining 50% lease time and would be allowed full usage privileges for its duration. The rejected client would react by sending out an additional lease renewal attempt when 87.5% of its lease time had elapsed. Any available DHCP server could respond to this DHCPREQUEST message with a DHCPACK and renew the lease. However, if the client received a DHCPNACK (negative) message, it would have to stop using the IP address immediately and start the leasing process over from the beginning.

When a client initializes TCP/IP, it will always attempt to renew its old address. Just like any other renewal, if the client has time left on the lease, it will continue to use the lease until its end. If, by that time, the client is unable to get a new lease, all TCP/IP functions will cease until a new, valid address can be obtained.

DHCP Lease Release

Yes, it's true—All good things must come to an end. Such is the case with leases. Since they specify a certain period of time, it's obvious that at some point the lease will end. Although they can be renewed repeatedly, it's important to keep in mind the fact that the lease process is an "at will" process. This means that if the client elects to cancel the lease by using the IPCONFIG / RELEASE utility, which is discussed later in this chapter, or is unable to contact the DHCP server before the lease elapses, the lease is automatically released. This is an important function that's useful for reclaiming extinct IP addresses formerly used by systems that have moved or switched to a non-DHCP address. An additional condition would occur when the IP address you're trying to snatch is reserved for a different system. In this case, you would find yourself unable to renew the lease, and eventually lose it as time expires.

Note that DHCP leases are not automatically released at system shutdown. A system that has lost it lease will attempt to release the same address that it had previously used.

Making DHCP Function

Now that you have an idea of what DHCP is, and what it can and can't do for you, the next step is to understand what's required to implement it and make it work. First, you need to make sure you have the right stuff on hand. There are three components essential for successful implementation:

A server   Under Windows NT, a DHCP server can be any Windows NT server, provided that it's running TCP/IP and is not itself a DHCP client. The server must have the DHCP server service up and running with a designated scope or range of available IP addresses to assign.

A client machine   The client can be practically any machine, including a Windows NT server, as long as it's not running the DHCP Server Service. Compatible running mates include Windows NT Workstation, Windows 95, Windows for Workgroups 3.11 with TCP/IP-32, and LAN Manager 2.2c (not the OS/2 version). Another potential candidate is Microsoft Network Client 3.0 for DOS, complete with a Real Mode TCP/IP driver.

A router If the DHCP server will function for multiple subnets, the router must support forwarding BootP broadcasts (RFC1542).

These requirements met, you can now move on to installing and configuring a DHCP server.

DHCP Server Installation and Configuration

Relax! As you will soon see, installing a DHCP server is much easier than you'd think—so don't be intimidated. Begin with any Windows NT server. After booting up and logging onto your server, proceed with the steps in Exercise 7.1.

EXERCISE 7.1

Installing and Configuring a DHCP Server

1. Click Start ➤ Setting ➤ Control Panel.

2. Double-click Network.

3. Click Services.

4. Click Add.

5. Select Microsoft DHCP Server, then select OK.

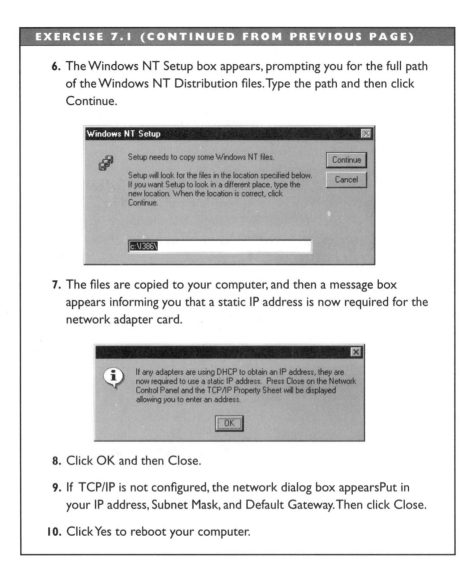

6. The Windows NT Setup box appears, prompting you for the full path of the Windows NT Distribution files. Type the path and then click Continue.

7. The files are copied to your computer, and then a message box appears informing you that a static IP address is now required for the network adapter card.

8. Click OK and then Close.

9. If TCP/IP is not configured, the network dialog box appearsPut in your IP address, Subnet Mask, and Default Gateway. Then click Close.

10. Click Yes to reboot your computer.

Defining the DHCP Scope

At a minimum, at least one scope must be defined per DHCP server, but you can assign multiple scopes. Since DHCP servers operate independently of each other and don't share information, it's very important to be sure that the IP addresses listed in that scope are unique. It's that sinister Networkland Law of Duplicates again! If two DHCP servers have a scope comprised of the same IP addresses, duplicates will be dispersed over your network, causing the grisly crash of one or both of the hapless clients that possess the same address.

In Exercise 7.2, you will define the scope of a DHCP server.

<table>
<tr><td>**Microsoft** ✓ **Exam** **Objective**</td><td>**Configure scopes by using DHCP Manager.**</td></tr>
</table>

EXERCISE 7.2

Creating a DHCP Scope

1. Click Start ➤ Programs ➤ Administrative Tools ➤ DHCP Manager to open the DHCP Manager Window.

2. Under DHCP Servers, click Local Machine.

3. On the Scope menu, click Create.

4. The Create Scope box appears.

5. Configure the scope by entering your IP pool information.

Start Address This is the first IP address in the range available for assignment to a DHCP client.

End Address This is the last IP address in the range available for assignment to a DHCP client.

Subnet Mask This is the subnet mask assigned to all DHCP clients of this server.

Exclusion Range Start Address This designates the first IP address in a special, exclusive range unavailable for assignment to DHCP clients. These addresses are generally reserved for hosts that must maintain static IP addresses for extended periods (e.g., the IP address for the DHCP or WINS server). If these addresses aren't corralled away from the normal available range, the operation of both the client with the static address and the DHCP client may fail.

Exclusion Range End Address This will designate the last IP address in the above-mentioned reserved range, unavailable for assignment to a DHCP client.

Lease Duration This will designate the amount of time a client system can lease an IP address. This option can be set to a specific number of days, hours, and minutes, or an unlimited span of time.

Name To ease management, it's advised to assign a name to the scope you're defining.

Comment This optional field is for identification purposes, and is used to describe your scope.

6. Once you've filled out the above information in the Create Scope dialog box, click OK. You'll then be asked to activate the scope. If you're ready to implement the scope at this time, select Yes.

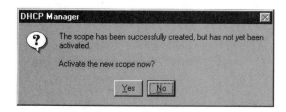

NOTE: If you are just now preparing a DHCP server and are not yet ready to start this scope, select No. You can start the scope at a later time by selecting Scope Active in the DHCP Manager program.

7. You will then receive a message stating, "No More Data Is Available." Click OK.

We will configure the scope in Exercise 7.3.

EXERCISE 7.3

Configuring DHCP Scope Options

1. Go to DHCP Manager and highlight the server.

2. On the DHCP Options menu, select Scope.

3. The DHCP Options: Scope dialog box appears.

4. Under Unused Options, select 003 Router and then click Add. The 003 Router option moves to the Active Options box.

5. Click Value. The DHCP Options: Scope dialog box expands to add the Router IP Address Values box.

6. Click Edit Array. The IP Address Array Editor dialog box appears.

7. Under New IP Address, type your default gateway address and then click Add.

IP Address Array Editor

General Information

Application: DHCP Options: Scope

Option: Router

OK

Cancel

Help

Data Entry

New IP Address:

Add ->

<- Remove

IP Addresses:
100.100.100.50

Server Name:

Resolve

8. The new IP Address appears under IP Addresses.

9. Click OK to return to the DHCP Options: Scope dialog box.

10. The new router is listed in the IP Address list.

11. Click OK.

12. A message box informs you that no more data is available.

13. Close DHCP Manager.

14. Exit DHCP Manager completely and restart it to view the new options.

DHCP Scope Options

For each scope member, options can be configured for the scope to provide additional configuration information to the scope members. The scope options contain an array of parameters that the DHCP administrator may configure. After the DHCP scope has been defined, there are three levels of scope options that become available for configuration.

Global Options

These exist at the default selection level. They provide the ability to deliver common information to all DHCP clients located on all subnets that access that particular DHCP server. An example of a global option is all the network's clients using the same WINS or DNS server.

Scope Options

These secondary level options are used to define information specific for a particular scope of IP addresses. A good example is appointing a specific gateway for each subnet to use. Scope options are always given priority over global options.

Client Options

Client options are specific to a certain IP address. For example, a client using a reserved IP address may have a specific configuration requirement. This option is given the highest priority—over both scope and global options.

Microsoft
✓ Exam
Objective

Install and configure a WINS server

- Import LMHOSTS files to WINS.
- Run WINS on a multihomed computer.
- Configure WINS replication.
- Configure static mappings in the WINS database.

Both global and scope options can be delineated from the DHCP Manager window by selecting from the Options pull-down menu. The options are listed as either active or unused. To control your selection, click the desired option, and then select Add or Remove. When options are highlighted, values may be assigned by clicking the Value button.

Because Microsoft clients only support a limited number of the DHCP functions, only those relative to Microsoft's TCP/IP implementations will be discussed. All other DHCP functions, such as Time Offset, Time Server, Name

Servers, Log Servers, Cookie Servers, LPR Servers, Impress Servers, etc, will only function on other operating systems, such as UNIX.

The Microsoft-compatible DHCP functions are discussed below:

003 Router assigns a default gateway to the client. This function is only enabled when the default gateway hasn't already been manually defined on that client.

006 DNS Servers indicates the IP address(es) of DNS servers to the client

046 WINS/NBT Node Type designates NetBIOS name resolution configuration:

- Broadcast/B-node

- Point to Point/P-node

- Mixed/M-node

- Hybrid/H-node

044 WINS/NBNS Servers designates the IP address(es) of WINS servers to the client. This option is only used if the client hasn't already been manually configured for a WINS server.

047 NetBIOS Scope ID verifies the local NetBIOS scope ID in a way that a NetBIOS-over-TCP/IP host will only communicate with other identically configured NetBIOS hosts.

After selecting from the various options listed above, one must appoint an appropriate value for your selection. These value types are similar to those found in common computer programming, as well as in the Windows NT registry. There are a total of six value types available to choose from. The data types can be thought of in the same context as setting up a database field type. For example, where you'd use a date field to express time, you'd instead use an IP address to designate a system's logical location. We've listed the data types for you below:

IP Address specifies the IP address of an object, such as a server or router that is added to the Options list. Typically, options with "server "or "router" in the name tend to use this value.

Long specifies a 32-bit numeric value commonly used as a value for the designation of timings, such as an *ARP Cache Time-out*

String defines a collection of *characters*, normally used as a value type for object names (e.g., a domain name)

WorD sets a 16-bit number value of a designated block size. "Max DG Reassembly Size" is an example of an option that uses this value type.

BytE establishes a numeric value designated by a single byte. This is typically used in situations where a single character (a character is one byte long) represents an option such as *WINS/NBT node* type. In this case, the value will be equal to 1, 2, 4, or 8.

Binary designates that a value is binary when set to on or off. It's commonly used when the need arises to enable or disable a specific set of functions or options. An example of a circumstance requiring this kind of action is when one is dealing with vendor-specific information.

DHCP Client Reservation

Often, in many networks, there are certain change-resistant machines such as servers that must always use the same IP address. To fulfill this need and shelter these sensitive devices, a special arrangement called a client reservation must be made with the DHCP server. Typically, client reservations are made so that machines that access other networks through a *firewall*, a device that secures a network by allowing only authorized systems to access the network, can function.

Another example of the need to reserve a particular IP address concerns systems that utilize DHCP, but not any additional services, such as WINS. A system such as this must have a manual entry in the WINS server so that other systems can be aware of its existence. Secondly, these non-WINS type clients must use some method of resolution, like a WINS proxy agent, so that they can communicate with other machines. Since DHCP is dynamic in nature, and the LMHOSTS file is static, they're incompatible—they won't communicate without help. Simply placing address entries in LMHOSTS on a system using DHCP without WINS, etc., would result in their incorrect resolution—perhaps (perish the thought), to an extinct IP address...Ouch! To make a client reservation, follow the steps in Exercise 7.4.

EXERCISE 7.4

How to Make a Client Reservation

1. Start DHCP Manager.

2. Double-click Local Machine.

3. The lightbulb icon and the IP address appear.

4. Click the light bulb icon.

5. The Option Configuration window displays an Active Scope option 003 Router.

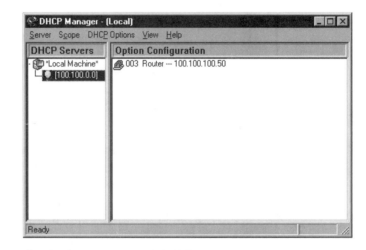

6. On the Scope menu, click Add Reservations.

7. The Add Reserved Clients dialog box appears.

EXERCISE 7.4 (CONTINUED FROM PREVIOUS PAGE)

8. In the IP Address box, type the IP address of the workstation you want reserved.

9. In the Unique Identifier box, type the physical address (hardware address) of the network adapter. (Do not include hyphens.)

10. In the Client Name box, type the name of the user, then click Add.

11. The Add Reserved Clients dialog box appears.

12. To return to DHCP Manager, click Close.

DHCP Relay

DHCP relay is an exceptional, money-saving feature for networks peppered with older routers that don't support this function. When a dynamic client computer that's located on the same subnet as a BootP relay agent requests an IP address, its request is forwarded right to the subnet's BootP relay agent. This agent is configured to forward the request directly to the correct computer—as long as it's running the Windows NT Server DHCP service. That computer then returns an IP address directly to the requesting client.

Microsoft ✓ ***Exam*** ***Objective***

Configure a Windows NT Server computer to function as an IP router

• Install and configure the DHCP Relay Agent

Configuration of the DHCP BootP relay agent is a two-step process. The first step is to install the DHCP Relay Agent Service onto the computer chosen to work as a BootP relay agent. Using the Microsoft TCP/IP Protocol Properties dialog box, the BootP agent can then be configured with the IP address of the computer that's running the Windows NT Server DHCP service. When that's done, the agent will know where to forward client requests for available IP addresses.

NOTE The DHCP Relay Agent Service is a Windows NT Server service.

The relay function is built into the Protocol module of TCP/IP and has two configuration options. The first is Seconds threshold, a time-to-live option restricting the time span within which a request must be answered. The second is Maximum hops, which specifies the maximum distance—in terms of routers—that a request can be forwarded. To configure this option, first select a seconds threshold (the default is 4) and then specify a maximum number of hops (the default is also 4). Next, select the Add button, specifying the IP address of the DCHP server that will answer client requests. You will install the DHCP Relay Agent Service in Exercise 7.5.

EXERCISE 7.5

Installing the DHCP Relay Agent Service

1. Click Start ➢ Settings ➢ Control Panel.

2. Double-click Network.

3. The Network Dialog box appears.

4. Click the Services tab.

5. The Services tab will display the list of Network Services currently running on this computer.

6. Click Add.

7. The Select Network Service dialog box displays the Network Services available.

8. Click DHCP Relay Agent.

9. Click OK.

10. The Windows NT Setup dialog box appears.

11. Type the path to the distribution files, then click OK.

12. The Network dialog box appears.

13. Click Close.

14. The Error-Unattended Setup dialog box appears. You are prompted to add an IP address to the DHCP Servers list.

> **Error - Unattended Setup**
>
> ❓ For the DHCP Relay service to start, there must be at least one DHCP server's IP address listed. Would you like to add an entry to the list?
>
> [Yes]   [No]

15. Click Yes.

16. The TCP/IP Properties dialog box appears.

17. Click the DHCP Relay tab, and then click Add.

18. The DHCP Relay Agent property sheet appears.

> **DHCP Relay Agent**
>
> DHCP Server: [Add]
> [   ]   [Cancel]

19. Type the IP address of the DHCP Server, and then click Add.

20. The IP address is added to the DHCP Servers list.

21. Click OK.

22. You are prompted to reboot your computer.

23. Click Yes.

BootP Relay is the software service component that enables a Windows NT server to forward BootP broadcasts. Unlike the DHCP Relay Agent Service, it's not configurable. It's essentially an intermediate step towards contacting a DHCP Server.

DHCP and the IPCONFIG Utility

TCP/IP is very adaptable, presenting its users with many opportunities for customization. It's fully routable and supports multiple internal functions. Unlike *NetBEUI,* which is nonroutable, and virtually nonconfigurable, traditional TCP/IP has not been *plug and play.* Plug and play means that when a software or hardware item is installed, it configures itself. You've plugged it in (installed it), and you're now free as a bird to work with it without further ado. For TCP/IP, DHCP has changed all this. TCP/IP now realizes unprecedented ease in implementation. Unfortunately, as invention and progress often serve to create efficiency and simplify things, they also tend to author whole new sets of problems. Suppose that, for whatever reason, you need to find out about the IP address, subnet mask, and default gateway that your system has been assigned. To answer this dilemma, Microsoft uses a command line utility called IPCONFIG. When IPCONFIG is executed, it displays all the basic, can't-live-without-it IP information you most often need:

- IP address

- Subnet mask

- Default gateway

If only things were always that simple! Nope—sad, but true, knowing this basic stuff may fail to do the trick when it comes to situations like the blood pressure–increasing inability to resolve a NetBIOS name. The good news is that Microsoft thought of that one. Should this unfortunate, yet commonplace event happen to you, type **IPCONFIG /ALL**. This will access the advanced listing information you may find highly useful in curing what ails your network. This beneficial information includes:

- Your system's host name

- NetBIOS node type (B-node, P-node, M-node, H-node)

- The assigned NetBIOS scope ID

- The IP address(es) of designated DNS servers

- NetBIOS resolution via DNS Enabled Status

- The IP address(es) of designated WINS servers

- IP Routing's Enabled Status

- WIN Proxy's Enabled Status

- DHCP's Enabled Status

- The Network Adapters Description

- The Hardware address of the Network Adapter

Renewing a Lease through IPCONFIG

As discussed earlier in this chapter, a DHCP lease is automatically renewed when 50% of the lease time gets used up. In the same vein—adhering to the same availability proviso—one can also renew a DHCP client's IP address lease manually via the IPCONFIG utility by executing **IPCONFIG/RENEW**. This function can be especially critical when a DHCP server goes down and you wish to maintain a new lease once the server is brought back up. This happens more often than one might think. For example, suppose you were upgrading the server and intended to have it down more than half of your client's lease period. Here's when IPCONFIG/RENEW hits a homer. With this cool little command, you can schedule a time for the server to be up, making it possible for all your users to renew their leases.

Releasing a Lease through IPCONFIG

In addition to renewing leases, you may need to cancel them. For example, if you want to move a system from one subnet to another, that system's IP address, subnet mask, and default gateway will probably all need to be changed. As a result, the machine's old information becomes obsolete, requiring lease cancellation. Typing **IPCONFIG /RELEASE** from the command line will generate a DHCPRELEASE message and cause all TCP/IP functioning on that client to cease immediately.

Also noteworthy is the fact that the DHCPRELEASE message isn't automatically generated when you shutdown a DHCP client. So, if one of your users is going to the Bahamas, resulting in their system's extended dormancy, IPCONFIG /RELEASE again comes in handy. Releasing their lease gives the server an opportunity to assign the lucky saps IP address to some less fortunate being's computer.

Maintaining the DHCP Database

There are three basic functions involved in maintaining the DHCP database—backup, restore, and compact. In most cases, you'll only be performing backups occasionally, and compacting the database on a weekly basis, or less. Only volatile, problematic, or extremely complicated network environments will require more vigilance on your part. To a degree, some functions described in this section are automatic. For example, if the system detects a corrupted database, it will automatically revert to its backup. Should this occur in a neglected network where no backup exists...you're in trouble! The following procedures are essential for ensuring your network's health and optimizing its performance. Understanding this section will help you prevent problems and preserve your sanity, as well as that of those who depend on you.

Backup

You can keep a backup copy of all information that is entered when configuring the server. This information includes scopes, client reservations, options, etc. The DHCP database will be backed up automatically every hour to the \%*SYSTEMROOT*%\SYSTEM32\DHCP\BACKUP\JET directory.

You can change the backup interval by modifying the registry entry key, located in HKEY_LOCAL_MACHINE\SYSTEM\CurrentControlSet\Services\ DHCPServer\Parameters\BackupInterval.

Note that a duplicate of the registry key for DHCP is stored in \%*SYSTEMROOT*%\SYSTEM32\DHCP\BACKUP, in a file called DHCPCFG.

Restore

This function of DHCP ensures that reliable data is served. If, for example, the DHCP server determines when initializing that its data is corrupt, it will automatically revert to the backup. You can force the DHCP server to manually restore the database in two ways, as shown in Exercises 7.6 and 7.7.

EXERCISE 7.6

Restoring the DHCP Database—First Way

1. Set the Restore Flag Option to 1. This option is stored in HKEY_LOCAL_MACHINE\CurrentControlSet\ Services\DHCPServer\Parameters.

2. Restart the computer. Once the system has rebooted, it will change the flag back to a 0.

EXERCISE 7.7

Restoring the DHCP Database—Second Way

Copy the contents of the backup directory (%*SYSTEMROOT*%\SYSTEM32\DHCP\ BACKUP\JET) to the DHCP directory (%*SYSTEMROOT*%\SYSTEM32\DHCP).

Compact

The ubiquitous Computerdom issue of More Space Needed is what this handy function addresses. Windows NT 4.0 is designed to automatically compact the DHCP database, so normally you should not need to run this procedure. However, if you are using NT Server 3.51 or earlier, after the DHCP database has been running a while, you should compact the database to improve DHCP performance. One executes it by running the JETPACK.EXE utility. You should compact the database whenever it approaches 30 Mb.

To compact your database, follow the steps in Exercise 7.8.

EXERCISE 7.8

Compacting the Database

1. Stop the DHCP server through the Service Manager in the Control Panel, or type **net stop dhcpserver** at a command prompt.

2. Change to the DHCP directory %*SYSTEMROOT*%\SYSTEM32 \DHCP, and run JETPACK DHCP.MDB *TEMP_FILE*.MDB.

NOTE: The temp filename is not important. Once JETPACK has completed compacting the database, *TEMP_FILE*.MDB (regardless of name), will have its contents copied back to the DHCP.MDB file and then be deleted.

3. Finally, restart the DHCP server either by rebooting, or by selecting Control Panel ➢ Service Manager, or by typing **net start dhcpserver** at a command prompt.

The Microsoft Windows NT 4.0 Resource Kit includes a command-line version of the DHCP Manager and a utility that detects unauthorized DHCP servers.

Knowledge of which files you're working with and how they perform with a DHCP server can be useful so we've included this little resource of DHCP files. It's provided for your information only—not as an exercise.

This alphabetical listing includes the filenames with a brief description of them, and should help you get a clear picture of the DHCP database.

DHCP.MDB This is the main DHCP database file. It's arguably the most important file in the DHCP directory that you'll work with.

DHCP.TMP This file is used internally by the DHCP server for temporary storage while running.

JET.LOG/JET*.LOG These are transaction log files which can be used in a jam by DHCP to recover data.

SYSTEM.MDB This is a storage file used by the DHCP server to track the structure of the database.

Summary

The purpose of DHCP is to control centrally IP-related information and eliminate the need to manually keep track of where individual IP addresses are allocated. Unless your network is very small, or is running applications that are incompatible with DHCP (e.g., routers that can't handle the BootP/DHCP protocol), using DHCP is generally a good idea.

IPCONFIG is a cool utility that can be very useful in resolving a mysterious NetBIOS name. Typing **IPCONFIG /ALL IPCONFIG /RENEW** can be especially useful at critical times, such as when a DHCP server goes down and you wish to maintain leases once the server is brought back up.

We closed the chapter with a discussion on maintaining the DHCP database. The functions involved in doing so are backup, restore, and compact. The very cool and economical JETPACK.EXE utility should be run periodically to keep your database working for you as the compact and efficient thing it should be.

You must understand DHCP and it's functions in a network environment when taking the NT TCP/IP 4.0 test. Go through the questions below to make sure you understand the objectives.

Review Questions

1. Your network is divided into seven subnets and you want to use DHCP to assign IP addresses to all computers on all subnets. You want to make sure that the two DNS servers are configured on each computer regardless of the subnet they are located on. How should you configure DHCP?

   A. By creating a global option

   B. By creating a local option

   C. By creating a scope option

   D. By creating a client option

2. You want to configure the DHCP Relay agent on your NT Server. What information must you supply?

   A. The computer name of the DHCP server

   B. The IP address of the DHCP server

   C. The IP address of a different DHCP relay agent of a remote subnet

   D. The IP address of the router to which DHCP requests should be forwarded

3. You have three NT Servers and you want to use DHCP to give them a unique address each time the server is started. What information must you supply when you add the client reservation for each of the servers?

   A. IP address

   B. Subnet mask

   C. Hardware address

   D. Lease period

4. You have 350 computers spread across eight subnets with two DHCP servers. You want each workstation to receive an IP address, even when one of the DHCP servers is down. What should you do?

   A. Create eight DHCP scopes on each DHCP server.

   B. Create four DHCP scopes on each DHCP server.

   C. Create two global DHCP scopes on each DHCP server.

   D. Create one global DHCP scope on each DHCP server.

5. Your company has multiple laptops and the users frequently connect them into different subnets. You want to automatically assign these laptops TCP/IP addresses. Which service must you use?

   A. DHCP

   B. DNS

   C. FTP

   D. SNMP

   E. WINS

6. You use DHCP to assign IP addresses to all computers on your network. You want your NT Servers to get the same unique IP address each time the server is started. What should you do?

   A. Create a client reservation for each server.

   B. Create an exclusion range of IP addresses to be assigned to the server.

   C. Specify an unlimited lease period for the servers only.

   D. Create a separate scope that contains the IP address for each server.

7. You have three subnets. One subnet has only laptop Windows 95 computers. The other two subnets have NT Workstations. You have one DHCP server to support all clients. You want the IP lease period for the laptop set to seven days. You want the NT Workstations lease set to thirty days. What should you do?

   A. Create one DHCP scope for all subnets. For each computer, create an exclusion range with a unique lease period.

   B. Create one DHCP scope for all subnets. For each workstation, create a client reservation with a 30-day lease period.

   C. Create one DHCP scope for each subnet. Specify the lease period as part of the scope's configuration.

   D. Create one DHCP scope for each subnet. Create a global option that specifies a lease period that is based on the operating system the client computer is running.

8. Your company has many laptops with Windows 95 that move from subnet to subnet. There is one WINS server on each subnet. You want to automatically assign the IP address for the WINS server on the subnet to which the laptop connects. Which service should you use?

A. DHCP

B. DNS

C. FTP

D. SNMP

E. WINS

9. You have two subnets with an NT Server on each subnet. One server is configured as a router between Subnet A and Subnet B. You have a different server running DHCP on Subnet A. All clients on Subnet B must be able to obtain IP addresses from the server on Subnet A. Which service should you install on a Windows NT Server computer on Subnet B?

A. RIP for IP

B. RIP for NWLink IPX/SPX Compatible Transport

C. The DHCP Relay Agent

D. WINS

10. You have four subnets with one DHCP server to support 100 NT Workstations and 10 NT Servers. DHCP needs to assign the same IP addresses to your servers every time they are started. Your boss gave you the following IP scheme to implement at work:

Gateways	1 through 19
Clients	20 through 99
Server	100 through 199
Clients	200 through 254

What are you going to do?

A. Create four DHCP scopes for each range of IP addresses.

B. Create three DHCP scopes for each type of host computer.

C. Create one DHCP scope that is configured to exclude a range of addresses for the gateways. Create a client reservation for each server.

D. Create one scope that is configured to exclude a range of addresses for the servers. Create a client reservation for each gateway.

E. Create one DHCP scope that is configured to reserve one range of addresses for the gateways and one range of addresses for the servers.

11. You want to install DHCP on your network consisting of three subnets. You place the server on one subnet, and all clients must be able to get IP addresses from this server. Which are two possible locations for DHCP relay agents?

A. On each subnet that does not contain the DHCP server

B. On the subnet that contains the DHCP server

C. On the routers between the subnets

D. On the DHCP server

12. You manage a network with four subnets, two DHCP servers, and three WINS servers. All workstations are configured for DHCP. You have been getting calls reporting that a duplicate IP address has been assigned. What is the most likely cause of the problem?

A. The client computers are not releasing the IP addresses when they shut down.

B. Each client computer is registering with more than one WINS server.

C. The DHCP servers have assigned all available IP addresses.

D. The DHCP servers are configured with scopes that have overlapping IP addresses.

13. **Situation:** Your network has four Windows NT Server computers, 10 Windows NT Workstation computers, 80 Windows 95 computers, and 10 UNIX machines. All machines only run TCP/IP. Users move their computers around the office constantly from one subnet to another. The UNIX machines do not move and do not use NetBIOS. One NT Server is running DHCP with scopes configured for all subnets. All Microsoft Windows-based computers are configured as DHCP clients.

Required results:

- All computers on all subnets must be able to access each other by host name.

- All computers must be able to receive an IP address from the DHCP server.

Optional desired results:

- All UNIX hosts should be able to access any NT Server running FTP by its host name.

- All clients should be able to access any UNIX host running an FTP or Telnet daemon.

Proposed solution:

- On the DHCP server, configure scopes with an exclusion range for the IP addresses of all UNIX computers.

- Configure all routers to forward all DHCP broadcast to all subnets.

- Install and configure a WINS server on the network.

- Configure DHCP to supply all DHCP clients with the IP address of the WINS server.

- On the WINS server, configure static mappings for each UNIX computer.

- Install a DNS server and configure DNS to use WINS for name resolution.

- Configure the DHCP server to supply all DHCP clients with the IP address of the DNS server.

Which results does the proposed solution produce?

A. The proposed solution produces the required results and produces both of the optional desired results.

B. The proposed solution produces the required results and produces only one of the optional desired results.

C. The proposed solution produces the required results but does not produce either of the optional desired results.

D. The proposed solution does not produce the required results.

14. Situation: Your network has 4 Windows NT Server computers, 10 Windows NT Workstation computers, 80 Windows 95 computers, and 10 UNIX machines. All machines only run TCP/IP. Users move their computers around the office constantly from one subnet to another. The UNIX machines do not move and do not use NetBIOS. One NT Server is running DHCP with scopes configured for all subnets. All Microsoft Windows-based computers are configured as DHCP clients.

Required results:

- All computers on all subnets must be able to access each other by host name.

- All computers must be able to receive an IP address from the DHCP server.

Optional desired results:

- All UNIX hosts should be able to access any NT Server running FTP by its host name.

- All clients should be able to access any UNIX host running an FTP or Telnet daemon.

Proposed solution:

- On the DHCP Server, configure scopes with an exclusion range for the IP addresses of all UNIX computers.

- Configure all routers to forward all DHCP broadcast to all subnets.

- Install and configure a WINS server on the network.

- Configure DHCP to supply all DHCP clients with the IP address of the WINS server.

- On the WINS server, configure static mappings for each UNIX computer.

Which results does the proposed solution produce?

A. The proposed solution produces the required results and produces both of the optional desired results.

B. The proposed solution produces the required results and produces only one of the optional desired results.

C. The proposed solution produces the required results but does not produce either of the optional desired results.

D. The proposed solution does not produce the required results.

CHAPTER

8

WINS: Windows Internet Name Service

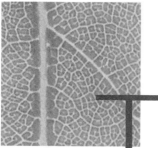

his chapter will address how the Windows Internet Name Service (WINS) reduces broadcast traffic associated with the B-node implementation of NetBIOS over TCP/IP. We'll take a look at installing and configuring a WINS server, WINS clients, and the WINS proxy agent. By the time you've made it to the other side of this chapter, you'll be armed with all you need to know regarding:

- WINS functions

- How WINS handles the resolution of NetBIOS names

- Installing and configuring WINS

- WINS client setup

- WINS replication

- How to maintain a WINS database

WINS Defined

NetBIOS B-node broadcasts create lots of traffic on networks. This being a less than desirable thing, Microsoft counter-created something called an *NBNS (NetBIOS Name Server)* as a solution, dubbing it *WINS (Windows Internet Name Service)*. A WINS server acts as network support by intercepting the legions of name-query broadcasts and processing them internally. This prevents inundating the network and consuming precious bandwidth. As a result, the network is relieved of stress—freed to function efficiently, unencumbered by its broadcast-related burdens. There's a whole bunch of interesting documentation about WINS in RFC 1001 and RFC 1002 that you can browse through sometime if you're interested. Figure 8.1 details a WINS function.

FIGURE 8.1

The functions of WINS

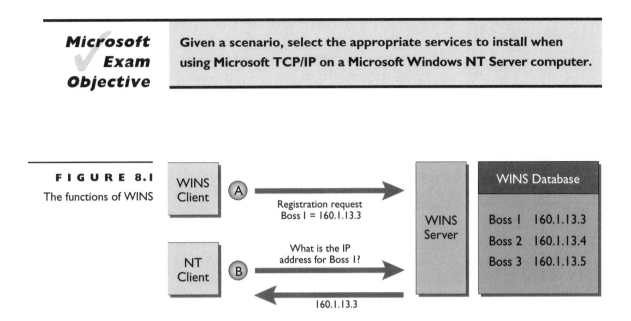

Before two NetBIOS-based hosts can communicate, the destination NetBIOS name must be resolved to an IP address. This is necessary because TCP/IP requires an IP address in order to establish communications. It can't achieve them through using a NetBIOS computer name.

The procedure is as follows:

Step A In a WINS environment, each time a WINS client starts up, it registers its NetBIOS name and IP address with the WINS server.

Step B When a WINS client initiates a command to communicate with another host, the resulting name-query request is sent directly to the WINS server instead of being broadcast all over the local network.

Step C If the WINS server finds the destination host's NetBIOS name and concurrent IP address mapping in its database, it returns this information to the WINS client. Because the WINS database obtains name/IP address mappings dynamically, its database entries are always current.

Why Use WINS?

Ahhh...Why do we love WINS? Let us count the ways! Yes, indeed. There's an abundance of benefits gained through employing a WINS server. The stand-out is its exceptional ability to substantially reduce traffic and effectively promote overall resolution speed. Since network broadcasts are sent directly to the WINS server, there is no need for congestion-producing B-node broadcasts. These broadcasts only darken the network doorstep if the server is unavailable or unable to resolve the needed address. Since WINS servers are the first contact, and are, in most cases, ready, willing, and able to satisfy name queries, the time spent resolving a NetBIOS name is markedly reduced. Additionally, Microsoft clients using WINS automatically register with the WINS server upon start-up, ensuring totally pristine, right-off-the-vine freshness of the contents of its database—more so than any other resolution service! Finally, because it's dynamic in nature, employing a WINS server fully eliminates a lot of the agonizingly boring work normally associated with database maintenance. As an extra bonus, you can even assign a second WINS server to a client for purposes of fault tolerance. WINS also provides internetwork and inter-domain browsing capabilities.

WINS/DNS Integration

In Windows NT 4.0, Microsoft's implementation of DNS is tightly integrated with WINS. This allows non-WINS clients to resolve NetBIOS names by querying a DNS server. Administrators now can replace any static entries for Microsoft-based clients in legacy DNS server zone files with the dynamic WINS/DNS integration. For example, if a non-Microsoft-based client wants to get to a Web page on an HTTP server that's DHCP/WINS enabled, the client queries the DNS server, the DNS server queries WINS, and the name is resolved and returned to the client. Prior to the WINS integration, there was no way to reliably resolve the name because of the dynamic IP addressing.

WINS is, therefore, only half of the answer to the name resolution problem, albeit an important half. We'll take that up in this chapter and look at DNS alternatives in the next chapter.

WINS in Action

When a WINS client starts, messages will be sent between the WINS client and the WINS server in order to register each of the WINS clients' names. Like DHCP, WINS messages occur in four modes: name registration, name renewal, name release, and name query/name resolution, as illustrated in Figure 8.2.

FIGURE 8.2

WINS works in four modes

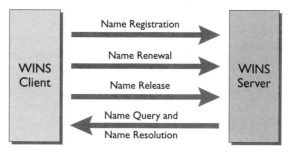

Name Registration

In the WINS environment, each client registers its name and corresponding IP address with its designated WINS server when it starts up. When a NetBIOS-based application or service is started, the client's NetBIOS name is also included in that package of information (see Figure 8.3). One type of service that is NetBIOS-dependent is the Messenger service used for the delivery of print notices, system events, and the like.

FIGURE 8.3

Name registration

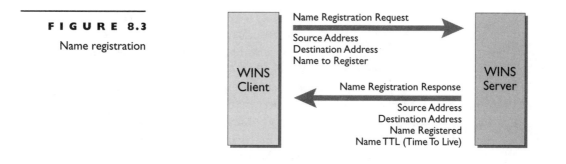

When a unique and valid name is received by the WINS server, it returns a message confirming registration, plus a specified *Time To Live (TTL) period* designating the duration of time that name can be used. With WINS, as with everything else in Computerdom, the existence of duplicate names is an offensive, frowned upon thing. If one of these dirty buggers is discovered during the WINS registration process, a WINS server will send out a challenge to its database's registered owner of the name in the form of a name query request. The challenge message is repeated three times, at 500 millisecond intervals—less if the server receives a reply. When the client happens to be a multihomed system, the above process is repeated for each IP address until the server either receives a reply or tries each address three times. If the current owner of the name responds, the WINS server rejects the request by sending a negative name request back to the machine attempting to claim the already-in-use NetBIOS name. If the current registered owner doesn't reply, then the name is deleted from the database, and a positive acknowledgment is sent to the requesting machine. If the primary WINS server doesn't respond after three tries, an attempt will then be made to contact a secondary server. If this effort is also unsuccessful, and no available server is found, the client will send out a B-node broadcast to validate its name and achieve registration among its peers.

NOTE The phrase "Time To Live" (TTL) is a common one in TCP/IP. Most often, it refers to notices sent out delimiting a period of time, or specifying the number of hops a message may go through before it's discarded. Obviously highly useful, it serves to phase out obsolete messages, and also prevents them from looping endlessly in circles among two or more routers. (Recall the "Counting to Infinity" scenario we presented earlier!)

Renewing Names

Similar to lease renewal, the process of renewing a name begins when a WINS client notifies the WINS server that it desires to continue its use of that name, and so its current Time To Live period now needs to be reset. Registered names associated with the WINS client are always done so on a temporary basis. This prevents confusion or worse if the name's current owner moves, receives a new IP address, or otherwise discontinues use of its name. Temporary registration permits the server to reassign the name elsewhere should any of these events occur. It's sort of an environmentally-friendly Networkland recycling program that's so popular, traffic gets really heavy en route to it. The name renewal process is shown in Figure 8.4.

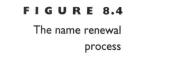

FIGURE 8.4

The name renewal process

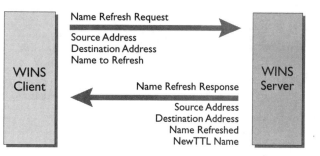

When the TTL period lapses to 50 percent of its original lease time, the WINS client sends a name renewal message to the primary WINS server. This message contains the client's name and both the source and destination IP address. If there's no response, the message will be resent once more at one eighth of the TTL. If there's still no response from the primary server, the client will then attempt renewal through the secondary WINS server, if one is configured. If the effort is successful, the WINS client will attempt to register with the secondary server as though it were the first attempt. If, after four attempts, the WINS client fails to contact the secondary WINS server, it'll switch back to the primary one. Once successful contact is made, either the primary or secondary WINS server will respond by sending the client a new TTL period. This process will continue as long as the client computer is powered-on, and as long as it remains a WINS client.

Releasing Names

WINS clients can also relinquish ownership of its name. It can accomplish this by sending a name release message, containing its IP address and name, during a proper shutdown. This will cause the entry to be removed from the WINS server's database. The WINS client will wait for confirmation in the form of a positive release message, comprised of the released name and a new TTL of zero, from the WINS server. At this point, it'll stop responding to its former NetBIOS name. If the IP address and name sent by the client don't match, the WINS server will return a negative release message. If no confirmation is received from the WINS server, the WINS client will then send up to three B-node broadcasts notifying all other systems, including non-WINS clients, to remove the now invalid name from their NetBIOS name caches. This process is illustrated in Figure 8.5.

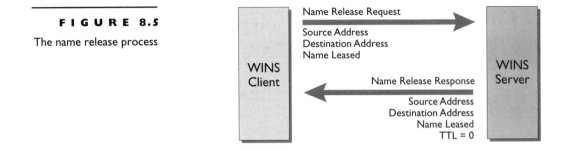

Name Query and Response

The WINS process is central to communication. Through it, names are resolved to IP addresses, which clearly identifies the devices involved and forms the basis for them to communicate. To get a picture of this process, think of making a phone call, and what you need to know to make it. First, you need the right number for the person you're trying to contact. For the call to be successful, you need an acknowledgment from the other end that you have, in fact, reached them. Think about phoning up someone who isn't home and doesn't have an answering machine. Because you didn't receive an acknowledgment from them, or their machine, you're left wondering if you actually reached them or not. Without the right access coordinates, plus a response from whomever or whatever's been contacted, communication just doesn't happen. This process describes name query and response, and the reason it's set up the way it is. Ideally, when a network is populated solely with WINS clients, the need for congestion-producing B-node broadcasts all but vanishes. Equipped with a fully functioning WINS server, most resolution traffic should be H-node over UDP port 137-NetBIOS Name Service. In Figure 8.6, we've detailed an expansion of how WINS, a NetBIOS Name Server, processes a request, or query. Try to make mental notes of how similar this process is to the one outlined for NetBIOS name servers covered in Chapter 6.

By default, WINS uses the H-node implementation of NetBIOS over TCP/IP. The NetBIOS Name Server is always checked for a NetBIOS name/IP address mapping before initiating a B-node broadcast. The process is as follows:

Step A Again, as with NetBIOS name resolution, begin with a command like **net use** or **net view**. We'll use **net use g: \\Alpine\public**. Initially, the system will always check the local address cache to try to resolve the name.

FIGURE 8.6

Name query and name
resolution

Prompt > Net use g: \\Alpine\\Public

NetBIOS Name Cache
NetBIOS Name\IP Address

Not
resolved

(A)

WINS
Client

Name Query Request

(B)

(Resend to secondary
server if not available)

WINS
Server

Second
WINS
Server

Name does not exsist

(C)

B-Node
Name Resolution

If it's found there, ARP will then proceed to resolve the hardware address. This deftly avoids adding unnecessary traffic on the network.

Step B If the process in Step A fails to resolve the name, a request is sent directly to the WINS server. If the primary server is up, and the name is found in its database, the information is returned to the requesting system. If the server fails to respond, the request is repeated twice before the client then switches to the secondary WINS server.

Step C If both the primary and secondary WINS servers fail to resolve the name, the client will revert to using a broadcast. If this is also unsuccessful, the system will then try checking the LMHOSTS file, HOSTS file, and finally, DNS.

NOTE

As soon as the host name is resolved as in steps A or B, ARP kicks in to ferret out the hardware address.

WINS Implementation

Before deciding whether or not to switch to or install WINS, it's wise to first assess your needs and be sure you understand the requirements necessary to implement it.

Prior Considerations

While it may be true that WINS servers are usually a helpful asset, they're not for every network. An example would be a small NetBIOS network existing within a larger, primarily UNIX-based internetwork. That network would likely be best off just using the DNS server and avoiding the cost of implementing a couple of WINS servers. Most often, if the decision is made to adopt WINS, two or more WINS servers need to be configured. This is because even though only one is actually required, the network will enjoy the advantages of fault tolerance in the event one of the servers goes down. The performance of each WINS server will vary according to that particular machine's hardware. For instance, the average high-end Pentium 200MHz can process about 1500 name registrations and 750 name queries per minute. You can enhance the performance of each WINS server by an estimated 25% by adding an auxiliary CPU. This is because each additional CPU adds a new, separate WINS process thread. It's also important to remember that your NIC card and disk drives can be the cause of bottlenecks. Performance for name registration can also be augmented by disabling logging though the WINS manager. However, this is generally a bad idea, because if the system crashes, you could lose your recent updates.

With the recommended two-server minimum execution of WINS, it's reasonable to expect to service up to roughly 10,000 clients. A good tactic to optimize performance is to set half the clients to one WINS server as their primary contact, and the other half to the other WINS server as their primary. For their secondary server, each client group would be configured with the opposite group's primary server.

Up to 2,500 clients as browse list can only hold this amount.

Server Requirements

By now you've decided to answer the pressing information processing question: "To WINS, or not to WINS?" If you've decided in favor of implementing WINS, you now need to know just what it'll take to do so.

For optimum performance, WINS servers should be Cray super-crunchers. Just kidding. There really aren't a lot of requirements placed on a WINS server, therefore, it can and should be added to any Windows NT 4.0 server that is running TCP/IP with a static, non-DHCP assigned IP address. If you elect to use DCHP, it changes things, but we'll tell you more about that a little later. For now, suffice it to say, if you're running DHCP, the WINS server will only function with a reserved address—using the same subnet mask and default gateway each time. The good thing about using DHCP is each client absolutely must know the WINS server's IP address. This can is easily updated to all clients through DHCP if the WINS server address should change.

There's no requirement for a WINS server to become a domain controller of any type.

Server Installation

The WINS service comes ready with Windows NT and will integrate seamlessly into the existing operating system as we shall soon see. It's a beautiful thing! Exercise 8.1 will help you install WINS on an NT Server.

Microsoft ✔ *Exam* *Objective*	**Install and configure a WINS server.** • Import LMHOSTS files to WINS. • Run WINS on a multihomed computer. • Configure WINS replication. • Configure static mappings in the WINS database.

EXERCISE 8.1

Installing a WINS Server

1. Click Start ➢ Settings ➢ Control panel ➢ Network.

2. Click the Services tab, then click Add.

3. Select Windows Internet Name Service, then click OK.

4. Type the path to your distribution files.

5. Click Close.

6. Click Yes in the dialog box requesting that you restart your computer.

WINS Server Configuration—Static Mapping for Clients

Most configurations for the WINS Server Service settings are automatic. Normally, few changes need to be made. However, things get a little more complicated when systems configured as WINS clients need to talk to those that aren't. For communication to happen in a mixed environment, manual entries must be made to the WINS server. This is due to the fact that non-WINS clients don't automatically register their names and so won't be recognized, making resolution for them impossible. The only alternative to manually adding entries to the WINS server is to add them to the workstation's LMHOSTS file.

To add a static mapping for any type of client, see Exercise 8.2.

Note that this procedure is not valid for systems that use DHCP if their IP addresses are not reserved. For example, if a non-WINS DHCP client were to change its IP address, the static name mapping would not be valid.

Suppose you've got this hideously long list of static mappings to add to your system. Employing the above procedure, you'll be ordering pizza for weeks, and your dog will forget who you are and go into attack mode upon your arrival back home. A quick alternative to plinking each one in is to use the WINS Manager's import function. It'll work with any text file that's in the same format as an LMHOSTS file.

Importing Your LMHOSTS File to WINS

All keywords with the exception of #DOM will be ignored. Those specified with the #DOM will be marked as an Internet group whose IP addresses will be added to a little group for that specified domain. With this shortcut, you can create unique group and Internet group settings.

EXERCISE 8.2

Configuring Static Entries for Non-WINS Clients

1. Start WINS Manager.

2. From the Mappings menu, click Static Mappings.

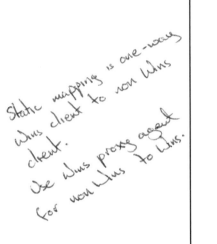

3. Click Add Mappings.

4. In the Name box, type the computer name of the non-WINS client.

5. In the IP Address box, type the IP address of the non-WINS client.

6. Under Type, select an option indicating whether this entry is a unique name or a type of specially named group described in the following list:

- **Unique** This will make an entry into the WINS database that allows for only one address for the given name. This is the most common choice for specifying non-WINS clients.

- **Multihomed** This is an extension of the unique name option that defines a name by referencing a system. However, because a multi-homed system can have multiple addresses (up to 25), it can be included with a given name. This type of computer is connected to more than one physical data link. The data links may or may not be attached to the same network.

- **Group** This is the same as a normal group where the IP addresses of individual clients are not stored. A normal group is the name to which broadcasts are sent, and is the domain name used for browsing. It's where domains and workgroups can be specified. This option is useful for functions involving broadcasts and required lists, as in domain browsing. This function enables a group of WINS clients to talk to a non-WINS domain by providing the group name for the WINS clients.

- **Internet Group** This is an extension of the normal group option and is used to gather up to 25 domain controllers, enabling them to communicate with each other. Like the group function above, a domain name is registered so it can be recognized as a single unit for purposes of creating cohesion among domain servers.

- **Domain Name** A NetBIOS name-to-address mapping that has 0x1C as the 16th byte. A domain group stores up to 25 addresses for members. For registrations after the 25th address, WINS over-writes a replica or, if none is present, the oldest registration.

7. After verifying the information you've entered, select Add. If you select Add and then realize you've made a mistake, you've got to close the current box and delete the entry from the Static Entry dialog box.

8. The entry is now in the database. The template will clear, allowing you to make additional entries.

Client Requirements

To implement WINS, the client machine requires configuration. A WINS client needs a computer running any of the following supported operating systems:

- Windows NT Server 4.0/3.5*x*

- Windows NT Workstation 4.0/3.5*x*

- Windows 95

- Windows for Workgroups with TCP/IP-32

- Microsoft Network Client 3.0 for MS-DOS (with TCP/IP)

- LAN Manager 2.2c for MS-DOS

Sorry—LAN Manager 2.2c for OS/2 isn't supported. Essentially, the only requirements for WINS clients are: They must be able to run a supported operating system/IP stack, and be configured with the IP address of both the primary and secondary (if there is one) WINS servers.

WINS Client Configuration

After the WINS server setup is complete, WINS clients can begin accessing it. In order for a client machine to be able to do this, it must first become a WINS client, configured with TCP/IP, with WINS enabled. This is accomplished by entering the IP address(es) for the WINS system(s) the client will be accessing. Exercise 8.3 illustrates the installation of WINS on NT clients and Windows for Workgroups.

For those clients who are also DHCP clients: When values (addresses) are entered into the WINS address slots, they will be given priority, automatically overriding any DHCP values.

Client Installation

Configuring a computer to be a WINS client requires that you add the IP address of the primary WINS server, and optionally, the IP address of a secondary WINS server. This can be done manually or automatically using DHCP. Exercises 8.3 and 8.4 assume that the TCP/IP transport is already loaded.

EXERCISE 8.3

Installing WINS Clients

1. For Windows 95 clients, go to Start ≻ Settings ≻ Control Panel ≻ Network.

2. Double-click TCP/IP.

3. Click the WINS tab.

4. Fill in the IP address for the primary and secondary WINS servers.

5. Close the Network dialog box and reboot.

EXERCISE 8.4

Installing Windows for Workgroups as a Client

1. From the Network group, open Network Setup.

2. Locate TCP/IP-32 3.11, then select Setup.

3. Inside TCP/IP configuration, enter the addresses for both the primary and secondary (if one exists) WINS server, then select OK.

4. Exit all applications, then shut down and restart your computer.

The DHCP Client

Clients can be configured for WINS even if they're also DHCP clients. DHCP uses two information fields to define WINS support.

The first field is defined by the addresses of the primary and secondary WINS servers in the 044 WINS/NBNS Servers blank. The second source is clarified by the type of node they've been configured to behave as. A WINS/ DHCP client must be configured to act as a hybrid node, specifying it thus: 046 WINS/NBT Node to 0x8 (H-node). 0x8 is the NetBIOS specification to define an H-node system. If you don't recall this, or need to review the various node types, refer back to Chapter 6.

Configuration for the Non-WINS Client

If you have computers on your internetwork that are not supported as WINS clients, they can resolve NetBIOS names on a WINS server using a WINS proxy agent (see Figure 8.7). Non-WINS clients can be configured to use WINS in an indirect manner. This process doesn't require changing anything on the non-WINS client itself. Instead, a WINS client that's located on the same network or subnet is used to act as a relay between the non-WINS machine and the WINS server. The machine acting as the relay is known as a WINS proxy agent. Using a WINS proxy agent to extend name resolution capabilities of a WINS server requires one proxy agent on each subnet that has non-WINS clients. This is not required if the network's routers are configured to forward B-node broadcasts (UDP 137 and 138), but is recommended to reduce broadcast traffic. You should have no more than two proxy agents per subnet, and the proxy agent must be a Windows-based WINS client—it cannot be a WINS server.

F I G U R E 8.7

Using a WINS proxy agent

A WINS proxy agent performs the two focal tasks of NetBIOS Name Registration and NetBIOS Name Resolution. The part these machines play in name registration is limited—they don't achieve actual, complete name registration of the non-WINS client. The proxy agent serves only to verify that no other machine is currently registered with the name being requested. It then proceeds to forward the query on to the WINS server for true registration.

This method is more thorough and fault tolerant because two machines, both the proxy agent and the WINS server, check up on the proposed name. The Proxy agent detects the resolution request, checks its own name cache for it, and sends the request on to the WINS server if the name isn't already in use. The WINS server then sends the actual resolution response back to the proxy agent, which then forwards it onward and back to the non-WINS client completing the process.

Exercise 8.5 shows you how to add the WINS proxy function.

EXERCISE 8.5

Configuring a WINS Proxy Agent

1. Use the Registry Editor to open HKEY_LOCAL_MACHINE\ System\CurrentControlSet\Services\NetBT\Parameters.

2. Set the Enable Proxy parameter to 1 (REG_DWORD).

3. Exit the Registry Editor.

4. Restart your computer.

Database Replication

Unlike DHCP servers that don't communicate with each other, WINS servers can be configured to replicate their database entries, sharing them with each other so that all servers across the network have synchronous name information. This also facilitates communication between WINS clients that've registered with different WINS servers. As an example, suppose your system has registered with the WINS server Alpine (see Figure 8.8) and your buddy's system registers with the WINS server Aspen. Not only will these systems enjoy full communication, they'll be able to resolve the names directly for each other because the WINS database is replicated between servers. This feature is not automatic, and requires configuration to become operative. When it has been configured, replication is automatically triggered any time the database changes (e.g., when names are registered and/or released). To configure a WINS server to function in this manner, it must be ordained as either a push or pull partner.

Push or Pull Partners

Push partners are WINS servers that function by sending update notices to pull partners whenever changes are made. Pull partners—also WINS servers—function by sending out requests to push partners, asking them for entries more recent than their current listings when they want to update their database contents. WINS servers can be defined as both push and pull, ensuring the most up to date information is registered. Only new listings added since the last time an update occurred will be replicated—not the entire database. To get a picture of this, take a peek at Figure 8.8.

F I G U R E 8.8

Determining whether a WINS server is a push or pull partner

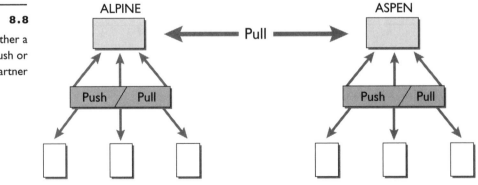

Determining If a Server Is a Push or Pull Partner

WINS database replication types can be determined by how a WINS server is used and the architecture of the network. If your network spans multiple sites across slow links, you'll want your servers to pull each other for updates. This is because pull requests can be predetermined to occur at specific times, like during lunch or evening, when the network's traffic is likely to be light. Alternately, if the links are fast, your concerns would have less to do with traffic, and your servers should be ordained as push partners. If you choose to set the server as a push, it's often a good idea to go ahead and configure it as both push and pull. By doing so, you'll be ensuring yourself that you're in possession of the most up-to-date WINS entries available.

In all, there are four ways in which replication takes place:

- Once configured as a replication partner, each server will automatically pull updates during initialization at startup.

- As a pull partner, the machine will query other WINS servers for updates at a chosen and specified time.

- As a push partner, the machine will advertise its updates when it reaches its threshold for number of changes. Both the threshold and the update interval are user definable.

- Finally, WINS databases may be manually replicated through the WINS manager.

WINS manager provides the ability to view the contents of the WINS database and search for specific entries. Exercise 8.6 should help clarify things.

The WINS Manager interface utility can be a little confusing the first time you work with it. It's helpful to understand that you have the ability to list, configure, and trigger replication partners from the Replications Partner dialog box.

Configuring Replication

If you happen to have two or more WINS servers, you can practice making replication partners. To add a replication partner for a WINS server, try Exercise 8.7.

WINS Automatic Replication Partners

If your network supports multicasting, the WINS server can be configured to automatically find other WINS servers on the network by multicasting to the IP address 224.0.1.24. This multicasting occurs by default every 40 minutes. Any WINS servers found on the network are automatically configured as push and pull replication partners, with pull replication set to occur every two hours.

If network routers do not support multicasting, the WINS server will find only other WINS servers on its subnet. Automatic WINS server partnerships are turned on by default. To disable this feature, use the Registry Editor to set UseSelfFndPnrs to 0 and McastIntvl to a large value.

EXERCISE 8.6

Viewing the NetBIOS Name/IP Address Mappings That Have Been Registered in the WINS Database

1. Start WINS Manager.

2. From the Mappings menu, click Show Database.

3. The Show Database dialog box appears.

Show Database - (Local)			

Display Options

Owner
- ○ Show All Mappings
- ⦿ Show Only Mappings from Selected Owner

Select Owner: Highest ID
- 150.150.29.215   1F5

Sort Order
- ○ Sort by IP Address
- ⦿ Sort by Computer Name
- ○ Sort by Expiration Date
- ○ Sort by Version ID
- ○ Sort by Type

Close
Help
Set Filter...
Clear Filter
Refresh
Delete Owner

Filter: None

Mappings		A	S	Expiration Date	Version ID
__MSBROWSE__-.[01h]	150.150.29.215	✔		8/1/97 10:45:59 AM	1F5
ADMIN[03h]	150.150.29.215	✔		8/1/97 10:47:40 AM	4
CMP[00h]	150.150.7.150	✔		7/31/97 6:18:16 PM	A
CMP[1Eh]	150.150.7.150	✔		7/31/97 6:18:16 PM	9
LAMTRAK[00h]	150.150.29.215	✔		8/1/97 10:45:59 AM	3
LAMTRAK[1Ch]	150.150.29.215	✔		8/1/97 10:45:59 AM	2
LAMTRAK[1Eh]	150.150.29.215	✔		8/1/97 10:43:59 AM	1
ONTKDHCP2[00h]	150.150.29.215	✔		8/1/97 10:45:59 AM	6
ONTKDHCP2[03h]	150.150.29.215	✔		8/1/97 10:45:59 AM	5
ONTKDHCP2[20h]	150.150.29.215	✔		8/1/97 10:45:59 AM	7

4. To view mappings for a specific WINS server, select Show Only Mappings from Selected Owner, and then from the Select Owner list, select the WINS server you want to view.

5. Select a Sort Order option to sort by IP Address, computer name, timestamp for the mapping, Version ID, or type. Under Sort Order, select how you want mappings sorted.

6. If you want to view only a range of mappings, click Set Filter, and then specify the IP addresses or NetBIOS names.

7. View the mappings in the Mappings box. Each mapping includes the following elements:

   A or S Indicates whether the mapping is dynamic or static. If there is a cross symbol in the A column, it indicates that the name is no longer active and will soon be removed from the database.

   Computer icon Indicates that the entry is a unique name

   Multiple Computers Represents a group, Internet group, or mutil-homed computer

   Name The registered NetBIOS name

   IP Address The IP address that corresponds to the registered name

   Expiration Date Shows when the entry will expire. When a replica is stored in the database, its expiration data is set to the current time plus the renewal interval on the receiving WINS server.

   Version ID A unique hexadecimal number assigned by the WINS server during name registration, which is used by the server's pull partner during replication to find new records.

8. To delete a WINS server and all database entries owned by that server, select a WINS server in the Select Owner list, and then click Delete Owner.

9. Click Close.

EXERCISE 8.7

Adding a Replication Partner for a WINS Server

1. Start WINS Manager, then select Replication Partners from the Server menu.

2. Choose Add, then enter the name or IP address of the new WINS server Partner.

3. Select OK to continue. Once the current WINS server communicates with the new partner, they'll appear in the address listing.

```
Replication Partners - (Local)                                  [X]
WINS Server                              Push  Pull
  🖳 150.150.28.215                        ✔     ✔        |   OK    |
  🖳 150.150.29.215                                       |  Cancel |

                                                          |  Help   |

                                                          |  Add... |

                                                          | Delete  |
 ─WINS Servers To List──────────────────────
  ☑ Push Partners   ☑ Pull Partners   ☑ Other           | Replicate Now |

 ─Replication Options──────      ─Send Replication Trigger Now──
  ☑ Push Partner  |Configure...|    |  Push  |   |  Pull  |
  ☑ Pull Partner  |Configure...|    ☐ Push with Propagation
```

At this point, you can either add additional servers by repeating the steps above, or set the partner type by selecting a WINS server from the list.

To set the partner type:

1. Elect either one or both of the Push/Pull Partner boxes from servers to list at the bottom of the dialog box, then select the Related Configure button.

2. When complete, select OK to continue.

3. From the Send Replication Now box, choose either Push or Pull to replicate your selected partners. You can also select Replicate Now to configure all systems at once. If you select Push with Propagation, those systems that receive updates will automatically share them with all their pull partners. If the partner finds no new entries, the Propagation command will be ignored.

4. Select OK to enter your changes.

Push partners are configured by setting the number of changes before the server sends out change notices. The number of requests a server receives should be used to determine the number of changes entered before the change notices are sent. The minimum setting is five changes. For a server that receives hundreds of registrations to be required to have every five changes notified across the network would be very wasteful and highly unnecessary. Although there are no wrong answers to what number of changes should occur before notices are sent, there are some that are more efficient and wiser than others. The same old network-oriented common sense applies here: Only send stuff out across the network as needed, avoiding unnecessary traffic. Always consider speed and efficiency—the things of performance. Don't create a setting that will require so many update notices—the replication process will be slowed to the point of decreased functionality.

As for pull partners...Here, your concerns are similar—defining a start time and an interval for replication. The determining factors for pull partner should be how much bandwidth you have at your disposal, and your transfer time. Again, there aren't any wrong settings for replication, but plan your update schedule for when the network is less busy.

Automated Cleanup

It's probably becoming pretty apparent by now that most of the data managed by WINS machines is maintained automatically, with the option for the network administrator to intervene at certain times. Often it's best to leave the majority of management functions to the internal system control of the WINS server, unaided by us humans. Controlling a WINS server pretty much comes down to setting things up, adding names, and removing them when necessary. There are some exceptions though. The related duties of database backup, restoration, and compression are definitely going to suffer without good ol' fashioned human support. Understanding that the name registration process is automatically handled by each WINS client may lead you to wonder about its opposite function—that of removing obsolete or incorrect names from the database.

Most of the database cleanup is accomplished automatically by controls set though the Configuration menu in the WINS Manager program. Once in, you'll be presented with a configuration screen listing four different timers:

Renewal Interval This delimits the intervals at which a WINS client is cued to renew its name with the WINS server. It's similar to the DHCP lease period discussed in Chapter 5. The default setting for this value is four days, or 96 hours.

Extinction Interval This sets the period of time between an entry being marked to be released and its subsequent extinction. Names are marked "release" when a WINS client terminates its session, changes its name, etc. At this point, the entry is considered deleted, but it's not automatically removed from the database. The default setting for this value is also four days, or 96 hours.

Extinction Time-out This option describes the time elapsed between an entry being marked as extinct, and when that entry is removed, or "zapped." This setting is the Lysol of database cleanup. The default setting for this value is again four days, or 96 hours, but it can also have a minimal value set for one day.

Verify Interval This sets the frequency at which a WINS server verifies the entries it doesn't own are still active (i.e., those depicting shared information from other servers). Both the default and minimal settings for this value equal 24 days, or 576 hours.

That's not all folks—there are two more options involved in the whole push or pull configuration fest. Let's say you want your server to pull other WINS servers for any new database entries, or other replication related stuff upon initialization. To do this, select the initial replication box located under Push Parameters, inside of which you'll find the spiffy option to set a retry count. This is like a replication insurance policy that ensures important changes are made even if your server is extremely busy, or temporarily unreachable. However, it's generally effective to simply push changes upon initialization, notifying other available WINS servers of changes when your server starts up. Since, in most cases, the servers that are up have more current information than those that are down, you may want to consider using both these methods. One final thing on push parameters—you can also set updates to automatically occur upon any IP address change. This is a highly mutable area, since when an entry is changed, it's often because DHCP has assigned a new address to it, or because the device has been moved to a different subnet.

If you're professionally managing this server, you should also select the Advanced button from the WINS Manager configuration panel to display additional options. This will reveal additional control opportunities described in the list below.

Logging Enabled turns on WINS server database event logging. As the name suggests, whenever changes are made to the database, they're recorded in the log.

Log Detailed Events specifies whether log entries are to be short and sweet or long-winded. It's used to add potentially telling details in the log, which can become quite handy when troubleshooting. Be warned, however... Nothing worthwhile in life is free! There's an abundance of overhead associated with this function that can turn your Porsche of a network into a Volvo. Steer clear of this one if speed and performance tuning are your goals.

Replicate Only with Partners determines whether your WINS server will communicate with other servers with which it's not already configured to push or pull entries. This is a really cool feature if you're running separate networks that shouldn't be communicating with each other. This function is enabled by default.

Backup On Termination automatically backs up the database when WINS Manager is closed.

Migrate On/Off replaces static information with the dynamic variety in the event of a conflict. For example, if you've made static entries, and the information you entered eventually changes, the WINS server will cause the database entries to "migrate" from static (S) to active/dynamic (A). A better name could be "evolve." If you're upgrading systems to Windows NT, use this option.

Starting Version Count (hex) specifies the highest version ID number for the Database. Usually, you will not need to change this value unless the database becomes corrupted and needs to start fresh.

Database Backup Path defines a local, non-network directory to which the WINS database will be backed up. This variable will be used along with automatic restore if the database is ever corrupted.

Maintaining the WINS Database

Now that you know the ins and outs on configuring replication partners, we'll give you the skinny on database control. The WINS Manager provides you with the tools you need to list, filter, and control name mappings.

As you now know, a NetBIOS name is 15 characters long, and up to 16 characters in total length. When reviewing the information list generated while showing the database mappings, you can determine what the 16th character is by examining the value in block brackets, located next to the NetBIOS name. Listed below are the five different types of entries possible for a registered name:

\\Computer-Name[00h] The registered name on the WINS client of the Workstation Service

\\Computer-Name[03h] The registered name on the WINS client of the Messenger Service

\\Computer-Name[20h] The registered name on the WINS client of the Server Service

\\User-Name[03h] The name of the user currently logged on to the computer, this name is used along with the messenger service for activities and communications like print notifications, net send, system events, etc. If a duplicate name is discovered because a user is logged on to more than one machine, only the first name will be registered.

\\Domain-Name[1Bh] This is the domain name as registered by the *Primary Domain Controller,* or *(PDC),* that's acting as the domain Master browser. It's useful for remote domain browsing. When prompted, a WINS server will produce the IP address of the system that registered the name.

Backing Up

Be a good scout—be prepared—back your stuff up! Doing so is the hallmark of the seasoned, "been there—done that," commemorative hat-wearing network professional. It is an aspect of the WINS database not to be ignored. Always keep a backup copy of all information entered when configuring the server. This backup becomes automatic after a 24 hour period lapses, and after a backup directory has been specified. To specify your backup directory, follow the steps in Exercise 8.8.

EXERCISE 8.8

Backing Up the WINS Database

1. From the WINS Manager Mapping menu, select Backup Database.

2. The Select Backup Directory dialog box appears.

3. Under Directories, select \%*SYSTEMROOT*%\SYSTEM32\WINS.

4. Choose OK.

5. Use the Registry Editor to open HKEY_LOCAL_MACHINE\SYSTEM\CurrentControlSet\Services\WINS.

6. On the registry menu, click Save Key.

7. In the Save Key dialog box, specify the path where you store backup versions of the WINS database file.

Restoration

Restoration ensures that reliable data is served. If the WINS server determines upon initialization that its data is corrupt, it will automatically revert to the backup. You can also manually force the WINS server to restore the database in two ways. The first way is by selecting Restore Database from the WINS manager mapping menu, and specifying the path where the backup directory is located. The second way is begun by deleting JET*.LOG, WINSTMP.MDB, and SYSTEM.MDB from the \%*SYSTEMROOT*%\SYSTEM32\WINS directory.

That done, proceed to copy SYSTEM.MDB from the Windows NT server distribution CD-ROM to the *%SYSTEMROOT%*\SYSTEM32\WINS directory. Finally, copy WINS.MDB from the backup directory to *%SYSTEMROOT%*\ SYSTEM32\WINS.

Compacting

This management function is executed by running the JETPACK.EXE utility. It should be run periodically when the database grows over 30MB in size to keep the database efficient. The size of the database depends on both the number and the type of entries in it. A unique or group entry uses only 50 to 70 bytes to record it, but an Internet group or multihomed entry will use a whopping 50 to 300 bytes depending on the number of IP addresses associated with it. On top of that, there are about 50 to 100 bytes of overhead needed to track time stamps and the other information that supports each entry. To compact a database, follow the steps in Exercise 8.9.

EXERCISE 8.9

Compacting the Database

1. Stop the WINS Server by selecting the Control Panel ➤ Services ➤ Windows Internet Name Service, or by typing **net stop WINS** at a command prompt.

2. Change to the WINS directory, *%SYSTEMROOT%*\SYSTEM32\ WINS, and run JETPACK WINS.MDB *TEMP_FILE*.MDB. Once JETPACK has completed compacting the database, the *TEMP_FILE* (regardless of name) will have its contents copied back to the WINS.MDB file, and will then be deleted.

3. Finally, restart the WINS server either by rebooting from Control Panel ➤ Services ➤ Windows Internet Name Service, or by typing **net start WINS** at a command prompt.

Below is a list of some of the files you'll be working with along with some information on how they perform in relation to the WINS server.

JET.LOG/JET*.LOG This file contains transaction log files which may be used by WINS to recover data if necessary.

SYSTEM.MDB This is a storage file that is used by the WINS server to track the structure of the database.

WINS.MDB This is the main WINS database file. It's the most important file you'll work with in the WINS directory. You'll most likely find yourself performing all maintenance operations with this file.

WINSTMP.MDB This temporary file is used and created internally by the WINS server. In the event of a crash, this file does not have to be removed.

Summary

The Windows Internet Name Service has an important advantage over DNS in NT 4.0 because WINS servers are dynamic; they're able to automatically add and change entries as needed. A WINS server acts as network support by intercepting the legions of name-query broadcasts and processing them internally, preventing these broadcasts from inundating the network and consuming precious bandwidth.

Key benefits to implementing WINS include:

- WINS servers are the first contact for name queries, and are most often able to satisfy them, so the time spent resolving a NetBIOS name is markedly reduced.

- Microsoft clients using WINS automatically register with the WINS server upon start-up, ensuring a current database better than any other resolution service.

- Because WINS is dynamic in nature, using a WINS server eliminates much of the tedious work normally associated with database maintenance.

- You can assign a second WINS server to a client for purposes of fault tolerance.

There aren't a lot of requirements placed on a WINS server, therefore, it can and should be added to any Windows NT server that is running TCP/IP with a static, non-DHCP-assigned IP address. If you're also running DHCP, the WINS server will only function with a reserved address—using the same subnet mask and default gateway each time. The problem with using DHCP is that each client must know the WINS server's IP address, which can become problematic if its address should change. There's no requirement for a WINS server to become a domain controller of any type.

Most configuration for the WINS server service settings are automatic. Communications become more complicated when systems configured as WINS clients need to talk to those that aren't. To ensure communication in a mixed environment, manual entries must be made to the WINS server. The only alternative to manually adding entries to the WINS server is to add them to the workstation's LMHOSTS file.

Unlike DHCP servers that don't communicate with each other, WINS servers can be configured to replicate their database entries, sharing them with each other so that all servers across the network have synchronous name information. When this feature has been configured, replication is automatically triggered any time the database changes. To function in this manner, the WINS server must be designated as either a push or pull partner. Push partners function by sending update notices to pull partners whenever changes are made, and pull partners function by sending out requests to push partners, asking them for entries more recent than their current listings when they want to update their database contents. You can set up the server as both push and pull to ensure possession of the most up-to-date WINS entries available.

It's very important to keep a backup copy of all information entered when configuring the server. This backup becomes automatic after a 24-hour period lapses, and after a backup directory has been specified.

Restoration ensures that reliable data is served. The compacting function is executed by running the JETPACK.EXE utility.

When considering the NT 4.0 TCP/IP test, you must understand how WINS replicates, how it works with other services like DHCP, and how to set and configure WINS in a multi-subnet network.

Review Questions

1. How many WINS servers are recommended for a network of 10,000 clients?

   A. 5

   B. 10

   C. 1

D. 2

E. 15

2. What are three benefits of a WINS server?

    A. Dynamic IP addressing.

    B. Reduces traffic.

    C. Can only be updated dynamically.

    D. Can resolve names across subnets. Internetwork and interdomain browsing capabilities without configuring and maintaining an LMHOSTS file at each computer.

3. How can a non-WINS client still use WINS for name resolution?

    A. By using broadcasts

    B. By using a proxy agent

    C. By using an LMHOSTS file

    D. Using a HOSTS table

    E. Using a DNS

4. How should you configure your WINS servers so users can resolve names across routers and non-WINS clients can use the WINS database to resolve names?

    A. Install a WINS server on each subnet.

    B. Install two WINS server, with each being a pull partner. Configure an LMHOSTS file on each WINS server.

    C. Install two WINS server, each as a pull server. Add static entries for the non-WINS clients.

    D. Install two WINS server, each as a push server. Add static entries for the non-WINS clients and a WINS proxy on each subnet.

5. You work at a large retail computer shop. A customer asks if a 386DX-25MHz system with 12MB of memory is enough to run the WINS service process. Is it? What should you ask of your customer before answering his question (besides his credit card number)? What suggestions should you make?

6. You are a network administrator for a computer manufacturer. Your company has a large network and needs to install WINS on it to help keep traffic down. You have a few OS/2 and UNIX computers that need to be registered in the WINS database. How do you do this?

7. You are installing two NT computers at your home office. After installing an NT Server running DHCP and WINS, you want to back up the WINS database. What are the steps to do this?

8. Situation: Your network has four Windows NT Server computers, 10 Windows NT Workstation computers, 80 Windows 95 computers, and 10 UNIX machines. All machines only run TCP/IP. Users move their computers around the office constantly from one subnet to another. The UNIX machines do not move and do not use NetBIOS. One NT Server is running DHCP with scopes configured for all subnets. All Microsoft Windows-based computers are configured as DHCP clients.

Required results:

- All computers on all subnets must be able to access each other by host name.

- All computers must be able to receive an IP address from the DHCP server.

Optional desired results:

- All UNIX hosts should be able to access any NT Server running FTP by its host name.

- All clients should be able to access any UNIX host running an FTP or Telnet daemon.

Proposed solution:

1. On the DHCP server, configure scopes with an exclusion range for the IP addresses of all UNIX computers.

2. Configure all routers to forward all DHCP broadcast to all subnets.

3. Install and configure a WINS server on the network.

4. Configure DHCP to supply all DHCP clients with the IP address of the WINS server.

5. Configure each Windows-based computer with a HOSTS file that contains entries for the UNIX computers.

Which results does the proposed solution produce?

A. The proposed solution produces the required results and produces both of the optional desired results.

B. The proposed solution produces the required results and produces only one of the optional desired results.

C. The proposed solution produces the required results but does not produce either of the optional desired results.

D. The proposed solution does not produce the required results.

9. Situation: Your network has four Windows NT Server computers, 10 Windows NT Workstation computers, 80 Windows 95 computers, and 10 UNIX machines. All machines only run TCP/IP. Users move their computers around the office constantly from one subnet to another. The UNIX machines do not move and do not use NetBIOS. One NT Server is running DHCP with scopes configured for all subnets. All Microsoft Windows-based computers are configured as DHCP clients.

Required results:

- All computers on all subnets must be able to access each other by host name.

- All computers must be able to receive an IP address from the DHCP server.

Optional desired results:

- All UNIX hosts should be able to access any NT Server running FTP by its host name.

- All clients should be able to access any UNIX host running an FTP or Telnet daemon.

Proposed solution:

1. Configure all routers to forward all DHCP broadcast to all subnets.

2. Install and configure a WINS server on the network.

3. Configure DHCP to supply all DHCP clients with the IP address of the WINS server.

Which results does the proposed solution produce?

A. The proposed solution produces the required results and produces both of the optional desired results.

B. The proposed solution produces the required results and produces only one of the optional desired results.

C. The proposed solution produces the required results but does not produce either of the optional desired results.

D. The proposed solution does not produce the required results.

10. **Situation:** You have five subnets and you want to install two DHCP servers on different subnets to assign IP addresses to Microsoft-based computers on the network.

Required results:

- The DHCP servers must be able to act as a backup if one server fails.

Optional desired results:

- Each server must get the same address each time it is started.

- The WINS and DNS server addresses must be provided to all DHCP clients.

Proposed solution:

1. Install the DHCP Relay Agent on each subnet.

2. Create a client reservation for each Windows NT server computer.

3. Define one scope on the first NT Server for each subnet. In each scope, define the range of IP addresses to be used on that subnet. Duplicate these settings on the other DHCP server.

Which results does the proposed solution produce?

A. The proposed solution produces the required results and produces both of the optional desired results.

B. The proposed solution produces the required results and produces only one of the optional desired results.

C. The proposed solution produces the required results but does not produce either of the optional desired results.

D. The proposed solution does not produce the required results.

11. Which name resolution mode should you specify on your DHCP Server if you want all clients to use WINS for name resolution before they use broadcasts?

A. B-node

B. P-node

C. M-mode

D. H-node

12. Which service must you use if you want your computers to dynamically resolve names through your complex intranetwork?

A. LMHOSTS

B. DNS

C. FTP

D. Telnet

E. WINS

13. How can your Windows workstations communicate by host name to a UNIX server?

A. Add a LMHOSTS file on the UNIX computer.

B. Add a static mapping for the name and IP address of the UNIX computer to the WINS database.

C. Configure the DNS Server address on the WINS server.

D. Create a TCP/IP session by Telnetting into the UNIX computer from the WINS server.

14. Which type of static entry must you add in your WINS database for a workstation with multiple NIC cards?

A. Unique

B. Group

C. Domain name

D. Internet group

E. Multihomed

15. How do you have two WINS servers update each others database dynamically?

A. Add LMHOSTS to each server.

B. Configure each WINS server as a WINS client of the other WINS server.

C. Configure a HOSTS table on each WINS Server.

D. Configure each WINS server both as a push partner and as a pull partner of the other WINS server.

16. What do you need to configure on your DHCP server for DHCP clients to resolve NetBIOS names dynamically? (Choose all that apply.)

A. The IP address of the WINS Server

B. The IP address of the DNS Server

C. The NetBIOS scope ID

D. The NetBIOS name resolution mode

17. Which service should you use so the computers on your network can resolve NetBIOS names without any administrative work?

A. TELNET

B. DNS

C. FTP

D. HOSTS

E. WINS

18. You have multiple subnets with a BDC on each subnet. What service should you use to allow all clients to be able to browse all subnets?

A. TELNET

B. DNS

C. FTP

D. LMHOSTS

E. WINS

19. You want all your Windows 95 clients to be able to resolve computer names without a HOSTS file. Which service should you use?

A. LMHOSTS

B. DNS

C. FTP

D. TELNET

E. WINS

20. What type of entries should you use to add entries into your WINS database for your UNIX computers?

A. Unique

B. Group

C. Domain name

D. Internet group

E. Multihomed

CHAPTER

9

DNS

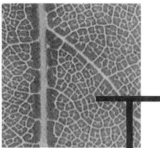

The onset of Active Directory for the Windows NT operating system is coming to us soon in Windows NT 5.0, and the Domain Name System (DNS) server will be much more important than it was in any prior Windows NT release. Because of this, installing and designing effective DNS implementations today will help tremendously when tomorrow's need to migrate to the next version of Windows NT materializes.

The use of the DNS service in the Microsoft Windows NT 4 operating system is currently optional. The DNS service that ships with Windows NT 4 is there if you want to use it, but there's presently nothing in Windows NT that requires you to do so. If you opt to use DNS, this chapter will show you how to do just that—but it won't stop there. Our focus will be on how best to design your DNS infrastructure in preparation for that imminent release of Windows NT Active Directory.

This chapter addresses installing and configuring DNS, integrating DNS and WINS, and using the DNS diagnostic tool NSLOOKUP.

This chapter will cover:

- Describing the structure and architecture that make up the domain name system

- Defining the domain name system (DNS) components

- Explaining how DNS is used to resolve names and IP addresses

- Describing the contents of the DNS database files

- Registering a DNS server with the parent domain

Where Did DNS Come From?

In the late '70s there were only a handful of networked computers, and all of the computer name-to-address mappings were contained in a single file called HOSTS. This was stored at the Stanford Research Institute's Network Information Center (SRI-NIC). Whenever anybody wanted to update their HOSTS file, they would download the latest HOSTS file from Stanford. This actually worked for a while, until more computers got on the network and managing the HOSTS file became too difficult. Bandwidth being pretty limited back then, Stanford got overloaded. One of the biggest problems centered around the HOSTS file being a flat name structure, requiring all computers across the whole Internet to have a unique name. The ARPNET was created to find the solution to this problem (along with a few others), which led to DNS, a distributed database using a hierarchical naming structure.

According to Dr. Paul Mockapetris, principal designer of DNS, the original design goal for DNS was to replace this cumbersome, singularly-administered HOSTS file with a lightweight, distributed database that would allow for hierarchical name space, distribution of administration, extensive data types, virtually unlimited database size, and reasonable performance.

The Domain Name System (DNS) is a set of protocols and services on a TCP/IP network that allows users of the network to utilize hierarchical, user-friendly names when looking for other hosts (computers) instead of having to remember and use their IP addresses. This system is used extensively on the Internet and in many private enterprises today. If you've used a Web browser, Telnet application, FTP utility, or other similar TCP/IP utilities on the Internet, then you have probably used a DNS server.

The DNS protocol's best-known function is mapping user-friendly names to IP addresses. For example, suppose the FTP site at Microsoft had an IP address of 157.55.100.1. Most people would reach this computer by specifying **ftp.microsoft.com** instead of its human being–alienating IP address. Besides being easier to remember, the name is more reliable. The numeric address could change for any number of reasons, but that name can remain in spite of the change.

The most popular implementation of the DNS protocol BIND was originally developed at Berkeley for the 4.3 BSD UNIX operating system. The name BIND stands for Berkeley Internet Name Domain. The primary specifications for DNS are defined in Requests for Comments (RFCs) 974, 1034, and 1035.

How DNS Works

DNS's job is to translate computer names into IP addresses. This is done by a hierarchical client/server-based distributed database management system. DNS works at the Application layer of the OSI reference model and uses TCP and UDP at the Transport layer.

The purpose of the DNS database is to translate computer names into IP addresses. In the DNS, the clients are called resolvers and servers are called name servers.

The domain name system is analogous to a telephone book. The user looks up the name of the person or organization that he wants to contact and cross-references the name to a telephone number. Similarly, a host computer contacts the name of a computer and a domain name server cross-references the name to an IP address.

Resolvers first send UDP queries to servers for increased performance and resort to TCP only if truncation of the returned data occurs.

Resolvers

The function of the resolvers is to pass name requests between applications and name servers. The name request contains a query. For example, the query might ask for the IP address of a WWW site. The resolver is often built into the application or is running on the host computer as a library routine.

Name Servers

Name servers take name requests from resolvers and resolve computer or domain names to IP addresses. If the name server is not able to resolve the request, it may forward the request to a name server that can resolve it. The name servers are grouped into different levels that are called domains.

Microsoft DNS

All right. That said, what's up with Microsoft DNS anyway, and why should you use it? Well, we'll start by telling you what it's not. First of all, know that the Microsoft DNS server isn't a port of the Berkeley BIND code. The Big M made up its collective mind not to port the BIND code in favor of writing their very own fully RFC-compliant code that's compatible with BIND instead. Why? Because, ever mindful of growth, they were trying to make it easy for themselves to add stuff like performance enhancements to it later. But fear not, the DNS server service in Windows NT 4 has been totally rewritten—it's not just the fumigated version—and rest assured that RFC compliance has been viciously tested. Yes folks, it *all* works.

Microsoft ✓ **Exam Objective**

Given a scenario, select the appropriate services to install when using Microsoft TCP/IP on a Microsoft Windows NT Server computer.

So what exactly *is* the Microsoft DNS server? Well, in accordance with the whole RFC thing, if an RFC-required feature isn't found in the Microsoft DNS product, it's considered a bug, so, primarily, the DNS server in Windows NT 4 is an RFC-compliant implementation of DNS. Because of this, it not only sustains all standard resource record types, it both creates and uses standard DNS zone files. Additionally, it can interoperate with other DNS servers and includes the DNS diagnostic utility NSLOOKUP—the definite article and standard of standards. Microsoft DNS doesn't stop there either—it goes above and beyond what's specified in RFCs with features like DNS Manager, a graphical administration utility that greatly eases administrative burdens, and dynamic updates through tight integration with WINS.

Let's expand on that…With Microsoft's DNS, network admininstrators now have freedom of choice—you have the option to turn off traditional DNS systems and choose the Microsoft Windows NT implementation instead. This gives you the ability to remove static entries for the Microsoft-based clients in the traditional DNS server zone files and opt for the WINS/DNS dynamic integration. Here's what we mean: Suppose you have a non–Microsoft-based client that wants to get out to a Web page on some HTTP server that's DHCP/WINS enabled. All that client would have to do is query the DNS server. That server then queries WINS, and the name's resolved and returned to the client. Because of dynamic IP addressing, before WINS integration you couldn't reliably resolve that name—nice touch, huh!

Microsoft DNS supports RFCs 1033, 1034, 1035, 1101, 1123, 1183 and 1536.

A Closer Look at DNS

Let's go back to DNS for a minute. A Domain Name System is composed of a distributed database of names that establish a logical tree structure called the *domain name space*. Each node, or domain, in that space is named and can contain subdomains. Domains and subdomains are grouped into zones to allow for distributed administration of the name space (we'll talk about zones more in a bit). The domain name identifies the domain's position in the logical DNS hierarchy in relation to its parent domain by separating each branch of the tree with a period (.). Figure 9.1 shows a few of the top-level domains, where the Microsoft domain fits, and a host called Tigger within the microsoft.com domain. If someone wanted to contact that host, they would use the fully-qualified domain name (FQDN) tigger.microsoft.com.

FIGURE 9.1

A DNS Hierarchy

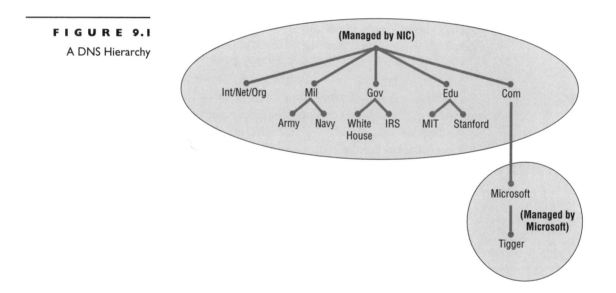

DNS Servers and the Internet

The root of the DNS database on the Internet is managed by the Internet Network Information Center (http://www.internic.com). The top-level domains were assigned organizationally, and by country. These domain names follow the International Standard 3166. Two-letter and three-letter abbreviations are used for countries, and various abbreviations are reserved for use by organizations, as shown in the following examples.

Three-Letter DNS Domain Names	Type of Organization
com	Commercial (for example, globalnet.com for Globalnet System Solutions Corporation)
edu	Educational (for example, mit.edu for Massachusetts Institute of Technology)
gov	Government (for example, whitehouse.gov for the White House in Washington, D.C.)
int	International organizations (for example, nato.int for NATO)
mil	Military operations (for example, army.mil for the Army)
net	Networking organizations (for example, nsf.net for NSFNET)
org	Noncommercial organizations (for example, fidonet.org for FidoNet)

Two-Letter DNS Domain Names	Type of Organization
de	Germany (Deutschland)
it	Italy
nz	New Zealand
us	United States

The Skinny on Domains

Each node in the DNS database tree, along with all the nodes below it, is called a *domain*. Domains can contain both hosts (computers) and other domains (subdomains). For example, the Microsoft domain microsoft.com could contain computers such as ftp.microsoft.com and subdomains such as sales.microsoft.com, which could and most likely do contain hosts such as appserver.sales.microsoft.com.

In general, domain names and host names have restrictions in their naming which only allow the use of characters a-z, A-Z, 0-9, and - (dash or minus sign). The use of characters such as the / (slash), . (period), and _ (underscore) is not allowed. We've had many a problem with clients creatively naming their hosts Server_1 and Server_2. These unfortunately-named NT Servers couldn't be registered with DNS.

Zones

Finally…it's time to enter the DNS Zone. A *zone* isn't some spaced-out individual, it's a portion of the DNS namespace whose database records exist and are managed in a particular zone file. A single DNS server can be configured to manage one or multiple zone files. Each zone is anchored at a specific domain node—referred to as the zone's root domain. Zone files don't necessarily contain the complete tree (that is, all subdomains) under the zone's root domain. For a comparison of domains and zones, take a look at Figure 9.2.

FIGURE 9.2

Domains and zones

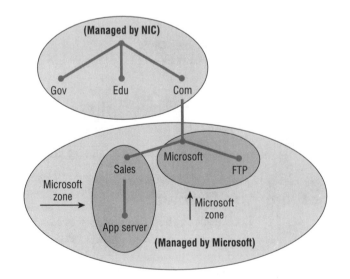

What are you looking at? Well, in this example, microsoft.com is a domain, but the entire domain isn't controlled by one zone file. Part of the domain is actually broken off into a separate zone file for sales.microsoft.com. Breaking up domains across multiple zone files may indeed be necessary to either distribute management of the domain to different groups, or to ensure efficiencies in data replication—zone transfers—which will be discussed soon.

Try not to confuse a zone with a domain. A zone is a physical file composed of resource records that defines a group of domains. A domain is a node in the DNS namespace and all subdomains below it.

Name Servers

DNS servers store information about the domain namespace and are referred to as name servers. Name servers generally have one or more zones for which they are responsible. The name server is then predictably said to have *authority* for those zones.

When you configure a DNS name server—as we shall soon see with the "NS" record—you're essentially telling it who all of the other DNS name servers are in the same domain.

Primary, Secondary, Master, and Caching-Only Servers

A *primary name server* is a name server that gets the data for its zones from local files. Changes to a zone, such as added domains or hosts, are carried out at the primary name server.

Secondary name servers get the data for their zones from another name server across the network that's the specific zone's authority. The process of obtaining this zone information—the database file—across the network is referred to as a zone transfer.

There are three reasons to have *secondary servers* within an enterprise network. Those reasons are:

> **Redundancy** Though this is usually something to avoid, it's prudent here. You need at least two DNS name servers serving each zone—a primary, and at least one secondary for (you guessed it) fault tolerance. As is true for other scenarios where fault tolerance is your goal, your strategic machines involved should be as independent as possible—that is, on different networks.

Remote locations You should also have secondary servers (or other primary servers for subdomains) in remote locations that have a large number of clients. You wouldn't want a whole legion of clients having to communicate across slow links for name resolution, now would you?

Reduce load on the primary Having secondary servers present reduces the load on your primary server.

Because information for each zone is stored in separate files, this primary or secondary designation is defined at a zone level. In other words, a given name server could be a primary name server for some zones and a secondary name server for others.

When defining a zone on a name server as a secondary, you must designate a name server from which it will obtain that zone information. The source of zone information for a secondary name server in a DNS hierarchy is referred to as a *master name server*, and it can either be a primary or secondary name server for the requested zone. When a secondary name server starts up, it contacts its master name server and initiates a zone transfer with it.

Use secondary servers as master servers when the primary is overloaded, or when there is a more efficient network path between "secondary to secondary" versus "secondary to primary."

Forwarders and Slaves

When a DNS name server receives a DNS request, it attempts to locate the requested information within its own zone files. If this fails because that server isn't authoritative for the domain requested, it must then communicate with other DNS name servers to resolve the request. Since, on a globally connected network, a DNS resolution request outside a local zone typically requires interaction with DNS name servers located outside of the company on the public Internet, it's a good idea to selectively enable specific DNS name servers in your company for this type of wide-area communication.

To address this issue, DNS allows for the concept of *forwarders*—specific DNS name servers selected to carry out wide-area communications across the Internet. All other DNS name servers within the company are configured with the IP addresses of the DNS name servers designated as forwarders to use them for this purpose. You do this configuration on a per server basis, not a per zone basis!

When a server that's configured to use forwarders receives a DNS request that it's unable to resolve through its own zone files, it passes the request along to one of the designated forwarders. The forwarder then carries out whatever communication is necessary to resolve the request, and returns the results to the requesting server, which, in turn, sends back the results to the original requester. If the forwarder is unable to resolve the query, the DNS server attempts to resolve the query on its own as it normally would.

Slaves are DNS servers that have been configured to use forwarders and have also been configured to return a failure message if the forwarder is unable to resolve the request. Slaves make no attempt to contact other name servers if the forwarder is unable to satisfy the request.

Master Name Server

When you define a zone on a name server as a secondary zone, you must designate another name server from which to obtain the zone information. The source of zone information for a secondary name server in a DNS hierarchy is referred to as a master name server. A master name server can be either a primary or secondary name server for the requested zone. When a secondary name server starts up, it contacts its master name server and initiates a zone transfer with that server.

Caching-Only Servers

Although all DNS name servers cache queries that they've resolved, *caching-only servers* are DNS name servers whose only job is to perform queries, cache the answers, and return the results—they aren't authoritative for any domains, and only contain information which they have cached while resolving queries.

When trying to determine when to use such a server, bear in mind that when these servers start up initially, they possess no cached information because they have to build up a store of it over time as they service requests. However, if you're dealing with a slow link between sites, there's much less traffic sent across that link because these servers don't perform zone transfers.

Name Resolution

There are three types of queries that a client can make to a DNS server: *recursive, iterative,* and *inverse.* During our little talk on name resolution, keep in mind that a DNS server can be a client to another DNS server at the same time.

Recursive Queries

In a recursive query, the queried name server is petitioned to respond with the requested data, or with an error stating either that the data of the requested type or the domain name specified doesn't exist. The name server *cannot* just refer the querier to a different name server.

Queries of this type are typically done by a DNS client (a resolver) to a DNS server. Also, if a DNS server is configured to use a forwarder, the request from this DNS server to its forwarder will be a recursive query.

Iterative Queries

In an iterative query, the queried name server gives back the best answer it currently has to the querier. This type of query is typically sent by a DNS server to other DNS servers, and happens after it's received a recursive query from a resolver.

Figure 9.3 demonstrates an example of both recursive and iterative queries. A client within the Microsoft Corporation is querying its DNS server for the IP address for www.whitehouse.gov.

1. The resolver sends a recursive DNS query to its local DNS server asking for the IP address of www.whitehouse.gov. The local name server is responsible for resolving the name and cannot refer the resolver to another name server.

2. The local name server checks its zones and finds no zones corresponding to the requested domain name.

3. The root name server has authority for the root domain and will reply with the IP address of a name server for the gov top-level domain.

4. The local name server sends an iterative query for www.whitehouse.gov to the gov name server.

5. The gov name server replies with the IP address of the name server servicing the whitehouse.gov domain.

6. The local name server sends an iterative query for www.whitehouse.gov to the whitehouse.gov name server.

7. The whitehouse.gov name server replies with the IP address corresponding to www.whitehouse.gov.

8. The local name server sends the IP address of www.whitehouse.gov back to the original resolver.

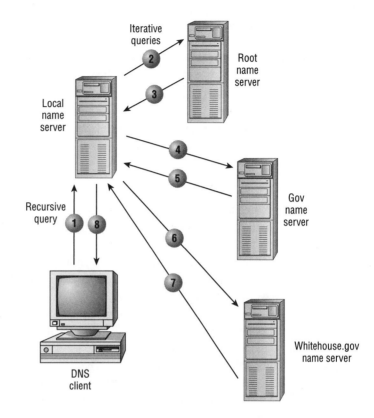

FIGURE 9.3

Recursive and iterative queries

Inverse Queries

Instead of supplying a name and then asking for an IP address, the client needs to first provide the IP address before it asks for the name. Since there's no direct correlation in the DNS name space between the domain names and the associated IP addresses they contain, only a thorough search of all domains could guarantee striking gold.

A special domain in-addr.arpa in the DNS name space was created to help get us all through this little catch. Nodes in the in-addr.arpa domain are named after the numbers in the dotted-octet representation of IP addresses, but because IP addresses get more specific from left to right, and domain names get less specific from left to right, the order of IP address octets must be reversed when building the in-addr.arpa tree. With this arrangement, administration of lower limbs of the DNS in-addr.arpa tree can be given to companies as they are assigned their Class A, B, or C subnet address.

Once the domain tree is built into the DNS database, a special pointer record is added to associate the IP addresses to the corresponding host names. In other words, to find a host name for the IP address 157.55.89.2, the resolver would query the DNS server for a pointer record for 2.89.55.157 .in-addr.arpa. If this IP address was outside the local domain, the DNS server would start at the root and sequentially resolve the domain nodes until arriving at 89.55.157.in-addr.arpa which should contain the resource PTR record for 2 (that is 157.55.89.2).

Caching and Time to Live

When a name server is processing a recursive query, it may be required to send out several queries to find the definitive answer. The name server caches all the received information during this process for a period of time specified in the returned data known as the time to live (TTL). Its duration is set by the name server administrator of the zone that contains the data. If yours is a volatile network that changes a lot, smaller TTL values will help ensure that data about your domain is more consistent across that network. But there's a catch—teensy TTLs also increase the load on your name server. Once data is cached by a DNS server, it starts decreasing the TTL (that is, begins a countdown) from its original value so it'll know when to flush the data from its cache. If a query comes in that can be satisfied by this cached data, the TTL that's returned with it equals the current amount of time left before flush time. Client resolvers also have data caches and honor the TTL value so that they too know when to flush.

DNS Files

Most DNS systems must be configured by editing text files, but as hinted at before, with Microsoft DNS, as with all Microsoft Windows-based products, there's a very cool interface to make that experience less odious than in times past. The new administration interface makes it a lot easier to configure both local and remote Microsoft DNS servers, and the DNS administrative tool configures the RFC-compatible text files for you. Time to pop that cork!

Even though the spiffy graphical user interface gives you the ability to modify the DNS files without an editor, you should still know the makeup of the DNS system configuration files. In RFC-compliant DNS systems, several files define the DNS system configuration and database. These files include the database, cache, reverse lookup, and 127 reverse lookup files. These files, explained in detail in the coming section, also exist in the Windows NT 4 DNS, and they too are RFC compliant.

The Database File (zone.dns)

A database file or zone file is the file which contains the *resource records* for the part of the domain for which the zone's responsible. Some of the common resource records are discussed below. Windows NT 4 supplies a file as a template to work with called PLACE.DNS. It's wise to edit and rename this file the same as the zone it represents before using it on a production DNS server, because it's the file that'll be replicated between masters and secondaries.

The Start of Authority

The first record in any database file is the Start of Authority (SOA) Record. The SOA defines the general parameters for the DNS zone. The following is an example of the parameters:

```
IN SOA <source host> <contact e-mail> <ser. no.> <refresh time>
<retry time> <expiration time> <TTL>
```

source host	The host on which this file is maintained
contact e-mail	The Internet e-mail address for the person responsible for this domain's database file
serial number	The "version number" of this database file that should increase each time the database file is changed
refresh time	The elapsed time (in seconds) that a secondary server will wait between checks to its master server to see if the database file has changed, and a zone transfer should be requested
retry time	The elapsed time (in seconds) that a secondary server will wait before retrying a failed zone transfer
expiration time	The elapsed time (in seconds) that a secondary server will keep trying to download a zone. After this time limit expires, the old zone information will be discarded.
time to live	The elapsed time (in seconds) that a DNS server is allowed to cache any resource records from this database file. This is the value that is sent out with all query responses from this zone file when the individual resource record doesn't contain an overriding value.

In order for a resource record to span a line in a database file, parentheses must enclose the line breaks.

In a zone file, the @ symbol represents the root domain of the zone. The "IN" in the following records is the class of data. It stands for Internet. Other classes exist, but none of them are currently in widespread use.

Any domain name in the database file which is not terminated with a period will have the root domain appended to the end.

Example:

```
@ IN SOA nameserver1.globalnet.com.todd.globalnet.com. (

1; serial number

10800; refresh [3 hours]

3600; retry [1hour]

604800; expire [7 days]

86400 ); time to live [1 day]
```

Setting the server's refresh interval means creating a balance between data consistency (accuracy of your data) and your network's load.

The Name Server Record

This lists the name servers for this domain, allowing other name servers to look up names in your domain. A database file may contain more than one name server record. The following is an example:

```
<domain> IN NS <nameserver host >
```

Example:

```
@ IN NS nameserver2.globalnet.com.

@ IN NS nameserver3.globalnet.com.
```

The Mail Exchange Record

This record tells us what host processes mail for this domain. If multiple mail exchange records exist, the resolver will attempt to contact the mail servers in order of preference from lowest value (highest priority) to highest value (lowest priority). By using the example records that follow, mail addressed to todd@globalnet.com is delivered to todd@mailserver0.globalnet.com first, if possible, and then to todd@mailserver1.globalnet.com if mailserver0 is unavailable.

```
<domain> IN MX <preference> <mailserver host>
```

Example:

```
@  IN MX 1 mailserver0
```

```
@  IN MX 2 mailserver1
```

The Host Record

A host record is used to statically associate hosts names to IP addresses within a zone. It should contain entries for all hosts that require static mappings, including workstations, name servers, mail servers, etc. These are the records that make up most of the database file when static records are used.

```
<host name> IN A <ip address of host>
```

Example:

```
tigger          IN   A   157.55.89.102

nameserver2     IN   A   157.55.89.12

mailserver1     IN   A   157.55.89.15
```

The Local Host Record

A local host record allows lookups for localhost.mmco.com to return 127.0.0.1.

```
localhost IN A 127.0.0.1
```

The CNAME Record

These records are sometimes called *aliases* but are technically referred to as *canonical name* (*CNAME*) entries. These records allow you to use more than one name to point to a single host.

Using canonical names makes it nice 'n easy to do stuff like host both an FTP server and a Web server on the same machine.

```
<host alias name> IN CNAME <host name>
```

Example:

Assume that www.globalnet.com and ftp.globalnet.com are on the same machine. Your zone file would then have the following entries in it, and look something like:

```
FileServer1    IN    A        157.55.89.41

FTP            IN    CNAME    FileServer1

www            IN    CNAME    FileServer1
```

But what if you decide to move the FTP server service away from the Web service? Well, all you'd have to do is change the CNAME in the DNS server for FTP, and add an address record for the new server like this:

```
FTP            IN    CNAME    FileServer2

FileServer2    IN    A        157.55.89.42
```

The Cache File (cache.dns)

The cache file contains host information needed to resolve names outside the authoritative domains, and contains names and addresses of root name servers. For users on the Internet, the default file provided with the Microsoft DNS service should suffice. For installations *not* connected to the Internet, the file should be replaced to contain the authoritative name servers for the root of your private network.

For a current Internet cache file see:

```
ftp://rs.internic.net/domain/named.cache
```

Example:

```
; DNS CACHE FILE

;

; Initial cache data for root domain servers.

;

; YOU SHOULD CHANGE:

; -Nothing if connected to the Internet. Edit this file only when
```

```
;   update root name server list is released.

;   OR

; -If NOT connected to the Internet, remove these records and
replace

;   with NS and A records for the DNS server authoritative for the

;   root domain at your site.

; Internet root name server records:

; last update: Sep 1, 1995

; related version of root zone: 1995090100

;

; formerly NS.INTERNIC.NET

   . 3600000 IN NS A.ROOT-SERVERS.NET.

A.ROOT-SERVERS.NET. 3600000 A 198.41.0.4

; formerly NS1.ISI.EDU

   . 3600000 NS B.ROOT-SERVERS.NET.

B.ROOT-SERVERS.NET. 3600000 A 128.9.0.107

; formerly C.PSI.NET

   . 3600000 NS C.ROOT-SERVERS.NET.

C.ROOT-SERVERS.NET. 3600000 A 192.33.4.12

; formerly TERP.UMD.EDU

  . 3600000 NS D.ROOT-SERVERS.NET.

D.ROOT-SERVERS.NET. 3600000 A 128.8.10.90

; formerly NS.NASA.GOV

   . 3600000 NS E.ROOT-SERVERS.NET.

E.ROOT-SERVERS.NET. 3600000 A 192.203.230.10

; formerly NS.ISC.ORG

   . 3600000 NS F.ROOT-SERVERS.NET.
```

```
F.ROOT-SERVERS.NET. 3600000 A 39.13.229.241

; formerly NS.NIC.DDN.MIL

   . 3600000 NS G.ROOT-SERVERS.NET.

G.ROOT-SERVERS.NET. 3600000 A 192.112.36.4

; formerly AOS.ARL.ARMY.MIL

   . 3600000 NS H.ROOT-SERVERS.NET.

; End of File
```

The Reverse Lookup File

This is a database file used for reverse lookups in particular IP DNS zones of host names when supplied with the IP numbers. The reverse lookup file allows a resolver to provide an IP address and request a matching host name. It contains SOA and name server records similar to other DNS database zone files, plus pointer records.

This DNS reverse-lookup capability is an important one because some applications provide a way to implement security based on the connecting host names. What does this mean? Well, if a client tries to link to a Network File System (NFS) volume with this security arrangement, the NFS server would then contact the DNS server, and do a reverse-name lookup on the client's IP address. If the host name returned by the DNS server isn't in the access list for the NFS volume, or if the host name isn't found by DNS, then the NFS mount request would be denied. This reverse-lookup capability is often used for troubleshooting reasons as well, but we're not going to go there quite yet.

Here are a couple example zones for different IP class networks.
Example Class C zone:

```
100.89.192.in-addr.arpa
```

Example Class B zone:

```
55.157.in-addr.arpa
```

The Pointer Record

Pointer records provide a static mapping of IP addresses to host names within a reverse-lookup zone. IP numbers are written in backward order and in-addr .arpa are appended to the end, creating the pointer record. As an example, looking up the name for 157.55.89.51 requires a pointer record (PTR) query for the name 51.89.55.157.in-addr.arpa.

```
<ip reverse domain name> IN PTR <host name>
```

Example:

```
51.89.55.157.in-addr.arpa. IN PTR mailserver1.mmco.com.
```

The Reverse Lookup File (Arpa-127.rev)

This is yet another database file. It's for the 127.in-addr.arpa domain, and used for reverse lookups of IP numbers in the 127 network, such as localhost. For example, if your network is in the Class C network address 193.128.152.0, then this file will be called 152.128.193.in-addr.arpa. The only things in this file that change are the SOA and NS records.

The Boot File

Although the boot file isn't actually defined in RFCs, and isn't needed in order to be RFC compliant, it is described here. We wanted to be thorough. This file is actually a part of the BIND specific implementation of DNS. Microsoft DNS can be configured to use a boot file if you're going to administer it through changes to the text files instead of using the DNS Administrator GUI.

The BIND boot file controls the startup behavior of the DNS server. Commands must start at the beginning of a line, and no spaces may precede commands. Recognized commands are: directory, cache, primary and secondary. The syntax for this file is as follows:

Directory Command   Specifies a directory where other files referred to in the boot file can be found.

```
directory <directory>
```

Example:

```
directory c:\winnt\system32\dns
```

Cache Command   Specifies a file used to help the DNS service contact name servers for the root domain. This command and the file it refers to *must* be present. A cache file suitable for use on the Internet is provided with Windows NT 4.

```
cache .<filename>
```

Example:

```
cache.cache
```

Primary Command   Specifies a domain for which this name server is authoritative, and a database file that contains the resource records for that domain (that is, zone file). Multiple primary command records could exist in the boot file.

```
primary <domain> <filename>
```

Example:

```
primary globalnet.com globalnet.dns
```

```
primary sales.globalnet.com sales.dns
```

Secondary Command   Specifies a domain for which this name server is authoritative, and a list of master server IP addresses from which to attempt downloading the zone information—rather than reading it from a file. It also defines the name of the local file for caching this zone. Multiple secondary command records could exist in the boot file.

```
secondary <domain> <hostlist> <local filename>
```

Example:

```
secondary test.globalnet.com 157.55.89.100 test.dns
```

Microsoft DNS Server

As you already know, Microsoft DNS is an RFC-compliant DNS server. It can create and use standard DNS zone files and supports all standard resource record types. It can also interoperate with non-Microsoft DNS servers and includes the DNS diagnostic tool NSLOOKUP. Microsoft DNS implements several features such as dynamic update through tight integration with WINS and easy administration through the graphical administration utility called DNS Manager.

Microsoft ✔ ***Exam*** ***Objective***

Install and configure the Microsoft DNS Server service on a Windows NT Server computer.

• Integrate DNS with other name servers.
• Connect a DNS server to a DNS root server.
• Configure DNS server roles.

Installing Microsoft DNS Server

Before we start our first exercise in Chapter 9, make sure your NT Server TCP/IP protocol is configured correctly. The DNS Server service obtains the default settings for the host name and domain name from Microsoft TCP/IP Properties. It creates default SOA, A, and NS records based on the specified domain name and host name. If the host name and domain name is not specified, then only the SOA record is created.

Exercise 9.1 will help you install DNS on your NT Server.

You should install the latest service packs for your NT Server. Remember to reinstall the service pack after installing any server services.

Administrating the DNS Server

To administrate and configure the NT DNS Server, run DNS Manager. Because the DNS server has no initial information about a user's network, the DNS server installs as a caching-only name server for the Internet. This means that the DNS server contains only information on the Internet root servers.

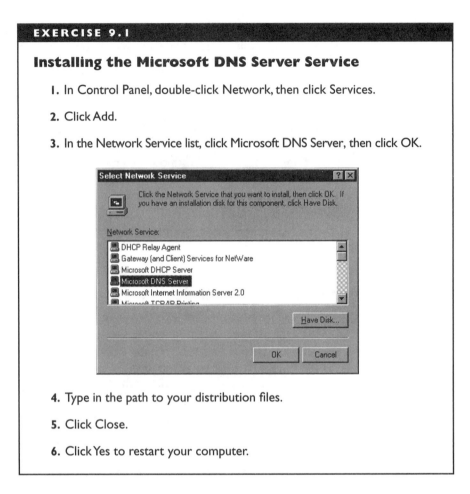

EXERCISE 9.1

Installing the Microsoft DNS Server Service

1. In Control Panel, double-click Network, then click Services.

2. Click Add.

3. In the Network Service list, click Microsoft DNS Server, then click OK.

4. Type in the path to your distribution files.

5. Click Close.

6. Click Yes to restart your computer.

For most DNS server configurations, additional information must be supplied to obtain the desired operation. For example:

Interfaces Specifies which interfaces DNS operates over on a multi-homed computer. By default, all interfaces are used.

Forwarders Configures your server to use another name server as a forwarder. The name server can also be configured as a slave to the forwarder.

Boot Method Displays which boot method the name server is using, either from the Registry or from the data files.

Manually Configuring DNS

The DNS server can be configured manually by editing files in the default installation path \%*SYSTEMROOT*%\SYSTEM32\DNS. Administration is identical to administration in traditional DNS. These files can be modified using a text editor. The DNS service must then be stopped and restarted.

Adding DNS Domains and Zones

The first thing you need to do is to determine the hierarchy for your DNS domains and zones. Once the domain and zone information has been determined, this must be entered into the DNS configuration using DNS manager. Let's start by adding the primary zone.

Exercise 9.2 will show you how to create a Primary zone in your DNS server.

EXERCISE 9.2

Adding a Primary Zone

1. Open the DNS Manager by going to Start ➢ Programs ➢ Administrative Tools ➢ Common ➢ DNS.

2. After DNS Manager opens, highlight Server List, go to the DNS menu, and choose New Server.

EXERCISE 9.2 (CONTINUED FROM PREVIOUS PAGE)

3. Enter the name or IP address of the DNS server to be added to the list, then click OK.

4. The server shows up under the Server List.

5. Right-click your computer name, and click New Zone.

6. Click Primary, then click Next.

Creating new zone for 150.150.29.215

Zone Type

- ⦿ Primary
- ○ Secondary:
  - Zone:
  - Server:

< Back   Next >   Cancel

7. In the Zone Name box, type your zone name.

8. Press the TAB key. Notice the zone GLOBALNET.COM.DNS is automatically entered in the Zone File box.

Creating new zone for 150.150.29.215

Zone Info

Zone Name: globalnet.com

Zone File: globalnet.com.dns

Enter the name of the zone and a name for its database.

< Back   Next >   Cancel

EXERCISE 9.2 (CONTINUED FROM PREVIOUS PAGE)

9. Click Next, then click Finish. Notice that the NS and SOA entries have been added.

10. Click the zone name, then click the DNS menu.

11. Click Properties.

12. Click the Notify tab.

```
Zone Properties - globalnet.com                    [?][X]

 General | SOA Record | Notify | WINS Lookup |

  ┌ Notify List ─────────────────────────────────────┐
  │ ┌──────────────────┐        ┌─────────┐          │
  │ │ ▌   .    .    .   │        │   Add   │          │
  │ └──────────────────┘        └─────────┘          │
  │ ┌──────────────────┐        ┌─────────┐          │
  │ │ 150.150.28.215   │        │ Remove  │          │
  │ │                  │        └─────────┘          │
  │ │                  │                             │
  │ │                  │                             │
  │ │                  │                             │
  │ └──────────────────┘                             │
  │                                                  │
  │ ☐ Only Allow Access From Secondaries Included on Notify List │
  └──────────────────────────────────────────────────┘

                            ┌──────┐   ┌────────┐
                            │  OK  │   │ Cancel │
                            └──────┘   └────────┘
```

13. In the Notify list box, type the IP address of the secondary DNS server for your domain (if you have one).

14. Click Add.

15. Click OK.

Adding Subdomains

After you have added all your zones to the server, subdomains under the zones can be added.

Exercise 9.3 will take you through the steps for adding subdomains to your DNS zone.

EXERCISE 9.3

Adding Subdomains

1. In DNS Manager, highlight the zone name. In the example it is globalnet.com.

2. Right-click and choose New Domain.

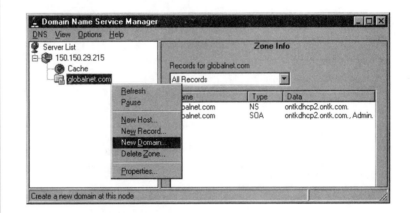

3. Enter the name of the new subdomain.

4. Click OK.

5. If multiple levels of subdomains are needed, create each successive subdomain through the New Domain Context menu option.

---

6. Configure the zone properties. Right-click the domain, in this example it is globalnet.com, and choose Properties to see the Zone Properties dialog box.

Zone Properties - globalnet.com

General | SOA Record | Notify | WINS Lookup

Zone File Name
```
globalnet.com.dns
```

Zone Type
- ○ Primary
- ○ Secondary

IP Master(s)

| | Add |
| Remove |
| Move Up |
| Move Down |

OK | Cancel

General Configures the zone file in which the resource records are stored and specifies whether this is a primary or secondary name server.

SOA Record Configures zone transfer information and the name server administrator mailbox.

Notify Specifies the secondary servers to be alerted when the primary server database changes. Also, additional security can be applied to the name server by specifying that only the listed secondary servers can contact this server.

WINS Lookup Enables the name server to query WINS to resolve names. A list of WINS servers can be configured in the dialog box. The WINS servers can be set on a per-name-server basis by selecting the Settings Only Affect Local Server checkbox. If this is not selected, secondary servers will also use the configured WINS servers.

DNS creates a key in the Registry for each zone for which the DNS will be authoritative. The keys are located in Hkey_Local_Machine\System\ CurrentControlSet\Services\DNS\Zones.

Adding Resource Records

The next step after the zones and subdomains are configured is to add the resource records. Exercise 9.4 shows you how to create a resource record.

EXERCISE 9.4

Creating a Resource Record

1. Select a zone or subdomain from the DNS Manager.

2. Right-click the domain or subdomain, and choose New Host or New Record from the menu bar.

3. To create a new host, type in the host name and IP address, and select Create a Pointer Record in the associated reverse lookup domain.

> **New Host**
>
> Enter the name of the new host for
> Sales.globalnet.com.
>
> Host Name: WINS Server
>
> Host IP Address: 150 .150 .44 .29
>
> ☑ Create Associated PTR Record
>
> Add Host
> Done

4. To create a new record, select which resource record type to create. A dialog box will display various fields specific to record type. The TTL field will display the default TTL from the SOA record for the zone file. A TTL value will be stored in the record only if it is changed from the default.

5. Enter the information, and click OK to add the resource record.

Configuring Reverse Lookup

A reverse lookup zone must be created for each network on which hosts in the DNS database reside. A reverse lookup zone helps to find a host name, given the host's IP address. Adding a reverse lookup zone is procedurally identical to adding any other type of zone, except for the name.

For example, if a host has an address of 189132.52.98, it would be represented in the in-addr.arpa domain as 98.52.132.189.in-addr.arpa. Furthermore, to enable this host to appear on a client that has its IP address, a zone would need to be added to the DNS for 52.132.189.in-addr.arpa. All pointer records for the network 189.132.52.0 would be added to this reverse lookup zone.

Exercise 9.5 outlines the steps for creating Reverse Lookup zone.

EXERCISE 9.5

Configuring a Reverse Lookup Zone for a Primary DNS Server

1. Open the DNS Manager, click the name of your computer.

2. On the DNS menu, click New Zone.

3. Click Primary, then click Next.

4. Type your reverse lookup zone name in the Zone Name box.

5. Tab to the Zone File box. The file is automatically inserted.

6. Click Next, then Finish.

7. Double-click the NS and SOA records, and notice the contents.

8. Click your reverse lookup zone name.

9. On the DNS menu, click Properties.

10. Click the Notify tab.

11. In the Notify list box, type the IP address of the secondary DNS server for your domain.

12. Click Add, then OK.

Integrating DNS and WINS

DNS in NT 4.0 is a static database of name-to-address mappings that must be manually updated. WINS dynamically registers name-to-address mappings and therefore requires less administration. As you may remember, DNS implements a hierarchical model, which allows the administration and replication of the database to be broken into zones. WINS is a flat name space and requires each WINS server to maintain a complete database of entries through replication.

The WINS Record

To integrate DNS with WINS, a new data record is defined as part of the database file. This is a unique WINS record to the DNS server. You enter it into the zone's root domain by placing the record in the database file. If a mapping is not found in the database file, DNS queries the WINS database (see Figure 9.4).

1. A client contacts its DNS server and requests the IP address of another host.

2. If the DNS server searches its database and does not find an address record for the host, the DNS server will look in the database file to see if it contains a WINS record.

FIGURE 9.4

Integrating DNS and WIN

Windows NT 4.0
DNS server

DNS name query:
Sales.Globalnet.com

NetBIOS name query:
<00> Sales

DNS
client

WINS server

3. Because the database file contains a WINS record, the DNS server converts the host portion of the name to a NetBIOS name and sends a request for this NetBIOS name to the WINS server.

4. If the WINS server is able to resolve the name, it returns the IP address to the DNS server.

5. The DNS server returns the IP address to the requesting client.

If a zone is configured for WINS resolution, all DNS servers that are authoritative for that zone must be configured for WINS resolution.

Enabling WINS Lookup

DNS can be configured to submit queries to a WINS server when a name-to-address mapping cannot be resolved by the DNS server by enabling WINS lookup.

Exercise 9.6 will show you how to enable WINS lookup in your DNS server.

EXERCISE 9.6

Enabling WINS Lookup

1. Open DNS Manager.

2. Select the zone and right-click.

3. Select Properties.

4. Click the WINS Lookup tab.

EXERCISE 9.6 (CONTINUED FROM PREVIOUS PAGE)

5. Check the Use WINS Resolution checkbox.

6. Enter the IP address of the desired WINS servers.

7. Click OK.

WINS Reverse Lookup

If you have a WINS-R record at the zone root, this instructs the DNS server to use NetBIOS node adapter status lookup for any reverse lookup requests for IP addresses in the zone root which are not statically defined with PTR records.

Enabling WINS reverse lookup is done by going to the WINS Reverse Lookup property page, then checking the Use WINS Reverse Lookup checkbox and entering the DNS Host Domain to be appended to the NetBIOS name before returning the response to the resolver.

WINS Time to Live

By going to the WINS Lookup property page in the Advanced dialog box, you can configure the WINS TTL. When a name-to-address mapping is resolved by the WINS server, the address is cached for the Cache Timeout Value. By default, this value is set to 10 minutes. If this address is forwarded to another DNS server, the TTL is also forwarded.

NSLOOKUP

The primary diagnostic tool is the NSLOOKUP utility. This enables users to interact with a DNS server and can be used to display resource records on DNS servers, including UNIX DNS implementations. This utility is automatically installed when DNS is installed in the NT server.

Lookup Modes

NSLOOKUP has two modes: interactive and non-interactive (or command line mode). If a single piece of data is needed, use non-interactive mode. If more than one piece of data is needed, interactive mode can be used.

The syntax for NSLOOKUP is as follows:

```
nslookup [-option…] [computer-to-find | -[server]]
```

-option Specifies one or more NSLOOKUP commands. For a list of commands, use the Help option in NSLOOKUP.

Computer-to-find If computer-to-find is an IP address and the query type is A or PTR, the name of the computer is returned. If computer-to-find is a name and does not have a trailing period, the default DNS domain name is appended to the name. To look up a computer outside of the current DNS domain, append a period to the name.

Server Use this server as the DNS name server. If the server is omitted, the currently configured default DNS server is used.

Summary

In the late '70s there were only a handful of networked computers, and all of the computer name-to-address mappings were contained in a single file called HOSTS.TXT. The ARPNET was created to find the solution to this problem (along with a few others), which led to DNS, a distributed database using a hierarchical name structure.

We covered a lot of ground in this very important chapter. We looked at the structure and components of the Domain Name System (DNS) and DNS database files, and found out how to resolve TCP/IP addresses. This chapter also covered installing, configuring DNS, integrating DNS and WINS, and using the DNS diagnostic tool NSLOOKUP.

If you're taking the NT 4.0 TCP/IP test, reread this chapter! It is very important that you understand Microsoft DNS front and back. Also, install DNS on a server, and go through the exercises again and again. Take a look at the exercise questions, and make sure you understand them completely.

Review Questions

1. Your computer on one subnet cannot connect to an NT server on a remote subnet by using the command **net use f:\\sales.acme.com\data**. When other computers on the local subnet try to run the same command, they can connect to the server either. You can ping the server by its IP address. What is the problem?

   A. The DNS server does not have an entry for sales.acme.com.

   B. Your workstation is not configured to use a DNS server.

   C. Your workstation is not configured as a WINS client.

   D. Your workstation is not configured to use TCP/IP.

2. You have NT Servers, UNIX computers, and NT Workstation computers on your network. You have three DNS servers for the acme.com domain. How can you configure your DNS server to use WINS to resolve NetBIOS names that are not in the DNS database?

   A. Configure only the primary DNS server to use WINS resolution, and it will update the other two DNS servers.

   B. Configure the primary DNS server to use WINS reverse lookup, and it will update the other two DNS servers.

   C. Configure all DNS servers to use WINS resolution.

   D. Configure all DNS servers to use WINS reverse lookup.

3. You want all client computers on your network to use one DNS server to resolve names that are not found on the WINS server. What must you do?

   A. Add an LMHOSTS table on each workstation with an entry of the WINS server and DNS server.

   B. Add a WINS entry in the workstation, reboot and then add the DNS entry. This will make the workstations look at the WINS server first.

   C. Configure the DNS server to enable WINS lookup for name resolution.

   D. Configure the WINS server to enable DNS for name resolution.

4. Which type of resource record must you add to your DNS server to allow users to connect to your NT server using multiple names?

   A. CNAME

   B. MX

   C. MINFO

   D. NS

   E. WKS

5. How should you configure your DNS server if you want to resolve Internet names and you already have a DNS server for intranet traffic?

   A. As a primary server

   B. As a secondary server

   C. As a forwarder

   D. As a caching only server

6. You want to install a second DNS server on your network for redundancy. How should you configure the backup DNS server?

   A. As a forwarder

   B. As a secondary server

   C. As a caching-only server

   D. As a primary server

7. Which type of resource record must you add on your DNS Server to identify your mail server?

   A. CNAME

   B. MX

   C. MINFO

   D. NS

   E. WKS

8. You have two DNS servers configured in a single zone and you want to install a third DNS server to provide load balancing for your large internetwork. How should you configure the third DNS server so it does not generate any zone transfer network traffic?

   A. Configure the DNS server to enable WINS lookup for name resolution.

   B. Configure the WINS server to enable DNS for name resolution.

   C. As a caching-only server

   D. As a forwarder

9. You want to enable Windows 95, UNIX, and Macintosh computers to use Internet Explorer to access your Web servers by using a host name. Which service should you use?

   A. DHCP

   B. DNS

   C. LMHOSTS

   D. HOSTS

   E. WINS

10. You are building a DNS server for your internetwork and are not going to connect it to the Internet. Which file on the DNS server should you modify?

A. Boot.ini

B. LMHOSTS

C. DNS

D. MX

11. All your NT computers are configured as both DHCP clients and WINS clients, and your UNIX workstations are configured to use DNS resolution. How can you make this is simple as possible for administration purposes?

A. Enable WINS resolution on the DNS server.

B. On the DNS server, configure an LMHOSTS file that contains one entry for each UNIX computer and preloads the NT computers.

C. Configure LMHOSTS on the NT computers and HOSTS on the UNIX computers.

D. On the WINS server, add an LMHOSTS table.

12. You are building a DNS server and want to use it to resolve names for the Internet and your intranet. How should you do it?

A. By using the default Boot file

B. By using the default Cache file

C. By configuring the DNS server to use WINS resolution

D. By configuring the WINS server to use DNS name resolution

13. What must you do to minimize the number of static records on your DNS server?

   A. Add an LMHOSTS to the DNS server.

   B. Configure the DNS server to enable WINS Reverse lookup for name resolution.

   C. Configure the DNS server to enable WINS lookup for name resolution.

   D. Add an LMHOSTS table to the WINS server.

14. Your users are complaining that they cannot connect to your NT Server by the NetBIOS name, but they can when they use the IP address. DHCP is configured to give the DNS server for name resolution. When you check the clients, you notice the DNS Server is different from the one that DHCP hands-out. How can this be?

   A. The client computers are on a different subnet then the DNS server.

   B. The DHCP Server is not working correctly.

   C. The client computer has been manually configured with a different IP address for the DNS server.

   D. The clients are using an LMHOSTS table for name resolution.

15. What should you do to resolve host names without any administrative overhead? (Choose three.)

   A. Install DNS.

   B. Install WINS.

   C. Configure DNS to use DHCP.

   D. Configure DNS to use WINS.

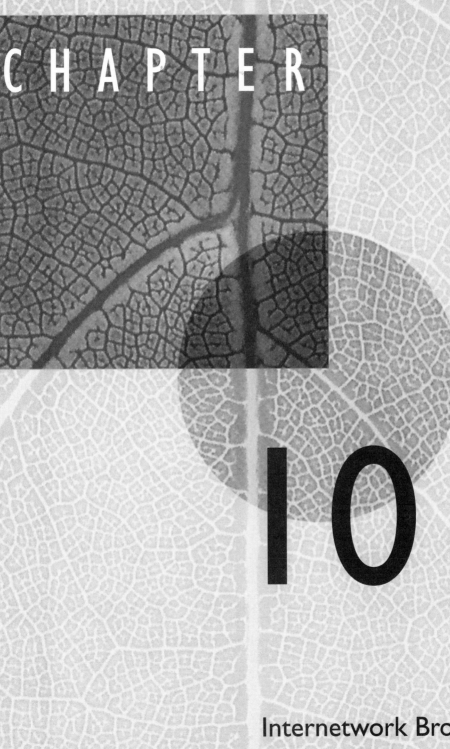

CHAPTER

10

Internetwork Browsing

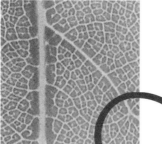

hapter 10's focus is on how to successfully browse for network resources across routers. It'll also examine some important issues centered around supporting this activity. We'll give you the skinny on configuring the LMHOSTS file to make browsing possible across domains for non-WINS clients, and how to prime LMHOSTS for use in logon validation and password changes in a domain. By the end of this chapter, Microsoft's Computer Browser service, and several other different types of browsers, should be as familiar as old friends.

When cruising through this chapter, you should aim to master the following:

- The Microsoft Windows NT Computer Browser service and how it works

- How the different types of browsers—master, preferred master, and backup—function

- How to configure LMHOSTS so non-WINS clients can browse across domains

- Configuring LMHOSTS for logon validation and password changes in a domain

A Browsing Brief

Before you can share something, you must first be aware of it, know how to find it, and obtain it. Browsing plays an important role in both finding and sharing currently available network resources. By providing a list of these resources, the computer browser service works to free most of the network's computer population from the burden of individually maintaining their own. This saves time and memory because this resource list is only distributed to a few, specially-designated machines.

Let's say you want to print something. Before you can, you need to locate and connect to a printer on your network. Without the help of a browser, your system would be reduced to a door-to-door solicitor, petitioning each system along the network corridor about what resources it has available until finally finding what it needs. Your system must then record and maintain that information for future use. All this would take up lots of CPU time, while reducing available memory on your workstation.

NT's browsing service reduces costs and adds efficiency in terms of network overhead. To find a particular resource, your workstation can simply contact the network's designated browser instead of generating network traffic by searching on its own to find the treasure you're after.

But How Do They Work?

Here's a step-by-step outline of basic Browser service behavior and operation:

1. After startup, every machine running a Browser service checks in with the master browser of their domain or workgroup. They're required to do so even if they don't have any shared resources to offer their group. Sometimes, under Windows NT, a system will possess hidden, administrative shares like "c$".

2. Like any introduction, the client's first time contacting the master browser is special. The first time the client tries to locate its available network resources, it asks the master browser for a list of backup browsers.

3. The client then asks for a list of network resources from one of the backup browsers.

4. The backup browser then provides the client with a list of domains and workgroups, plus a list of local servers appointed for the client's particular workgroup or domain.

5. The client's user then picks a local server, domain, or workgroup in order to view another list of available servers.

6. Lastly, the client's user chooses a server to look for the right machine with which to establish a session for using their desired resource. The user then contacts that server.

Browser Forms and Functions

The task of providing a list of network resources to clients is broken down into various roles, which are carried out by the corresponding computer.

Master Browser The machine that builds, maintains, and distributes the master list of all available network resources (known as a *browse list*)

Domain Master Browser A system specially cast and designated to play the role of master browser by a network administrator. At startup, this system arrogantly proclaims itself to be the network's master browser. If it finds another machine trying to horn in on its rightful network position in its absence, the domain master browser will force an "election" between itself and the upstart. Networks not being democracies, these elections most often result in the domain master browser reclaiming its throne. The only exception to this being if that "little upstart" machine also happens to be a *primary domain controller (PDC)*. PDCs always function as the master browser of the domain—their reign is not to be challenged.

Backup Browser These systems act as relay stations. They receive copies of the browse list from the master browser, and upon request, distribute them to clients.

Potential Browser This is a system that has the capacity of becoming a browser, but isn't one, and won't become one unless specifically commanded to do so by the master browser.

Non-Browser This computer is configured so that it won't maintain a browser list. These are most often client systems.

Windows NT Workstation, Windows NT Server, Windows for Workgroups, and Window 95 computers can perform the master browser and backup browser roles. However, only a Windows NT Server acting as a PDC can perform the domain master browser role.

Browser Criteria

Browser criteria serve as a means of determining the hierarchical order of the different types of computer systems in the workgroup or domain. Each browser computer has certain criteria, depending on the type of system it is. These criteria include:

- The operating system

- The operating system version

- Its current role in the browsing environment

The following is a hypothetical list of computers in a domain. They're presented in the order in which they would win an election, and organized into three criteria categories.

Criteria Category #1: Operating System

- Windows NT Server that is the PDC

- Windows NT Server

- Windows NT Workstation

- Windows 95

- Windows for Workgroups

Criteria Category #2: Operating System Version

- 4.0

- 3.51

- 3.5

- 3.1

Criteria Category #3: Current Browser Role

- Preferred Master browser

- Master browser

- Backup browser

- Potential browser

This criteria ranking is observed and referred to during an election. These elections are held to determine which computer should be the master browser in the event that the current master browser becomes unavailable.

The Browser Election

As the name implies, the master browser oversees the entire browsing environment. There's only one master browser for each domain or workgroup. In a domain that spans subnets, there's a domain master browser. If the computer that's designated as the master browser shuts down for any reason, another computer needs to be selected to be the master browser. This is done through a browser election, which ensures that only one master browser exists per workgroup or domain. An election is instituted when any of the following events occur:

- A client computer can't locate a master browser.

- A Backup browser attempts to update its network resource list, and can't locate the master browser.

- A computer that's been designated as a preferred master browser comes online.

Configuring Browsers

To determine whether a Windows NT computer will become a browser, the browser service looks in the Registry when the computer initializes for the following parameter:

```
\HKEY_LOCAL_MACHINE\SYSTEM\CurrentControlSet\Services\
Browser\Parameters\MaintainServerList.
```

Microsoft ✓ *Exam Objective*   **Configure and support browsing in a multiple-domain routed network.**

For performance tuning and optimization purposes, it's possible to both configure and prevent a computer from becoming a browser.

The `MaintainServerList` parameter can contain the following values:

Parameter	Value
No	This computer never participates as a Browser server.
Yes	This computer becomes a Browser server. At startup, this computer attempts to contact the master browser to get a current browse list. If the master browser cannot be found, the computer forces one to be elected. This computer either is elected as the master browser or becomes a backup browser. Yes is the default value for Windows NT Server domain controller computers.
Auto	Depending on the number of currently active browsers, this computer may or may not become a Browser server. It's referred to as a *potential browser*. This computer is notified by the master browser as to whether it should become a backup browser. Auto is the default value for Windows NT Workstation and Windows NT Server—non-domain controller computers.

Browser Announcements

Master browsers and backup browsers each have their own roles to play in the operation of the browsing environment. Browsers need to communicate with each other and must provide service to client computers. When a computer that's running the server service comes online, it must inform the master browser that it's available. The computer does this by announcing itself on the network.

Servers

Each computer periodically announces itself to the master browser by broadcasting on the network. Initially each computer announces itself once per minute. As the computer stays running, the announcement time is extended to once every 12 minutes. If the master browser hasn't heard from a computer after three announcement periods elapse, it'll remove the computer that hasn't kept in touch from the browse list.

Important! This means that there could be a 36-minute delay between the time a server goes down and the time that server is removed from the browse list. Computers appearing in the list could possibly be unavailable.

Backup Browsers

In addition to announcing themselves, backup browsers contact the master browser every 15 minutes to obtain an updated network resource (browse list), and a list of workgroups and domains. The backup browser caches these lists, and forwards them to any clients that send out a browse request. If the backup browser can't find the master browser, it forces an election.

Master Browsers

Master browsers also periodically announce themselves to backup browsers with a broadcast. When backup browsers receive this announcement, they refresh their master browser name with any new information.

Master browsers receive announcements from the following systems:

- Windows NT 4.0/3.51 Workstation

- Windows NT 4.0/3.51 Server

- Windows NT 3.1 Workstation

- Windows NT 3.1 Advanced Server

- Windows 95

- Windows for Workgroups

- LAN Manager systems

Master browsers will return lists of backup browsers to these systems for their local subnet:

- Windows NT 4.0/3.51 Workstation

- Windows NT 4.0/3.51 Server

- Windows NT 3.1 Workstation

- Windows NT 3.1 Advanced Server

- Windows 95

- Windows for Workgroup clients

When a system starts, and its `MaintainServerList` parameter is set to `Auto`, the master browser is responsible for telling the system whether to become a backup browser or not.

> The list of resources that the master browser maintains and returns to the backup browsers is limited in size to 64K of data. This limits the number of computers that can be in a single workgroup's or domain browse list to 2,000-3,000 computers.

Cruising an Internetwork

Many a problem can arise when trying to browse around networks that require a hop or two across routers to reach. A big reason for this is because master browsers receive notices via B-node broadcasts—and as you've learned, routers won't let those pass through to different subnets. Also, domains that span routers are very prevalent in TCP/IP internetworks. On Microsoft networks, the browser service relies heavily on NetBIOS name broadcasts for getting information from connecting systems. Microsoft has come up with two great solutions for machines with that ol' Travelin' Jones—one dependent on WINS, and the other on the LMHOSTS file.

On the Wing with WINS

Recall that WINS solves the whole NetBIOS broadcast jam by dynamically registering names. Machines running WINS maintain and store all that name-related stuff (like IP addresses) in their databases where the information is readily available to the remote TCP/IP hosts that require it when contacted to establish communications. WINS clients, configured to operate compatibly with a WINS server, automatically register their names with them upon startup. This makes clean, broadcast-less identity referencing routinely available to all—except, of course, non-WINS clients, which we'll be discussing next. For a visual reference to what we've been talking about, see Figure 10.1.

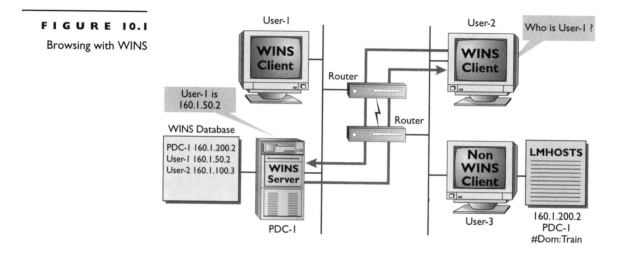

If you happen to be running the client component Windows for Workgroups with TCP/IP32, you'll have to replace the VREDIR.386 file with the one supplied on the Windows NT Server 3.5x distribution CD.

The LMHOSTS File and Domain Functions

Non-WINS clients can be internetwork browsing's problem children. The fact that non-WINS clients register using B-node broadcasts presents a major problem if the system designated as the domain's master browser is somewhere over the rainbow on a different subnet. Why? Simple—its registration broadcast won't be forwarded. On the client end of things, receiving messages that the browser service isn't available or viewing empty resource lists are also potential pitfalls.

Microsoft
✓ **Exam**
Objective

Configure HOSTS and LMHOSTS files.

To address these dilemmas, Microsoft added a pair of tags to the LMHOSTS file: #PRE and #DOM. These tags enable the non-WINS client to communicate with a domain controller to do three very important things:

- Register with it

- Verify a user account

- Change passwords

Because user validation is required to operate login scripts and user profiles, and because broadcasts are used for replication of the domain database, special care should be used when configuring domain controllers when there isn't a WINS server around. To ensure your non-WINS clients will function well, be sure an entry is added for each domain controller present in the domain. Domain controllers that are also non-WINS machines should have a listing of all other domain controllers in their databases. This'll prove very handy if one of the servers is ever promoted to primary domain controller at any point in the future.

LMHOSTS file entries on each subnet's master browser must first list the IP address, followed by the domain browser's NetBIOS name. Then come the tags, #PRE and #DOM, followed by the domain name. They should look something like this:

```
137.37.9.9  master-browser_name #PRE #DOM: domain-name

137.37.9.10 domain-controller_name #PRE #DOM: domain-name
```

Domain Functions

The #PRE tag tells TCP/IP to preload the resolution information into memory, while the #DOM tag alerts the client machine that it has reached a domain controller. #DOM is significant for the directing of data during broadcasts. These addresses indicate to the router to forward broadcasts to certain addresses. All this means that you're essentially making a broadcast and then directing it to a special place, so the #PRE tag must always precede the #DOM tag. See Figure 10.2 for a visual illustration of LMHOSTS in action.

FIGURE 10.2

Using LMHOSTS to browse across subnets

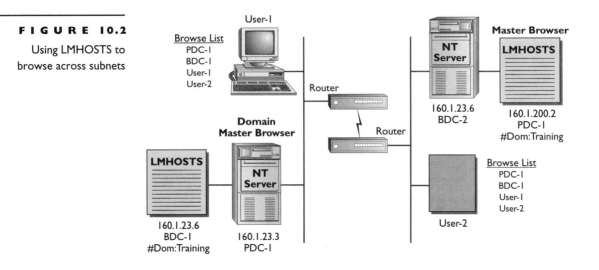

Certain tasks executed by Windows NT network services will cause broadcasts to be sent out to all computers located within a Microsoft domain. For instance, when logging into a domain or changing a password, a broadcast will be transmitted to the domain to find a domain controller able to authenticate the logon request, and/or change the user's password. Another situation that will induce broadcasts is when a domain controller replicates the domain user account database. To do this, the primary domain controller sends a broadcast out to all backup domain controllers that populate the domain, directing them to request a replication of updated changes made in the domain accounts database. (See Figure 10.3.)

Remember that for Windows for Workgroups, the presence of a Windows NT server domain is required for WAN browsing because Workgroups do not define a domain controller. For a Windows for Workgroups client to be capable of WAN browsing, it must first log onto a domain.

Exercise 10.1 will show you how to configure your LMHOSTS file.

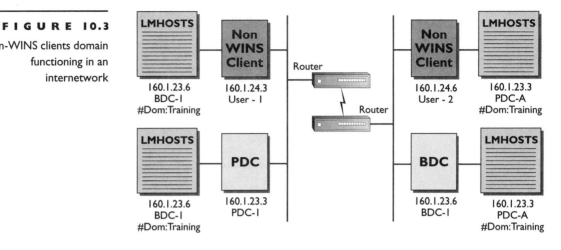

FIGURE 10.3

Non-WINS clients domain
functioning in an
internetwork

EXERCISE 10.1

Configuring the LMHOSTS File

1. First, prepare your LMHOSTS file with the appropriate entry to logon to another computer on your domain.

2. Stop the WINS Server service. From the command prompt, type **net stop wins**.

3. From the command prompt, verify that you have no existing connections to your other computer. Type **net use *othercomputername*\ ipc$ /d**. (Replace *othercomputername* with the name of your computer.)

4. Purge the NetBIOS name cache. Type **nbstat -R**, and then press Enter (the R must be uppercase).

5. Try to browse by typing **Net View *othercomputername***.

---

6. Notice the error that occurs when a remote host does not exist in the LMHOSTS file or when the entry is invalid.

7. Use Notepad to create a file in the \WINNT\SYSTEM32\DRIVERS\ETC directory named LMHOSTS.

8. Add the following entry to the file:

IP_Address *othercomputername* #PRE DOM:domain

9. Save the file, and then exit Notepad.

Now add the LMHOSTS file mapping for the other computer's domain controller to the NetBIOS name cache for browsing and logon validation.

1. Clear the NetBIOS name cache and load #PRE entries. Type **nbstat -R**, and then press Enter.

2. View the NetBIOS name cache. Type **nbstat -c**, and then press Enter.

3. Notice the entry that appears. Hopefully, it's your other computer!

4. Start the WINS Server service by typing **net start wins** at the command prompt.

Summary

Microsoft's computer browsing service works to free most of the network's computer population from the burden of individually maintaining their own network resource database lists. This saves time and memory because this resource list is only distributed to a few specially designated machines. Windows NT Computer Browsing service is a highly efficient way of swiftly locating active network resources.

The LMHOSTS strategy is a different story. Being that a non-WINS client's registration broadcasts aren't forwarded, ensuring smooth browsing with one requires a little finesse. So, Microsoft has added a pair of tags to the LMHOSTS file: #PRE and #DOM. But remember, certain tasks executed by Windows NT network services will cause broadcasts to be sent out to all computers located within a Microsoft domain. This happens when logging into a domain or changing a password, or when a domain controller replicates the domain user account database.

When taking the NT TCP/IP 4.0 test, remember your LMHOSTS file and what the #PRE and #DOM is used for.

Review Questions

1. You want to have users browse your local NT network, but you do not want to configure anything. Which NT Service should you use?

   A. DNS

   B. WINS

   C. LMHOSTS

   D. Windows NT Computer Browser service

2. What's the function of the master browser?

   A. Update the LMHOSTS file.

   B. Update the WINS database.

   C. The master browser collects and maintains the master list of available network resources, and it distributes this list to Backup browsers.

   D. The master browser collects and maintains the backup list of available network resources, and it distributes this list to Master browsers.

3. You want your non-wins clients to use an LMHOSTS file to resolve names across routers. How should you configure the LMHOSTS?

A. master_browser ip_address #PRE #DOM:domain_name

B. ip_address master_browser #DOM:domain_name #PRE

C. ip_address master_browser #PRE #DOM:domain_name

D. ip_address master_browser #PRE:domain_name #DOM

4. You want your non-wins clients to resolve a remote NT Server name of Sales in the Acme domain with an ip address of 192.168.100.1. How should you configure your the non-wins clients?

A. With an LMHOST table and the following entry:

```
Sales        192.168.100.1      #PRE:ACME      #DOM
```

B. With an LMHOSTS table And the following entry:

```
192.168.100.1      ACME      #PRE      #DOM:      SALES
```

C. With an LMHOSTS table And the following entry:

```
192.168.100.1      SALES      #PRE      #DOM:      ACME
```

D. With a host table And the following entry:

```
192.168.100.1      ACME      #PRE      #DOM:      SALES
```

5. You try to connect to a server in the browse list but cannot. How could a server appear in the browse list but not be available?

A. You can, it's a user error.

B. The server could be down. It is possible that the server is down but is still listed in the browse list.

C. You need to reboot the NT Server.

D. You need to reboot your workstation.

6. You have three networks tied together with a router. The router has a capacity for NetBIOS name broadcasts. For optimum performance, should you use the LMHOSTS files and WINS, or should you simply let the router pass NetBIOS name broadcasts?

7. Unclear on the issue of browsers, Management invites you into a meeting to clear up the matter. They want to know what types of browsers systems running Windows NT Workstation or NT Server can use. What do you tell them?

8. A student of yours knows that Microsoft has added a pair of tags to the LMHOSTS file: #PRE and #DOM, and the student remembers that these tags enable the non-WINS client to communicate with a domain controller to accomplish three very important things. However, this student is unable to recall exactly which three things and asks you. What would you answer?

9. You want to import the file that contains computer name-to-IP address mappings into the WINS database on your server. Which file should you import?

   A. The DHCP.MDB file from a DHCP server

   B. The CACHE.DNS file from a DNS server

   C. The HOSTS file

   D. The LMHOSTS file

10. Why would you use an LMHOSTS file instead of a HOST file?

   A. When you cannot connect to a WINS Server

   B. When your DNS server is down

   C. When you want to preload NetBIOS names into cache

   D. When you want to preload host names into cache

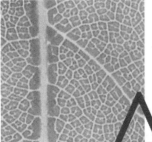

As discussed in Chapter 1, TCP/IP affords an extremely high degree of flexibility when operating within a diverse environment populated with many different platforms. The fundamental benefit of using TCP/IP is that it provides the wonderful ability to smoothly connect to, and interoperate with, different types of hosts. Disparate systems, such as VAX, Macintosh, UNIX, mainframes, etc., all use TCP/IP. Within each set of diversified systems, there exist subsets of systems that are more TCP/IP-oriented than others—for instance, all machines running UNIX, such as Sun workstations, SunOS, IBM's AIX, AT&T's System 5, etc. For systems like these, mutual, common ground is found in the interface of the tools that allow them to interoperate. These systems, and their shared, correlative functions, are what we're going to focus on in this chapter. For example, we'll show you how a NetBIOS-based host is able to achieve fluid communication with dissimilar systems whose only parallel is the fact that they're using TCP/IP as their communication protocol.

Here's a list of stuff to keep in mind while you're reading through this chapter:

- Dissimilar communication environments

- Communication between NetBIOS and foreign host systems

- Software requirements for achieving communication with Microsoft operating systems

- Usage of TCP/IP utilities as provided by Microsoft

- The Windows NT FTP server

- TCP/IP printing issues

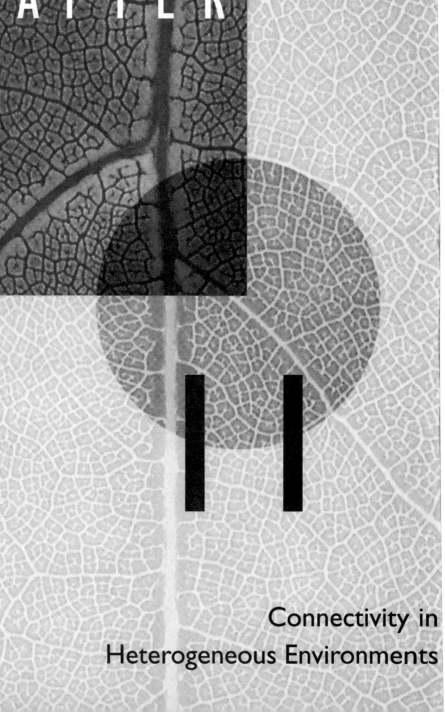

CHAPTER

11

Connectivity in
Heterogeneous Environments

Making Connections

As we said, TCP/IP provides a flexible means by which dissimilar computing environments may effectively communicate with each other. Without thinking in terms of a network, think of two systems communicating through asynchronous modems. Regardless of what operating systems these two systems may be running, they can "talk," provided they do so using the same parameters and protocols for communication. TCP/IP serves as an organizational model by establishing a set mode of communication despite the operating system in use. Here's a sample list of some common operating systems that can use TCP/IP to interoperate for file and print services.

- Apple Macintosh
- DEC VAX systems
- DOS systems with TCP/IP
- IBM Mainframes (among others)
- Internet objects
- LAN Manager
- NFS HOSTS
- OS/2 Systems with TCP/IP
- TCP/IP-based printers
- Windows 95
- Windows NT
- Windows for Workgroups
- UNIX-based systems

The only requirements for connecting between these disparate operating systems are that they're running TCP/IP as their communication protocol, and using their respective utilities and services in some specific ways that we'll describe later in the chapter.

A Microsoft client such as Windows NT, Windows 95, or Windows for Workgroups can interoperate with an RFC-compliant, NetBIOS-based, SMB (Server Message Block) server using the Windows Redirector. It accomplishes interoperation through use of standard Windows commands over a common set of communication protocols like TCP/IP or NetBEUI. Two examples of machines that can operate in this manner are a UNIX host that's running LAN Manager for UNIX, and a DEC VAX, running Pathworks. Both LAN Manager for UNIX and DEC's VAX system running Pathworks operate similarly to Windows NT when it's running on platforms other than Intel platforms.

TCP/IP Utilities and the WINDOWS NT Command

Many of the TCP/IP-based networking features are built directly into Windows NT. The type of network function you're attempting to perform will also determine whether you'll be using a Windows NT internal function, or a TCP/IP utility. The chosen function will further define the requirements for carrying it out. Here are a few network truisms to abide by while working with Windows NT and TCP/IP commands:

- The same protocol must be used on both systems attempting communication with each other for connectivity and communication to result.

- Network connections from a command line are achieved through the net use command.

- Applications on other systems are accessed though Windows NT's native environment, and are processed at the client (distributed) rather than processed by the server host (centralized).

- Windows NT can use NetBIOS names—not just IP address names—to communicate via the net use and net view line commands. This is done for reasons of maintaining compatibility with other protocols, like NetBEUI, that don't use IP addresses and don't accommodate the overhead of additional program processing well.

- The NetBIOS scope parameter must match all other hosts' scope parameters. This allows NetBIOS networks to be divided and organized. Systems set for one scope don't communicate with those set for another scope. Therefore, two systems can have the same NetBIOS name as long as they're using different scopes.

- Remote hosts—those located on other subnets—must be resolved by a supported method such as WINS, LMHOSTS, etc.

How to Interoperate with an RFC-Compliant NetBIOS Host

When Windows NT isn't attempting to communicate with an RFC-compliant NetBIOS-based host (Windows for Workgroups, Windows 95, Windows NT, LAN Manger, LAN Manager for UNIX, etc.), but is trying to talk to a foreign TCP/IP system, different rules apply. While it's true that a number of common functions work great within a common realm, they're not understood and shared among foreign hosts that use tools uniquely and specifically defined for their way of communicating. Here are some ins and outs to know when communicating with foreign TCP/IP hosts.

- You must use TCP/IP—NetBEUI won't talk to TCP/IP, nor will IPX or any other non-IP protocol.

- Only commands supported by the specific TCP/IP utility, such as FTP, TELNET, etc., may be used to communicate with the foreign system.

- Applications that are accessed on the foreign system are run centrally at the foreign system—not at your local system. This is because different systems use different compilers, CPU commands, and memory instructions, which are generally not platform-independent.

- TCP/IP utilities can either use the host name or the IP address.

- Both local and remote host names that are used in TCP/IP utilities must be resolved in the HOSTS file, DNS, WINS, B-node broadcast, or in the LMHOSTS file.

There's a distinct difference in how TCP/IP communication is established between similar and foreign hosts. While these differences may seem trivial, they're important to understand. Grasping these similarities and differences will greatly assist you later in debugging and configuring large TCP/IP environments.

TCP/IP Utilities the Microsoft Way

TCP/IP utilities follow their own specific set of rules. This conformity provides for standardization and ease of use when moving from one machine to the next through various operating systems. Microsoft provides FTP, LPD, LPQ, LPR, REXEC, RSH, RCP, Telnet, and TFTP TCP/IP utilities. The majority of the commands presented here are similar in implementation to their UNIX-based counterparts. And yes, just like UNIX, they're usually case-sensitive. They can be divided into three categories:.

- Command utilities: REXEC, RSH, and Telnet

- Transfer utilities: RCP, FTP, TFTP, and WWW

- Printer utilities: LPD, LPR, and LPQ

Microsoft ✓ *Exam* *Objective*   **Given a scenario, identify which utility to use to connect to a TCP/IP-based UNIX host.**

Command Utilities

REXEC (Remote Execution)

The Remote Execute connectivity command will run a process on a remote system equipped with the REXEC server service. The REXEC service is password protected. Only upon receiving a valid password will this function proceed. The command format is as follows:

```
REXEC host {-1 username} {-n} command
```

This command line is broken down like this:

host: specifies the host name or IP address of the system that is not the default

-l username: specifies a valid user on the remote system when this is not the default

-n: redirects the input for REXEC to null, if you don't want input

command: specifies the execution line you wish to run on the host

RSH (Remote Shell)

The Remote Shell utility allows a user to issue a command to a remote host without logging into it. Password protection isn't provided; however, the designated user name must exist in the *.rhosts file* on the UNIX server that's running the RSH daemon. This command is commonly used with UNIX systems for executing program compilers. The command format looks like this:

```
RSH host {-1 username} command
```

host: specifies the host name or IP address of the system where the remote commands are run

-l username: designates a valid user on the remote system when this is not the default (it must be in an .rhosts file located in the user's home directory)

command: is the UNIX command to be run on the remote host

Telnet

The Telnet connectivity command initiates terminal emulation with a remote system running a Telnet service. Telnet provides DEC VT 100, DEC VT 52, or TTY emulation through the connection-based services of TCP. This program provides a way for users to execute any command as if sitting right there in front of the host it's to be performed on. Telnet has similarities to Novell's Rconsole utility, but can also be thought of as a text-based network version of Symantec's PC Anywhere remote control utility because it's limited to those machines (a workstation or server) running a Telnet server program. The Telnet program requires TCP/IP on both the client and server, and requires an account set up on the server being contacted. Microsoft Windows NT doesn't provide the server process, but it does provide a client interface. Security is furnished by the requirement of a user name and password identical to those used when logging onto the system directly. Telnet sometimes serves up a full graphical display beyond text. If this occurs, it's usually a form of X Window.

If you've installed TCP/IP and connection utilities from Windows NT, you have access to the Telnet program. To establish a connection, simply type **Telnet** plus the destination name or IP address. If no destination is specified, the Telnet terminal screen will be displayed. At this point, choose Remote System from the Connect menu. The Connect dialog box will appear. Then, in the Host Name box, type the host name or IP address of the Telnet server, and choose Connect. When logging onto the Telnet server, enter your user account and the corresponding password. You'll then be able to talk to the remote host as though you were sitting there in front of it.

By default, Telnet uses port 23. Depending on the service—SMTP, FTP, Telnet, Time, Login, Whois, BootP, etc.—the service can be redirected by a command line, through which you can use a different port. (A port specifies the remote port you want to connect to, providing compatibility with applications.) This is very handy for talking to other services. For example, for direct communication to an SMTP mail port 25, you would type **TELNET host 25**.

Non-Standardization Problems   In general, Telnet works fine with computers of all kinds. But some host computers just plain won't talk to you unless you're an IBM 3270-type dumb terminal, so there is another program, tn3270. Tn3270 is a variation of Telnet that emulates an IBM 3270 full-screen type terminal. The main things to know about tn3270 are that 3270-type terminals have a *lot* of functions.

Not all implementations of tn3270 are equal, so don't be totally shocked if you Telnet to an IBM site using tn3270, work for awhile, and get the message, "Unexpected command sequence—program terminated." It means that your tn3270 couldn't handle some command that the IBM host sent it. And IBM terminal emulation can be a real pain in the neck when it comes to key mapping. On the IBM terminal are a set of function keys labeled PF1, PF2, and so on. As there are no keys labeled like that on a PC or a Mac, what key should you press to get PF4, for instance? Well, it's Esc-4 on some implementations of tn3270, F4 on some others, and there doesn't seem to be any real agreement either on what the key is, or what the key should be. Make sure that you have the documentation for your tn3270 somewhere around before you start Telnetting to an IBM host.

There is no tn3270 shipped with NT.

Why Use Telnet?   What is Telnet good for, anyway? Several things. First, it is the way to access a number of specialized basic information services. For instance, many large libraries put their entire card catalog on Telnet servers. University researchers can then look for an item, and request it through inter-library loan. Another example can be found by Telneting to InterNIC. The

InterNIC keeps track of all registered IP addresses on the Internet. Just type **Telnet internic.net,** and you're in. This is what you'd see:

```
UNIX(r) System V Release 4.0 (rs1)

****************************************************************
**********

* -- InterNIC Registration Services Center --

* For wais, type:     WAIS <search string> <return>

* For the *original* whois type:  WHOIS [search string] <return>

* For referral whois type:   RWHOIS [search string] <return>

* For user assistance call (703) 742-4777

# Questions/Updates on the whois database to
HOSTMASTER@internic.net

* Please report system problems to ACTION@internic.net

****************************************************************
**********

Please be advised that use constitutes consent to monitoring

(Elec Comm Priv Act, 18 USC 2701-2711)

6/1/94

We are offering an experimental distributed whois service called
referral

whois (RWhois). To find out more, look for RWhois documents, a
sample

client and server under:

gopher: (rs.internic.net) InterNIC Registration Services ->

  InterNIC Registration Archives -> pub -> rwhois

  anonymous ftp: (rs.internic.net) /pub/rwhois

Cmdinter Ver 1.3 Sun Jun 22 15:37:39 1997 EST

[ansi] InterNIC >
```

Another use for Telnet might be a commercial firm that wants to offer an online ordering service: You just log on, browse the descriptions of the items available, and place an order electronically. A third, somewhat technical, reason for using Telnet is that it can be used as a debugging tool. Using Telnet, you can essentially impersonate different applications, like FTP and mail.

The final reason for using Telnet is simply its original reason for existence—remote login to a service on a distant host. That has become a feature of much less value than it was when it first appeared, largely because of the way that we now use computers. Twenty years ago, you would have had a dumb terminal on your desk. Today, you are likely to have a computer on your desk, a computer with more computing power than a mainframe of twenty years ago. We are less interested today in borrowing someone else's computing power than we are in borrowing their information—with their permission, of course. Specifically, we often seek to transfer files to and from other computers over an intranet. For that reason, we'll consider transfer utilities next.

Transfer Utilities

RCP (Remote Copy)

RCP is used to copy files between local and remote UNIX hosts, or between two remote hosts. The Remote Copy tool is used in a similar manner as FTP for copying files, except it doesn't require user validation. Like RSH, the designated user name must exist in the .RHOSTS file located on the UNIX server that's running the RCP daemon. It's also commonly used with UNIX systems. The command format is as follows:

```
RCP {-abhr}{host1.}{user1:}source {host2.}{user2:}path/destination
```

Host1/host2 is the name, or IP address, of the destination or source system. If the `host.user:` portion is omitted, the host is assumed to be the local computer.

User1/User2 specifies valid users that exist on the destination and source systems (usernames must be in the .RHOSTS file), and source/destination is the full path designating where files are copied.

The switch options are as follows:

-a   Set by default, this option sets transfers to ASCII, and specifies for translation UNIX/DOS text formatting for cr-lf, (carriage return/linefeed, DOS hex 0d 0a), and lf, (linefeed, UNIX hex 0a).

-b   Sets transfers to binary with no translation.

-h   Sets the transfer of hidden files.

-r   Recursively copies the contents of all subdirectories of the source to the destination. Both the source and destination must be directories. It's equal to the DOS /S command with XCOPY.

FTP

The File Transfer Protocol (FTP) is used to copy files to and from a system running an FTP server over TCP, and is therefore quite obviously connection-oriented. The host may be UNIX, VAX, Windows NT, or any other system running an FTP server process. Although this utility uses both user and password protection, it can be configured to allow anonymous usage. Unlike Telnet, Microsoft does provide a daemon or server service for FTP to run. In most Internet applications, when using FTP with "anonymous" as a user ID, an e-mail account is used as the password, as it can be logged to show an audit trail.

If you've installed TCP/IP and connection utilities with Windows NT, you already have the FTP program. Because no icon is created from a command prompt, type **ftp** and the destination name or IP address.

The command line with options is:

```
ftp {options} host command
```

If no destination host is specified, the FTP terminal screen will appear. When it does, type **open** to establish your connection. As with Telnet, you'll then be prompted for a login name and password. Once connected, you have a variety of options available to you. You can view these options by typing **help** or ?. Doing so will yield the following information:

!   DOS shell to command prompt. Type **Exit** to return.

?   Command listing or ? *Command* displays the command description. It works the same as Help.

append   This allows you to add to a file.

ASCII   Sets the transfer mode type to ASCII. It is used for text files.

bell	Inserts a little beep when the command is completed
Bye	Closes an FTP session, and exits the FTP program
Binary	Sets the transfer mode type to Binary. It is used for files other than text.
cd	Change directory on FTP server (must include a space following cd). It also uses .. (double dots) for going back a directory, and / for specifying root.
close	Closes an FTP session
debug	Toggles the debug mode
delete	Removes a remote file
dir	Lists a directory of files—similar to ls -l in UNIX
disconnect	Closes an FTP session
get	Retrieves a file
Glob	Toggles meta-character expansion of local filenames
hash	Toggles printing. # (hash signs) for each data block transferred
help	Command listing or help *Command* displays the command description. It is the same as ?.
literal	Sends arguments, verbatim, to the remote FTP server. A single FTP reply code is expected in return.
lcd	Changes directory locally
ls	Lists a directory of files. (It uses ls -l for all information.)
mdelete	Removes multiple remote files
mdir	Provides a directory of multiple remote directories
mget	Downloads multiple files from the remote system
mkdir	Makes a directory on the remote system
mls	Provides a directory of multiple remote directories
mput	Uploads multiple files to the remote system

open	Begins an FTP session
prompt	Toggles interactive prompting on multiple commands
put	Uploads a file
pwd	Prints a working directory (like cd in DOS)
quit	Exits the FTP session
Quote	Sends arguments, verbatim, to the remote FTP server. A single FTP reply code is expected in return. Quote is identical to Literal.
recv	Downloads a file
rename	Renames a file
rmdir	Removes a directory
remotehelp	Gets a Help listing from the FTP server
send	Uploads a file
status	Shows the current status of FTP connections
trace	Toggles packet tracing
type	Sets the transfer type
user	Sends new user information
verbose	Toggles the verbose mode

As you can see, there's a ton of commands, and while it's not important to memorize them, you should be aware of their existence and how to find them. Many new GUI FTP programs have been created by third parties in an effort to simplify the FTP process. However, most FTP systems use the same commands in a manner that complies to the standard.

TFTP

The Trivial File Transfer Protocol (TFTP), also discussed in detail in Chapter 2, is equal to FTP without security. Using UDP to communicate in place of TCP, this program will communicate with a host running the TFTP server software. As with Telnet, Microsoft only provides the client portion of TFTP. The server part must come from a third party source, or be used from another operating system such as a UNIX server. The command format is as follows:

```
TFTP [-i] host [GET | PUT] source [destination]
```

-I	Specifies binary image transfer mode, also called octet. If -i is omitted, the file is transferred in ASCII mode.
source / destination	Is the full path designating where files are copied to and from
get	Transfers destination (specifies where to transfer) on the remote computer to source (specifies what file to transfer) on the local computer
put	Transfers source (specifies what file to transfer) on the remote computer to destination (specifies where to transfer) on the local computer

WWW

Web browsers such as Microsoft Internet Explorer and Netscape Navigator use HTTP to transfer pages of data from a Web server. The WWW follows a client/server model and uses the HTTP protocol between the client and the server.

System requirements for the client:

A Web browser There are several World Wide Web clients available, some of which can be freely downloaded from the Internet.

System requirements for the server:

The World Wide Web service The server responds with the status of the transaction, successful or failed, and the data for the request. After the data is sent, the connection is closed and no state is retained by the server. Each object in an HTTP document requires a separate connection.

Web browsers support the following data transfer benefits:

Web browsers support many data types A Web browser can automatically download and display text files and graphics, some can even play video and sound clips, and launch helper applications for known file types.

Web browsers support many protocols Web browsers support several data transfer protocols, including FTP, Gopher, HTTP, and NNTP.

FTP versus Telnet

Now let's review what we've seen so far. First, you use the FTP program to log onto a remote system, in a manner similar to Telnetting onto a remote system. In fact, it's so similar, some people have trouble understanding why there's a difference between Telnet and FTP. Telnet is for terminal emulation into another facility's computing power; FTP is for transferring files to and from another facility's computers. Once you FTP to another site, you'll find that the site usually has its files organized into a set of directories arranged in a tree structure. You move FTP's attention from one directory to another with the cd command.

You also may have a tree-structured directory on your system; if you wish to tell FTP to transfer to or from a particular directory, then you use the local cd command, or lcd. You use the binary command to tell FTP that you're going to transfer files that aren't simple ASCII. The get command requests that the remote system give you a file, and the put command requests that the remote system *accept* a file from you. And there you have the basics of FTP.

Printer Utilities

Microsoft TCP/IP Network Printing Support provides the ability to:

- Print to a printer attached to a Windows NT 4.0 print server from a UNIX host (LPDSVC service).

- Print to printers attached to UNIX hosts from any computer that can connect to a Windows NT computer. The Windows NT computer communicates with the UNIX printer using the LPR and LPQ utilities.

- Print to printers that use a network interface with TCP/IP.

Microsoft ✓ ***Exam Objective*** | **Configure a Windows NT Server computer to support TCP/IP printing.**

As mentioned previously, Microsoft provides three utilities to allow TCP/IP printing with NT:

- LPD
- LPQ
- LPR

Once you've installed and configured the TCP/IP printer support, you can connect to the printer using Print Manager or the LPR command. LPQ and LPR are client applications that communicate with LPD on the server.

LPD

The LPD (Line Printer Daemon) runs as a service on the Windows NT computer Line Printer Daemon Service (LPDSVC), and enables any computer with TCP/IP and LPR to send print jobs to the Windows NT computer. See the section "Installing a TCP/IP-based Printer" later in this chapter.

The configuration parameters for the TCP/IP Print Server are located under the following Registry key:

HKEY_LOCAL_MACHINE\SYSTEM\CurentControlSet\Services\ LPDSVC\Parameters

LPQ

LPQ (Line Printer Queue) allows a user to view the print queue on an LPD server. It displays the state of a remote LPD queue. The command format is this:

```
lpq -Sserver -Pprinter -l
```

The different parts of the command are:

-Sserver	The name or IP address of the host providing the LPD service
-Pprinter	The name of the print queue
-l	Specifies that a detailed status should be given

LPR

For command-line situations, or when you're printing from a UNIX host, use the LPR (Line Printer) command-line utility. The Line Printer utility allows jobs to be sent to a printer that is serviced by a host running an LPD server.

To send the print jobs, LPR makes a TCP connection to the LPD service using ports 512 and 1023. The command format looks like this:

```
lpr -Sserver -PPrinter [-CClass] [-JJobname] [-oOption] [-x] [-d]
filename
```

The different parts of the command are:

Sserver	The name or IP address of the host providing the LPD service
-Pprinter	The name of the print queue
-Cclass	The job classification for use on the banner page
-Jjob	The job name to be printed on the banner page
-oOption	Indicates the type of the file (the default is text file; use -ol for binary files such as postscript)
-x	For compatibility with SunOS 4.1x or prior version
-d	For sending a data file first

Exercise 11.1 will show you how to install a TCP/IP printer on your NT computer.

EXERCISE 11.1

Installing a TCP/IP-Based Printer

To install the TCP/IP-based printer, you do the following:

1. In the Control Panel, double-click Network. The Network dialog box appears.

2. Click the Services tab. The Services property sheet appears.

3. Click Add. The Select Network Services dialog box appears.

4. Click Microsoft TCP/IP Printing and then click OK. The Windows NT Setup box appears, prompting you for the full path of the Windows NT distribution files.

5. Type **C:\I386** (or the folder in which your distribution files are located), and then click OK. The appropriate files are copied to your workstation, and then the Network dialog box appears.

EXERCISE 11.1 (CONTINUED FROM PREVIOUS PAGE)

6. Click Close. A Network Settings Change message box appears, indicating that the computer needs to be restarted.

7. Click Yes.

8. Log on as Administrator.

9. In the Control Panel, double-click Services. The Services dialog box appears.

10. Select TCP/IP Print Server, and then click Start.

11. Click Close.

Exercise 11.2 shows you how to create a TCP/IP-based printer.

EXERCISE 11.2

Creating a TCP/IP-Based Printer

1. In the Control Panel, double-click Printer. The Printers window appears.

2. Double-click Add Printer. The Add Printer Wizard dialog box appears.

3. Click My Computer and then click Next.

4. Click Add Port. The Printer Ports dialog box appears.

5. Click LPR Port and then click New Port. The Add LPR Compatible Printer dialog box appears.

6. In the Name or Address of Server Providing LPD box, type your own IP address.

7. In the Name of Printer or Print Queue on That Server box, type **name_of_printer**, and then click OK.

8. Click Close.

EXERCISE 11.2 (CONTINUED FROM PREVIOUS PAGE)

9. Click Next.

10. Complete the Add Printer Wizard dialog box by entering the Share name, if necessary.

11. An Insert Disk message box prompts you for a floppy disk.

12. Click OK. A Windows NT Setup dialog box appears, prompting you for the location of the Windows NT Server distribution files.

13. Type in the path to the distribution files.

14. An icon should appear with the TCP/IP printer that was created.

Exercise 11.3 shows you how to print to a TCP/IP based printer by using Print Manager.

EXERCISE 11.3

Printing to a TCP/IP-Based Printer by Using Print Manager

1. In the Printers window, double-click Add Printer. The Add Printer Wizard dialog box appears.

2. Click Network Printer Server and then click Next. The Connect to Printer dialog box appears.

3. In the Printer box, type the name of your TCP/IP printer. The Add Printer Wizard prompts you to make this printer the default printer.

4. Click Yes and then click Next.

5. Click Finish. An icon representing the printer will be created in the Printers window.

6. Start Notepad. Then create and print a short document.

Microsoft Internet Information Server

Windows NT 4.0 introduces the Microsoft Internet Information Server. It's both a network file and an application server. This next section explains the design principles and architecture behind the Internet Information Server, which supports three protocols: HTTP, FTP, and Gopher. We've included some exercises to give you experience installing the Internet Information Server and configuring the protocols. To install the following items, select Control Panel ➤ Network ➤ Services tab.

Internet Service Manager Installs the administration program for managing services

World Wide Web Service Creates a WWW publishing server

Gopher Service Creates a gopher publishing server

FTP Service Creates a File Transfer Protocol (FTP) publishing server

ODBC Drivers and Administration Installs Open Database Connectivity (ODBC) drivers

Before installing the Microsoft Internet Information Server, you need to close all open applications—even the Control Panel window—or you're likely to get an open file error message. Also, if you intend to install the Gopher service, it's a good idea to declare an Internet domain name in the TCP/IP configuration (under the DNS tab). If you don't define an Internet domain name, you'll be notified to set one during the installation to ensure that Gopher operates properly.

Exercise 11.4 will help you install Microsoft's Internet Information Server. This will be version 2, which is included on the Server CD. We will upgrade to version 4 later in this chapter.

EXERCISE 11.4

Installing Microsoft's Internet Information Server

1. Select Control Panel ➢ Network ➢ Services tab. Click your right mouse button on Network Neighborhood, and then choose Properties. Select Add. You will be presented with a list of services.

2. Select Internet Information Server v2.0.

NOTE: When installing Microsoft NT Version 4.0 Server, the Install Internet Information Server icon appears by default on the desktop. Double-click the icon.

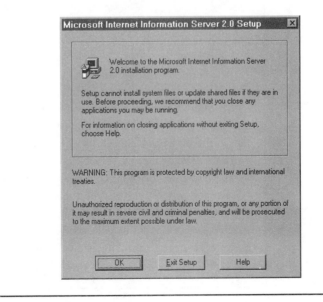

3. Type in the path to the Distribution files.

A Welcome screen will appear, notifying you to close all background applications. Close all other programs and then click OK.

4. You'll be given a menu listing all the service components (as listed above). Click on the adjacent box to select each desired component. Note that there's one extra item—Help and Sample Files. Select this option if you want to install online Help and sample HyperText Markup Language (HTML) files. Then click OK to continue.

A list of directories is presented for the locations of World Wide Web, FTP, and Gopher Publishing.

This is the path of the home (root) directory for each service you're installing. It's your option to accept the default directory, and place all files to be published in that directory. By default, and unless configured otherwise, the files in that directory, plus all subdirectories, will be available to clients. If you have existing files to be published, as in HTML files, type the fully qualified path to them or relocate the files to the new home directory, making adjustments where necessary in the documents to reflect the directory change. Of note—the Setup program doesn't allow network shares to be specified as root publishing directories. If your files are stored on a network share, you'll need to use Internet Service Manager to configure your publishing directories after setup's completed.

5. Click OK to continue.

6. You'll then be asked if it's OK to create directories. Choose Yes.

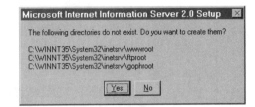

If you're installing the Gopher service and haven't declared an Internet Domain Name, you will receive a warning at this point. Click OK.

Also, if you're configuring your system with FTP, you may receive the following warning regarding the anonymous user account: "Your computer's guest account is enabled for network access." This means that any user can access the FTP service, regardless of whether they've been granted access to do so. Do you want to disable the guest access to the FTP service on this computer? This question is an individual judgment call. Do you want anonymous access? This is your decision.

The final phase in configuring the Installation involves the *ODBC (Open Database Connectivity)* drivers.

ODBC allows the Internet utilities to interface with a database—usually via *SQL Server.* In the Install In Drivers dialog box, you'll be prompted to select SQL Server. Then select OK to complete the installation.

You'll need to provide access to set up the ODBC drivers and data sources by using the ODBC *applet* icon in the Windows NT Control Panel. If you have an application running that uses ODBC, you may see an error message telling you that one or more components are in use. If so, close all applications and services—in this case the ones that use ODBC. You have the option of entering the Advanced section of the SQL dialog box to gain access to how the selected drivers are installed, managed, and translated.

In the Advanced Installation Options dialog box, you'll choose whether you want to perform a version check, install the driver manager, or look manually at each module's version by clicking on the Versions button. This will reveal the currently installed version of the MS Code Page Translator, the ODBC Driver Manager, and SQL Server. Click OK to complete the installation.

If after installation is complete, you decide to remove a Microsoft Internet Information Server component, you'll need to use the procedure in Exercise 11.5.

Removing the Microsoft Information Server

1. Choose Start ➢ Programs, then choose Microsoft Internet Server (Common).

2. Run the Internet Information Server Setup.

3. A Welcome screen will appear, notifying you to close all background applications. Close all other programs and then click on OK.

4. A menu will appear, asking you if you would like to Add/Remove Components, Repeat last install, or Remove All. If you add components, the instructions are the same as in the last exercise. If you select to remove all components or repeat the last installation, you will be prompted for confirmation before continuing.

Internet Service Manager

All of the services that you've installed for the Microsoft Internet Information Server can be managed by the Internet Services Manager, located in the Microsoft Internet Server (Common). This program is designed to assist you in the configuration and enhancement of your internetwork services. By using a single program to manage Internet services, you're able to manage all Internet services running on any Windows NT system in your network in a streamlined manner.

Service Manager Views

Depending on the number of systems running internetwork services, you can choose from three control view formats, found in Microsoft Internet Service Manager's View menu.

Report View

This selection provides an alphabetical listing of all selected computers. A host's name may appear more than once since each installed service is shown on a separate line. While in the Report view, you may sort by any column simply by clicking on the header. This view tends to be most useful when you're managing one or two systems running Internet Server. This is the default view.

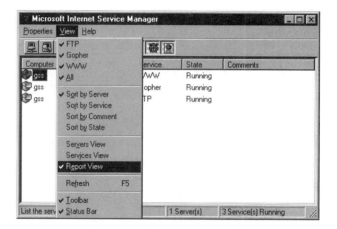

Servers View

This view is ideal for larger installations of Internet Information Server. It's the computer name of all systems running any of the Peer Web services. Click the plus symbol next to a server name to display which services that server is running. You can also double click on the server name. Double-click a service name to see its property sheets. This display is an easy to view tree that displays the services as traffic lights—Red (stopped), Yellow (paused), and Green (running).

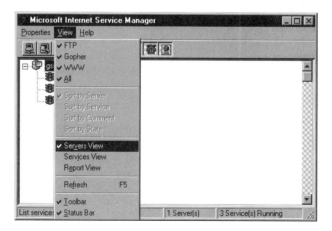

Services View

This is the most efficient way to determine where a particular service is running. All systems running a service such as FTP will be listed under that grouping. Click the plus symbol next to a service name to see which servers are running that service, or double-click on the service. Double-click the computer name under a service to see the property sheets for the service running on that computer.

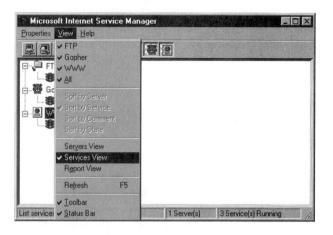

Service Manager Functions

No matter which view you choose, you'll be able to perform similar functions. The main reason behind changing views is to refine and assist the management process. You'll notice that all functions are included in the button bar, and that they're identical to those in the pull-down menus. The three functions performed in the manager are Connecting to a Server, Services Control, and Service Configuration.

Connect to Server

This can be selected through either the connect button, or the pull-down menu under Properties. This function is used to enable you to attach to the server you wish to manage. Use the Find All Servers button or pull-down menu to locate systems dynamically.

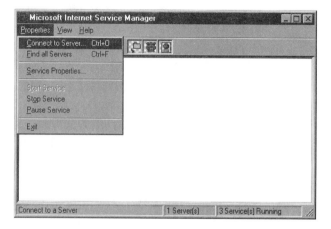

Services Control

This provides the ability to stop, start, or pause a service. Ordinarily, this type of function is done though the Server Manager or Control Panel. However, for many users this activity is difficult and cumbersome. Because of this, improvements were in order, and you can now simply use either the button bar or the pull-down menus.

Service Configuration

This is only accessible by double-clicking the leaf item in the displayed tree—there is no button bar or pull-down menu for this one. When you double-click the desired item, you'll access a setup page. The page is very similar to other service pages. They only vary slightly from service to service.

The configuration for each service is discussed in the following sections.

Unlike Windows NT 3.5x, the services are configured with a new anonymous account created by setup, rather than defaulting to the guest account. The new account name is called IUSR_computername. It uses a randomly generated password and privilege to log on locally. When Peer web services are installed on domain controllers, this account is added to the domain database automatically. After setup has completed installation, you can change the username and password for the account from the Service Property sheet inside the Internet Service Manager. The new username and password must match the same username and password in the Windows NT User Manager. The WWW, FTP, and gopher services use the IUSR_computername user account by default when anonymous access is allowed (not Guest). Rights for this account can be configured like all others, through User Manager. File permissions can be set on NTFS drives for IUSR_ computername, with Windows NT Explorer.

FTP Management

Under Microsoft Windows NT 4.0, FTP management is performed though the Internet Service Manager. As With Windows NT 3.5x, you can use any FTP client, including most Web browsers, to connect to the FTP server. To see the configuration of a host system with the FTP service, double-click the server from the Services View. You'll then be presented with the property sheets, including Service, Messaging, Directories, Logging, and Advanced.

Service

This sheet is the same as the configuration screen in Windows NT 3.5x. However, there are a few minor differences. First, maximum connections defaults to 1,000 rather than 20. Also, the connection timeout has increased from 10 minutes (3.5x) to 15, which is now measured in seconds (900 by default). Additionally, anonymous username, as discussed earlier, has been changed to IUSR_computername. Two new features to this screen are the addition of a comment field to describe the purpose of the FTP service, and the Current Sessions Manager—previously managed from the FTP Manager in Control Panel under Windows NT 3.5x. No additions or changes have been made to the Current Sessions Manager.

Messages

This isn't a truly new feature to the FTP service, since previously you could make these entries though the Registry editor under 3.5x. However, what's new about this sheet is that it now provides a Welcome message (logging on), an Exit message (logging off), and a Maximum connections message (limit of users logged on).

Directories

This sheet offers the configuration of directories—a feature not fully offered by Windows 3.5x. By default, all files and subdirectories will be available, if placed in the home directory. The home directory is the location where you should place all FTP materials. Although there can be only one home directory, you can choose to add and create virtual directories.

Virtual directories aren't visible to users, and can only be seen if the client machine knows the alias of the virtual directory. These directories are commonly used to distribute files that aren't open to the public, but still use anonymous names and passwords. With both home and virtual directories, you can designate the data storage area on another system. The input fields for a username and password in the Add or Edit dialog box are no longer grayed out if the directory is on an alternate system.

Keep in mind that when you use the network, you must provide a valid ID and password for the server that you're attaching the FTP service to. Errors will be displayed and reported on each entry line on the directory sheet. The point at which you add directories (home or virtual) is also the point at which you'll designate read and write access. As with 3.5x, security will be limited according to the anonymous account's file permissions. Finally, due to limitations that some browsers impose—that the FTP listing be styled in UNIX format—you may choose your directory listing system as UNIX or MS-DOS. This is a global setting for all directories. Some other function features are listed below.

Special Directories This can be used within the home directories to control the root directory displayed to FTP users. These directories must be physical subdirectories—they can't be specified by using virtual directories.

Username Directories These are directories within the home directory with names that match a particular username. If a user logs on with a username that has a matching directory in the home directory, that directory is used as the root. FTP username directories aren't created by default during setup.

Anonymous Directory This is also a directory within the home directory. If a user logs on using the password Anonymous, the directory name Anonymous is used as the root.

Annotated Directories Each directory can contain a file that can be used to summarize the information that the directory contains, and automatically provide access to remote browsers. This is done by creating a file called FTPSVC.CKM in the FTP directory. Most of the time, you'll want to make this a hidden file so that directory listings don't display it. From an FTP client, you would type **Site ckm** at the command prompt, or use the Registry Editor to enable annotated directories by adding the following value:

```
HKEY_LOCAL_MACHINE\SYSTEM\CurrentControlSet\Services\
MSFTPSVC\Parameters
```

```
AnnotateDirectories REG_DWORDRange: 0 or 1Default = 0 (directory
annotation is off).
```

This Registry entry doesn't appear by default in the Registry, so you must add an entry if you want to change its default value. If Directory Annotation is enabled on your FTP service, Web browsers may display error messages when browsing your FTP directories. You can eliminate such errors by limiting each annotation file to one line, or by disabling Directory Annotation.

Logging

This sheet allows you to enable FTP service logging. It can be enabled by checking the Enable Logging box. You may either send the logs to a file or to an *SQL/ODBC database*. If you elect to send it to a file, you may specify the location where you'd like the log files placed. Also, you have the option to open a new log daily (Inyymmdd.log), weekly (Inyymmww.log), monthly (Inyymm.log), or when the file reaches a designated size (INETSRVn.log). The filenames for the log vary according to the trigger you use, as shown in each set of parentheses ending with a .log extension. If you decide to send the information to an SQL/ODBC database, you must provide an ODBC data source name, the Table, and a username and password along with it.

![FTP Service Properties for tcpip dialog box showing the Logging tab with Enable Logging checked, Log to File selected with Daily option and log file directory C:\WINNT35\system32\LogFiles, and Log to SQL/ODBC Database options including ODBC Data Source Name (DSN), Table, User Name, and Password fields. Log file name: INyymmdd.log]

Advanced

This sheet limits access to the FTP server in two ways: source systems and network utilization.

FTP Service Properties for tcpip

Service | Messages | Directories | Logging | Advanced

By default, all computers will be:

⊙ Granted Access
○ Denied Access

Except those listed below:

Access	IP Address	Subnet Mask
🔒 Denied	160.1.23.123	

Add...
Edit...
Remove

☐ Limit Network Use by all Internet Services on this computer
Maximum network use:
4,096   KB/S

OK   Cancel   Apply   Help

The functions presented here were offered in a limited manner, at best, in Windows NT 3.5x.

By default, all systems are granted access. If you want to limit access, you have three options. First, you can grant access to all computers with the exclusion of those you add as single computers, or a certain group of computers. Second, you can deny access to all computers, with the exception of those you add as single computers or a group of computers. When adding a single computer, use the button with the three dots to look up a host name from DNS (if registered) to get that system's IP address. When adding a group of computers, this option (host name lookup) isn't available; however, you now have the option to specify a subnet mask. The last way the Advanced sheet allows you to limit access to the FTP server is by setting a maximum network utilization in terms of kilobytes per second. This is done by clicking the box next to the Limit Network Use By All Internet Services on This Computer dialog box. As you have probably figured out, this option affects all Internet services, WWW, FTP, and Gopher.

Gopher Management

We talked about Gopher in Chapter 2, and although it's not shiny and new to TCP/IP, support for it is a new feature to Windows NT 4.0. To refresh your memory, a Gopher service is a function you can use to create links to other computers or services, annotate your files and directories, and create custom menus. The implementation that is included with Windows NT is full-featured, including something called Gopher Plus Selector Strings. This allows the server to return additional information to the client, like administrator name, modification date, and MIME type. From the Internet Service Manager, all configuration functions are the same as those for FTP, with the exception that there isn't an option to specify messages, or an option to specify read/write access from the directory sheet.

All Gopher files should be placed in the gopher home directory: (\INETSRV\ GOPHROOT), by default. This makes browsing the gopher directories a breeze for clients. Tag files can be created to enable links to other computers or services, to annotate your files and directories, and to create custom menus. The gopher service will make the following available under a specified directory tree:

- Tags and how they are to be stored

- Indexes to speed up searches

- Activity log records

To enable Wide Area Information Search (WAIS) index searching, you must change the following entry in the Windows NT Registry from 0 (disabled) to 1(enabled): HKEY_LOCAL_MACHINE\SYSTEM\CurrentControlSet\ Services\GopherSVC\CheckForWAISDB.

Gopher Tag Files

Tag files allow you to jazz up the standard gopher display sent to clients with additional material, and also to provide links to other systems. Tag files are responsible for all the information about a file that's sent to a client. This information must include the name of the file to be displayed for the client. Typically, tag files contain a display name, host name, and port number. If you're utilizing Gopher Plus, you can add more information to each tag file, such as the server administrator's name and e-mail address, the file's creation date, and its last modification date. In order to use these features, you must first create the file, and then store it on the gopher server. The tags for your gopher site can be created with the gdsset utility. For information syntax on this utility, type **gdsset** by itself on a command line. You'll then be presented with the following information:

```
Usage: gdsset [-crl] [-g<GopherItemType>] [-f <FriendlyName>][-s
<Selector>] [-h<HostName>] [-p<PortNumber>]-D<Directory> -d
<filename> [-a <AdminName>] [-e <AdminEmail>]-c change (edit/
create) the existing tag information(Default is to create a new
tag information)-r read and dump the tag information on console-d
specifies that given file is actually a directory-g specifies
gopher object type.
```

The Gopher Object Type is a single character—usually a digit number from 0 to 9. The default type is 9 for binary. See the following Gopher type codes for complete details (valid when -r is not used):

-f **<FriendlyName>** specifies Friendly Name for object (valid when -r is not used).

-l specifies that link information is to be set for write (valid when -r is not used).

-s **<Selector>** specifies the selector for link (valid when -l is used).

-h<HostName> specifies the Host for link (valid when -l is used).

-p<PortNumber> specifies the Port number for link (valid when -l is used).

-a <AdminName> specifies the Administrator Name, defaults to the service administrator's name in the Service dialog box of the Microsoft Internet Service Manager.

-e <AdminEmail> specifies the Administrator Email, defaults to the service administrator's e-mail name in the Service dialog box of the Microsoft Internet Service Manager.

Note that this command line automatically sets the hidden file attribute on the tag files you create. Typical use of the command is as follows:

```
gdsset -c -g# -f description of file -a administrator's name -e
e-mail
```

The remainder of the command options are typically for supporting advanced features such as providing links to other hosts. Also, this command can be used in *batch mode*, or *nested batch* with the for command. Refer to online help for more details on performing this action. After the information has been set for a file, you can quickly determine its accuracy by using the gdsset -r filename command.

Gopher Type Codes

The following is a list of all the possible type codes for Gopher. Again, if not specified, the default is 9 for binary. These codes are used following -g in the gdsset command.

0 A file, usually a flat text file

1 A gopher directory

2 A CSO phone-book server

3 An error

4 A Macintosh file in Binhex format

5 An MS-DOS binary archive

6 A UNIX Uuencoded file

7 An index-search server

8 A Telnet session

9 A binary file

c A calendar or calendar of events

g A graphic interchange file (GIF) graphic

h An HTML World Wide Web hypertext page

i An in-line text that is not an item

I Another kind of image file

m A BSD format mbox file

P A PDF document

T A TN3270 mainframe session

: A bitmap image (use Gopher plus information for type of image)

Tag files are hidden files. Use the ATTRIB command, Explorer, or File Manager to set the hidden attribute for tag files. On drives formatted with a FAT file system, the tag filename uses the same name as the file it describes, with .GTG as the file extension appended to the 8.3 name. The name then becomes 8.3.3. For example, if the content filename is SAMPLE.TXT, the tag filename would be SAMPLE.TXT.GTG. The tag files on FAT can be edited with most ASCII text editors. On drives formatted using NTFS, :GTG is appended to the filename instead of .GTG. In this case, if the content filename is SAMPLE.TXT, then the tag filename would be SAMPLE.TXT:GTG. Unlike FAT files, NTFS tag files can't be edited by most text editors because they're stored in an alternate data stream. If a tag file is stored on an NTFS volume, you must first manually move the tag file before you move the corresponding data files. When you move the tag file you'll have to modify the hidden attribute both before and after the move. Again, hiding and unhiding files is done through the ATTRIB command, File Manager, and Explorer.

World Wide Web Service

Before we get caught up in the Web, it's important to understand the terminology involved. Here's a list of key terms and their definitions:

Internet: A global network of computers

Intranet: Refers to any TCP/IP network that is not connected to the Internet

World Wide Web (WWW): A graphical, easy-to-navigate interface for looking at documents on the Internet

Hyperlinks: Shortcuts on WWW documents to aid in connecting to other pages, downloading files, etc.

Uniform Resource Locator (URL): The standard naming convention on the Internet; for example, http://www.microsoft.com/home.html

Web Browser: A tool for navigating and accessing information on the Web (e.g. Internet Explorer, Mosaic and Netscape Navigator, etc.)

HyperText Transport Protocol (HTTP): A protocol specification used to respond to browser requests. Your workstation can be configured to provide FTP and gopher services.

HTML: The document standard for Internet Web pages

Windows NT 4.0 adds Web services to its suite of TCP/IP applications. Now you can create and design your own intranet or Internet Web page quickly and easily. Traditionally, this service has been performed by UNIX-based hosts or Windows NT systems utilizing third-party vendor software. The software is generally costly, and in many cases, more than just a bit of a challenge to configure.

In Windows NT 4.0, the configuration method is the same whether you'll be using your system on the Internet or an intranet. The only major differences from one implementation to the next deal with how security is configured. With a Windows NT workstation, just as sharing files doesn't make your workstation a dedicated file server, publishing Web pages doesn't make your workstation a dedicated Internet server. If you need a dedicated Internet server with advanced administration capabilities and the ability to respond to a multitude of simultaneous connections, you should use Microsoft Internet Information Server. It's included with Windows NT Server Version 4.0.

Web pages are constructed in HTML (hypertext markup language), which includes both hypertext and hyperlinks. This is the standard document form that Web browsers support. HTML enables a Web page to make connections and reference other Web pages both locally and on foreign hosts, even if they're part of an entirely different network. Although you can create these files in practically any text editor, it's generally a good idea to use a product such as Internet Assistant for Word (free from Microsoft), Netscape Navigator's Editor, or another HTML-specific editor. Doing so will ensure proper formatting and reduce debugging time, and allow you to link to any SQL/ODBC database. This support can be added by setting up the ODBC drivers and data sources using the ODBC applet in the Windows NT Control Panel.

During installation, if you have an application running that uses ODBC, you might receive an error message telling you that one or more components are in use. If this happens, before continuing, close all applications and services that use ODBC. When setting up peer Web services, you'll find that most Internet browsers, such as Internet Explorer (ships with NT 4.0), structure their addressing sequence in URL format. URL syntax is a specific sequence of protocol, domain name, and path to the requested information.

Configuring Web Service

Configuring the Web Service sheets can be achieved through the Internet Service Manager. Most configuration functions are the same as FTP's, with some exceptions. First, there's no option to specify messages, since it's done by the HTML Web page. The other configuration differences are discussed below.

Service

The configuration is the same as FTP's with the exception that password authentication is done at three levels:

- Allow Anonymous

- Basic (Clear Text)

■ Windows NT Challenge/Response

The anonymous configuration is the most common on the Internet, and is generally used to allow the public to see your Web page. When this is the only configured password authentication option, the user will be logged in as the anonymous account regardless of name or password. Basic, or clear text, is a simple level of password protection. As with FTP, passwords are sent unencrypted and therefore may be viewed with a packet analyzer. Depending on your needs, this can be a drag. By Default, the basic option isn't enabled, but basic authentication can be encoded when used in conjunction with *Secure Sockets Layer (SSL),* which ensures usernames and passwords are encrypted before transmission. All browsers support basic authentication. *Windows NT Challenge/Response* is a system by which the service will honor requests by clients to send user account information using the Windows NT Challenge/ Response authentication protocol. This protocol uses a one-way algorithm— a mathematical formula that can't be reversed—to prevent passwords from being transmitted. The Windows NT Challenge/Response authentication process is started automatically when an access denied error is encountered on an anonymous client request.

Directories

This sheet is primarily the same in concept as FTP's configuration, however there are a few distinct differences. First, notice that by default this sheet lists both a home directory and a virtual directory named scripts. This provides a secure place to locate your scripts files, as well as creates a public Web home directory. Next, you can select the enable default document to select a specific Web page, in HTML, to be delivered to your Web browser when it's not even specified to do so. Simply type the name of the default document in the designated dialog box. You can also enable directory browsing on the directory sheet. Directory browsing allows a user to be presented with a hypertext listing of directories and files so they can navigate freely through your directory structure.

You can choose Edit Properties to add or modify directory entries. You have the same Virtual Directory options as with FTP. This allows you to add directories outside the home directory, including those that reside on other hosts. See the FTP Directory sheet for complete details on doing this. Also, as with FTP, virtual directories won't appear in WWW directory listings; you must create explicit links in HTML files for the user, or the user must know the URL in order to access virtual directories. You can also virtualize a server by clicking on the box next to Virtual Server. This will allow you to specify an IP address for the entry.

Finally, as with FTP, the Web service uses access control. It must match any existing NTFS rights to work. These rights include Read, Execute, and Require Secure SSL Channel. Read should be selected for information directories, but it's not a good idea to use this option for directories containing programs. Execute allows clients to run any programs in a given directory. This box is selected by default for the directory created for programs. Put all your scripts and executable files into this directory. Do not select this box for directories containing static content. Select the Require secure SSL channel (Not Installed) box if using Secure Sockets Layer (SSL) security to encrypt data transmissions. This must be installed with the key manager in order work.

Key Manager

The key manager is used to create a Secure Socket Layer security encryption implementation. The key manager may be launched by selecting Start ➤ Programs (Microsoft Internet Server (Common). Key manager is a central tool that can be used to manage all security keys on any NT-based system with Microsoft's Peer Web Services. You can connect to a remote system by choosing the Servers pull-down menu, or by using the tool bar.

To create a new key, select Create New Key in the Key pull-down. Fill in the information in this dialog box, then click OK to create two files. The first file is a key file containing a key pair. The second file is a certificate request file. When your request is processed, the provider will return a certificate to you. Below is the New Key dialog box; fill in the information as explained below.

Key Name: A descriptive name for the key you are creating

Password: Specifies a password to encrypt the private key

Bits: Generates a key pair—by default 1024 bits long; options are 1024, 512 or 768 bits

Organization: Your company name

Organizational Unit: The division or department within your company; for example, Sales

Common Name: The domain name of the server; for example, www.company.com

Country: Two-letter ISO Country designation; for example, US, FR, AU, UK, and so on

State/Province: The full, non-abbreviated name of your state or province

Locality: The full name of the city where your company is located

Request File: The name of the request file that'll be created or accepted by default. Accepting default automatically copies the Key Name you have designated, and attaches an .REQ extension to it to create the request filename. For example, if you have typed security in the Key Name box, the default request filename will become SECURITY.REQ.

Do not use commas in any field. Commas are interpreted as the end of that field and will generate an invalid request without even giving you so much as a warning!

When you've filled in all the information, click OK. Retype your password when prompted, and click OK again. Your key will appear in the Key Manager window under the computer name. Once completed, you'll need to contact VeriSign's Web site at www.verisign.com to get details on how to get a certificate to activate your key. The key generated by Key Manager isn't valid for use on the Internet until you obtain a valid key certificate for it from the proper key authorities. Until you do so, the key can't be used, and will lie dormant on its host computer.

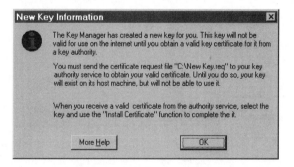

Once you have your key, you should then select the Key Graphic and use the Key pull-down to select Install Certificate. This will validate the key and give you a date range during which the key is usable. A summary for the key reflecting the information that you gave when you created it appears in the lower-right corner of the screen. When installing the key, you'll be prompted to select or type in the IP address of the server to which you want to apply the Secure Sockets Layer key. Your choices are none, default, or to specify or select an address.

Applying Your Certificate to Your Server

After you complete your certificate request, you will receive a signed certificate from the certification authority. Consult your certification authority for complete details. It'll look something like the following example:

```
-----BEGIN CERTIFICATE-----

JIEBSDSCEXoCHQEwLQMJSoZILvoNVQECSQAwcSETMRkOAMUTBhMuVrM

mIoAnBdNVBAoTF1JTQSBEYXRhIFN1Y3VyaXR5LCBJbmMuMRwwGgYDVQ

QLExNQZXJzb25hIEN1cnRpZm1jYXR1MSQwIgYDVQQDExtPcGVuIE1hc

mt1dCBUZXN0IFN1cnZ1ciAxMTAwHhcNOTUwNzE5MjAyNzMwWhcNOTYw

NTEOMjAyOTEwWjBzMQswCQYDVQQGEwJVUzEgMB4GA1UEChMXU1NBIER

hdGEgU2VjdXJpdHksIEluYy4xHDAaBgNVBAsTE1B1cnNvbmEgQ2VydG

1maWNhdGUxJDAiBgNVBAMTG09wZW4gTWFya2V0IFR1c3QgU2VydmVyI

DExMDBcMA0GCSqGSIb3DQEBAQUAA0sAMEgCQQDU/71rgR6vkVNX40BA

q1poGdSmGkD1iN3sEPfSTGxNJXY58XH3JoZ4nrF7mIfvpghNi1taYim

vhbBPNqYe4yLPAgMBAAEwDQYJKoZIhvcNAQECBQADQQBqyCpws9EaAj

KKAefuNP+z+8NY8khckgyHN2LLpfhv+iP8m+bF66HNDU1Fz8ZrVOu3W

QapgLPV90kIskNKXX3a

------END CERTIFICATE-----
```

Beautiful, isn't it?! Copy and save the text to a file, using a tool such as Notepad, and give it a name you can remember—something like CERTIF.TXT. Then use Key Manager to install your signed certificate onto the server. Exercise 11.6 will lead you through the steps of installing a certificate.

If you don't specify an IP address while installing your certificate, the same certificate will be applied to all virtual servers created on the system. If you're hosting multiple sites on a single server, you can specify that the certificate only be used for a given IP address by adding the specific IP address, for example: 160.191.82.54.

EXERCISE 11.6

Installing a Certificate

1. Select Programs ➤ Microsoft Internet Server ➤ Common ➤ Key Manager.

2. Next choose Key ➤ Create New Key.

3. Fill in your information in the dialog box, then choose OK.

Your final step to completing the setup is to commit to the changes. You may do this by either exiting the program, or using the pull-down menu.

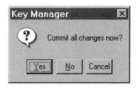

Installing IIS Version 4

When installing IIS 4, you can either upgrade from an existing version (except IIS 4 betas) or install a shiny new version.

To obtain a copy of IIS 4, go to the Microsoft Web site (www.microsoft.com) and either order the CD for IIS version 4, or download the installation files. On a 28.8 modem this will take around four hours!

Let's take a look at how we can install version 4. But, first make sure you have Service Pack 3 installed, and then download the appropriate IIS version 4 files from the Microsoft Web site. (It must be IE v4.01 to install the NT Option Pack.)

1. Put the CD in your server. It should automatically open Internet Explorer.

2. Click Install.

3. Click Installing Windows NT Option Pack.

4. Install Service Pack 3 if it isn't already installed.

5. Click Setup Windows NT 4.0 Option Pack

6. If you do not have Internet Explorer installed, a dialog box will appear, asking if it is OK to do so (see Figure 11.1).

FIGURE 11.1

Install Internet
Explorer 4.0 prompt

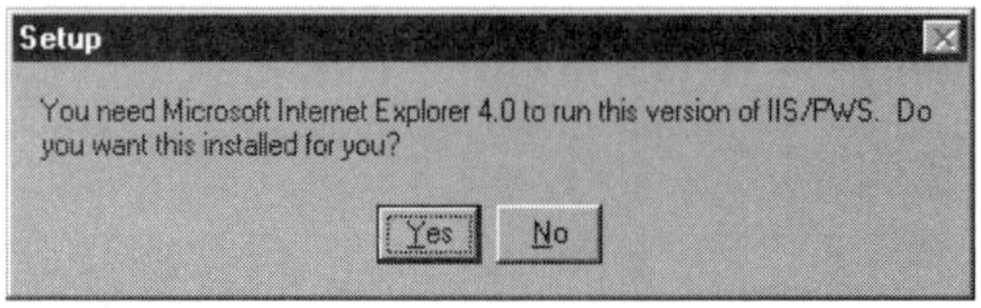

7. If you choose yes, you'll wait a few minutes and then...you guessed it, the computer will reboot! Figure 11.2 shows the reboot screen you will get.

FIGURE 11.2

The reboot screen

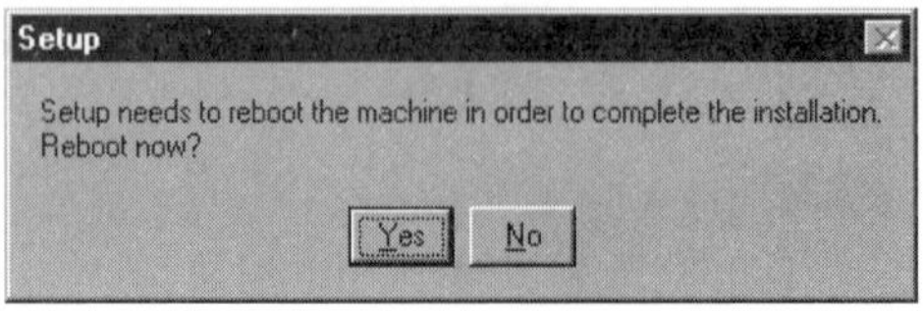

8. After it reboots, the computer will take a few minutes to update the files it has copied. It will then display screen shown in Figure 11.3.

9. Click Next.

10. Because I already have IIS version 2 installed, Setup wants to know if I just want to upgrade the installed components (Upgrade Only) or if I want to add new components (Setup Plus). I choose Setup Plus. (See Figure 11.4.)

FIGURE 11.3

Setup NT 4.0 Option
Pack continued

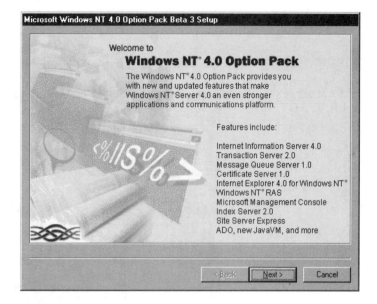

FIGURE 11.3

Setup NT 4.0 Option
Pack continued

FIGURE 11.4

Upgrade or Upgrade
Plus screen

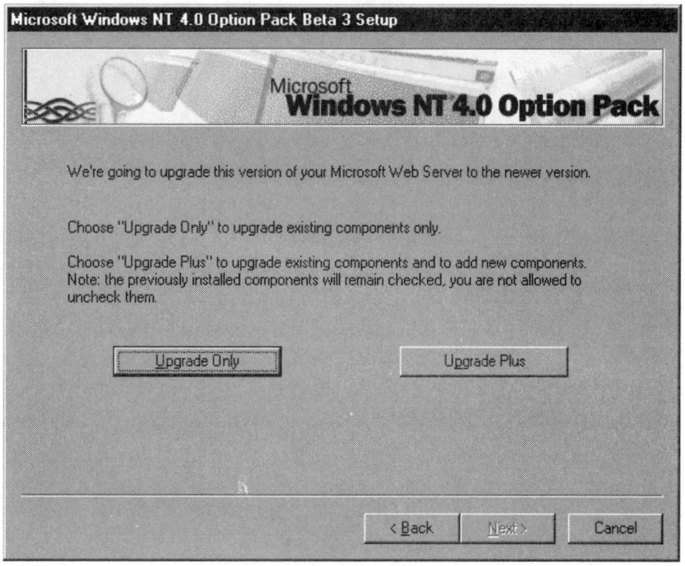

11. The screen shown in Figure 11.5 appears and gives you your upgrade options. You can add the new components that are listed here, but you cannot delete any that were already installed.

FIGURE 11.5

Upgrade options

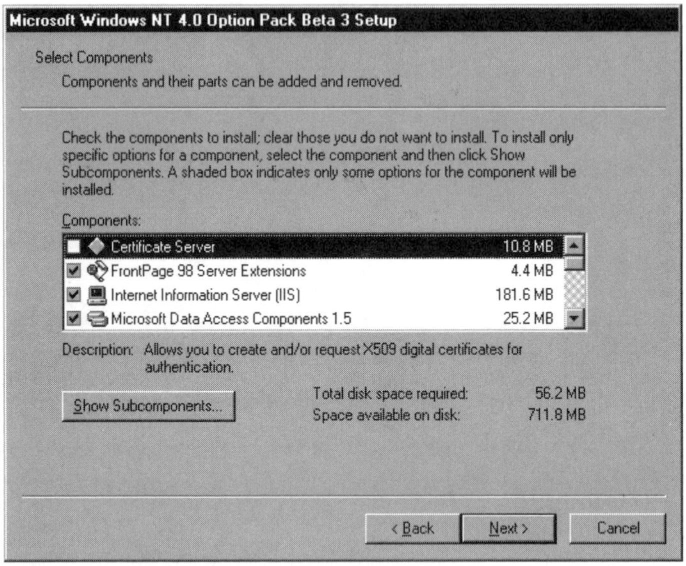

12. Click Next after choosing the components you want.

13. For any new components you choose, you need to create a new directory. Setup walks you through creating new directories for any of the new components you checked, as shown in Figure 11.6.

14. The screen in Figure 11.7 shows you the status of your installation as Setup finishes copying files.

15. After Setup is done coping files, you will see the screen shown in Figure 11.8. Click Finish.

16. The will take a few seconds to finalize the settings, and then it will ask you to reboot.

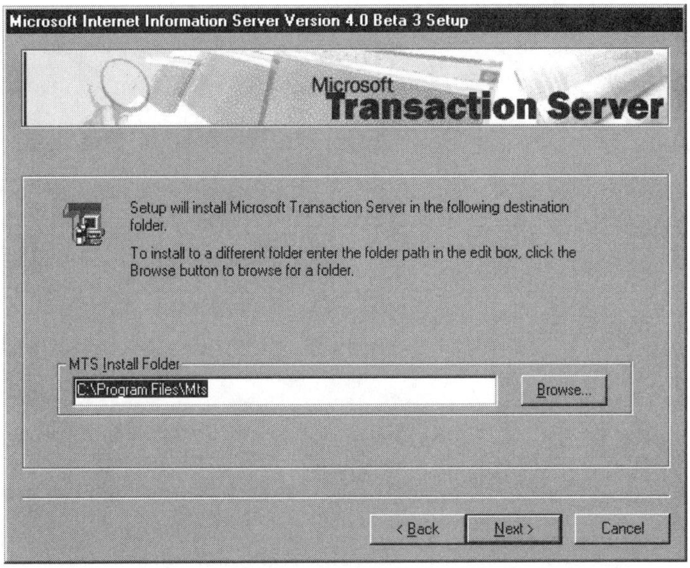

FIGURE 11.6

Creating new directories

FIGURE 11.6

Creating new directories

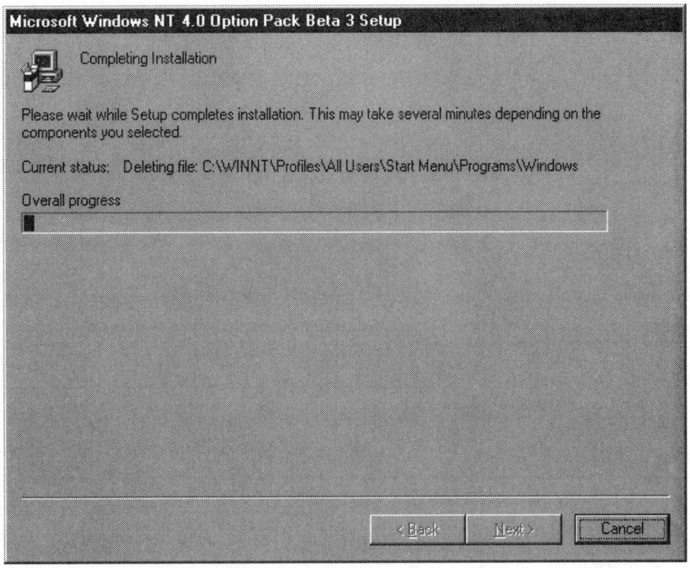

FIGURE 11.7

Setup status

FIGURE 11.8
We're done! Click finish.

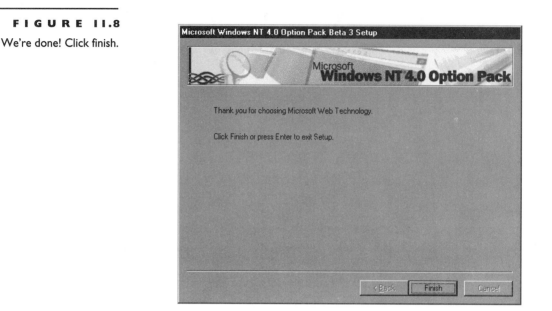

TCP/IP Dial-Up Networking with RAS

Dial-up networking (DUN) is the method for establishing connections to external computer hosts. It works with the Remote Access Service (RAS) to extend network connectivity to external clients. DUN can run on both NT Server and NT Workstation.

Microsoft
✓ ***Exam***
Objective

Configure a RAS server and dial-up networking for use on a TCP/IP network.

Remote Access Service (RAS)

RAS is an NT Service that runs on either NT Workstation or NT Server. A remote RAS client can access and operate everything a standard network-attached client can, but it will be slower. NT Server can support 256 simultaneous RAS connections, but NT Workstation can only run a single RAS connection, whether inbound or outbound.

Network protocols such as NetBEUI, NWLink, and TCP/IP must be encapsulated when being sent over a phone line and then decapsulated on the other end. The protocols are encapsulated in what are called Line Protocols. Examples of line protocols are SLIP and PPP.

You can install both RAS and DUN during set up of NT or anytime after. To set up RAS after NT is configured, add the RAS service from the Network applet in Control Panel.

Summary

The first concept we focused on in this chapter was how communication occurs within a diversified communication environment. Some important things to remember when communicating to foreign TCP/IP hosts are:

- You must use TCP/IP. NetBEUI won't talk to TCP/IP, and nor will IPX.

- Only commands supported by the specific TCP/IP utility, such as FTP, TELNET, etc., may be used to communicate with the foreign system.

- Applications that are accessed on the foreign system are run centrally at the foreign system—not at your local system.

- TCP/IP utilities can use either the host name or the IP address.

- Both local and remote host names that are used in TCP/IP utilities must be resolved in the HOSTS file, DNS, WINS, b-node broadcast, or LMHOSTS file.

Microsoft provides FTP, LPQ, LPR, REXEC, RSH, RCP, Telnet, and TFTP TCP/IP utilities, which can be organized into three divisions as follows:

- Command utilities: REXEC, RSH, and Telnet

- Transfer utilities: RCP, FTP, and TFTP

- Printer utilities: LPR and LPQ

The majority of the commands presented in the chapter for these utilities are similar in implementation to their UNIX-based counterparts, and like UNIX, they're usually case-sensitive.

In the next section, we discussed the Internet Information Server, the most important being the platform-independent FTP service. Even though Microsoft's is run on Windows NT, and others are run on UNIX, there aren't any major differences between them from the client viewpoint. On a network that's directly connected to the Internet, you can retrieve a file from a remote FTP site simply by typing start ftp, opening the site by name or IP address, listing the file, and using the get command.

The last issue we covered was internetwork printing. Microsoft TCP/IP Network Printing Support provides the ability to:

- Print to a printer attached to a Windows NT print server from a UNIX host (LPDSVC service).

- Print to printers attached to UNIX hosts from any computer that can connect to a Windows NT computer. The Windows NT computer communicates with the UNIX printer using the LPR and LPQ utilities.

- Print to printers that use a network interface with TCP/IP.

- When taking the NT TCP/IP 4.0 test, you must understand how to FTP to a remote site and how to troubleshoot problems associated with not being able to ftp to remote sites. You also must be able to understand the different printing commands used with NT Server 4.0. Make sure that you go through the following questions and that you understand them completely.

Review Questions

1. You have a TCP/IP print device directly connected to your NT Server. How do you configure the NT Server to forward the documents to the print device?

   A. Redirect the jobs using LPR.

   B. Redirect the jobs using LPQ.

   C. Install the TCP/IP printing service on the server.

   D. Install the TCP/IP printing service on the print device.

2. You have a UNIX computer with a print device connected. Business requirements dictate that users be able to print to this print device. How should the users send their output to this print device?

   A. On their workstations, capture a logical printer port to the UNC name for the printer.

   B. On their workstations use the LPR utility.

   C. On their workstations use the LPQ utility.

   D. On their workstations install the TCP/IP Printing service.

3. You have an NT Server with a print device connected. How can you configure the server so your UNIX workstations can print to the printer using LPR?

   A. On the NT Server, install the TCP/IP printing service.

   B. On the Unix computers, install the TCP/IP Printing service.

   C. Create a printer share.

   D. Give the printer an IP address.

   E. Add the LPR Server Service to the NT Server.

4. You have an NT Server with a print device connected and want your NT workstations to be able to use this printer. How should you configure the NT Server?

   A. Assign an IP address to the printer and give this address to the UNIX users.

   B. Install the LPR utility on the server.

   C. Create a printer share.

   D. Install the TCP/IP printer service on the NT Server.

5. You have a print device connected to a UNIX computer running the LPD. What should you do to allow NT Workstation users to print to this device but have the printer still be managed by your NT Server? (Choose all that apply.)

   A. Install the LPR utility on your NT workstations.

    B. Install the TCP/IP printing service on the server.

    C. Install the SNMP service on all workstations.

    D. Create a shared printer on the server that uses an LPR port to send documents to the UNIX print device.

6. You want your users to be able to access your NT Server on the Internet and download files. Which service must you use on your NT Server?

    A. DHCP

    B. DNS

    C. FTP

    D. SNMP

    E. WINS

7. You want your UNIX users to be able to connect to a remote NT Server. However, when they run the command ftp 172.16.31.2 to connect to the remote server, they cannot connect. They *can* connect to a local NT Server. What could the problem be?

    A. No DNS server is defined on the UNIX workstations.

    B. The workstations are not configured with a default gateway.

    C. The NT server is not configured with a default gateway.

    D. The UNIX workstation are not configured to use WINS.

    E. The NT Server is not running the FTP service.

8. You want to view the documents that have been sent to a UNIX TCP/IP printer. Which utility should you use?

    A. FTP.EXE

    B. LPQ.EXE

    C. LPR.EXE

    D. TELNET.EXE

9. You want to run a remote program on a UNIX computer. What utility should you use?

    A. FTP.EXE

    B. LPQ.EXE

    C. LPR.EXE

    D. TELNET.EXE

10. Which utility should you use to copy files from a UNIX computer to your NT Workstation?

    A. FTP.EXE

    B. LPQ.EXE

    C. LPR.EXE

    D. TELNET.EXE

11. You want to print a text document on a UNIX print device. Which utility should you use?

    A. FTP.EXE

    B. LPQ.EXE

    C. LPR.EXE

    D. TELNET.EXE

12. You can connect to a remote NT Server using FTP through NT Explorer. However, you cannot connect when you type **ftp sales.acme.com**. What could be wrong?

    A. DNS is not defined on your workstation.

    B. You do not have a default gateway configured on your workstation, or it is incorrect.

    C. The NT Server does not have a default gateway configured.

    D. The SNMP service is not running.

13. You are working at a Windows NT workstation that is not configured for DNS. The HOSTS file on your workstation contains the following entries:

131.107.32.9	sales	#sales FTP server
131.107.8.254	corp Web server	#intranet Web server
131.107.16.67	UNIX developer	#UNIX computer/ developers
131.107.16.12	developer	#developers FTP server

When you ftp to developer, you connect to a Windows NT Server on a remote subnet, but when you try ftp 131.107.16.12, it fails. What is most likely the problem?

A. The host name assigned to the server is not Developer.

B. The IP address assigned to the FTP server is not 131.107.16.12.

C. The HOSTS file on your workstation is not returning the correct host name for the FTP server.

D. The FTP server is not running TCP/IP.

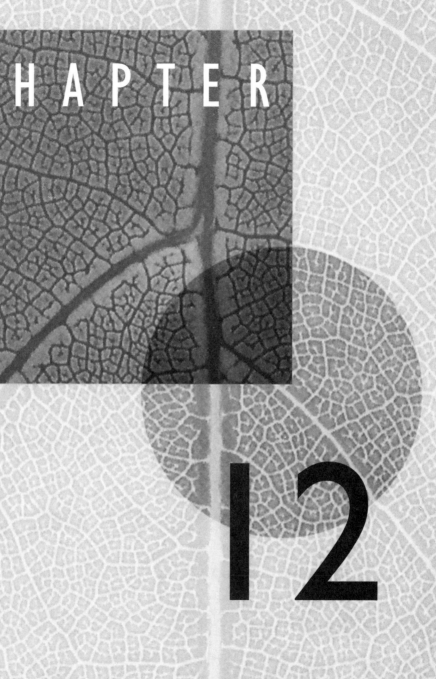

CHAPTER

12

Microsoft SNMP Services

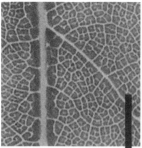

In this chapter we're going to look at Simple Network Management Protocol (SNMP). Sound simple? Not really. SNMP is actually a pretty complex protocol, but it *is* simple to administrate—that's the beauty of it!

We'll start out by explaining the purpose of SNMP and the different operations performed by an SNMP agent and an SNMP manager. Then we'll define Management Information Base (MIB) and show you how to install and configure the Microsoft SNMP service.

An SNMP Overview

SNMP (Simple Network Management Protocol) is one very important protocol in the TCP/IP suite. It allows you to monitor and manage a network from a single workstation or several workstations, called SNMP managers. SNMP is actually a family of specifications that provide a means for collecting network management data from the devices residing in a network. It also avails a method for those devices to report any problems they are experiencing to the management station. From an SNMP manager, you can query the network's devices regarding the nature of their functions. Examples of machines you'd want to monitor include:

- Computers running Windows NT

- Lan Manager servers

- Routers and gateways

- Minicomputers or mainframe computers

- Terminal servers

- Wiring hubs

Figure 12.1 shows the network administrator at an SNMP management station making queries to various devices on the internetwork. A router can be queried for the contents of its routing table, or for statistics relating to the amount of traffic it's forwarding. A mainframe computer can be surveyed to determine which ports are listing for requests, or for what connections have been established with clients. A Windows NT computer can also be monitored, and can alert the manager of pertinent events, such as when a particular host is running out of hard disk space. Regardless of the type of device that is queried, the SNMP agent on the device is able to return meaningful, highly useful information to the manager.

FIGURE 12.1

SNMP Managers and SNMP Agents

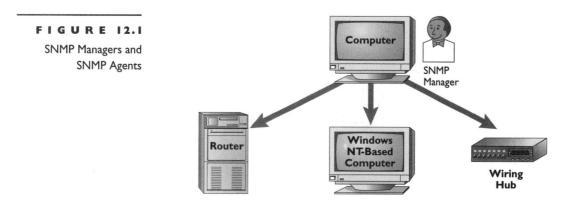

SNMP is defined in RFC 1157.

Management Systems and Agents

SNMP uses a distributed architecture consisting of management systems and agents. It works like this: The manager first submits a request to the agent either to obtain or to set the value of a networking variable within the agent's Management Information Base (MIB). The agent satisfies the request according to the community name accompanying the request. A community name can be compared to a password, and will be discussed more thoroughly later in the chapter.

The SNMP protocol is simple in that only five types of commands are defined within it. They are:

- GetRequest: The command used by the manager to request information from an agent.

- GetNextRequest: Also employed by the manager, this command is used if the information desired is contained within a table or array. The manager can use this command repeatedly until the complete contents of the array have been acquired.

- GetResponse: The queried agent uses this command to satisfy a request made by the manager.

- SetRequest: The manager uses this command to change the value of a parameter within the agent's MIB.

- Trap: A special command the agent uses to inform the manager of a certain event.

Figure 12.2 outlines the primary function of the management system—requesting information from an agent. A management system is any computer running the SNMP management software. This system can initiate the `GetRequest`, `GetNextRequest`, and the `SetRequest` operations.

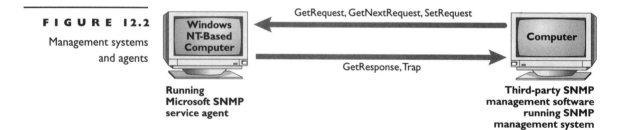

FIGURE 12.2

Management systems and agents

An SNMP agent is any computer running SNMP agent software—most often, a server or router. The chief obligation of an SNMP agent is to perform the tasks initiated by the `GetRequest`, `GetNextRequest`, and `SetRequest` commands, as required by a management system. The Microsoft SNMP service is the SNMP agent software. The only operation initiated by an agent is through the `trap` command, which alerts management systems to an extraordinary event, such as a password violation.

MIB: The Management Information Base

A MIB describes the objects, or entries, that are to be included in the SNMP agent database. For this reason, SNMP agents are sometimes referred to as MIBs. Objects in a MIB must be defined so that developers of the management station software will know which objects are available, the object names, and their related values. This information is included in a MIB specification.

A MIB records and stores information about the host it is running on. An SNMP manager can request and collect information from an agent's MIB, as well as inspect or alter the objects contained therein. For example, from the SNMP manager you can examine the number of sessions that have taken place on a certain remote host. The Microsoft SNMP service supports Internet MIB II, Lan Manager MIB II, DHCP MIB, and WINS MIB. Here's a description of each of these tools.

Internet MIB II A superset of the previous standard, Internet MIB I. It defines 171 objects essential for either fault or configuration analysis. Internet MIB II is defined in RFC 1213.

LAN Manager MIB II for Windows NT Contains a set of objects specifically designed to support computers running Windows NT. It defines approximately 90 objects that include items such as statistical, share, session, user, and logon information. Most LAN Manager MIB II objects have read-only access because of the insecure nature of SNMP.

DHCP MIB Windows NT includes a DHCP MIB that defines objects to monitor DHCP server activity. This MIB (DHCPMIB.DLL) is automatically installed when the DHCP server service is installed. It contains approximately 14 objects for monitoring DHCP, such as the number of DHCP discover requests received, the number of declines, and the number of addresses leased out to clients.

WINS MIB Windows NT includes a WINS MIB that defines objects to monitor WINS server activity. This MIB (WINSMIB.DLL) is automatically installed when the WINS server service is installed. It contains approximately 70 objects for monitoring WINS, such as the number of resolution requests successfully processed, the number of resolution requests that failed, and the date and time of the last database replication.

Microsoft's SNMP Service

In order to take advantage of Microsoft's NT SNMP services, you must have an SNMP manger that can monitor and display SNMP alerts. The Microsoft SNMP service provides SNMP agent services to any TCP/IP host that's running the SNMP management software. Microsoft SNMP service can run on Windows NT, as long as it's also running TCP/IP.

Microsoft ✔️ *Exam* *Objective*	**Given a scenario, identify which tool to use to monitor TCP/IP traffic.**

There are two methods that the Microsoft SNMP service management software can employ to collect information about devices. One way is to have devices send alerts to an SNMP manager or to any other manger within the community. Another method is to have the SNMP manager poll devices every few seconds, minutes, or hours.

By adding the public community to the alert list, any management station within the community will receive alerts and be able to make changes to the configuration.

Microsoft's SNMP service can use a HOSTS file, DNS, WINS, or the LMHOSTS file to perform host name-to-IP address translation, and toidentify which hosts it will report information to and receive requests from.It also enables counters for monitoring TCP/IP performance using Performance Monitor.

Planning and Preparing for Implementation

If you plan to use the SNMP service with a third-party manager, you'll need to:

- Record the IP addresses and host names of participating hosts.

- Add host name/IP address mappings to the appropriate name resolution resource.

- Identify the third-party management systems and Microsoft SNMP agents.

Host Names and IP Addresses

When installing the SNMP service on an agent, make sure you have the host names or IP addresses of the hosts to which your system will send SNMP traps, as well as those to which your system will respond regarding SNMP requests.

Host Name Resolution

The SNMP service uses normal Windows NT host name resolution methods to resolve host names to IP addresses. If you use host names, be sure to add all host name/IP address mappings of the participating computers to the appropriate resolution sources (such as the HOSTS file, DNS, WINS, or the LMHOSTS file).

Management Systems and Agents

A management system is any computer running the TCP/IP transport and third-party SNMP manager software. The management system requests information from an agent. To use the Microsoft SNMP service, you need at least one management system.

An SNMP agent is a Windows NT-based computer running the Microsoft SNMP service. The agent provides the management system with requested status information and reports any extraordinary events.

Defining SNMP Communities

Before you install SNMP, you'll need to define an SNMP community. A community is a group to which hosts running the SNMP service belong. A community parameter is simply the name of that group by which SNMP communities are identified. The use of a community name provides some security and context for agents receiving requests and initiating traps, and does the same for management systems and their tasks. An SNMP agent won't respond to a request from a management system outside its configured community, but an agent can be a member of multiple communities at the same time. This allows for communications with SNMP managers from different communities. Figure 12.3 illustrates how a community name is used.

In Figure 12.3, Host A can receive and send messages to Host Manager B because they are both members of the Public 1 Community. Hosts C through E can receive and send messages to Manager F because all these machines are members of the default public community.

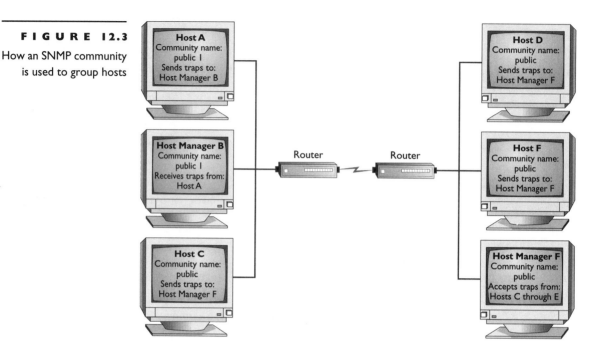

FIGURE 12.3

How an SNMP community
is used to group hosts

SNMP Installation and Configuration

Okay, now we're going to talk about installing and configuring the SNMP service on a Windows NT computer. If you want to monitor TCP/IP with Performance Monitor, you'll need to install the SNMP service. Also, if you want to monitor a Windows NT-based computer with a third-party application, you'll need to configure the SNMP service.

Microsoft
✓ *Exam*
Objective

Configure SNMP.

SNMP Service Security

There is minimal-level security available with SNMP that is inherent in the processes of management and agent systems when initiating and receiving requests and traps. However, don't allow yourself to be lulled into a false sense of security! If your SNMP-managed network is connected to the Internet, or any public internetwork, a firewall should be in place to prevent intrusion from outside SNMP management consoles. When installing SNMP, keep in mind the following security configuration options:

Send Authentication Trap Used if you want the computer to send a trap for a failed authentication. When the SNMP service receives a management request that does not contain or match the community name, the SNMP service can send a trap to the trap destination.

Accepted Community Names This specifies community names from which the computer will accept requests. A host must belong to a community that appears in this list for the SNMP service to accept requests from that host. Typically, all hosts belong to the community-named public.

Accept SNMP Packets from Any Host By default, this option is checked. Accepts packets from everybody.

Only Accept SNMP Packets from These Hosts If checked, the computer should only accept packets from hosts that have specific IP or IPX addresses, plus the host name that's in the associated box.

Exercise 12.1 will show you how to install and configure the SNMP Service on NT Server.

EXERCISE 12.1

Installing and Configuring the SNMP Service

1. From the Control Panel, double-click Network.

2. From the Network Settings dialog box, click Add.

3. Click the Services tab and then click Add. The Select Network Services dialog box appears.

---

4. Click SNMP Service and then click OK.

5. Type the path to the distribution files.

6. After the appropriate files are copied to the computer, the SNMP Service Configuration dialog box appears. Configure the following parameters:

Send Trap with Community Names The community name to which traps are sent. A management system must belong to the designated community to receive traps. The default community name for all hosts is Public.

The Trap Destination The trap destination consists of names or IP addresses of hosts to which you want the SNMP service to send traps. If you use a host name, make sure it can be resolved so the SNMP service can map it to the IP address.

SNMP Agent Services

A Simple Network Management Protocol agent is a database of information about a device, and/or its environment, which is installed on the device designated for management or monitoring. Data contained in the agent database depends on the specific function of the devices that are to be monitored. The agent in the managed device doesn't volunteer information, because doing so would take away from its primary function. The only exception to this rule is that an agent will send an alarm to the management station if a critical threshold is crossed. Microsoft SNMP agent services give a Windows NT-based computer the ability to provide an SNMP management system with the information on activity that occurs at different layers of the Internet Protocol suite.

Assuming that TCP/IP and SNMP have already been installed, click SNMP Properties to access a menu, which is broken down into three parts: Agent, Traps, and Security. The SNMP configuration that you'd enter is the same information that you would enter under Windows NT 3.5*x*.

To configure the SNMP Agent, select the Agent tab on the Microsoft SNMP Properties page. Under Service, select the type of service to report. Select all boxes that indicate network capabilities provided by your NT computer. SNMP must have this information to manage the enabled services. Notice that Applications, Internet, and End-to-End are default services.

The SNMP agent generates trap messages that are then sent to an SNMP management console—the trap destination. Trap destinations are identified by a computer name, IP address, or IPX address of the "host of hosts" on the network to which you want the trap messages sent. The trap destination must be a host that is running an SNMP manager program. To configure the trap destination on a Windows NT 4.0 computer, use the Traps tab in the Microsoft SNMP Properties page to enter the host name, IP address, or the IPX address of the computer(s) running an SNMP manager program.

Community names provide a rudimentary security scheme for the SNMP service. You can add and delete community names by using the Security tab on the Microsoft SNMP Properties page. You can also filter the type of packets that the computer will accept. You must configure the SNMP service with at least one community name. The default name is Public.

Exercise 12.2 will show you how to configure the SNMP Agent on your NT computer.

EXERCISE 12.2

Configuring the SNMP Agent

1. In the Microsoft SNMP Properties dialog box, click the Agent tab.

2. Fill in the Contact and Location Information on the Agent page.

EXERCISE 12.2 (CONTINUED FROM PREVIOUS PAGE)

3. Choose the Service types, or accept the defaults.

4. Choose the Traps tab.

Microsoft SNMP Properties

Agent | Traps | Security

The SNMP Service provides network management over TCP/IP and IPX/SPX protocols. If traps are required, one or more community names must be specified. Trap destinations may be host names, IP addresses, or IPX addresses.

Community Name:

Globalnet

Add

Remove

Trap Destinations:

GlobalnetServ2
160.1.43.189
GlobalnetServ1

Add... Edit... Remove

OK Cancel Apply

5. Add a new Community Name if needed; Public is the default.

6. Add the Trap Destination host or hosts.

7. Choose the Security tab.

8. Add any new names under Accepted Community Names, then choose Add.

9. Choose OK.

10. Restart the computer.

How to Spot SNMP Service Errors

After SNMP is installed, you can then view SNMP errors from the Event Viewer system log. The Event Viewer will record all events occurring with the system components of SNMP—even failure of the SNMP service to start. The Event Viewer is the first place you should look to identify any possible problems relevant to the SNMP service.

The **SNMPUTIL** Utility

The SNMPUTIL.EXE utility is available only in the Windows NT 4.0 Resource Kit. This utility verifies whether the SNMP service has been correctly configured to communicate with SNMP management stations. SNMPUTIL makes the same SNMP calls as an SNMP management station, as shown in the following example:.

```
snmputil command agent community object_identifier_(OID)
```

The valid commands are:

get   Get the value of the requested object identifier

getnext   Get the value of the next object following the specified object identifier

walk   Step (walk) through the MIB branch specified by the object identifier

If you wanted to determine the number of DHCP server addresses leased by a DHCP server named MAXamillion in the public community, you would issue the following command:

```
snmputil getnext MAXamillion Public .1.3.6.1.4.1.311.1.3.2.1.1.1
```

The command will respond with the OID and counter value for the object ID in question, which is the number of IP leases that are issued.

How SNMP Works

Figure 12.4 illustrates how SNMP works and responds to a third-party management system request:

1. A third-party SNMP management system running on Host 1 requests the number of active sessions from a Microsoft SNMP agent. The SNMP management system uses the host name to send the request. The request is passed by the application to socket (UDP port) 161. The host name is resolved by using the HOSTS file, DNS, WINS, B-node broadcast, or LMHOSTS.

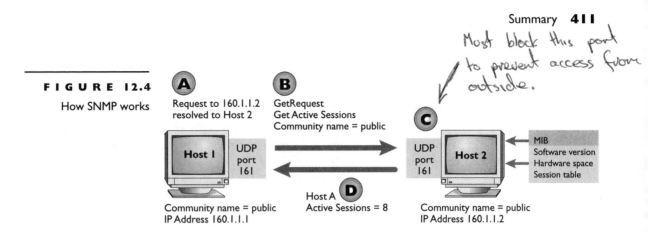

Most block this port to prevent access from outside.

FIGURE 12.4

How SNMP works

2. An SNMP message that contains the GetRequest command is formed to discover the number of active sessions with the community name of public.

3. The Host 2 Microsoft SNMP agent receives the message and verifies the community name, as well as if the message has been corrupted in any way. If the community name is wrong, or the message got corrupted somewhere along the way, it's discarded. If the message is valid and the community name is correct, then the host verifies the IP address to make sure the address is authorized to accept messages from the management station.

4. An SNMP message stating that eight sessions are active is then sent back to the SNMP manager.

Summary

SNMP permits the monitoring and managing of a network from a single workstation or several workstations, called SNMP managers. It's a family of specifications that provide a means for collecting network management data from the devices residing in a network. With an SNMP manager, you can query the network's devices regarding the nature of their functions.

A MIB describes the objects, or entries, that are to be included in the SNMP agent database. SNMP agents are sometimes referred to as MIBs. An SNMP manager can request and collect information from an agent's MIB. It can also inspect or alter the objects contained in it. The Microsoft SNMP service supports Internet MIB II, LAN Manager MIB II, DHCP MIB, and WINS MIB.

The security available with SNMP is minimal. If your SNMP-managed network is connected to the Internet, or any public internetwork, a firewall should be in place to prevent intrusion from outside SNMP management consoles.

The NT TCP/IP test will cover a couple of SNMP objectives. Be sure and understand Security (or lack of), how to send and receive traps, and how SNMP works with Performance Monitor. The questions below will help you get an understanding.

Review Questions

1. How do you prevent your NT server running SNMP from being managed by unauthorized SNMP management stations?

   A. Rename the administrator account on the server.

   B. Configure the server to accept SNMP packets from specified hosts only.

   C. Convert your NT partitions to NTFS.

   D. Define a password for the SNMP community name.

2. How do you configure your NT Server to send trap messages to an SNMP management station?

   A. Enter the IP address of the SNMP management station on your NT Server.

   B. Enter the Server name of the SNMP management station.

   C. Enter the community name defined on the SNMP management station.

   D. Enter the guest account information to connect in the background.

3. What utility should you run on a UNIX station and an NT Server to view TCP/IP protocol statistics for the Windows NT Server from the UNIX computer?

   A. On the UNIX computer run a protocol analyzer and on the NT Server run the Network Monitor.

   B. On the UNIX computer run a SNMP Management program and on the NT Server run the SNMP Server service.

   C. On the UNIX computer run a Network Monitor and on the NT Server run the protocol analyzer.

   D. On the UNIX computer run an ftp client and on the NT Server run the ftp server service.

4. How can you collect statistics for all TCP/IP traffic on the NT Servers on your network by using Performance Monitor?

   A. Run DHCP on each server.

   B. Configure each server to use WINS.

   C. Install the SNMP service on each server.

   D. Run the NET.EXE utility on each server.

   E. Run the FTP Server service on each server.

5. You want to add SNMP to your NT workstation, but you don't want just anybody getting in and changing your MIBs. What security option should you put in place to stop SNMP packets from being tweaked by unwanted visitors?

6. Your company's network manager has set up your NT workstation to respond to SNMP requests coming from an SNMP management system. While doing so, he told you all about the sort of stuff the management system will be requesting. What are the operations he told you will be requested by the SNMP management system?

7. Which of the following statements about SNMP with NT are false? (Choose all that apply.)

A. NT can send SNMP traps to a SNMP manger.

B. Windows 95 can send SNMP traps to an NT Server.

C. NT Workstation and Server can send SNMP traps to an NT Server.

D. NT Server can send SNMP traps to a UNIX SNMP manager.

8. What are the default communities for NT running SNMP? (Choose two.)

A. Read=Private

B. Write=Public

C. Write=Private

D. Read=Public

9. What is a MIB?

A. A MIB describes the objects, or entries, that are to be included in the DLL's needed to run SNMP on your NT Server.

B. A MIB describes the objects, or entries, that are to be included in the SNMP agent database.

C. A MIB is a DLL needed to run SNMP in NT.

D. A MIB is a DLL needed to send traps to an NT Server.

10. Where should you look on your NT Server for SNMP errors?

A. In the SNMP error log kept in C:\winnt\system 32

B. In the Event Viewer

C. In the Performance Log

D. In the %winnt_root%\system32\etc\snmplog.err

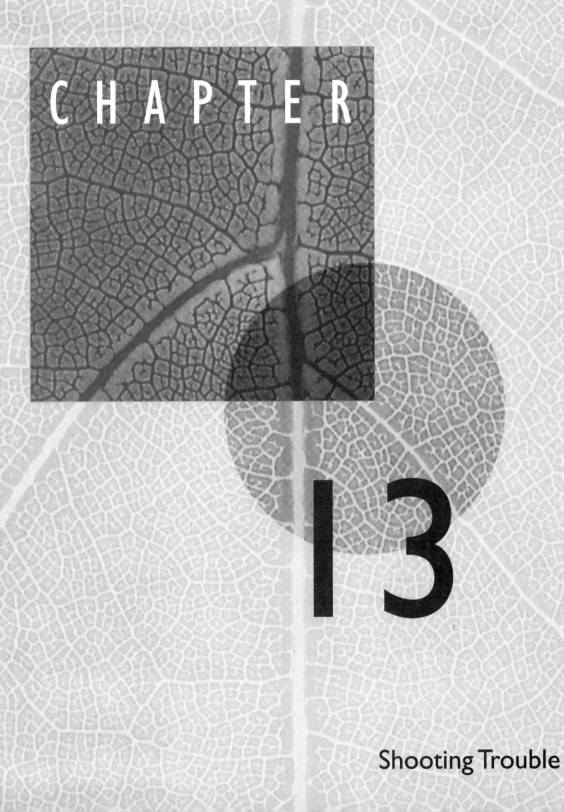

CHAPTER

13

Shooting Trouble

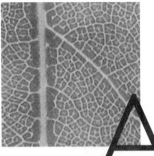

All through this book, you've had opportunities to see what happens when TCP/IP is incorrectly configured. In this chapter, we'll examine some common TCP/IP problems, present some important guidelines for avoiding networking dilemmas, and cover troubleshooting tips for an IP network.

By the time you've reached the end of this chapter, you should be able to:

- Accurately identify common TCP/IP related problems.

- Use Microsoft Windows NT utilities to successfully diagnose TCP/IP related problems.

Getting to the Source

Although it may certainly seem during a major network outage that you've found and are experiencing an entirely new, never-before-encountered network problem, 99 percent of the computer puzzles you'll experience on the job won't be new ones at all. Rest assured. It's highly likely your problem isn't unique, but rather common, with a proven, successful method to lead you happily toward its solution. In the networking industry, contacts are your best friends, so the old adage of never burning your bridges at work strongly applies. The network world is a small world after all, and you just never know when you might need the insights of a former colleague!

When an outage occurs on a network—large or small—time-honored problem-solving strategies like staying calm, thinking logically, and the good ol' process of elimination also apply. Lots of network problems can be grouped into categories. It's important to understand these different categories, and then work deductively through them until the culprit's exposed. Many Microsoft TCP/IP-related problems can be grouped into the following categories:

Source Category	Typical Associated Problems
Configuration	If your network configuration is incorrect, it can result in one or more services not starting when you bring up your NT Workstation or Server.
IP addressing	The host can hang up when trying to communicate with other hosts. This could be caused by the existence of an improper subnet address or duplicate IP address. Windows NT will give you a pop-up message if there are duplicate IP addresses on your network.
Subnet addressing	Related to the above, if your host has an improper subnet address assigned to it, it may not be able to talk to other local or remote hosts.
Resolution	You can ping a host with an IP address, or connect to a network drive using a host's IP address, but you cannot establish a connection using only its host name.

The problem implicates its source. Identifying the source narrows down the field of possible causes and expedites finding a solution. For example, if you ping to Host Bob, and receive an error stating, "host unknown," you can then ping Host Bob from the host's IP address, 160.1.56.89. If the ping is successful, a resolution problem is the culprit, and you can begin troubleshooting the resolution methods used on your network. If the ping was unsuccessful, you can start troubleshooting Host Bob for connectivity issues.

Tools for Diagnosis

TCP/IP has been around for quite a while, so there's a whole bunch of tools around to help you troubleshoot problems related to it. Some of these tools can be used to locate the source, while others can be employed to track errors. Microsoft Windows NT includes plenty of utilities that can prove very helpful when attacking a TCP/IP network-related problem.

Microsoft ✓ *Exam* *Objective*	**Use Microsoft TCP/IP utilities to diagnose IP configuration problems.** • Identify which Microsoft TCP/IP utility to use to diagnose IP configuration problems.

The following TCP/IP tools are included with Microsoft NT:

Tool	Purpose
PING	Verifies connections between hosts by sending ICMP echo packets to the specified IP address
ARP	Gathers hardware addresses of local hosts and your default gateway. You can view the ARP cache and check for invalid or duplicate entries.
NETSTAT	Checks your current connections and protocol-related statistics of your TCP/IP host
NBTSTAT	Reports statistics and connections for NetBIOS over TCP/IP
IPCONFIG	Displays TCP/IP configuration settings for a host. This utility is particularly useful when the host obtains address information dynamically from DHCP, or a host name from WINS.
TRACERT	A route reporting utility that sends ICMP echo requests to an IP address and reports ICMP errors that are returned. TRACERT produces a report that lists all of the routers crossed in the process.
ROUTE	Used to view or modify the local routing table
SNMP	Used to remotely manage network devices by collecting, analyzing, and reporting data about the performance of network components

Event Log	Tracks errors and certain noteworthy events
Performance Monitor	A versatile tool that can be used to analyze performance and detect bottlenecks. Remember, Microsoft SNMP must be enabled on a host in order to monitor TCP/IP counters.
Registry Editor	The fault-tolerant database in which configuration data is stored for Windows NT. REGEDIT32 is the editor that allows you to browse and edit the configuration of the host.
Network Monitor	Captures incoming and outgoing packets to analyze a problem
NSLOOKUP	Displays information from DNS name servers

General Guidelines to Follow

When faced with a troubleshooting dilemma, it's a good idea to keep some simple guidelines in mind to help you stay focused. In a difficult, high-pressure situation, these guidelines can prevent you from duplicating your efforts. Often, in a "network down" predicament, people panic and just start recklessly resetting routers, rebooting servers, and so on. After these attempts, when the network still doesn't function, they call on someone else, who then enters the situation, and begins resetting routers, and rebooting servers—taking up critical time with redundant approaches, and getting everyone nowhere fast! It's so important to approach these often complicated quandaries in a sensible, logical manner—with a plan—so if you do get stumped, you can turn the problem over to someone and equip them with organized knowledge of exactly what you've already done. Also important is the documentation of the error and solution path for other colleagues who may come across that very problem later. Figure 13.1 shows the different layers of the DoD reference model and the different protocols related to each layer. A firm understanding of the different layers and the protocols that are specified at each layer will help you intelligently troubleshoot network problems—and make you sound smart in meetings, too!

Microsoft ✓ *Exam* *Objective*

Given a scenario, identify which tool to use to monitor TCP/IP traffic.

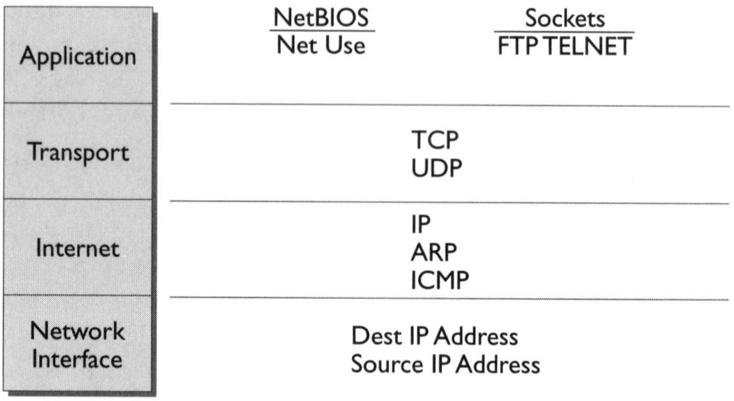

FIGURE 13.1

Protocols at each layer of the Internet Protocol suite

netbios

ping

Application	NetBIOS	Sockets
	Net Use	FTP TELNET
Transport		TCP
		UDP
Internet		IP
		ARP
		ICMP
Network Interface		Dest IP Address
		Source IP Address

Using Figure 13.1 as a troubleshooting guide, let's say that a user calls, complaining that they can't log on to the NT domain. Begin by analyzing the bottom layer of the DoD model, working up through the model to the Application layer until a likely problem source is established. You must determine that the protocols at each layer of the TCP/IP suite can communicate with those operating at the layers above and below.

- First, try to ping the device in question. If you can ping the host, then you have verified IP communication between the Network Interface layer and the Internet layer. Why? Because ping uses ARP (Address Resolution Protocol) to resolve the IP address to a hardware address. If pinging worked, then the resolution was successful, meaning the culprit isn't in the lower layers.

- Next, try to either telnet or net use to the host. If you can establish a session, you have successfully verified TCP/IP communication from the Network Interface layer through the Application layer. At this point you will have to go to the host in question to find out what the user is typing in. The problem can sometimes be something as simple as a domain name being spelled incorrectly.

■ If you are unable to resolve the problem, try using a network analyzer like Network General's Sniffer or Microsoft Network Monitor to help you discover the problem.

Verifying IP Communications

Pinging a host is a very popular way of troubleshooting problems. It can be a great place to start—sometimes leading you straight to the problem. If you can ping a host on a remote network, you have verified connectivity through routers, gateways, bridges, and possibly other network devices. That's a pretty good test. Your first weapon when trouble strikes is to try to ping the host. If pinging the host by its host name doesn't work, then try pinging with the host's IP address. If the ping is successful when using just the IP address, then you have a resolution problem.

Microsoft
✓ *Exam*
Objective

Diagnose and resolve IP addressing problems.

Here are some general guidelines to keep in mind when pinging a host:

■ First, ping the local host address of 127.0.0.1. This will tell you if the host can see itself on the network and if TCP/IP is loaded correctly.

■ Next, ping your IP address to check the correct configuration. If this doesn't work, select Control Panel ➤ Network and check for IP address, subnet, and default gateway entry errors.

■ If you're successful pinging your own IP address, ping the default gateway next. If this doesn't work, check your configuration again, and then check to make sure the router is up and working.

■ Next, ping the IP address of a remote host located on the other side of the router to verify that the router and WAN are working correctly. If this doesn't work, make sure that IP routing is enabled on all router interfaces. (Typically this is on by default, but someone could have accidentally disabled it.) Also, make sure the remote host is up and functioning.

If all is successful and all problems seem to be fixed, throw caution to the wind and try pinging the host by its host name. If things still aren't working, it's time to troubleshoot your resolution methods, like HOSTS file, WINS, LMHOSTS, and DNS. Refer to previous chapters if you get stuck.

Verifying TCP/IP Session Communications

After you ping your network to death and fix the problem, or find that all is well, the next step is to establish a session with the remote host. .

Microsoft ✓ ***Exam*** ***Objective*** | **Diagnose and resolve name resolution problems.**

You can use a few different methods to verify communication between the Network Interface layer and the Application layer.

- To connect to a host using its NetBIOS name, make a connection using the net use or net view command. An example would be **net use G: \\ Alpine\share**. If this isn't successful, make sure you're using the correct NetBIOS name, and that the host has a NetBIOS name. Also, make sure the destination host is in your LMHOSTS file (entered correctly) if the destination host is located on a remote network.

- If you're still having problems connecting with the NetBIOS name, it's time to check Scope IDs. Each host can be given an extension on their NetBIOS name to keep hosts from seeing each other on the network. Check to make sure that the Scope ID is the same as yours.

- To connect to a host that is not NetBIOS-based, use the Telnet or FTP utility to make a connection. If by chance this was unsuccessful, make sure the remote host has TCP/IP running and that it also has a Telnet or FTP daemon running. Additionally, make sure you have the correct permission on the remote host to enable you to perform Telnet or FTP. If you're still unsuccessful, check your HOSTS file to make sure the entry for the remote host is correct.

Summary

Network problems can be grouped into categories. Solid problem-solving skills begin with an understanding of the different categories, and how to work deductively through them until the culprit is exposed.

Remember, the problem implicates its source. Therefore, identifying the source narrows down the field of possible causes and expedites finding a solution.

Microsoft Windows NT includes plenty of utilities that can prove very helpful when attacking a TCP/IP network-related problem. Some of these tools can be used to locate the source, while others can be employed to track errors. They are:

- PING
- ARP
- NETSTAT
- NBTSTAT
- IPCONFIG
- TRACERT
- ROUTE
- SNMP
- Event Log
- Performance Monitor
- Registry Editor
- NSLOOKUP

Next, we explored some general guidelines to keep in mind when going after nasty network gremlins. The basic key to success is to approach networking puzzles in a logical manner, with a plan, so if you get stumped, you can turn the problem over to someone who knows what you've already done.

It's important to document the problem and the solution path for other colleagues who may come across it later.

When taking the NT TCP/IP 4.0 test, be sure and understand all the different tools included with NT and what they do. The questions below will help you get an idea of what they are looking for.

Review Questions

1. You have an NT workstation on Subnet 1, and your NT Server is on Subnet 2. You receive a "Network name not found" error when typing the command **net use f : \\sales.acme.com\leads**. The IPCONFIG utility shows you the following output:

Host name:	wksta1.acme.com
DNS Server:	
Node Type:	Hybrid
NetBIOS scope ID:	
IP routing enabled:	No
WINS Proxy Enabled:	No
NetBIOS resolution Uses DNS:	No
Description:	ELNK3 Ethernet Adapter
Physical Address:	00-20-AF-BE-B2-63
DHCP Enabled:	Yes
IP Address:	98.46.9.38
Subnet mask:	255.255.240.0
Default Gateway:	98.46.18.1
DHCP Server:	98.46.6.136

Primary WINS Server:	98.46.6.136
Secondary WINS Server:	98.46.6.137
Lease Obtained:	Sunday, May 24, 1998 12:42:03 PM
Lease Expires:	Wednesday, May 27, 1998 12:42:03 PM

What is most likely the cause of the problem?

A. You cannot specify a host name in a FQDN path.

B. The workstation is not configured correctly.

C. The workstation does not have a hosts table.

D. The workstation does not have an LMHOST file.

2. Which utility should you use to collect TCP/IP protocol statistics, save the statistics in log files for later analysis, and export the statistics for use in a spreadsheet?

A. NETSTAT.EXE

B. NBTSTAT.EXE

C. Performance Monitor

D. Network Monitor

3. Which two utilities can you use to view the routing tables on a Windows NT Server computer?

A. ROUTE.EXE

B. NETSTAT.EXE

C. NBTSTAT.EXE

D. IPCONFIG.EXE

E. ARP.EXE

4. Which utility should you use to purge the server's NetBIOS name cache?

A. ROUTE.EXE

B. NETSTAT.EXE

C. NBTSTAT.EXE

D. IPCONFIG.EXE

E. ARP.EXE

5. What utility should you use to view a list of all current TCP/IP connections to your NT Server?

A. ROUTE.EXE

B. NETSTAT.EXE

C. NBTSTAT.EXE

D. IPCONFIG.EXE

E. ARP.EXE

6. Which two NT Server utilities can you use to view both IP statistics and Ethernet statistics?

A. Network Monitor

B. NET.EXE

C. NETSTAT.EXE

D. IPCONFIG.EXE

E. NBTSTAT.EXE

7. What NT Server utility should you use to view a chart of TCP/IP protocol statistics?

A. Performance Monitor

B. Network Monitor

    C. IPCONFIG.EXE

    D. NBTSTAT.EXE

    E. NETSTAT.EXE

8. Which utility let you view TCP/IP protocol statistics from the last time your NT Server was started?

    A. NET.EXE

    B. NETSTAT.EXE

    C. NBTSTAT.EXE

    D. IPCONFIG.EXE

    E. Network Monitor

9. What utility can you type at a command line to view the list of IP address-to-physical address mappings for your NT Server?

    A. Network Monitor

    B. NET. EXE

    C. NBTSTAT. EXE

    D. TELNET.EXE

    E. ARP.EXE

10. What command line utility can you use to view a list of NetBIOS names that are currently cached on your NT Server?

    A. NET. EXE

    B. FTP. EXE

    C. NBTSTAT. EXE

    D. Network Monitor

    E. WINS.EXE

11. You have a remote NT Server running as an FTP server. When you use NT Explorer you can connect, but it fails when you use the command **ftp sales.acme.com.** What is the most likely cause of the problem?

    A. No DNS server defined on your workstation.

    B. No Default Gateway defined on your workstation.

    C. No Default Gateway defined on the remote server.

    D. No DNS configuration on the remote server.

12. From your NT workstation you can connect to a remote server by using the command **ftp sales.acme.com.** However, you cannot connect through NT Explorer when specifying the computer name. What is the most likely cause of the problem?

    A. No DNS server defined on your workstation.

    B. No Default Gateway defined on your workstation.

    C. No Default Gateway defined on the remote server.

    D. No WINS configuration on the remote server.

13. At your NT workstation you attempt to connect to an NT Server by using the command **ftp sales.acme.com.** You receive the message "Bad IP address." Pinging the server was successful. What could the problem be? Choose all that apply.

    A. No DNS server defined on your workstation.

    B. No Default Gateway defined on your workstation.

    C. There is no entry in the DNS server for sales.acme.com.

    D. The LMHOSTS file does not contain an entry for sales.acme.com.

14. Your Windows NT workstation cannot talk to a host in another building, but it works locally. Your co-workers' workstations are working fine. What is the troubleshooting step you should take?

15. Your Windows NT workstation cannot talk on the network either locally or remotely. What are the troubleshooting steps you should take?

16. You have just installed TCP/IP and cannot ping hosts by their NetBIOS name on your network. Your IP address, subnet mask, and default gateway are correct. What is the problem?

MCSE: TCP/IP for NT Server 4 Study Guide, Third Edition

Exam 70-059: Objectives

NOTE Exam objectives are subject to change at any time without prior notice and at Microsoft's sole discretion. Please visit Microsoft's Training & Certification Web site (www.microsoft.com/Train_Cert) for the most current listing of exam objectives.

NETWORK PRESS SYBEX

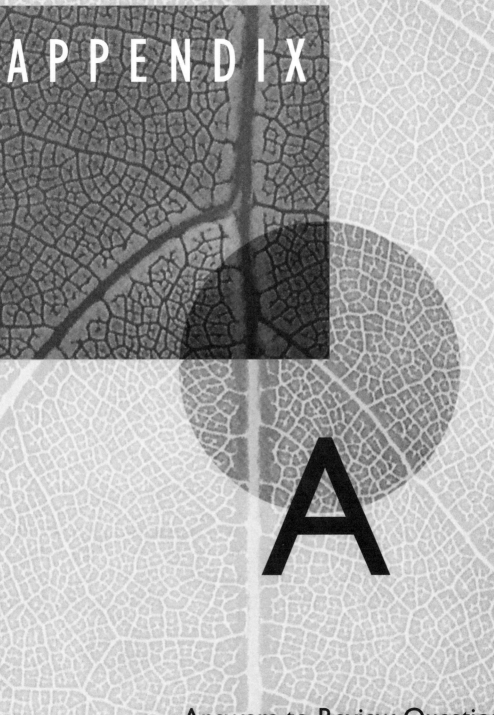

APPENDIX

A

Answers to Review Questions

Chapter 1

1. What is TCP/IP?

   A. A collection of packets sent through the Internet

   B. A collection of packages for use on the Internet

   C. A suite of protocols that provide routing and addressing in wide-area networks, and connectivity to a variety of hosts.

   D. A freeware program

   Answer: C

   Explanation: TCP/IP is just two popular protocols in the Internet Protocol Suite. All of the protocols together make the TCP/IP suite. These protocols allow addressing of hosts and routing.

2. What are the layers in the DOD four-layer model used by TCP/IP?

   A. Process/Application

   B. Session

   C. Network Access

   D. Internet

   E. Host-to-Host

   F. Transport

   Answer: A, E, D and C respectively

   Explanation: The DOD model was created before the OSI model and only comprises of four layers: Process/Application, Host-to-Host, Internet, and Network Access.

3. What core TCP/IP protocols are provided with Microsoft TCP/IP?

   A. TCP

   B. UDP

C. DUP

D. ICMP

E. PI

F. IP

G. PAR

H. ARP

I. CTP

Answer: A, B, D, F and H

Explanation: Microsoft includes in its operating system the TCP/IP protocol suite. Included are TCP, UDP, ICMP, IP and ARP.

4. What parameters are required for a TCP/IP host to communicate in a wide-area network?

   A. IP Address

   B. Subnet Mask

   C. Zip Code

   D. Default Gateway

   E. Login Name

   Answer: A, B and D

   Explanation: For a TCP/IP host to communicate in a wide-area network, the minimum configuration for a TCP/IP host is a valid IP address, subnet mask, and default gateway.

5. It's Monday morning. Just as you arrive at your desk, your boss calls you into his office, and says he read about TCP/IP in a Microsoft magazine over the weekend. Because he now knows that all Microsoft products are fabulous, he's set on having someone implement MS TCP/IP at all

twelve branch office sites. He says that because of your quality work over the past few months, you're his first choice. However, before he names you the project's leader, he wants you to give him a complete explanation of TCP/IP and how it will meet his networking needs. Can you? Try it.

Answer: The acronym TCP/IP stands for *Transmission Control Protocol/Internet Protocol.* Essentially, it's a set of two communication protocols that an application can use to package its information for sending across a network, or networks. TCP/IP also refers to an entire collection of protocols, called a protocol suite. This collection includes application protocols for performing tasks such as e-mail, file transfers, and terminal emulation.

6. To get a jump on the competition, you need to find some information on a new, highly efficient protocol being developed. Where would you find this information? How would you access it and through which server? If you have access to the Internet, try this as an exercise on your computer.

Answer: FTP to DS.INTERNIC.NIC or e-mail rfc-info@isi.edu, including the message: **help: ways_to_get_rfcs.**

7. Your boss tells you she spent lunch at the gym, where she overheard a great way to look up information on the Internet. She tells you that it organizes subjects into a menu system and allows you to access the information on each topic listed. She's frustrated because she can't remember what its called—can you?

Answer: Gopher organizes topics into a menu system and allows you to access the information on each topic listed.

8. You are the senior communication technician for a small computer store. The sales staff is complaining that they cannot deliver or receive mail on their TCP/IP computers. All other applications on the network seem to work properly. The location of the problem is likely to be on *which layer* of the DOD model?

Answer: The Application/Process layer of the DOD is responsible for sending and receiving mail using the Simple Mail Transfer Protocol.

9. The IS department is planning to implement TCP/IP. Your manager, who knows and understands the OSI reference model, asks you, "What are the layers in the four-layer model used by the DOD for TCP/IP, and how does each layer relate to the OSI reference model?" What do you tell him?

Answer: The four layers of the DOD model and how each relates to the OSI model are shown below:

DOD	OSI
Process/Application layer	Application, Presentation, and Session
Host-to-Host or Transport	Transport
Internet	Network
Network Access	Data Link and Physical

10. You are the network administrator for a large accounting office. They have seven offices, all connected. You get a call from a remote office complaining that their workstations cannot connect to the network. After talking with them for a few minutes, you discover that network connectivity is down at all seven offices. What layer of the DOD model is likely at fault?

Answer: The Network Access layer is responsible for network connectivity.

11. The accounting department calls you about two workstations in their department, complaining that "they're taking turns like twins, with only one being able to log in to the network at a time." All the other workstations in the department are fine. What's the problem, and how do you fix it?

Answer: Two workstations with the same hardware address (MAC address) can only work one at a time. Change out the network card. Yes, this does happen, but typically you would duplicate IP addresses. We have seen both Ethernet and Token Ring cards with duplicate IP addresses.

12. You're the network manager for a large aircraft company. The reservationists have been griping for two weeks about the slow response of their computers. You've narrowed the problem down to noise on the thin-net coax cabling. Which layer of the DOD model is responsible?

    Answer: The Network Access layer is responsible for the physical specifications of the cabling. Make sure the specifications of the cable, such as length and terminators, are correct.

13. Your co-worker calls you because she is confused about the differences between the OSI reference model and the DOD model. She can't figure out where packets are framed with the hardware address and a cyclic redundancy check. What do you tell her?

    Answer: The Data Link layer of the OSI model is responsible for framing and hardware addressing, while the Network Access layer is responsible for the DOD model.

14. You're in an interview for an important position at a good company. You've studied hard and know your TCP/IP. The interviewer asks you, "What is the connectionless protocol at the Internet layer of the DOD model, and what is its function?" Do you stare back blankly, mouth agape, or answer confidently with...?

    Answer: The Internet Protocol. The complex task of routing is performed at the Internet layer.

15. After you breeze through that last question, the interviewer then asks you, "At what layer are messages segmented, and what protocol is used for segmenting them?" What's your answer?

    Answer: TCP at the Host-to-Host layer. TCP takes large blocks of information from an application and breaks them down into segments, which it then numbers and sequences so that the destination's TCP protocol can order the segments back into the large block the application intended. After these segments have been sent, TCP waits for acknowledgment for each one from the receiving end's TCP, retransmitting the ones not acknowledged.

16. Your pal just landed a job as a Help Desk operator and is brushing up on her TCP/IP protocols to prepare for her first day. She calls you with this question: "Ones and zeros are extracted from the cable and formed

into logical groups called frames. The hardware destination is then checked, and a cyclic redundancy checksum is performed. If the hardware address is correct, and the CRC matches its original mathematical algorithm, the packet is then sent to which protocol at which layer?" What do you tell her?

Answer: Ones and zeros are extracted from the cable and formed into logical groups called frames. The hardware destination is then checked, and a cyclic redundancy checksum is performed. If the hardware address is correct and the CRC matches its original mathematical algorithm, the packet is sent to IP at the Network layer to verify the IP address. If the IP address is valid, it is then sent to UDP or TCP at the Host-to-Host layer.

17. You're a software developer who enjoys writing video games to play on the Internet with TCP/IP. You want to use the fastest protocol at the Transport layer of the OSI model to ensure no delay when blowing up all the Morphofreaks. What protocol do you use? Also, at what corresponding layer of the DOD model would this protocol run?

Answer: UDP (User Datagram Protocol) at the Host-to-Host layer. Unlike TCP, which receives streams of data, UDP receives upper-layer blocks of information and breaks them into segments. Like TCP, it gives each segment a number for reassembly into the intended block at the destination. However, UDP does *not* sequence the segments.

18. Your UNIX diskless workstations cannot logon to the host. After troubleshooting, you notice that when they boot up, the hardware address is sent to the host, but the host rejects them. Which protocol is asleep on the job?

Answer: BootP (Boot Program). When a diskless workstation is powered on, it broadcasts a BootP request on the network. A BootP server hears the request and looks up the client's MAC address in its BootP file. If it finds a match, BootP assigns an IP address to the host.

19. You need to install network management to keep track of network errors and to baseline for future growth. Which protocol do you use, and which layer of the DOD does it operate on?

Answer: The Simple Network Management Protocol can get information about your network and help you baseline. It runs at the Process/Application layer.

Chapter 2

1. You want to collect the TCP/IP frames that are received by your Windows NT Server computer, and then save the data in a file to analyze later. Which utility should you use?

   A. NETSTAT.EXE

   B. Performance Monitor

   C. NBTSTAT.EXE

   D. Network Monitor

   Answer: D

   Explanation: Network Monitor is used like a sniffer to analyze traffic. Because of the nature of the data, often it is useful to save some of the frames for review. NETSTAT is used to review all inbound/outbound connections to a server; however, it has nothing to do with framing. Performance Monitor measures and counts data statistics, not their content. NBTSTAT is used for NETBIOS over TCP/IP statistics, which has no specification for reviewing frames.

2. You need to determine whether the TCP/IP configuration is initialized or if a duplicate IP address is configured on your NT Workstation. Which utility should you use?

   A. ARP.EXE

   B. NBTSTAT.EXE

   C. NETSTAT.EXE

   D. IPCONFIG.EXE

   E. PING.EXE

   Answer: D

   Explanation: IPCONFIG will list the IP address information assigned to each adapter. If a duplicate address has been detected, the address will be disabled. ARP is for resolving IP addresses to MAC hardware addresses—obviously not your choice. NBTSTAT is used to show NETBIOS over TCP/IP status, such as NetBIOS caching—again, not your choice. Finally PING is used to verify that an address is reachable. However, if you were pinging your own address, obviously your would get a response—again, not useful in this situation.

3. You have four NT Server computers, and you want to find out which computers send the most traffic to each server. What should you do to find out?

A. Use Performance Monitor on each server.

B. Use Network Monitor on each server.

C. Use NETSTAT.EXE on each server.

D. Use NBTSTAT.EXE on each server.

E. Use ROUTE.EXE on each server that is functioning as a router.

Answer: B

Explanation: Network Monitor acts as a sniffer to review traffic connections in the instance noted above. Performance Monitor will only show quantity information. NETSTAT is useful for reviewing connections; however, it does not display which information is good and which is bad. NBTSTAT shows the NETBIOS cache, but provides no connection information of any value. ROUTE usually is used to review how information is set, but again, has little functionality for displaying bad information.

4. You have a network ID of 150.150.0.0 and you need to divide it into multiple subnets. You need 600 host IDs for each subnet, with the largest amount of subnets available. Which subnet mask should you assign?

A. 255.255.224.0

B. 255.255.240.0

C. 255.255.248.0

D. 255.255.252.0

Answer: D

Explanation: First examine all available masks in binary. By going through each mask, we should find that D would give us the results we need. 252.0 in binary is 11111100.00000000. All the zeros represent the hosts and all the ones represent the subnets. We have 6 bits for subnets and 10 bits for hosts. This will yield 1022 (1024, less all 0s and all 1s) hosts and 62 (64, less all 0s and all 1s) subnets.

5. You have a network ID of 150.150.0.0 with eight subnets. You need to allow the largest possible number of host IDs per subnet. Which subnet mask should you assign?

A. 255.255.224.0

B. 255.255.240.0

C. 255.255.248.0

D. 255.255.252.0

Answer: B

Explanation: First examine all available subnets. You should find that B would meet the requirements. 240.0 in binary is:11110000.00000000. This tells us that we have 12 bits used for the host ID in the Class B network and four bits used for the subnets. This will yield 4094 (4096, less all 0s and all 1s) hosts and 14 (16, less all 0s and all 1s) subnets.

6. You have a network ID of 206.17.45.0 and you need to divide it into multiple subnets. You need 25 host IDs for each subnet, with the largest amount of subnets available. Which subnet mask should you assign?

A. 255.255.255.192

B. 255.255.255.224

C. 255.255.255.240

D. 255.255.255.248

Answer: B

Explanation: Because you need 25 hosts, you must reserve five bits for the network ID. That yields 30 IDs (2^5–2). This leaves three bits for subnetting, which is six subnets (2^3–2). Therefore, the answer is 11100000 or 224.

7. You have a Class A network address with 60 subnets. You need to add 40 new subnets in the next two years and still allow for the largest possible number of host IDs per subnet. Which subnet mask should you assign?

A. 255.240.0.0

B. 255.248.0.0

C. 255.252.0.0

D. 255.254.0.0

Answer: D

Explanation: Because you need 100 subnets, you must reserve seven bits for the network ID to equal 126 subnets (2^7-2). This gives 17 bits for the hosts, which equals 131,070 hosts per subnet. You should probably never do this in real life.

8. You want to capture and view packets that are received by your Windows NT computer. Which utility should you use?

   A. NETSTAT.EXE

   B. Performance Monitor

   C. IPCONFIG.EXE

   D. Network Monitor

   Answer: D

   Explanation: Network Monitor is used to analyze traffic. Because of the nature of the data, often it is useful to save some of the frames for review. NETSTAT will show TCP/IP connections, but not data information. Performance Monitor is used for gathering statistical information; however, it will not show the contents of any data. IPCONFIG will display your IP and DHCP information, but, again, will show no information.

9. You have a Class B network, and you plan break it up into seven subnets. One subnet will be connected to the Internet, but you want all computers to have access to the Internet. How should you assign the subnet mask for the networks?

   A. By using a default subnet mask

   B. By creating a custom subnet mask

   C. By assigning a subnet mask of 0.0.0.0

   D. By assigning a subnet mask that has the IP address of the router

   Answer: B

Explanation: Because you require seven networks, you will need at least a mask of 255.255.240.0 (which gives you 14 subnets). If you used the default mask, 255.255.0.0, this would provide zero subnets but 65,534 hosts.

10. You need to come up with a TCP/IP addressing scheme for your company. How many host IDs must you allow for when you define the subnet mask for the network? (Choose all the correct answers.)

    A. One for each subnet

    B. One for each router interface

    C. One for each WAN connection

    D. One for each network adapter installed on each host

    Answer: B and D

    Explanation: Note the key words, *host IDs*. Each interface on a router must have an IP address. (The only exception is a Cisco router running without IP.) However, as a default gateway—Ethernet, Token Ring, Serial, and so on—that interface must still be addressed. Also, each PC must have an IP address assigned to it.

11. You have a Class B network address divided into 30 subnets. You will add 25 new subnets within the next two years. You need 600 host IDs for each subnet. Which subnet mask should you assign?

    A. 255.192.0.0

    B. 255.254.0.0

    C. 255.255.248.0

    D. 255.255.252.0

    Answer: D

    Explanation: Because you need 55 subnets, you must reserve six bits for the network ID to equal 62 (2^6–2) subnets, and 10 bits, or 1022 (1024–2), for the host ID. 11111100.00000000, or 252.0, gives us this answer.

12. You have a network ID of 206.17.250.0 and you need to divide it into nine subnets. You need to provide for the largest possible number of host IDs per subnet. Which subnet mask should you assign?

    A. 255.255.255.192

    B. 255.255.255.224

    C. 255.255.255.240

    D. 255.255.255.248

    Answer: C

    Explanation: Because you need nine subnets, you must reserve four bits for the network ID to equal 14 (2^4–2) subnets, and four bits, or 14 (2^4–2), for the host ID. 11110000, or 240, gives us this answer.

13. You have a Class C network address divided into three subnets. You will need to add two subnets in the next two years. Each subnet will have 25 hosts. Which subnet mask should you assign?

    A. 255.255.255.0

    B. 255.255.255.192

    C. 255.255.255.224

    D. 255.255.255.248

    Answer: C

    Explanation: Because you need five subnets, you must reserve three bits for the network ID to equal six subnets (2^3=8–2), and five bits, or 30 (2^5–2), for the host ID. 11100000, or 224, gives us this answer.

14. You need to come up with a TCP/IP addressing scheme for your company. How many network IDs must you allow for when you define the subnet mask for the network? (Choose all the correct answers.)

    A. One for each subnet

    B. One for each host ID

    C. One for each router interface

D. One for each WAN connection

E. One for each network adapter installed on each host

Answer: A and D

Explanation: Each host on the network must have a unique IP address. However, you are only required to have one Network ID per network. Each set of hosts must share a common network ID, as well as connections between networks, which are the WAN connections.

15. You need to come up with a TCP/IP addressing scheme for your company. Which two factors must you consider when you define the subnet mask for the network? (Choose two.)

A. The number of subnets on the network

B. The number of host IDs on each subnet

C. The volume of network traffic on each subnet

D. The location of DNS servers

E. The location of default gateways

Answer: A and B

Explanation: There are two components that are determined by the subnet mask: the number of subnets and the number of workstations. The network traffic is secondary to your consideration. DNS is just a filler answer and has no relational value. The location of the Default gateway may be on a different planet; nonetheless, each subnet will still require a default gateway.

16. You have a Class C network address of 206.17.19.0 with four subnets. You need the largest possible number of host IDs per subnet. Which subnet mask should you assign?

A. 255.255.255.192

B. 255.255.255.224

C. 255.255.255.240

D. 255.255.255.248

Answer: B

Explanation: Because you need four subnets, you must reserve three bits for the network ID to equal six subnets (2^3-2), and five bits, or 30 (2^5-2), for the host ID. 11100000, or 224, gives us this answer.

17. You have a Class C network address of 206.17.88.0 and you need the largest amount of subnets, with up to 12 hosts per subnet. Which subnet mask should you assign?

    A. 255.255.255.192

    B. 255.255.255.224

    C. 255.255.255.240

    D. 255.255.255.248

    Answer: C

    Explanation: Because you need 12 hosts per subnet, you must reserve four bits for the Host ID to equal 14 hosts per network (2^4-2), and four bits, or 14 (2^4-2) for the network ID. 11110000, or 240, gives us this answer.

18. A user can ping the IP address of her workstation, but she cannot ping the IP address of any other computer. This user also cannot connect to any workstation through NT Explorer. What is most likely the problem?

    A. The workstation is configured with an invalid default gateway address.

    B. The workstation is configured with an invalid subnet mask.

    C. The workstation is configured with a duplicate IP address.

    D. The workstation is not configured to use WINS.

    Answer: B

    Explanation: It is most likely for the subnet mask to be causing problems. When NT detects a duplicate IP address it will automatically shut down the protocol (usually displaying a conflict message), and PING would say that all designations are unreachable (unless your IP address was 0.0.0.0, then loopback 127.0.0.1 would be OK). The default gateway does not matter because the user can't even see her neighbor. Also, WINS does not matter because if name resolution were used, the system would attempt to broadcast for it.

19. You need to check connectivity with TCP/IP to an NT server on a remote subnet. Which utility should you use?

    A. ARP.EXE

    B. NETSTAT.EXE

    C. NBTSTAT.EXE

    D. PING.EXE

    E. ROUTE.EXE

    Answer: D

    Explanation: PING is used to test for a valid connection to a remote IP address. ARP is used to resolve an IP address to a MAC address; however, it does not test connectivity. NETSTAT informs you of the network connections, but it will only check the established connection, not the connectivity. NBTSTAT will check the NETBIOS over TCP/IP naming, but it has nothing to do with a valid path. ROUTE is used in static router mappings, which may be valid or invalid because the utility does not check for validity.

20. You need to perform network capacity planning for various types of IP traffic, and you want to analyze and decode TCP/IP packets. Which utility should you use?

    A. NETSTAT.EXE

    B. Performance Monitor

    C. NBTSTAT.EXE

    D. Network Monitor

    Answer: D

    Explanation: Network Monitor is like a network sniffer. It has the ability to capture and decode network traffic and can be used to analyze traffic. Also useful, but not part of the solution, would be to see how much traffic is sent to a specific network card by using Performance

Monitor. However, this will not let you analyze or decode the packets. NETSTAT and NBTSTAT have no correlation to the task at hand.

21. You need to get an IP address assigned so you can broadcast your company on the Internet. Who do you contact?

    Answer: NIC (Network Information Center). However, typically you would go through your ISP to get your IP addresses.

22. You need to send a broadcast message on the network informing users that the server is going down. When you send the multicast transmission, which address will IP use to broadcast the message to all users?

    Answer: 255.255.255.255 or 11111111.11111111.11111111.11111111

23. The NIC assigns you a Class B address for your company's network. How many octets define the network portion of the address?

    Answer: The first two octets (16 bits) in a Class B network are reserved for the network address.

24. The NIC has assigned a Class C address for your new Internet Web server. How many bits can you use for the host address?

    Answer: In a Class C address, eight bits are reserved for host addresses.

25. You look in your workstation configuration and notice there's an IP address of 127.0.0.1. What does this mean?

    Answer: 127.0.0.1 is the loopback address for the local host, so you can test your workstation without loading up the network with a bunch of stuff unnecessarily.

26. You decide you want to subnet your Class B network with a mask of 255.240.0.0. When implemented it does not work. Why?

    Answer: The first two octets of a Class B subnet mask must be 255.255.

27. Your boss read in a Microsoft magazine that creating subnets will help her network run more efficiently. She's decided to implement this, and wants you to lead the project. She wants you to outline what the advantages of subnetting the network are so she can justify the project to her

superiors in a meeting this afternoon. What will you equip her with? Take a minute to create a list of the benefits of subnetting for her.

Answer:

- Reduced network traffic

- Optimized network performance

- Simplified management

- Facilitates spanning large geographic distances

28. You have four offices and 25 nodes at each office. Which subnet mask would you assign to your Class C network address of 201.201.201.0?

Answer: 255.255.255.224. This subnet address would give you six subnets with 30 nodes per subnet.

29. You have a Class B network address of 187.32.0.0. Which subnet address would give you at least 200 subnets?

Answer: 255.255.255.0. All bits in the third octet used for subnetting would give you 254 subnets, each with 254 nodes.

30. Your network is not assigned an address by the NIC and you do not need to be on the Internet. You create a Class A address of 36.0.0.0 with a subnet mask of 255.255.0.0. How many subnets can you use, and how many hosts can be on each subnet?

Answer: 254 subnets, each with 65,534 hosts. All bits in the second octet are used for subnets, which leaves the second and third octet (16 bits) for hosts.

31. Your IS manager asks you if there is some kind of computer that will map host names to IP addresses for groups of computers called domains. What do you tell him?

Answer: Network Information Services (NIS)

32. You're called upon to help train a new network Help Desk employee who is confused about the Domain Name System. How do you explain it to her?

Answer: The Domain Name System (DNS) is a mechanism that helps users to locate the name of a host and to map a name to an IP address on machines throughout the Internet.

33. The CIO of your company is assessing the knowledge level of his network operating system staff. He calls to ask you the difference between NIS and DNS. What do you say?

Answer: The major difference between NIS and DNS is that an NIS server covers a smaller area. NIS servers relate only to a group of computers, not the entire Internet. DNS covers a large area and is typically on the Internet.

Chapter 3

1. You have four Class C network addresses: 203.200.5.0, 203.200.6.0, 203.200.7.0 and 203.200.8.0. You want to combine these addresses into one logical network to increase the host IDs that you can have on one subnet. Which subnet mask should you assign?

A. 255.255.252.0

B. 255.255.254.0

C. 255.255.255.252

D. 255.255.255.254

Answer: A

Explanation: In opposition to subnetting, supernetting borrows bits from the network ID and masks them as the host ID for more efficient routing. To combine the above three addresses, the destination of a packet is determined by ANDing the destination IP address and the subnet mask of the routing entry.

Network ID	Subnet Mask	Subnet Mask In Binary
203.200.5.0	255.255.252.0 =	1111111.111111 11.11111100.000 00000

Because we have a Class C network, our subnet mask only could be:

A 255.255.252.0 or B 255.255.254.0. Answers C and D are incorrect for Class C Supernetting.

We need to combine four networks, and 254 would only give us one bit with two subnets. So, without working at it, the answer must be A. However, to work it out anyway: 252 gives us two bits or 4 subnets. Perfect!

2. You can ping all the computers on your subnet and your default gateway, but you cannot ping any of the computers on a remote subnet. Other users on your subnet can ping computers on the remote subnet. What could be the problem?

   A. The subnet mask on the router is invalid.

   B. The subnet mask on your computer is invalid.

   C. The default gateway address on your computer is invalid.

   D. The computers on the remote subnet are not configured for TCP/IP.

   E. The route to the remote subnet has not been established on the router.

   Answer: B and C

   Explanation: If the subnet is incorrect on your computer, the router will think you're either on a different network or on a network it doesn't know about, and discard the packet. Also, just because you can ping the default gateway doesn't mean your workstation actually is configured with the correct default gateway.

3. Using Windows NT Explorer, your Windows NT Workstation can connect to a remote server, but not to a server on your local subnet. What is most likely the cause of the problem?

   A. Invalid default gateway address on your workstation

   B. Invalid default gateway address on the local server

   C. Invalid subnet mask on your workstation

   D. Invalid subnet mask on the remote server

   Answer: C

   Explanation: An invalid subnet mask on your workstation would mean that your system is seeing different network assignments. Assuming the router was within the scope of your network, you would still be able to see other networks. However, without going though a router, if a PC was on the same network, but your PC was configured to be on a different network, the local connection would fail. If the gateway address was incorrect, your system would not be able to talk to other networks. The gateway on the local server would make no difference because it is a local communication. And finally, regardless of what the subnet is on the remote server, your PC is still communicating to it as it should (as a remote network).

4. Using Windows NT Explorer, your Windows NT Workstation cannot connect to a local server, but all other users can. When you run Network Monitor, you notice that each time the workstation attempts to connect to the server, it broadcasts an ARP request for the default gateway. What is most likely the cause of the problem?

   A. Invalid default gateway address on the workstation

   B. Invalid subnet mask on the workstation

   C. The workstation has a duplicate IP address.

   D. The workstation is not configured to use WINS.

   Answer: B

   Explanation: Your system is viewing the server as if it were on a different network, and that is why it is trying to talk to the gateway. Since your PC is local, the gateway address does not matter. Also, if your workstation had a duplicate IP address, it would not try ARP with the gateway. WINS would not matter in this scenario because all systems are regarded as local.

5. Your NT Workstation cannot connect to a remote server, but all other workstations can. The network is configured as follows: two subnets, one router. The router has two interfaces: Network A with 167.191.32.1 and Network B with 167.191.64.1. All computers use a subnet mask of 255.255.240.0. You are located on Network B. When you run IPCONFIG on your workstation, you receive the following output:

IP Address	167.191.82.17
Subnet Mask	255.255.240.0
Default Gateway	167.191.64.1

What is most likely the cause of the problem?

A. IP address on workstation is invalid.

B. Subnet mask on workstation is invalid.

C. Default gateway on workstation is invalid.

D. IP address on server is invalid.

E. Default gateway on server is invalid.

Answer: A

Explanation: Because you are on subnet B, the default gateway of 167.191.64.1 is correct. Because the default gateway is correct, the IP address must be invalid for the 64 subnet. Using a 240 mask, you have utilized four bits, or 2^4, or 14 subnets (16–2). This mask has a range of 16 to 31, 32 to 47, 48 to 63, 64 to 79, 80 to 95, and so on. The workstation IP address of 167.191.82.17 is on the 80 subnet and is an invalid host ID in the 167.191.64.0 network.

6. You are troubleshooting a Windows NT Server computer on a TCP/IP network. The server is located on a subnet with a network ID of 167.170.2.0. The default gateway address is 167.170.2.1. Users on a remote subnet cannot access the server. You run ipconfig /all at the server and receive the following output:

Host Name	pdctest
DNS Servers	
Node Type	Hybrid
NetBIOS scope ID	
IP Routing Enabled	no
WINS Proxy Enabled	no
NetBIOS Resolution Uses DNS	no
Physical Address	00-20-AF-CA-E5-27
DHCP Enabled	no

IP Address	167.170.2.223
Subnet Mask	255.255.0.0
Default Gateway	167.170.2.1
Primary WINS Server	167.170.2.46

What is most likely the cause of the problem?

A. Subnet mask is incorrect.

B. NetBIOS scope ID is incorrect.

C. NetBIOS node type is incorrect.

D. IP address is out of range for this subnet.

Answer: A

Explanation: The clue is in the fact that you are informed that the network ID is 167.170.2.0. Because the question defines the first three numbers, this can lead to the conclusion that the IP subnet mask is wrong because it only defines the first two octets. The NETBIOS type is the default, and should have no effect in this context. The noted type of Hybrid just states that the system will talk to the WINS server, then broadcast to find an IP address. However, that has nothing to do with the workstation's problem. Finally, as for the IP address being out of range, that notion is far fetched because a mask of 255.255.0.0 or 255.255.255.0 would be valid. What you need to remember for a question like this is to look for the wrong answers.

7. You have five Windows NT Server computers all configured as static routers. Which utility should you use to identify the path that a packet takes as it passes through the routers?

A. Network Monitor

B. ROUTE.EXE

C. TRACERT.EXE

D. IPCONFIG.EXE

E. NETSTAT.EXE

Answer: C

Explanation: TRACERT (trace route) is a common TCP/IP command that is used to follow gateways until the final target is reached. Network Monitor could tell you the same information; however, you would have to monitor every segment of your network that individually connects each segment until a path is established. IPCONFIG also will not tell you anything useful except your default gateway, which will tell little for multiple paths. NETSTAT will show the ultimate connections, but will state nothing about the intermediates.

8. You have an NT Server on a remote subnet. You cannot ping this server by its IP address, but you can ping your default gateway and all other computers on the remote subnet. What could the problem be? (Choose two.)

   A. The server is not WINS enabled.

   B. The server has an invalid subnet mask.

   C. The server has an invalid default gateway address.

   D. Your workstation is configured with an invalid subnet mask.

   E. Your workstation is configured with an invalid default gateway address.

   Answer: B and C

   Explanation: If the server's subnet is invalid, it may potentially not see the remote workstation as being on a different network. As with having a bad IP gateway, this will cause the server to attempt to respond to the incorrect path. Because we are talking about the system's IP address, WINS does not even come into the picture. Because we can ping all other remote subnet computers, we obviously do not have a problem with our subnet mask and/or default gateway.

9. You can connect through NT Explorer to all workstations on your local subnet, but cannot connect to any workstations or servers on a remote subnet. Which IP address should you ping first to diagnose the problem?

   A. The local server

   B. The default gateway

C. The remote server

D. None, TCP/IP isn't loaded

E. None, reboot the router

Answer: B

Explanation: Obviously, the first step to sending packets to the remote network is the default gateway. Because you can already communicate to the local server, that would be pointless; and the remote server would only be your choice if you wanted to work backwards. The clue that you don't want to do this is that the question mentions workstations and servers on the remote subnet. If TCP/IP was not loaded, then nothing would communicate; and rebooting the router does no good if the problem is something other than a router hang-up.

10. Your Windows NT Workstation cannot connect to a remote Windows NT Server using NT Explorer. All other computers can connect to the remote NT Server. You run Network Monitor and notice that each time the workstation attempts to connect to the server, the workstation broadcasts an ARP request for the remote server's IP address. What is most likely the cause of the problem?

    A. The workstation is configured with an invalid default gateway address.

    B. The workstation is configured with an invalid subnet mask.

    C. The workstation is configured with a duplicate IP address.

    D. The workstation is not configured to use WINS.

    Answer: B

    Explanation: Your computer thinks the remote server is on your network. This indicates that the subnet mask is wrong. Because you system is sending an immediate ARP, this indicates that the default gateway is not even referenced. Also, if the IP address was a duplicate, you would lose the IP interface. As for WINS, the ARP message would never be issued if the name was not resolved to an IP address.

11. You have a RAS server that is connected to an Internet Service Provider via ISDN. You want your Windows 95 workstations to use the RAS server to access the Internet. How should the default gateway addresses be configured?

   A. The default gateway address on the RAS server specifies the IP address of the ISP's router interface to your internal network.

   B. The default gateway address on the RAS server specifies the IP address of the ISP's router interface to the Internet.

   C. The default gateway address on each Windows 95 computer specifies the IP address of the ISP's router interface to your internal network.

   D. The default gateway address on each Windows 95 machine specifies the IP address of the RAS server's network interface to your internal network.

   Answer: D

   Explanation: The question is asking how the default gateways should be configured on your Windows 95 workstations. The default gateway on the hosts should be set to the interface on the server on your internal network.

12. Your NT Server has three network adapters. You configure the server to route TCP/IP packets, and you want it to be able to automatically update its routing tables by using routing information from other routers on the network. Which service must you install on the Windows NT Server computer?

   A. RIP for IP

   B. RIP for NWLink IPX/SPX Compatible Transport

   C. The DHCP Relay Agent

   D. The DHCP Service

   Answer: A

   Explanation: RIP for IP will automatically update routing tables from other routers. IPX and DHCP are not used and do not matter in the above context.

13. You have five multihomed Windows NT Server computers running TCP/IP and routing TCP/IP packets. You want to configure the routing tables on these servers with a minimum of administrative effort. What should you do?

    A. Use NETSTAT.EXE to configure the routing tables.

    B. Use ROUTE.EXE to configure the routing tables.

    C. Install the DHCP Relay Agent.

    D. Install RIP for IP.

    Answer: D

    Explanation: RIP for IP will automatically update routing tables from other routers. NETSTAT will show current connections but has no low management-routing value. ROUTE is useful for routing, but is very interactive. This is not a minimum of administrative effort. DHCP is not used and does not matter in the above context.

14. You have a multihomed Windows NT Server that you want to configure as a TCP/IP static router. What two steps must you complete?

    A. Enable IP forwarding.

    B. Configure each network adapter with a unique subnet mask.

    C. Configure each network adapter with an IP address, and ensure that each IP address is from a different subnet.

    D. Configure each network adapter with an IP address, and ensure that each IP address is from a different address class.

    Answer: A and C

    Explanation: If you did not get this one, you really need to consider re-reading the entire static router section. First, you have two network cards that you want to forward packets between. Easy—enable forwarding. A packet comes in one card and out the other. Next, each card must be in a different subnet/network.

15. You have installed two routers on one subnet to provide redundancy. When one router fails, users start complaining that they cannot access remote subnets, even though you have a second router on the network. What should you do to prevent this problem from occurring the next time a router fails?

A. Configure each workstation with multiple default gateway addresses.

B. Configure each workstation with multiple IP addresses.

C. Install a WINS server on each subnet.

D. Install the DHCP Relay Agent on both routers.

Answer: A

Explanation: This question is also very easy. Use multiple default gateways such that if one is not available, the next in line is used. Consider that neither WINS or DHCP is a requirement to the above network, and configuring multiple addresses on a workstation will not reduce the number of points of failure or provide redundancy if the router fails.

16. The network is configured as follows: two subnets, one router. The router has two interfaces: Network A with 167.191.32.1 and Network B with 167.191.64.1. All computers use a subnet mask of 255.255.224.0. Your NT Workstation cannot connect to a remote server on Network A, but all other workstations on Network B can. You are located on network B. When you run IPCONFIG on your workstation, you receive the following output:

IP Address	167.191.82.17
Subnet Mask	255.255.224.0
Default Gateway	167.191.32.1

What is most likely the cause of the problem?

A. IP address on workstation is invalid.

B. Subnet mask on workstation is invalid.

C. Default gateway on workstation is invalid.

D. IP address on server is invalid.

E. Default gateway on server is invalid.

Answer: C

Explanation: Your workstation is configured with the wrong gateway. The gateway that you have selected is on Network A.

17. The network is configured as follows: two subnets, one router. The router has two interfaces: Network A with 167.191.32.1 and Network B with 167.191.64.1. All computers use a subnet mask of 255.255.224.0. Your NT Workstation cannot connect to a remote server on Network A, but all other workstations on Network B can. You are located on Network B. When you run IPCONFIG on your workstation, you receive the following output:

IP Address	167.191.96.17
Subnet Mask	255.255.224.0
Default Gateway	167.191.64.1

What is most likely the cause of the problem?

A. IP address on workstation is invalid.

B. Subnet mask on workstation is invalid.

C. Default gateway on workstation is invalid.

D. IP address on server is invalid.

E. Default gateway on server is invalid.

Answer: A

Explanation: The IP address on the workstation is not valid for the 64 subnet. The valid hosts for subnet 64 are 167.191.64.1 to 167.191.95.254.

18. Situation: You are installing an NT TCP/IP server with three network adapters. You also plan to use this server as a router.

Required results:

- The new server must be configured to route TCP/IP.

Optional desired results:

- The server must dynamically update its routing tables.

- The server must provide IP addresses to all clients located on all subnets.

- The server must be able to send trap messages across the network to a Windows NT workstation computer.

Proposed solution:

- Install TCP/IP and configure one IP address for each of the server's network adapters.

- Install PPTP on the server.

- Install DHCP on the server and configure one scope for each subnet.

- Install SNMP on the server and configure SNMP to forward traps messages to the workstation.

Which results does the proposed solution produce?

A. The proposed solution produces the required result and produces all of the optional desired results.

B. The proposed solution produces the required result and produces only two of the optional desired results.

C. The proposed solution produces the required result but does not produce any of the optional desired results.

D. The proposed solution does not produce the required result.

Answer: D

Explanation: Installing and configuring TCP/IP and one IP address for each adapter is fine as long as IP routing is selected. However, because IP routing is not specified, the router will not work. Additionally, DHCP will provide network numbers as stated per scope per subnet, and SNMP will manage the management. However, to dynamically update its routing tables, you must use RIP so that the NT router can communicate with the remote router to update its routing table automatically.

19. **Situation:** You are installing an NT TCP/IP server with three network adapters. You also plan to use this server as a router.

Required result:

■ The new server must be configured to route TCP/IP.

Optional desired results:

■ The server must dynamically update its routing tables.

■ The server must provide IP addresses to all clients located on all subnets.

■ The server must be able to send trap messages across the network to a Windows NT workstation computer.

Proposed solution:

■ Install TCP/IP and configure one IP address for each server's network adapters.

■ Enable IP forwarding on the server.

■ Install PPTP on the server.

■ Install the DHCP Relay Agent on the server.

Which results does the proposed solution produce?

A. The proposed solution produces the required result and produces all of the optional desired results.

B. The proposed solution produces the required result and produces only two of the optional desired results.

C. The proposed solution produces the required result but does not produce any of the optional desired results.

D. The proposed solution does not produce the required results.

Answer: C

Explanation: Installing TCP/IP and assigning addresses with IP forward on the server satisfies the router components. However, you must add RIP for dynamic routing, DHCP server to assign IP addresses (with one scope per subnetwork), and SNMP to manage TCP/IP traps.

20. **Situation:** You are installing an NT TCP/IP server with three network adapters. You also plan to use this server as a router.

Required result:

■ The new server must be configured to route TCP/IP.

Optional desired results:

■ The server must dynamically update its routing tables.

■ The server must provide IP addresses to all clients located on all subnets.

■ The server must be able to send trap messages across the network to a Windows NT workstation computer.

Proposed solution:

■ Install TCP/IP and configure one IP address for each server's network adapters.

■ Enable IP forwarding on the server.

■ Install RIP for IP on the server.

■ Install DHCP with scopes for all subnets.

Which results does the proposed solution produce?

A. The proposed solution produces the required result and produces all of the optional desired results.

B. The proposed solution produces the required result and produces only two of the optional desired results.

C. The proposed solution produces the required result but does not produce any of the optional desired results.

D. The proposed solution does not produce the required results.

Answer: B

Explanation: The solution lacks SNMP to send traps to the Windows NT workstation computer.

21. **Situation:** You are installing an NT TCP/IP server with three network adapters. You also plan to use this server as a router.

Required result:

- The new server must be configured to route TCP/IP.

Optional desired results:

- The server must dynamically update its routing tables.

- The server must provide IP addresses to all clients located on all subnets.

- The server must be able to send trap messages across the network to a Windows NT workstation computer.

Proposed solution:

- Install TCP/IP and configure one IP address for each server's network adapters.

- Enable IP forwarding on the server.

- Install DHCP with scopes for all subnets.

- Install SNMP on the server and configure SNMP to forward trap messages to the workstation.

- Install a third-party SNMP manager on the server.

Which results does the proposed solution produce?

A. The proposed solution produces the required result and produces all of the optional desired results.

B. The proposed solution produces the required result and produces only two of the optional desired results.

C. The proposed solution produces the required result but does not produce any of the optional desired results.

D. The proposed solution does not produce the required results.

Answer: B

Explanation: In order to automatically update the router table, the router requires IP. The SNMP manager on the server will not do anything and does not affect the result either way.

22. Assign the missing IP and subnet mask values for each customer below:

Beginning IP address	192.24.0.1
Ending IP address	192.24.7.8
Subnet Mask	
Beginning IP address	192.34.16.1
Ending IP address	
Subnet Mask	255.255.240.0
Beginning IP address	
Ending IP address	192.24.11.254
Subnet Mask	255.255.252.0
Beginning IP address	192.24.14.1
Ending IP address	
Subnet Mask	255.255.254.0

Answer:

Beginning IP address	192.24.0.1
Ending IP address	192.24.7.8
Subnet Mask	255.255.248.0
Beginning IP address	192.34.16.1
Ending IP address	192.34.31.254
Subnet Mask	255.255.240.0

Beginning IP address	192.24.8.1
Ending IP address	192.24.11.254
Subnet Mask	255.255.252.0
Beginning IP address	192.24.14.1
Ending IP address	192.24.15.254
Subnet Mask	255.255.254.0

Chapter 4

1. What is IP address resolution?

   A. Resolving duplicate IP addresses

   B. The successful mapping of an IP address to its hardware address

   C. Resolving invalid subnet masks

   D. Resolving errors when IP tries to resolve an IP address to a hardware address

   Answer: B

   Explanation: Before an IP address can be mapped to a host name, its hardware address must be known.

2. How do you resolve IP addresses locally?

   A. By typing Resolve IP address ip-address

   B. By typing ARP -s ip-address

   C. With an ARP request and an ARP reply

   D. With an RARP request and an RARP reply

   Answer: C

   Explanation: When a host does not know the hardware address of a destination host, it ARPs the host asking for its hardware address. The host then replies with an ARP, which includes its hardware address. To do this, however, it must know the hosts IP address.

3. How does your computer resolve IP addresses remotely?

A. It sends an ARP to the destination machine.

B. It sends an RARP to the destination machine.

C. It sends an RARP to the default gateway.

D. It sends an ARP to the default gateway.

Answer: D

Explanation: When it is determined by the sending host that the destination is on a remote network, it then ARPs the default gateway for its hardware address. After the default gateway replies with its hardware address, the sending host sends the frame with the destination of the default gateway. Once the default gateway receives the frame, it is its responsibility to forward the packet to the correct destination host.

4. Which is true about the ARP cache?

A. It's cleared out every time the computer is rebooted.

B. The ARP cache stores only dynamic IP and hardware addresses.

C. The ARP cache stores only static IP and hardware addresses.

D. It's permanent.

Answer: A

Explanation: Every time a host reboots, the cache is cleared. This is because the cache is only kept in RAM.

5. What's the maximum lifetime of an entry in the ARP cache?

A. Two minutes

B. As specified by the system administrator

C. Ten minutes

D. ARP entries are permanent and can only be removed by typing **ARP -d**.

Answer: C

Explanation: The maximum lifetime of an ARP entry is 10 minutes. However, if it is not used in two minutes, it is deleted; otherwise, it is deleted after 10 minutes. NT keeps a separate ARP cache for each IP address.

6. Aside from the initial entry into the cache, if the destination system isn't contacted again, how long will the entry remain in the cache?

   A. Ten minutes

   B. Two minutes

   C. Five minutes

   D. Until deleted

   Answer: B

   Explanation: Same as the explanation for question number five.

7. Under Windows NT, if the cache fills up, what happens to old and new entries?

   A. If their lifetime expires, old entries are deleted, and new ones added.

   B. Regardless of whether or not an old entry's lifetime has expired, it is deleted in favor of adding the new one.

   C. Old entries are cached for future use, and new ones added to the ARP table.

   D. Nothing

   Answer: B

   Explanation: If an ARP cache reaches its maximum capacity before entries expire, the oldest entry is deleted so that a new entry can be added.

8. You're a computer science professor at a major university. One of your students wants to know why an IP address needs to be resolved. She asks "Why is it necessary to know both the software and hardware addresses—why isn't knowing the hardware address enough?" What do you tell her?

    Answer: An IP address must be resolved to determine which host owns it. IP addresses are easier to work with in that they follow a logical system. Hardware addresses tend to be a lot less friendly and difficult to manage. Knowing both also reduces the risk of error. In addition, different network technologies have different hardware addressing schemes. IP uses a single addressing scheme for cross-platform compatibility. Therefore, it is necessary to map one to the other.

9. You're being interviewed for a network specialist position. Your potential employer asks, "In what way could an incorrect subnet mask cause a problem? When would this problem occur, and who, if anyone, would notice?" How would you answer?

    Answer: Incorrect subnet masks cause problems when a host is attempting to determine if an address is local or remote. The reason is that during this process a host will examine the subnet mask to determine which portions of the address are network-based and which are node-based. If a remote machine is discovered on the local network, a broadcast storm can result, causing systems to time-out and hang. It would affect the entire network, and, therefore, many would notice.

10. When you go to a DOS prompt and type **ARP –g**, what do you see? (Choose all that apply.)

    A. IP to NetBIOS names that have been resolved

    B. The IP Cache

    C. The entries in the ARP cache

    D. IP to MAC addresses that have been resolved

    Answer: C, D

    Explanation: By typing ARP –g, you can see the hardware (MAC) addresses that have been resolved from an IP address.

Chapter 5

1. You're trying to connect to workstations by using their host name, and you receive errors. You check the HOSTS file on the workstation, and it contains the following entries:

127.0.0.1	#localhost loopback diagnostic	
150.170.16.200	#AtLibrary atLibrary &	# Lib Server
150.170.3.2	#router2 Router2	# Engr $ router
150.170.3	#net3 Net3	# Engineering Dept

What must you do to the HOSTS file on the workstation?

A. Remove all the $ characters.

B. Remove all the & characters.

C. Remove the first # character from each line.

D. Change the IP address in the last line to 142.170.3.0.

Answer: C

Explanation: The basic problem with the above host file is that no names have been assigned to any of the IP addresses. The # character is used to input a comment. In this case, all the host names will be read as comments and not understood for HOST name-to-IP address resolution.

2. What is a domain name?

A. The Microsoft implementation of a NetBIOS name server

B. A text file in the same format as the 4.3 BSD UNIX file

C. A hierarchical name that is implemented using a Domain Name Server (DNS)

D. A flat name that is implemented using a Domain Name Server (DNS)

Answer: C

Explanation: Domain names are given to corporations by the InterNIC. These names are used to help map IP addresses to host names. It is a lot easier for someone to type **www.microsoft.com** than an IP address.

3. What is host name resolution?

    A. A B-node broadcast on the local network for the IP address of the destination NetBIOS name

    B. The process of mapping a host name to an IP address

    C. A hierarchical name that is implemented using a Domain Name Server (DNS)

    D. A local text file that maps IP addresses to the NetBIOS computer names

    Answer: B

    Explanation: Host name resolution is a way for computers to resolve names from IP addresses to human names.

4. What is true of a host name?

    A. The NAMEHOST utility will display the host name assigned to your system.

    B. It is an alias assigned to a computer by an administrator to identify a TCP/IP host.

    C. A host name never corresponds to an IP address that is stored in a HOSTS file or in a database on a DNS or WINS server.

    D. Host names are not used in Windows NT commands.

    E. A host name cannot be used in place of an IP address when using PING or other TCP/IP utilities.

    Answer: B

    Explanation: A host name is a way for humans to remember a computer. Host names are easier for most users to logon to, or copy and send data to, than IP addresses.

5. Which are common problems associated with host name resolution? (Choose all correct answers.)

A. Multiple entries for the same host on different lines

B. Host name is misspelled

C. Case-sensitivity

D. IP address is invalid

Answer: A, B, and D

Explanation: Typically, what administrators find in HOSTS files are duplicate entries, misspelled names, and invalid or old IP addresses.

6. You have enabled all Windows NT name resolving techniques: WINS, b-node broadcast, and LMHOSTS, in addition to the HOSTS file and DNS. But none of these methods resolves a host name. What is the only way to communicate with this host?

Answer: If none of the methods work to solve the host's name, the only way to communicate with the host is to specify the IP address.

7. When resolving names with a HOSTS file, the local names are being resolved while none of the remote host names are being resolved. What would stop the remote host names from being resolved?

Answer: The default gateway is not defined or incorrect.

8. When resolving names with a HOSTS file, you notice that a host name is being resolved incorrectly. When checking the HOSTS file, you don't see a problem, as the name is spelled correctly and the IP address is correct. What else could be wrong?

Answer: There are multiple entries for the same host on different lines.

9. Your company needs to resolve names on the Internet for its customers trying to look up information on the state of the company. What service will you use to resolve names?

Answer: Domain Name System

10. On Windows NT, the HOSTS file is stored where?

A. In the %SYSTEMROOT% directory

B. In the %SYSTEMROOT% \SYSTEM32 directory

C. In the %SYSTEMROOT% \SYSTEM32\DRIVERS\ETC directory

D. In the %SYSTEMROOT% \SYSTEM32\ETC directory

Answer: C

Explanation: The HOSTS and LMHOSTS is stored in the %SYSTEM-ROOT\SYTEM32\DRIVERS\ETC directory.

Chapter 6

1. What are some of the key words that can be included in your LMHOSTS file? (Choose all that apply.)

A. #PRE

B. #LAST

C. #INCLUDE

D. #MH

Answer: A, C, and D

Explanation: These are some of the predefined key words that can be used to help modify your LMHOSTS file.

2. What is a P-Node? (Choose all that apply.)

A. A broadcast to resolve names

B. A method to resolve names from a NBNS

C. A method to resolve names from a DNS server

D. A method to resolve names from a WINS server

Answer: B and D

Explanation: NBNS and WINS are the same thing! This method of operation provides an effective and efficient means for resolving names directly from a NetBIOS Name Server (NBNS) such as WINS.

3. What is the function of the LMHOSTS file?

   A. To resolve DNS names of remote hosts

   B. To resolve UNIX names of remote hosts

   C. To resolve NetBIOS names of remote hosts

   D. To resolve a MAC address to a NetBIOS name

   Answer: C

   Explanation: Windows NT uses the NetBIOS interface. This means Microsoft has to have a way to resolve its Windows interface to a host name. The LMHOSTS file can do this.

4. Which methods are used to resolve NetBIOS names? (Choose all that apply.)

   A. Local Broadcast

   B. LMHOSTS file

   C. NBNS

   D. HOSTS file

   E. DNS

   Answer: All of the above

   Explanation: As the explanation for question 3 explains, Microsoft needs a way to resolve its NetBIOS interface to a host name. These are the five methods.

5. On Windows NT systems, LMHOSTS is maintained in

   A. %SYSTEMROOT%\SYSTEM\DRIVERS\ETC

   B. %SYSTEMROOT%\SYSTEM32\DRIVERS\HOSTS

C. %SYSTEMROOT%\SYSTEM32\DRIVERS\ETC

D. %SYSTEMROOT%\SYSTEM\UNIX\ETC

Answer: C

Explanation: The LMHOSTS is, by default, placed in the ETC directory. You will also find the HOSTS, NETWORKS, PROTOCOL, and SERVICES files there.

6. What does the NBTSTAT utility do?

   A. Checks the state of current NetBIOS over TCP/IP connections

   B. Checks the state of current WinSOCK over TCP/IP connections

   C. Checks the state of current TCP/IP packet throughput

   D. Checks the status of your network

   Answer: A. Checks the state of current NetBIOS over TCP/IP connections.

   Explanation: This program is useful for troubleshooting and pre-loading the NetBIOS name cache. Here is the command syntax:

   - **nbtstat -n**: Lists the NetBIOS names registered by the client

   - **nbtstat -c**: Displays the NetBIOS name cache

   - **nbtstat -R**: Manually reloads the NetBIOS name cache using entries in the LMHOSTS file with a #PRE parameter

7. You are trying to connect to a 3.51 NT Server with the net use *server_name* command. That works OK, but when you try net use \\IP _address, it gets a bad command or filename. You checked the IP address and it is correct. What could the problem be?

   Answer: The net use command requires a NetBIOS name when connecting to 3.51 and below. For example, to connect to a server with an IP address of 192.123.45.67, you could not type **NET USE F: \\192.123.45.67\share**. The actual name is required, and therefore, the system must still resolve the name. However, this is now possible when connecting to an NT version 4 computer.

8. You get calls from users complaining that NetBIOS names are not being resolved all the time. "It's flaky," says one user. You open the LMHOSTS file and find some errors: a misspelled name, some old IP addresses, and a couple of misplaced comments. What effect can these erroneous entries have on the LMHOSTS file?

Answer:

- A misspelled name will keep the LMHOSTS file from resolving the name.

- An old IP address will cause the resolved name to be misdirected. (This is worse than one being resolved, because you will be directed to the wrong system, if one at all.)

- A misplaced comment will generally have no effect as long as it does not disrupt the standard format of the LMHOSTS file.

9. While cleaning out the LMHOSTS file, you found entries that started with #PRE. Where should you locate the LMHOSTS entries with the #PRE identifier? Why?

Answer: Entries should be placed at the END of the LMHOST file. These entries are only read when TCP/IP initializes, and are not read again.

10. You have been promoted to network manager. Your first job is to make sure you are using all of the company's bandwidth properly. Which node modes should you use? Which mode will be the most efficient for your network?

Answer: If all of the destination hosts you need to resolve NetBIOS names are on the same subnet, then Microsoft's Enhanced B-mode is most efficient. However, because this is hardly the case, the best overall efficiency tends to come from H-node, M-node, and P-node systems. This is largely due to the fact that they have little waste in finding their target system. H-node and M-node systems are equally reliable; however, the H-node is more desirable because it is less chatty. In the purest sense, Microsoft's Enhanced B-node can generate the least traffic if all required systems are pre-loaded into memory. As this is not commonly the case, usually P-node systems are regarded as the most silent. Given a choice, use an H-node system.

11. Someone in your office deleted the # signs in the LMHOSTS file because they thought they were comments. After you replaced the # signs, and the phones stopped ringing (two hours later!), this staff member wants to know what the # identifiers that are used in the LMHOSTS file are used for. What do you tell her?

Answer:

1. #PRE (for loading resolution names into memory)

2. #DOM (discussed later, for domain validation)

3. #INCLUDE (for including a remote system's LMHOSTS files)

4. #BEGIN_ALTERNATE (beginning of alternate block inclusion search)

5. #END_ALTERNATE (end of alternate block inclusion search)

6. # (comments and text)

Chapter 7

1. Your network is divided into seven subnets and you want to use DHCP to assign IP addresses to all computers on all subnets. You want to make sure that the two DNS servers are configured on each computer regardless of the subnet they are located on. How should you configure DHCP?

A. By creating a global option

B. By creating a local option

C. By creating a scope option

D. By creating a client option

Answer: A

Explanation: Because all systems will use the same two DNS servers, you want to use a global option.

2. You want to configure the DHCP Relay agent on your NT Server. What information must you supply?

   A. The computer name of the DHCP server

   B. The IP address of the DHCP server

   C. The IP address of a different DHCP relay agent of a remote subnet

   D. The IP address of the router to which DHCP request should be forwarded

   Answer: B

   Explanation: The IP address of the DHCP server is a direct path. A name requires resolution and is not nearly so quick. The IP address of a different DHCP relay would be pointless. Where is it going to relay the information? The IP address of the router is the default gateway. If it was configured with BootP, you wouldn't need the relay.

3. You have three NT Servers and you want to use DHCP to give them a unique address each time the server is started. What information must you supply when you add the client reservation for each of the servers?

   A. IP address

   B. Subnet mask

   C. Hardware address

   D. Lease period

   Answer: A and C

   Explanation: For each permanent reservation, you must supply the IP address that you want to reserve. You also must supply the hardware address of the Network board in the system to which you are assigning the reserved address. The hardware address is always unique to each network interface adapter.

4. You have 350 computers spread across eight subnets with two DHCP servers. You want each workstation to receive an IP address, even when one of the DHCP servers is down. What should you do?

   A. Create eight DHCP scopes on each DHCP server.

   B. Create four DHCP scopes on each DHCP server.

   C. Create two global DHCP scopes on each DHCP server.

   D. Create one global DHCP scope on each DHCP server.

   Answer: A

   Explanation: Each DCHP server is configured independently with a range of IP addresses that do not overlap each other. Each server will have one scope per subnet.

5. Your company has multiple laptops and the users frequently connect them into different subnets. You want to automatically assign these laptops TCP/IP addresses. Which service must you use?

   A. DHCP

   B. DNS

   C. FTP

   D. SNMP

   E. WINS

   Answer: A

   Explanation: Dynamic Host Configuration Protocol (DHCP) is the mechanism used to assign IP addresses to systems on-the-fly. DNS and WINS are used for name resolution, FTP is used for file transfer, and SNMP is used for management.

6. You use DHCP to assign IP addresses to all computers on your network. You want your NT Servers to get the same unique IP address each time the server is started. What should you do?

   A. Create a client reservation for each server.

   B. Create an exclusion range of IP addresses to be assigned to the server.

C. Specify an unlimited lease period for the servers only.

D. Create a separate scope that contains the IP address for each server.

Answer: A

Explanation: Creating a client reservation for each server will ensure the same IP address is assigned each time the system is rebooted. Note that an exclusion range would work, but it would not be assigned via DHCP. Also, an unlimited lease period would work; however, there is no way for the DHCP server to determine which assignment went to servers, which went to workstations, and so on. A separate scope would only work if all the servers were on the same network where the separate scope was not attempting to share the range with another scope.

7. You have three subnets. One subnet has only laptop Windows 95 computers. The other two subnets have NT Workstations. You have one DHCP server to support all clients. You want the IP lease period for the laptop set to seven days. You want the NT Workstations lease set to thirty days. What should you do?

A. Create one DHCP scope for all subnets. For each computer, create an exclusion range with a unique lease period.

B. Create one DHCP scope for all subnets. For each workstation, create a client reservation with a 30-day lease period.

C. Create one DHCP scope for each subnet. Specify the lease period as part of the scope's configuration.

D. Create one DHCP scope for each subnet. Create a global option that specifies a lease period that is based on the operating system the client computer is running.

Answer: C

Explanation: A DCHP scope independent of other scopes has the ability to set the lease time. Configure the period of the lease per scope. Note that you can't create a single scope of all subnets and client reservations. This would not make sense because you already know which subnets need 30 days. There is no option to define a lease period based on OS.

8. Your company has many laptops with Windows 95 that move from subnet to subnet. There is one WINS server on each subnet. You want to automatically assign the IP address for the WINS server on the subnet to which the laptop connects. Which service should you use?

   A. DHCP

   B. DNS

   C. FTP

   D. SNMP

   E. WINS

   Answer: A

   Explanation: Dynamic Host Configuration Protocol (DHCP) is the mechanism used to assign IP address to systems on-the-fly. DHCP will also deliver other specified information including WINS server, node types, and so on. DNS and WINS are used for name resolution but not for attribution assignments; FTP is used for file transfer, and SNMP is used for management/monitoring.

9. You have two subnets with an NT Server on each subnet. One server is configured as a router between Subnet A and Subnet B. You have a different server running DHCP on Subnet A. All clients on Subnet B must be able to obtain IP addresses from the server on Subnet A. Which service should you install on a Windows NT Server computer on Subnet B?

   A. RIP for IP

   B. RIP for NWLink IPX/SPX Compatible Transport

   C. The DHCP Relay Agent

   D. WINS

   Answer: C

   Explanation: The DHCP Relay Agent has the ability to forward IP addressing requests to a specific destination. If a router does not support BootP/DHCP, the relay agent is required. RIP is used to provide routing information to the router, but does not do anything for DHCP broadcasts. WINS is simply a name resolution tool and will do nothing for DHCP requests.

10. You have four subnets with one DHCP server to support 100 NT Work-
    stations and 10 NT Servers. DHCP needs to assign the same IP addresses
    to your servers every time they are started. Your boss gave you the fol-
    lowing IP scheme to implement at work:

    Gateways   1 through 19

    Clients   20 through 99

    Server   100 through 199

    Clients   200 through 254

    What are you going to do?

    A. Create four DHCP scopes for each range of IP addresses.

    B. Create three DHCP scopes for each type of host computer.

    C. Create one DHCP scope that is configured to exclude a range of
    addresses for the gateways. Create a client reservation for each
    server.

    D. Create one scope that is configured to exclude a range of addresses
    for the servers. Create a client reservation for each gateway.

    E. Create one DHCP scope that is configured to reserve one range of
    addresses for the gateways and one range of addresses for the servers.

    Answer: C

    Explanation: The question is easy; the answers are not. The best answer
    seems to be C. But remember, you are still required to have four
    scopes—one per subnet.

11. You want to install DHCP on your network consisting of three sub-
    nets. You place the server on one subnet, and all clients must be able to
    get IP addresses from this server. Which are two possible locations for
    DHCP relay agents? (choose two)

    A. On each subnet that does not contain the DHCP server

    B. On the subnet that contains the DHCP server

    C. On the routers between the subnets

D. On the DHCP server

Answer: A and C

Explanation: Obviously, the subnet without a DHCP will require a relay agent if the router on that subnet does not support BootP forwarding and broadcasting. Secondly, if the router does support BootP forwarding and broadcasting, it will act as the DHCP relay agent. Note that having a relay on the same subnet will not do anything because the DHCP request is a broadcast that will be picked up by the DHCP server anyway. Also, placing the DHCP relay on the server itself would have no effect either. The only time answers B and D would have any value would be if there were another DHCP server on another subnet. However, the question does not state that.

12. You manage a network with four subnets, two DHCP servers, and three WINS servers. All workstations are configured for DHCP. You have been getting calls reporting that a duplicate IP address has been assigned. What is the most likely cause of the problem?

   A. The client computers are not releasing the IP addresses when they shut down.

   B. Each client computer is registering with more than one WINS server.

   C. The DHCP servers have assigned all available IP addresses.

   D. The DHCP servers are configured with scopes that have overlapping IP addresses.

Answer: D

Explanation: Each DHCP server is configured independently of the others. When IP ranges overlap one another, it is possible to get duplicate IP addresses. As of NT 4.0 (with the current service pack updates and registry changes), DHCP can ping the address before assigning it, thereby reducing the possibility of this occurrence. An IP address is assigned a lease period and at the end of the lease, the address may be reassigned. Therefore, answer A does not apply. The WINS servers do not control DCHP IP address assignments, so answer B does not apply. If all IP address are assigned, your system simply will not be assigned one, so answer C does not apply either.

13. Situation: Your network has four Windows NT Server computers, 10 Windows NT Workstation computers, 80 Windows 95 computers, and 10 UNIX machines. All machines only run TCP/IP. Users move their computers around the office constantly from one subnet to another. The UNIX machines do not move and do not use NetBIOS. One NT Server is running DHCP with scopes configured for all subnets. All Microsoft Windows-based computers are configured as DHCP clients.

Required results:

- All computers on all subnets must be able to access each other by host name.

- All computers must be able to receive an IP address from the DHCP server.

Optional desired results:

- All UNIX hosts should be able to access any NT Server running FTP by its host name.

- All clients should be able to access any UNIX host running an FTP or Telnet daemon.

Proposed solution:

- On the DHCP server, configure scopes with an exclusion range for the IP addresses of all UNIX computers.

- Configure all routers to forward all DHCP broadcasts to all subnets.

- Install and configure a WINS server on the network.

- Configure DHCP to supply all DHCP clients with the IP address of the WINS server.

- On the WINS server, configure static mappings for each UNIX computer.

- Install a DNS server and configure DNS to use WINS for name resolution.

- Configure the DHCP server to supply all DHCP clients with the IP address of the DNS server.

Which results does the proposed solution produce?

A. The proposed solution produces the required results and produces both of the optional desired results.

B. The proposed solution produces the required results and produces only one of the optional desired results.

C. The proposed solution produces the required results but does not produce either of the optional desired results.

D. The proposed solution does not produce the required results.

Answer: B

Explanation: Because all computers (including UNIX) on all subnets must be able to access each other by host name, we need a DNS. Because the DNS is set up to use WINS, and WINS is configured with static mapping for the UNIX machines, we have met this requirement. However, nowhere is any provision made for setting up the UNIX systems as DNS clients. We have a gray area in defining that all computers must be able to receive an IP address from the DHCP Server because the UNIX systems may not support this function. Nonetheless, we could think that setting them up as with an exclude range in DHCP can be ample DHCP assignment/support. All UNIX hosts must be configured to use the DNS in such a way that the hosts are able to access any NT Server running FTP by its host name. Also, all clients should be able to access any UNIX host running an FTP or Telnet daemon.

14. **Situation:** Your network has 4 Windows NT Server computers, 10 Windows NT Workstation computers, 80 Windows 95 computers, and 10 UNIX machines. All machines only run TCP/IP. Users move their computers around the office constantly from one subnet to another. The UNIX machines do not move and do not use NetBIOS. One NT Server is running DHCP with scopes configured for all subnets. All Microsoft Windows-based computers are configured as DHCP clients.

Required results:

■ All computers on all subnets must be able to access each other by host name.

■ All computers must be able to receive an IP address from the DHCP server.

Optional desired results:

■ All UNIX hosts should be able to access any NT Server running FTP by its host name.

■ All clients should be able to access any UNIX host running an FTP or Telnet daemon.

Proposed solution:

■ On the DHCP server, configure scopes with an exclusion range for the IP addresses of all UNIX computers.

■ Configure all routers to forward all DHCP broadcast to all subnets.

■ Install and configure a WINS server on the network.

■ Configure DHCP to supply all DHCP clients with the IP address of the WINS server.

■ On the WINS server, configure static mappings for each UNIX computer.

Which results does the proposed solution produce?

A. The proposed solution produces the required results and produces both of the optional desired results.

B. The proposed solution produces the required results and produces only one of the optional desired results.

C. The proposed solution produces the required results but does not produce either of the optional desired results.

D. The proposed solution does not produce the required results.

Answer: D

Explanation: Because all computers (including UNIX) on all subnets must be able to access each other by host name, we need a DNS. This was not included in the solution, so it fails the first requirement. We have a gray area in defining that all computers must be able to receive an IP address from the DHCP server because the UNIX systems may not support this function. Nonetheless, we think that setting them up with an exclude range in DHCP is ample DHCP assignment/support. Also, the proposed solution for all Windows-based clients being able to access any UNIX host running an FTP or Telnet daemon is met by usage of WINS.

Chapter 8

1. How many WINS servers are recommended for a network of 10,000 clients?

   A. 5

   B. 10

   C. 1

   D. 2

   E. 15

   Answer: D

   Explanation: Typically, one server can handle all of the clients; however, the second server should be used for redundancy.

2. What are three benefits of a WINS server?

   A. Dynamic IP addressing.

   B. Reduces traffic.

   C. Can only be updated dynamically.

   D. Can resolve names across subnets. Internetwork and interdomain browsing capabilities without configuring and maintaining an LMHOSTS file at each computer.

   Answers: B, C, D

   Explanation: WINS stops broadcasts as clients are looking to resolve names to IP addresses. WINS is a dynamic database and WINS clients register with the database upon bootup. You can also register static addresses for non-WINS clients into the WINS database. Also, because routers don't pass broadcasts by default, WINS can be used to resolve names in large intranetworks.

3. How can a non-WINS client still use WINS for name resolution?

   A. By using broadcasts

   B. By using a proxy agent

C. By using an LMHOSTS file

D. Using a HOSTS table

E. Using a DNS

Answer: B

Explanation: By using a Microsoft Proxy agent, non-WINS clients communicate with the NT computer running proxy services, and the proxy computer in turn communicates with the WINS server.

4. How should you configure your WINS servers so users can resolve names across routers and non-WINS clients can use the WINS database to resolve names?

   A. Install a WINS server on each subnet.

   B. Install two WINS server, with each being a pull partner. Configure an LMHOSTS file on each WINS server.

   C. Install two WINS server, each as a pull server. Add static entries for the non-WINS clients.

   D. Install two WINS server, each as a push server. Add static entries for the non-WINS clients and a WINS proxy on each subnet.

   Answer: D

   Explanation: D is a good choice because you have two WINS servers, hopefully on different subnets, and proxies for the subnets without a WINS server.

5. You work at a large retail computer shop. A customer asks if a 386DX-25MHz system with 12MB of memory is enough to run the WINS service process. Is it? What should you ask of your customer before answering his question (besides his credit card number)? What suggestions should you make?

   Answer: A 386DX-25MHz system would not work because WINS needs to run on an NT Server. NT Server requires a minimum 486DX33 to run.

6. You are a network administrator for a computer manufacturer. Your company has a large network and needs to install WINS on it to help keep traffic down. You have a few OS/2 and UNIX computers that need to be registered in the WINS database. How do you do this?

Answer: By using a WINS proxy agent. A WINS proxy agent extends the name resolution capabilities of the WINS server to non-WINS clients by listening for broadcast name registrations and broadcast resolution requests, and then forwarding them to a WINS server.

7. You are installing two NT computers at your home office. After installing an NT Server running DHCP and WINS, you want to back up the WINS database. What are the steps to do this?

Answer:

1. From the WINS Manager Mapping menu, choose Backup Database.

2. Specify the location for saving backup files.

3. If you want to back up only the changes that have occurred since the last backup, select Perform Incremental Backup.

4. Choose OK.

The WINS database is backed up automatically every 24 hours after you specify the backup directory.

8. Situation: Your network has four Windows NT Server computers, 10 Windows NT Workstation computers, 80 Windows 95 computers, and 10 UNIX machines. All machines only run TCP/IP. Users move their computers around the office constantly from one subnet to another. The UNIX machines do not move and do not use NetBIOS. One NT Server is running DHCP with scopes configured for all subnets. All Microsoft Windows-based computers are configured as DHCP clients.

Required results:

■ All computers on all subnets must be able to access each other by host name.

■ All computers must be able to receive an IP address from the DHCP server.

Optional desired results:

- All UNIX hosts should be able to access any NT Server running FTP by its host name.

- All clients should be able to access any UNIX host running an FTP or Telnet daemon.

Proposed solution:

1. On the DHCP server, configure scopes with an exclusion range for the IP addresses of all UNIX computers.

2. Configure all routers to forward all DHCP broadcast to all subnets.

3. Install and configure a WINS server on the network.

4. Configure DHCP to supply all DHCP clients with the IP address of the WINS server.

5. Configure each Windows-based computer with a HOSTS file that contains entries for the UNIX computers.

Which results does the proposed solution produce?

A. The proposed solution produces the required results and produces both of the optional desired results.

B. The proposed solution produces the required results and produces only one of the optional desired results.

C. The proposed solution produces the required results but does not produce either of the optional desired results.

D. The proposed solution does not produce the required results.

Answer: D

Explanation: Because all computers (including UNIX) on all subnets must be able to access each other by host name, you need a DNS or HOSTS file on each UNIX system. This was not included in the solution. We have a gray area in defining that all computers must be able to receive an IP address from the DHCP server because the UNIX systems may not support this function. Nonetheless, I think that setting them up with an exclude range in DHCP is ample DHCP assignment/support.

9. Situation: Your network has four Windows NT Server computers, 10 Windows NT Workstation computers, 80 Windows 95 computers, and 10 UNIX machines. All machines only run TCP/IP. Users move their computers around the office constantly from one subnet to another. The UNIX machines do not move and do not use NetBIOS. One NT Server is running DHCP with scopes configured for all subnets. All Microsoft Windows-based computers are configured as DHCP clients.

Required results:

- All computers on all subnets must be able to access each other by host name.

- All computers must be able to receive an IP address from the DHCP server.

Optional desired results:

- All UNIX hosts should be able to access any NT Server running FTP by its host name.

- All clients should be able to access any UNIX host running an FTP or Telnet daemon.

Proposed solution:

1. Configure all routers to forward all DHCP broadcast to all subnets.

2. Install and configure a WINS server on the network.

3. Configure DHCP to supply all DHCP clients with the IP address of the WINS server.

Which results does the proposed solution produce?

A. The proposed solution produces the required results and produces both of the optional desired results.

B. The proposed solution produces the required results and produces only one of the optional desired results.

C. The proposed solution produces the required results but does not produce either of the optional desired results.

D. The proposed solution does not produce the required results.

Answer: D

Explanation: Because all computers (including UNIX) on all subnets must be able to access each other by host name, we need a DNS or HOSTS file on each UNIX system—neither exist. Also, because the UNIX systems are not NetBIOS based, they will not register with the WINS server. Furthermore, this network contains multiple subnets so broadcasting for address resolution will not work. Therefore, not all systems can access each other by host name and not all clients will be able to access any UNIX host running an FTP or Telnet daemon. Additionally, no special arrangements have been made for the UNIX systems with the DHCP server.

10. **Situation:** You have five subnets and you want to install two DHCP servers on different subnets to assign IP addresses to Microsoft-based computers on the network.

Required results:

■ The DHCP servers must be able to act as a backup if one server fails.

Optional desired results:

■ Each server must get the same address each time it is started.

■ The WINS and DNS server addresses must be provided to all DHCP clients.

Proposed solution:

1. Install the DHCP Relay Agent on each subnet.

2. Create a client reservation for each Windows NT server computer.

3. Define one scope on the first NT Server for each subnet. In each scope, define the range of IP addresses to be used on that subnet. Duplicate these settings on the other DHCP server.

Which results does the proposed solution produce?

A. The proposed solution produces the required results and produces both of the optional desired results.

B. The proposed solution produces the required results and produces only one of the optional desired results.

C. The proposed solution produces the required results but does not produce either of the optional desired results.

D. The proposed solution does not produce the required results.

Answer: D

Explanation: The basic problem is that you are duplicating identical scopes between two DHCP servers. This will cause duplicate IP addresses (with the exception that NT 4.0 with current service packs and registry changes will ping the address before assigning it). Also, while the client reservation for the NT servers has been created on the DHCP systems, the DHCP servers are not assigning WINS and/or DNS to the clients.

11. Which name resolution mode should you specify on your DHCP Server if you want all clients to use WINS for name resolution before they use broadcasts?

A. B-node

B. P-node

C. M-mode

D. H-node

Answer: D

Explanation: An H-node is a hybrid configuration in which a system will first check with the WINS server before making any broadcast for name resolution.

12. Which service must you use if you want your computers to dynamically resolve names through your complex intranetwork?

A. LMHOSTS

B. DNS

C. FTP

D. Telnet

E. WINS

Answer: E

Explanation: WINS is a centralized database that will automatically register and resolve computer names. DHCP is used to assign addresses to machines but not to resolve them. DNS will resolve names but will not register them automatically. FTP is used to transfer files, and it is thrown into the question as a filler. The same is true for SNMP, which is used for TCP/IP management.

13. How can your Windows workstations communicate by host name to a UNIX server?

    A. Add a LMHOSTS file on the UNIX computer.

    B. Add a static mapping for the name and IP address of the UNIX computer to the WINS database.

    C. Configure the DNS Server address on the WINS server.

    D. Create a TCP/IP session by Telnetting into the UNIX computer from the WINS server.

Answer: B

Explanation: By adding a static mapping, you enable the WINS-enabled clients to resolve an IP address to a system that is not registered with the WINS database.

14. Which type of static entry must you add in your WINS database for a workstation with multiple NIC cards?

    A. Unique

    B. Group

    C. Domain name

    D. Internet group

    E. Multihomed

Answer: E

Explanation: By definition, a system with multiple adapters is said to be multihomed. This is due to the fact that the system will appear on multiple subnets with the same NetBIOS name.

15. How do you have two WINS servers update each others database dynamically?

A. Add LMHOSTS to each server.

B. Configure each WINS server as a WINS client of the other WINS server.

C. Configure a HOSTS table on each WINS Server.

D. Configure each WINS server both as a push partner and as a pull partner of the other WINS server.

Answer: D

Explanation: Establishing the partners as push, pull, or both does Replication of the WINS database. This means that as changes occur, they will be either pushed up or pulled down after a duration of time. Doing both ensures the most up-to-date configuration.

16. What do you need to configure on your DHCP server for DHCP clients to resolve NetBIOS names dynamically? (Choose all that apply.)

A. The IP address of the WINS Server

B. The IP address of the DNS Server

C. The NetBIOS scope ID

D. The NetBIOS name resolution mode

Answer: A, D

Explanation: In addition to specifying the WINS server's IP address, you must define the mode of NetBIOS name resolution that each client will use—B-node, P-node, M-node, and H-node.

17. Which service should you use so the computers on your network can resolve NetBIOS names without any administrative work?

A. TELNET

B. DNS

C. FTP

D. HOSTS

E. WINS

Answer: E

Explanation: Because all of your PCs are NetBIOS based, you should use the WINS server service to resolve names. DHCP is used for IP address distribution, FTP for file transfer, and SNMP for TCP/IP management. Although DNS would work, because all PCs are NetBIOS based, the better solution is the WINS server. It is automatic and will come first in the name resolution search order.

18. You have multiple subnets with a BDC on each subnet. What service should you use to allow all clients to be able to browse all subnets?

    A. TELNET

    B. DNS

    C. FTP

    D. LMHOSTS

    E. WINS

    Answer: E

    Explanation: WINS will maintain a centralized database of systems that may be browsed by clients. DNS will work for name resolution. However, that is not browsing. DHCP is used for IP address distribution, FTP for file transfer, and SNMP for TCP/IP management.

19. You want all your Windows 95 clients to be able to resolve computer names without a HOSTS file. Which service should you use?

    A. LMHOSTS

    B. DNS

    C. FTP

D. TELNET

E. WINS

F. Answer: E

G. Explanation: In truth, both DNS and WINS will work for this function. However, because all PCs will support WINS, it is a better choice. It is automatic for registering, offers browsing, requires little management, and so on. Nowhere in the question is there any mention of systems that do not support WINS.

20. What type of entries should you use to add entries into your WINS database for your UNIX computers?

A. Unique

B. Group

C. Domain name

D. Internet group

E. Multihomed

Answer: A

Explanation: A unique address states that the IP address is assigned to just one system. A group is typically registered for a workgroup between Windows for Workgroups, Windows 95, and Windows NT systems. A domain name is typically registered by a primary domain controller. An Internet group generally is used similar to a domain type of name. And multihomed is used for systems with multiple network adapters.

Chapter 9

1. Your computer on one subnet cannot connect to an NT server on a remote subnet by using the command **net use f:\\sales.acme.com\data**. When other computers on the local subnet try to run the same command, they can connect to the server either. You can ping the server by its IP address. What is the problem?

A. The DNS server does not have an entry for sales.acme.com.

B. Your workstation is not configured to use a DNS server.

C. Your workstation is not configured as a WINS client.

D. Your workstation is not configured to use TCP/IP.

Answer: B

Explanation: If there were no entry for sales.acme.com on the DNS server, no one would be able to connect to the remote server. WINS is not likely to have a FQDN. The best answer is that the workstation is not configured with an IP address for a DNS server.

2. You have NT Servers, UNIX computers, and NT Workstation computers on your network. You have three DNS servers for the acme.com domain. How can you configure your DNS server to use WINS to resolve NetBIOS names that are not in the DNS database?

A. Configure only the primary DNS server to use WINS resolution, and it will update the other two DNS servers.

B. Configure the primary DNS server to use WINS reverse lookup, and it will update the other two DNS servers.

C. Configure all DNS servers to use WINS resolution.

D. Configure all DNS servers to use WINS reverse lookup.

Answer: C

Explanation: If a zone is configured for WINS resolutions, all DNS servers that are authoritative for that zone must be configured for WINS resolution.

3. You want all client computers on your network to use one DNS server to resolve names that are not found on the WINS server. What must you do?

A. Add an LMHOSTS table on each workstation with an entry of the WINS server and DNS server.

B. Add a WINS entry in the workstation, reboot and then add the DNS entry. This will make the workstations look at the WINS server first.

C. Configure the DNS server to enable WINS lookup for name resolution.

D. Configure the WINS server to enable DNS for name resolution.

Answer: C

Explanation: You cannot configure the WINS server to look in DNS for name resolution. However, you can configure DNS to look in WINS if it cannot resolve the name.

4. Which type of resource record must you add to your DNS server to allow users to connect to your NT server using multiple names?

   A. CNAME

   B. MX

   C. MINFO

   D. NS

   E. WKS

   Answer: A

   Explanation: Multiple names can be assigned by using the CNAME resource type. CNAME allows a system to respond to multiple names according to which different services (WWW, FTP, Gopher, and so on) may be associated with it. However, it is important to note that names can be assigned with no association whatsoever.

5. How should you configure your DNS server if you want to resolve Internet names and you already have a DNS server for intranet traffic?

   A. As a primary server

   B. As a secondary server

   C. As a forwarder

   D. As a caching only server

   Answer: C

   Explanation: Because the DNS server has no initial information about a user's network, the DNS server installs as a caching-only name server for the Internet. This means that the DNS server contains only information about the Internet root server. By making it a forwarder, it will forward all Internet requests to the Primary DNS Server on the Internet.

6. You want to install a second DNS server on your network for redundancy. How should you configure the backup DNS server?

   A. As a forwarder

   B. As a secondary server

   C. As a caching-only server

   D. As a primary server

   Answer: B

   Explanation: By definition, a secondary server will provide redundancy for the DNS server. Remember that there are three reasons to have a secondary server: redundancy, faster access for remote locations, and reduced load. Creating a new zone does not duplicate information, caching only notes those addresses it has already resolved.

7. Which type of resource record must you add on your DNS Server to identify your mail server?

   A. CNAME

   B. MX

   C. MINFO

   D. NS

   E. WKS

   Answer: B

   Explanation: The designation for a mail server is MX. MX records specify a mail exchanger for a domain name.

8. You have two DNS servers configured in a single zone and you want to install a third DNS server to provide load balancing for your large internetwork. How should you configure the third DNS server so it does not generate any zone transfer network traffic?

   A. Configure the DNS server to enable WINS lookup for name resolution.

   B. Configure the WINS server to enable DNS for name resolution.

   C. As a caching-only server

   D. As a forwarder

   Answer: C

   Explanation: Generally, you want to load-balance by adding a secondary server. However, because the question also states that you should not have generated any zone traffic, the only possible solution is to add the new server as a caching-only server. When queries are made, that server will check the other DNS servers for information and store it for its time-to-live period. These servers improve in response as they are run over time.

9. You want to enable Windows 95, UNIX, and Macintosh computers to use Internet Explorer to access your Web servers by using a host name. Which service should you use?

   A. DHCP

   B. DNS

   C. LMHOSTS

   D. HOSTS

   E. WINS

   Answer: B

   Explanation: The domain name service (DNS) is the mechanism that is used to resolve HOST names to IP addresses. Although WINS can be used in the same fashion, it lacks support for the Macintosh systems. The DNS service is supported without issue.

10. You are building a DNS server for your internetwork and are not going to connect it to the Internet. Which file on the DNS server should you modify?

A. Boot.ini

B. LMHOSTS

C. CACHE.DNS

D. MX

Answer: C

Explanation: For installations not connected to the Internet, the CACHE.DNS file should be replaced to contain the name server's authoritative domains for the root of the private network.

11. All your NT computers are configured as both DHCP clients and WINS clients, and your UNIX workstations are configured to use DNS resolution. How can you make this is simple as possible for administration purposes?

A. Enable WINS resolution on the DNS server.

B. On the DNS server, configure an LMHOSTS file that contains one entry for each UNIX computer and preloads the NT computers.

C. Configure LMHOSTS on the NT computers and HOSTS on the UNIX computers.

D. On the WINS server, add an LMHOSTS table.

Answer: A

Explanation: By enabling WINS Lookup, DNS can be configured to submit queries to a WINS server when the DNS server cannot resolve a name-to-address mapping.

12. You are building a DNS server and want to use it to resolve names for the Internet and your intranet. How should you do it?

A. By using the default Boot file

B. By using the default Cache file

C. By configuring the DNS server to use WINS resolution

D. By configuring the WINS server to use DNS name resolution

Answer: B

Explanation: The cache file contains host information that is needed to resolve names outside authoritative domains. It contains names and addresses of root name servers. The default file provided with the Microsoft Windows NT version 4.0 DNS Server has the records for all of the root servers on the Internet.

13. What must you do to minimize the number of static records on your DNS server?

A. Add an LMHOSTS to the DNS server.

B. Configure the DNS server to enable WINS Reverse lookup for name resolution.

C. Configure the DNS server to enable WINS lookup for name resolution.

D. Add an LMHOSTS table to the WINS server.

Answer: C

Explanation: By enabling WINS lookup, you can configure DNS to submit queries to a WINS server when a name-to-address mapping cannot be resolved by the DNS server.

14. Your users are complaining that they cannot connect to your NT Server by the NetBIOS name, but they can when they use the IP address. DHCP is configured to give the DNS server for name resolution. When you check the clients, you notice the DNS Server is different from the one that DHCP hands-out. How can this be?

A. The client computers are on a different subnet then the DNS server.

B. The DHCP Server is not working correctly.

C. The client computer has been manually configured with a different IP address for the DNS server.

D. The clients are using an LMHOSTS table for name resolution.

Answer: C

Explanation: If a PC has a DNS server manually listed, it will take precedence over DHCP.

15. What should you do to resolve host names without any administrative overhead? (Choose three.)

   A. Install DNS.

   B. Install WINS.

   C. Configure DNS to use DHCP.

   D. Configure DNS to use WINS.

   Answer: A, B, D

   Explanation: If you have the DNS refer to the WINS server, it will appear as if the DNS is dynamic.

Chapter 10

1. You want to have users browse your local NT network, but you do not want to configure anything. Which NT Service should you use?

   A. DNS

   B. WINS

   C. LMHOSTS

   D. Windows NT Computer Browser service

   Answer: D

   Explanation: The Windows NT Browsing service, by default, requires no configuration. You can install Microsoft NT and not even think about browsing unless you have multiple subnets. If you have multiple subnets, you should use WINS or LMHOSTS.

2. What's the function of the master browser?

    A. Update the LMHOSTS file.

    B. Update the WINS database.

    C. The master browser collects and maintains the master list of available network resources, and it distributes this list to Backup browsers.

    D. The master browser collects and maintains the backup list of available network resources, and it distributes this list to Master browsers.

Answer: C

Explanation: The master browser gives the browse list to the backup browsers, which then distribute it to the clients.

3. You want your non-wins clients to use an LMHOSTS file to resolve names across routers. How should you configure the LMHOSTS?

    A. master_browser ip_address #PRE #DOM:domain_name

    B. ip_address master_browser #DOM:domain_name #PRE

    C. ip_address master_browser #PRE #DOM:domain_name

    D. ip_address master_browser #PRE:domain_name #DOM

Answer: C

Explanation: The PDC of each domain should be the master browser of the domain. One important thing to keep in mind when using the LMHOSTS file is to keep it short. If you have a long LMHOSTS file, it could slow down the resolution.

4. You want your non-WINS clients to resolve a remote NT Server name of Sales in the Acme domain with an ip address of 192.168.100.1. How should you configure your the non-wins clients?

    A. With an LMHOST table and the following entry:

```
Sales        192.168.100.1      #PRE:ACME      #DOM
```

B. With an LMHOSTS table And the following entry:

```
192.168.100.1        ACME       #PRE      #DOM:      SALES
```

C. With an LMHOSTS table And the following entry:

```
192.168.100.1        SALES      #PRE      #DOM:      ACME
```

D. With a host table And the following entry:

```
192.168.100.1        ACME       #PRE      #DOM:      SALES
```

Answer: C

Explanation: ip_address master_browser #DOM:domain_name #PRE is the way you must create an entry in an LMHOSTS file. An LMHOSTS file should be copied to each domain PDC to ensure browsing problems do not exist.

5. You try to connect to a server in the browse list but cannot. How could a server appear in the browse list but not be available?

   A. You can; it's user error.

   B. The server could be down. It is possible that the server is down but is still listed in the browse list.

   C. You need to reboot the NT Server.

   D. You need to reboot your workstation.

   Answer: B

   Explanation: Each computer periodically announces itself to the master browser by broadcasting on the network. Initially, each computer announces itself once per minute. As the computer stays running, the announcement time is extended to once every 12 minutes. If the master browser hasn't heard from a computer after three-announcement period's elapse, it will remove the computer that hasn't kept in touch from the browse list.

6. You have three networks tied together with a router. The router has a capacity for NetBIOS name broadcasts. For optimum performance, should you use the LMHOSTS files and WINS, or should you simply let the router pass NetBIOS name broadcasts?

Answer: Good question! Depends on your network. It would be easier to just let the broadcasts fly across the network. You wouldn't have to worry about creating or updating the LMHOSTS file and WINS. However, this would be at the cost of network bandwidth—a big expense! If you have a small to medium size Ethernet network, and the bandwidth usage is around two to three percent, it should be OK to let those broadcasts fly. On the other hand, if the bandwidth usage is five percent or higher, think about creating LMHOSTS files and installing WINS servers. Another solution is to let the broadcasts fly and see what the user's response time is when allowing broadcasts to go through the router, or routers. If they don't seem to notice any delay, give them all the time they need. It's a good idea to plan for the future by having your LMHOSTS and WINS servers ready to go when needed.

7. Unclear on the issue of browsers, Management invites you into a meeting to clear up the matter. They want to know what types of browsers systems running Windows NT Workstation or NT Server can use. What do you tell them?

Answer:

- Master browser

- Domain master browser

- Backup browser

- Potential browser

- Non-browser

8. A student of yours knows that Microsoft has added a pair of tags to the LMHOSTS file: #PRE and #DOM, and the student remembers that these tags enable the non-WINS client to communicate with a domain controller to accomplish three very important things. However, this student is unable to recall exactly which three things and asks you. What would you answer?

Answer:

- Registration
- Verification of a user account
- Changing of passwords

9. You want to import the file that contains computer name-to-IP address mappings into the WINS database on your server. Which file should you import?

   A. The DHCP.MDB file from a DHCP server

   B. The CACHE.DNS file from a DNS server

   C. The HOSTS file

   D. The LMHOSTS file

   Answer: D

   Explanation: The WINS server offers a migration type of utility to read an LMHOSTS file with the Import function. Keep in mind that because DHCP is dynamic and always changing, it would be too involved and likely to change to be useful. The CACHE.DNS is typically a listing or requested information that the DNS has built up, and the HOSTS file is more HOST name-oriented than NetBIOS.

10. Why would you use an LMHOSTS file instead of a HOST file?

   A. When you cannot connect to a WINS Server

   B. When your DNS server is down

   C. When you want to preload NetBIOS names into cache

   D. When you want to preload host names into cache

   Answer: C

   Explanation: LMHOSTS allow you to preload NetBIOS names that have been resolved to an IP address into cache. The HOSTS table is used to resolve HOST names, not NetBIOS names.

Chapter 11

1. You have a TCP/IP print device directly connected to your NT Server. How do you configure the NT Server to forward the documents to the print device?

   A. Redirect the jobs using LPR.

   B. Redirect the jobs using LPQ.

   C. Install the TCP/IP printing service on the server.

   D. Install the TCP/IP printing service on the print device.

   Answer: C

   Explanation: You want the NT Server to behave as a print server, so you will require TCP/IP printing services. There is no such thing as installing the print service on the print device; however, it is useful to configure the device with an IP address. The LPQ utility is used to view a queue of a system running LPD. The LPR command is used to send jobs to a printer that it services by a host running LPD. However, LPR is a client utility and will not establish your NT unit as a print server.

2. You have a UNIX computer with a print device connected. Business requirements dictate that users be able to print to this print device. How should the users send their output to this print device?

   A. On their workstations, capture a logical printer port to the UNC name for the printer.

   B. On their workstations use the LPR utility.

   C. On their workstations use the LPQ utility.

   D. On their workstations install the TCP/IP Printing service.

   Answer: B

   Explanation: The LPR utility allows jobs to be sent to a printer that is serviced by a host running an LPD server. If the device is on a UNIX system, there will be no UNC name (UNC names are NetBIOS based). The LPQ command allows you to see items in the UNIX print queue.

3. You have an NT Server with a print device connected. How can you configure the server so your UNIX workstations can print to the printer using LPR?

A. On the NT Server, install the TCP/IP printing service.

B. On the Unix computers, install the TCP/IP Printing service.

C. Create a printer share.

D. Give the printer an IP address.

E. Add the LPR Server Service to the NT Server.

Answer: A

Explanation: The TCP/IP printing service is the Microsoft equivalent to the LPD print server on a UNIX-based machine. This service will allow UNIX clients using the LPR utility to print to a device on a Windows NT Server.

4. You have an NT Server with a print device connected and want your NT workstations to be able to use this printer. How should you configure the NT Server?

A. Assign an IP address to the printer and give this address to the UNIX users.

B. Install the LPR utility on the server.

C. Create a printer share.

D. Install the TCP/IP printer service on the NT Server.

Answer: C

Explanation: If you wanted NT Workstations to print to a printer connected to an NT server, you would just create a share. If you want UNIX to print to it, you would install TCP/IP Printing Services.

5. You have a print device connected to a UNIX computer running the LPD. What should you do to allow NT Workstation users to print to this device but have the printer still be managed by your NT Server? (Choose all that apply.)

   A. Install the LPR utility on your NT workstations.

   B. Install the TCP/IP printing service on the server.

   C. Install the SNMP service on all workstations.

   D. Create a shared printer on the server that uses an LPR port to send documents to the UNIX print device.

   Answer: B and D

   Explanation: To configure Windows NT Print Manager to use an LPD print server, you must add the Microsoft TCP/IP printing support and configure a printer to use the LPR print monitor.

6. You want your users to be able to access your NT Server on the Internet and download files. Which service must you use on your NT Server?

   A. DHCP

   B. DNS

   C. FTP

   D. SNMP

   E. WINS

   Answer: C

   Explanation: FTP will allow systems to transfer files regardless of their operating system. WINS and DNS are used for name resolution, DHCP for IP address assignment to clients, and SNMP for TCP/IP management.

7. You want your UNIX users to be able to connect to a remote NT Server. However, when they run the command ftp 172.16.31.2 to connect to the

remote server, they cannot connect. They *can* connect to a local NT Server. What could the problem be?

A. No DNS server is defined on the UNIX workstations.

B. The workstations are not configured with a default gateway.

C. The NT server is not configured with a default gateway.

D. The UNIX workstation are not configured to use WINS.

E. The NT Server is not running the FTP service.

Answer: B

Explanation: Because the server is located remotely, the workstation is most likely not configured with a default gateway. This would prevent you from connecting to a remote subnet. Because you are not connecting via IP address, clearly you are beyond the point that DNS/WINS name resolution would make any difference. Also, because your PC is initializing communication, the server's default gateway will not matter. Finally, FTP permissions would not have an impact on the connection, just the security.

8. You want to view the documents that have been sent to a UNIX TCP/IP printer. Which utility should you use?

A. FTP.EXE

B. LPQ.EXE

C. LPR.EXE

D. TELNET.EXE

Answer: B

Explanation: LPQ is used to view items in a UNIX print queue. FTP is used to transfer files with UNIX hosts. LPR is used to send files to a UNIX print server, and TELNET is used to run UNIX programs remotely.

9. You want to run a remote program on a UNIX computer. What utility should you use?

   A. FTP.EXE

   B. LPQ.EXE

   C. LPR.EXE

   D. TELNET.EXE

   Answer: D

   Explanation: TELNET is used to open a remote session to a UNIX computer and run a program (which is processed at the UNIX system). FTP is used to transfer files, and LPQ and LPR are used for printer-related functions.

10. Which utility should you use to copy files from a UNIX computer to your NT Workstation?

    A. FTP.EXE

    B. LPQ.EXE

    C. LPR.EXE

    D. TELNET.EXE

    Answer: A

    Explanation: FTP is used to copy files from a UNIX host. LPQ and LPR are printer related. Telnet is used to open a remote session.

11. You want to print a text document on a UNIX print device. Which utility should you use?

    A. FTP.EXE

    B. LPQ.EXE

    C. LPR.EXE

    D. TELNET.EXE

    Answer: C

Explanation: The line printer (LPR) utility should be used to send a text file to a UNIX-based TCP/IP print server. FTP is used to transfer files to systems, not printers. LPQ is used to view a UNIX print queue but not to print. Telnet has nothing to do with printing whatsoever.

12. You can connect to a remote NT Server using FTP through NT Explorer. However, you cannot connect when you type **ftp sales.acme.com**. What could be wrong?

   A. DNS is not defined on your workstation.

   B. You do not have a default gateway configured on your workstation, or it is incorrect.

   C. The NT Server does not have a default gateway configured.

   D. The SNMP service is not running.

   Answer: A

   Explanation: In this scenario, you can connect to the NetBIOS name (which may be resolved by WINS), but not to the HOST name. WINS should be able to resolve this as a HOST name, but somewhere along the line it is not resolving the HOST name. This is most likely an issue at the DNS. Obviously, this can not be a gateway problem because NT Explorer works, thus verifying the transport.

13. You are working at a Windows NT workstation that is not configured for DNS. The HOSTS file on your workstation contains the following entries:

131.107.32.9	sales	#sales FTP server
131.107.8.254	corp Web server	#intranet Web server
131.107.16.67	UNIX developer	#UNIX computer/ developers
131.107.16.12	developer	#developers FTP server

When you ftp to developer, you connect to a Windows NT Server on a remote subnet, but when you try ftp 131.107.16.12, it fails. What is most likely the problem?

A. The host name assigned to the server is not Developer.

B. The IP address assigned to the FTP server is not 131.107.16.12.

C. The HOSTS file on your workstation is not returning the correct host name for the FTP server.

D. The FTP server is not running TCP/IP.

Answer: B

Explanation: This is a confusing question because the comments in the question (listed with # signs) are misleading. However, when you ftp to developer, Windows NT will search the HOSTS file for the first occurrence of the host name developer, which appears on the third line. All things said and done, developer is being resolved to 131.107.16.67. The second entry with developer is never reached. Because the question denotes success associated with 131.107.16.67 and failure with 131.107.16.12, it is clear that the file's comments are incorrect.

However, depending on your view of the question, you may have interpreted that FTP was not running correctly on 131.107.16.12 and that developer was just by accident. So let's step through why none of the other answers fit.

First of all, A could be correct if you were to read into the question that you should have been telneting to UNIX. But that still overlooks the fact that you have the second developer name. Next, C could not be correct because we know which name is being returned. The failure would still stand. Finally, D would not apply because FTP is part of TCP/IP.

Chapter 12

1. How do you prevent your NT server running SNMP from being managed by unauthorized SNMP management stations?

   A. Rename the administrator account on the server.

   B. Configure the server to accept SNMP packets from specified hosts only.

   C. Convert your NT partitions to NTFS.

   D. Define a password for the SNMP community name.

   Answer: B

   Explanation:. Renaming the administrator account, even though it is a good idea, won't make any difference to SNMP. You can configure the Server to accept only packets from specified hosts in the SNMP Properties Security tab.

2. How do you configure your NT Server to send trap messages to an SNMP management station?

   A. Enter the IP address of the SNMP management station on your NT Server.

   B. Enter the Server name of the SNMP management station.

   C. Enter the community name defined on the SNMP management station.

   D. Enter the guest account information to connect in the background.

   Answer: A, C

   Explanation: There are two pieces of information required in setting up an SNMP service on an NT Server. The first is the IP address of the server that you want messages to be sent to. The second is the community name that is defined on the SNMP management system.

3. What utility should you run on a UNIX station and an NT Server to view TCP/IP protocol statistics for the Windows NT Server from the UNIX computer?

   A. On the UNIX computer run a protocol analyzer and on the NT Server run the Network Monitor.

   B. On the UNIX computer run a SNMP Management program and on the NT Server run the SNMP Server service.

   C. On the UNIX computer run a Network Monitor and on the NT Server run the protocol analyzer.

   D. On the UNIX computer run an ftp client and on the NT Server run the ftp server service.

   Answer: B

   Explanation: You need to use an SNMP management software such as HP's OpenView on your UNIX computer, which utilizes the SMNP service at the NT Server.

4. How can you collect statistics for all TCP/IP traffic on the NT Servers on your network by using Performance Monitor?

   A. Run DHCP on each server.

   B. Configure each server to use WINS.

   C. Install the SNMP service on each server.

   D. Run the NET.EXE utility on each server.

   E. Run the FTP Server service on each server.

   Answer: C

   Explanation: SNMP provides a variety of information to a management system and must be loaded on every server you want to manage with SNMP.

5. You want to add SNMP to your NT workstation, but you don't want just anybody getting in and changing your MIBs. What security option

should you put in place to stop SNMP packets from being tweaked by unwanted visitors?

Answer: To specify security settings, choose the Security tab to open the SNMP Security Configuration dialog box. Choose Only Accept SNMP Packets from These Hosts. If checked, this computer should accept packets only from hosts that have specific IP or IPX addresses and the host name in the associated box.

6. Your company's network manager has set up your NT workstation to respond to SNMP requests coming from an SNMP management system. While doing so, he told you all about the sort of stuff the management system will be requesting. What are the operations he told you will be requested by the SNMP management system?

Answer: The primary function of an SNMP agent is to perform the GetRequest, GetNextRequest, and SetRequest operations requested by a management system. An agent is any computer running SNMP agent software, typically a server or router.

7. Which of the following statements about SNMP with NT are false? (Choose all that apply.)

   A. NT can send SNMP traps to a SNMP manger.

   B. Windows 95 can send SNMP traps to an NT Server.

   C. NT Workstation and Server can send SNMP traps to an NT Server.

   D. NT Server can send SNMP traps to a UNIX SNMP manager.

   E. Answer: B, C: NT by default cannot be an SNMP manager. It can, however, send SNMP traps to a third party SNMP manager.

8. What are the default communities for NT running SNMP? (Choose two.)

   A. Read=Private

   B. Write=Public

   C. Write=Private

   D. Read=Public

   Answer: C, D: The default communities are write=private and read=public.

9. What is a MIB?

   A. A MIB describes the objects, or entries, that are to be included in the DLL's needed to run SNMP on your NT Server.

   B. A MIB describes the objects, or entries, that are to be included in the SNMP agent database.

   C. A MIB is a DLL needed to run SNMP in NT.

   D. A MIB is a DLL needed to send traps to an NT Server.

Answer: B: MIBs tell the SNMP manger what information can be collected from a TCP/IP device running an SNMP agent.

10. Where should you look on your NT Server for SNMP errors?

   A. In the SNMP error log kept in C:\winnt\system 32

   B. In the Event Viewer

   C. In the Performance Log

   D. In the %winnt_root%\system32\etc\snmplog.err

Answer: B: After SNMP is installed, you can view SNMP errors from the Event Viewer system log. The Event Viewer will record all events occurring with the system components of SNMP—even failure of the SNMP service to start. The Event Viewer is the first place you should look to identify any possible problems relevant to the SNMP service.

Chapter 13

1. You have an NT workstation on Subnet 1, and your NT Server is on Subnet 2. You receive a "Network name not found" error when typing the command **net use f : \\sales.acme.com\leads**. The IPCONFIG utility shows you the following output:

Host name:	wkstal.acme.com
DNS Server:	
Node Type:	Hybrid
NetBIOS scope ID:	

IP routing enabled:	No
WINS Proxy Enabled:	No
NetBIOS resolution Uses DNS:	No
Description:	ELNK3 Ethernet Adapter
Physical Address:	00-20-AF-BE-B2-63
DHCP Enabled:	Yes
IP Address:	98.46.9.38
Subnet mask:	255.255.240.0
Default Gateway:	98.46.18.1
DHCP Server:	98.46.6.136
Primary WINS Server:	98.46.6.136
Secondary WINS Server:	98.46.6.137
Lease Obtained:	Sunday, May 24, 1998 12:42:03 PM
Lease Expires:	Wednesday, May 27, 1998 12:42:03 PM

What is most likely the cause of the problem?

A. You cannot specify a host name in a FQDN path.

B. The workstation is not configured correctly.

C. The workstation does not have a hosts table.

D. The workstation does not have an LMHOST file.

Answer: B

Explanation: It is possible to specify an FQDN in a net use command. The problem in this instance is that the user does not have a DNS server configured.

2. Which utility should you use to collect TCP/IP protocol statistics, save the statistics in log files for later analysis, and export the statistics for use in a spreadsheet?

A. NETSTAT.EXE

B. NBTSTAT.EXE

C. Performance Monitor

D. Network Monitor

Answer: C

Explanation: Performance Monitor is used to gather and monitor statistics. This utility has the ability to log and export statistics that are of use in a spreadsheet.

3. Which two utilities can you use to view the routing tables on a Windows NT Server computer?

A. ROUTE.EXE

B. NETSTAT.EXE

C. NBTSTAT.EXE

D. IPCONFIG.EXE

E. ARP.EXE

Answer: A and B

Explanation: The Route Print and Netstat –R commands can be used to view routing tables on an NT Server.

4. Which utility should you use to purge the server's NetBIOS name cache?

A. ROUTE.EXE

B. NETSTAT.EXE

C. NBTSTAT.EXE

D. IPCONFIG.EXE

E. ARP.EXE

Answer: C

Explanation: NBTSTAT is the utility used to work with the NetBIOS name cache on a Windows NT system. ROUTE is used to direct traffic in a network, NETSTAT is used to view TCP/IP statistics, IPCONFIG shows IP configuration information, and ARP is used to resolve IP addresses to hardware addresses.

5. What utility should you use to view a list of all current TCP/IP connections to your NT Server?

   A. ROUTE.EXE

   B. NETSTAT.EXE

   C. NBTSTAT.EXE

   D. IPCONFIG.EXE

   E. ARP.EXE

   Answer: B

   Explanation: NETSTAT displays protocol statistics and the current state of TCP/IP connections. ROUTE is used to direct traffic in a network, NBTSTAT is used to show NetBIOS over TCP/IP information, IPCONFIG is used to show IP configuration information, and ARP is used to resolve IP addresses to hardware addresses.

6. Which two NT Server utilities can you use to view both IP statistics and Ethernet statistics?

   A. Network Monitor

   B. NET.EXE

   C. NETSTAT.EXE

   D. IPCONFIG.EXE

   E. NBTSTAT.EXE

   Answer: A and C

   Explanation: NETSTAT displays protocol statistics and the current state of TCP/IP connections. Network Monitor has the ability to display limited Network statistics. NET.EXE issues network commands, IPCONFIG.EXE shows TCP/IP configuration information, and NBTSTAT.EXE shows NetBIOS over TCP/IP statistics.

7. What NT Server utility should you use to view a chart of TCP/IP protocol statistics?

A. Performance Monitor

B. Network Monitor

C. IPCONFIG.EXE

D. NBTSTAT.EXE

E. NETSTAT.EXE

Answer: A

Explanation: Performance Monitor is the utility to view a chart of TCP/IP protocol statistics as they are occurring. NETSTAT, NBTSTAT, and IPCONFIG are all text based. Network Monitor acts like a sniffer for analyzing data, not statistics.

8. Which utility let you view TCP/IP protocol statistics from the last time your NT Server was started?

A. NET.EXE

B. NETSTAT.EXE

C. NBTSTAT.EXE

D. IPCONFIG.EXE

E. Network Monitor

Answer: B

Explanation: NETSTAT is the utility for reviewing the current TCP/IP statistics. The NET issues network commands, NBTSTAT reviews NetBIOS over TCP/IP, IPCONFIG shows how a workstation running TCP/IP is configured, and Network Monitor sniffs out current (as in immediately occurring) packet-related information.

9. What utility can you type at a command line to view the list of IP address-to-physical address mappings for your NT Server?

A. Network Monitor

B. NET. EXE

C. NBTSTAT. EXE

D. TELNET.EXE

E. ARP.EXE

F. Answer: E

G. Explanation: ARP is used to display and modify the physical address-to-IP address translation. ARP will display the current list of IP addresses-to-physical addresses.

10. What command line utility can you use to view a list of NetBIOS names that are currently cached on your NT Server?

A. NET. EXE

B. FTP. EXE

C. NBTSTAT. EXE

D. Network Monitor

E. WINS.EXE

Answer: C

Explanation: NBTSTAT is the utility used to show and work with Net-BIOS over TCP/IP. NBTSTAT –c will list the names that are currently cached on the NT system.

11. You have a remote NT Server running as an FTP server. When you use NT Explorer you can connect, but it fails when you use the command **ftp sales.acme.com**. What is the most likely cause of the problem?

A. No DNS server defined on your workstation.

B. No Default Gateway defined on your workstation.

C. No Default Gateway defined on the remote server.

D. No DNS configuration on the remote server.

Answer: A

Explanation: In the scenario, you can connect to the NetBIOS name (which may be resolved by WINS), but not the HOST name. WINS should be able to resolve this as a HOST name, except that somewhere along the line it is not. This is most likely an issue at the DNS. Obviously, this cannot be a gateway problem because NT Explorer works.

12. From your NT workstation you can connect to a remote server by using the command **ftp sales.acme.com**. However, you cannot connect through NT Explorer when specifying the computer name. What is the most likely cause of the problem?

A. No DNS server defined on your workstation.

B. No Default Gateway defined on your workstation.

C. No Default Gateway defined on the remote server.

D. No WINS configuration on the remote server.

Answer: D

Explanation: Because the FTP command works, this verifies both the host name and transport mechanisms. That means that choice A can be eliminated because the workstation is resolving the HOST name. Both B and C can be eliminated because the gateways are part of the transport. That leads us to the conclusion that either the server must not have registered with the WINS server or the server is not configured to use WINS.

13. At your NT workstation you attempt to connect to an NT Server by using the command **ftp sales.acme.com**. You receive the message "Bad IP address." Pinging the server was successful. What could the problem be? Choose all that apply.

A. No DNS server defined on your workstation.

B. No Default Gateway defined on your workstation.

C. There is no entry in the DNS server for sales.acme.com.

D. The LMHOSTS file does not contain an entry for sales.acme.com.

Answer: A and C

Explanation: If your PC has an incorrect IP address, you will obviously have an inability to resolve a host's name. Also, if there is no entry for the system in the DNS, you, again, will not be able to resolve the name. If your PC had an incorrect DNS name, you would have no success pinging the server. The ARP cache has not correlation for name-to-IP resolution, and NetBIOS is not used in FTP.

14. Your Windows NT workstation cannot talk to a host in another building, but it works locally. Your co-workers' workstations are working fine. What is the troubleshooting step you should take?

Answer: Check your configuration. Either your subnet mask is incorrect or your default gateway is entered incorrectly.

15. Your Windows NT workstation cannot talk on the network either locally or remotely. What are the troubleshooting steps you should take?

Answer: First, ping your local host address of 127.0.0.1. If you're successful, then ping your IP address. If that works, take a look at your configuration and check your subnet mask and default gateway. Also, don't forget to check your cable.

16. You have just installed TCP/IP and cannot ping hosts by their NetBIOS name on your network. Your IP address, subnet mask, and default gateway are correct. What is the problem?

Answer: Either your resolution methods are not working (i.e. HOSTS file, LMHOSTS, WINS, or DNS), or the remote host either doesn't have a NetBIOS name or is not functioning correctly.

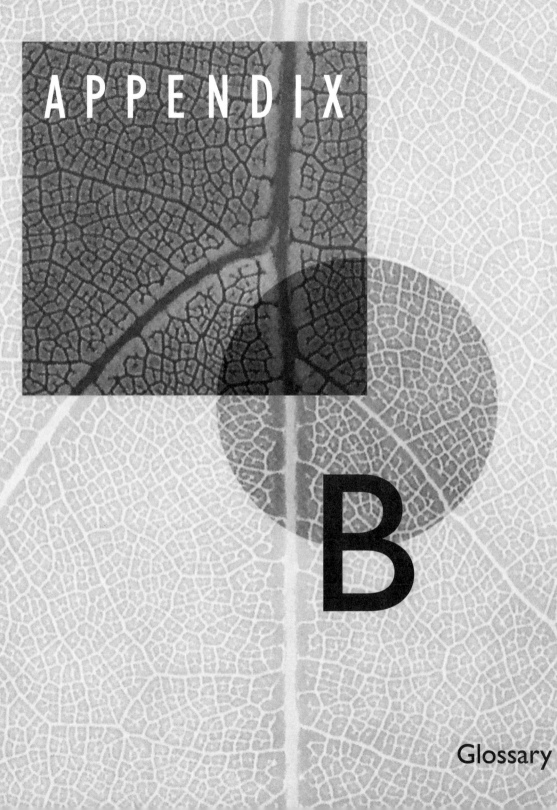

APPENDIX

B

Glossary

Abstract Syntax Representation, Revision #1 (ASN.1)

A description of a data structure that is independent of machine-oriented structures and encodings.

Address

In TCP/IP, an IP address is a 32-bit numeric identifier assigned to a node. The address has two parts, one for the network identifier and the other for the node identifier. All nodes on the same network must share the network address and have a unique node address. For networks connected to the Internet, network addresses are assigned by the Internet Activities Board (IAB).

Addresses also include IPX addresses—the internal network number and external network number—and the MAC (Media Access Control) address assigned to each network card or device.

Advanced Research Projects Agency Network (ARPANET)

A packet-switched network developed in the early 1970s. The "father" of today's Internet. ARPANET was decommissioned in June 1990.

Agents

In the client/server model, the part of the system that performs information preparation and exchange on behalf of a client or server application.

American National Standards Institute (ANSI)

A nonprofit organization responsible for the ASCII (American Standard Code for Information Interchange) code set, as well as numerous other voluntary standards.

Application Layer

The layer of the OSI model that interfaces with user mode applications by providing high-level network services based upon lower-level network layers. Network file systems like named pipes are an example of Application layer software. See *Named Pipes, Open Systems Interconnection.*

Application Program Interface (API)

A set of routines that an application program uses to request and carry out lower-layer services performed by the operating system.

Archie

A program that helps Internet users find files. Participating Internet host computers download a listing of their files to Archie servers, which index these files. Users can then search this index and transfer these files using FTP. Archie functions as an archive search utility, hence its name.

ARP (Address Resolution Protocol)
IP address to hardware address translation protocol.

Asynchronous Data Transmission
A type of communication that sends data using flow control rather than a clock to synchronize data between the source and destination.

Autonomous System
Internet TCP/IP terminology for a collection of gateways (routers) that fall under one administrative entity and cooperate using common Interior Gateway Protocol (IGP).

Bandwidth
In network communications, the amount of data that can be sent across a wire in a given time. Each communication that passes along the wire decreases the amount of available bandwidth.

Batch Program
An ASCII file that contains one or more Windows NT commands. A batch program's filename typically has a .bat or .cmd extension. When you type the filename at the command prompt, the commands are processed sequentially.

Binary
The numbering system used in computer memory and in digital communication. All characters are represented as a series of 1s and 0s. For example, the letter A might be represented as 01000001.

Binding
A process that establishes the initial communication channel between the protocol driver and the network adapter card driver.

Bits
In binary data, each unit of data is a bit. Each bit is represented by either 0 or 1, and is stored in memory as an ON or OFF state.

Boot Partition
The volume, formatted for either an NTFS, FAT, of HPFS file system, that contains the Windows NT operating system's files. Windows NT automatically creates the correct configuration and checks this information whenever you start your system.

Bridge

A device that connects two segments of a network and sends data to one or the other based on a set of criteria.

Browser

A computer on a Microsoft network that maintains a list of computers and services available on the network.

Browsing

The process of requesting the list of computers and services on a network from a browser.

Buffers

A reserved portion of memory in which data is temporarily held pending an opportunity to complete its transfer to or from a storage device or another location in memory.

Carrier Sense, Multiple Access with Collision Detect (CSMA/CD)

Different devices on a network may try to communicate at any one time, so access methods need to be established. Using the CSMA/CD access method, a device first checks that the cable is free from other carriers and then transmits, while continuing to monitor the presence of another carrier. If a collision is detected, the device stops transmitting and tries later. In a CSMA network with collision detection, all stations have the ability to sense traffic on the network.

Checksum

A number that is calculated based on the values of a block of data. Checksums are used in communication to ensure that the correct data was received.

Circuit Switching

A type of communication system that establishes a connection, or circuit, between the two devices before communicating and does not disconnect until all data is sent.

Client

Any device that attaches to the network server. A workstation is the most common type of client. Clients run client software to provide network access. A piece of software which accesses data on a server can also be called a client.

Client/Server Network

A server-centric network in which some network resources are stored on a file server, while processing power is distributed among workstations and the file server.

Coaxial Cable
One of the types of cable used in network wiring. Typical coax types include RG-58 and RG-62. The 10base2 system of Ethernet networking uses coaxial cable. Coaxial cable is usually shielded. The Thicknet system uses a thicker coaxial cable.

Communication Protocol
For computers engaged in telecommunications, the protocol (i.e., the settings and standards) must be the same for both devices when receiving and transmitting information. A communications program can be used to ensure that the baud rate, duplex, parity, data bits, and stop bits are correctly set.

Connection-Oriented
The model of interconnection in which communication proceeds through three well-defined phases: connection establishment, data transfer, connection releases. Examples: X.25, Internet TCP and OSI TP4, registered letters.

Connectionless
The model of interconnection in which communication takes place without first establishing a connection. Sometimes called datagram. Examples: LANs, Internet IP, OSI, CLNP, UDP, ordinary postcards.

Consultative Committee on International Telegraphy and Telephony (CCITT)
A committee, sponsored by the United Nations, that defines network standards, including X.400 and X.500. This committee has been recently renamed to International Telecommunications Union/Telecommunications Standardization Sector (ITU/TSS).

Control Panel
Windows family utility containing management tools.

CSNET (Computer+Science Network)
A large computer network, mostly in the U.S. but with international connections. CSNET sites include universities, research labs, and some commercial companies. Now merged with BITNET to form CREN.

Cyclic Redundancy Checksum (CRC)
A redundancy check in which the check key is generated by a cyclic algorithm. Also, a system checking or error checking performed at both the sending and receiving station after a block check character has been accumulated.

Daemon Program

A utility program that runs on a TCP/IP server. Daemon programs run in the background, performing services such as file transfers, printing, calculations, searching for information, and many other tasks. This is similar to a TSR program in DOS. Daemons are fully supported by UNIX, however.

DARPA (Defense Advanced Research Projects Agency)

The U.S. government agency that funded the ARPANET.

Data Frames

Logical, structured packets in which data can be placed. The Data Link layer packages raw bits from the Physical layer into data frames. The exact format of the frame used by the network depends on the topology.

Data Link Layer

The OSI layer that is responsible for data transfer across a single physical connection, or series of bridged connections, between two network entities.

Data Packet

A unit of data being sent over a network. A packet includes a header, addressing information, and the data itself. A packet is treated as a single unit as it is sent from device to device.

Data Transfer Rate

The data transfer rate determines how fast a drive or other peripheral can transfer data with its controller. The data transfer rate is a key measurement in drive performance.

Datagram

A packet of information and associated delivery information, such as the destination address, that is routed through a packet-switching network.

Dedicated Line

A transmission medium that is used exclusively between two locations. Dedicated lines are also known as leased lines or private lines.

Default Gateway

IP uses the default gateway address when it cannot find the destination host on the local subnet. This is usually the router interface.

Device Driver

A piece of software that allows a workstation or server to communicate with a hardware device. For example, disk drivers are used to control disk drives, and network drivers are used to communicate with network boards.

DHCP (Dynamic Host Configuration Protocol)

A method of automatically assigning IP addresses to client computers on a network.

DoD Networking Model

A four-layer conceptual model describing how communications should take place between computer systems. The four layers are Process/Application, Host-to-Host, Internet, and Network Access. DoD is the acronym for Department of Defense, the government agency that provided the original funding for the development of the TCP/IP protocol suite.

Domain

A logical grouping for file servers within a network, managed as an integrated whole.

Domain Controller

Primary server within a domain and primary storage point for domain-wide security information.

Domain Names

The name by which a domain is known to the network.

DNS (Domain Name System)

The distributed name/address mechanism used in the Internet.

Dumb Terminal

A workstation consisting of keyboard and monitor, used to put data into the computer or receive information from the computer. Dumb terminals were originally developed to be connected to computers running a multi-user operating system so that users could communicate directly with them. All processing is done at and by the computer, not the dumb terminal. In contrast, a smart terminal contains processing circuits which can receive data from the host computer and later carry out independent processing operations.

EGP (Exterior Gateway Protocol)

A reachability routing protocol used by gateways in a two-level internet. EGP is used in the Internet core system.

Error Control

An arrangement that combines error detection and error correction.

Error Correction

A method used to correct erroneous data produced during data transmission, transfer, or storage.

Ethernet

The most popular Data Link layer standard for local area networking. Ethernet implements the carrier sense multiple access with collision detection (CSMA/CD) method of arbitrating multiple computer access to the same network. This standard supports the use of Ethernet over any type of media including wireless broadcast. Standard Ethernet operates at 10Mbps. Fast Ethernet operates at 100Mbps. See *Data Link Layer*.

FDDI (Fiber Distributed Data Interface)

A network specification that transmits information packets using light produced by a laser or light-emitting diode (LED). FDDI uses fiber-optic cable and equipment to transmit data packets. It has a data rate of up to 100Mbps and allows very long cable distances.

File Transfer Protocol (FTP)

A TCP/IP protocol that permits the transferring of files between computer systems. Because FTP has been implemented on numerous types of computer systems, file transfers can be done between different computer systems (e.g., a personal computer and a minicomputer).

Frame

A data structure that network hardware devices use to transmit data between computers. Frames consist of the addresses of the sending and receiving computers, size information, and a checksum. Frames are envelopes around packets of data that allow them to be addressed to specific computers on a shared media network. See *Ethernet, FDDI, Token Ring*.

FTP

See *File Transfer Protocol*.

Full-Duplex

A method of transmitting information over an asynchronous communications channel, in which signals may be sent in both directions simultaneously. This technique makes the best use of line time but substantially increases the amount of logic required in the primary and secondary stations.

Gateway

In e-mail systems, a system used to send and receive e-mail from a different e-mail system, such as a mainframe or the Internet. Gateways are supported by Message Handling Services (MHS).

Gopher

An Internet tool that organizes topics into a menu system that users can employ to find information. Gopher also transparently connects users with the Internet server on which the information resides.

GOSIP (Government OSI Profile)

A U.S Government procurement specification for OSI (Open Systems Interconnection) protocols.

Half-Duplex

A method of transmitting information over a communication channel, in which signals may be sent in both directions, but only one way at a time. This is sometimes referred to as local echo.

Handshaking

In network communication, a process used to verify that a connection has been established correctly. Devices send signals back and forth to establish parameters for communication.

Hardware Address

See *Media Access Control (MAC) Address*.

Hop

In routing, a server or router that is counted in a hop count.

Hop Count

The number of routers a message must pass through to reach its destination. A hop count is used to determine the most efficient network route.

Host
An addressable computer system on a TCP/IP network. Examples would include endpoint systems such as workstations, servers, minicomputers, mainframes, and immediate systems such as routers. A host is typically a system that offers resources to network nodes.

Host Name
A TCP/IP command that returns the local workstation's host name used for authentication by TCP/IP utilities. This value is the workstation's computer name by default, but it can be changed by using the Network icon in Control Panel.

Host Table
The HOSTS or LMHOSTS file that contains lists of known IP addresses.

Host-to-Host Layer
The DoD model layer that references to the Transport layer of the OSI model.

Hub
An Ethernet Data Link layer device that connects point-to-point Physical layer links, such as twisted pair or fiber-optic cables, into a single shared media network. See *Data Link Layer, Ethernet*.

IAB (Internet Activities Board)
The technical body that oversees the development of the Internet suite of protocols (commonly referred to as TCP/IP). It has two task forces (the IRTF and the IETF), each charged with investigating a particular area.

ICMP (Internet Control Message Protocol)
A protocol at the Internet layer of the DoD model that sends messages between routers and other devices, letting them know of congested routes.

IEEE (Institute of Electrical and Electronics Engineers)
A professional ANSI-accredited body of scientists and engineers based in the United States. IEEE promotes standardization, and consults to the American National Standards Institute on matters relating to electrical and electronic development. The IEEE 802 Standards Committee is the leading official standard organization for LANs.

IESG (Internet Engineering Steering Group)
The executive committee of the IETF.

IETF (Internet Engineering Task Force)

One of the task forces of the IAB. The IETF is responsible for solving short-term engineering needs of the Internet. It has over 40 Working Groups.

IGP (Interior Gateway Protocol)

The protocol used to exchange routing information between collaborating routers in the Internet. RIP and OSPF are examples of IGPs.

Integrated Services Digital Network (ISDN)

A new network standard that allows high-speed communication over ordinary category 3 or 5 copper cabling. It may someday replace conventional phone systems with high-speed, digital lines.

International Standards Organizations (ISO)

A worldwide federation of national standards bodies whose objective is to promote the development of standardization and related activities in over 90 countries, with a view to facilitating international exchange of goods and services.

Internet

A global network made up of a large number of individual networks interconnected through the use of TCP/IP protocols. The individual networks comprising the Internet are from colleges, universities, businesses, research organizations, government agencies, individuals, and other bodies. The governing body of this global network is the Internet Activities Board (IAB). When the term *Internet* is used with an upper-case *I*, it refers to the global network, but with a lower-case *i*, it simply means a group of interconnected networks.

Internet Address

A 32-bit value displayed in numbers that specifies a particular network and a particular node on that network.

Internet Layer

The layer in the DoD model that relates to the Network layer of the OSI model.

Internet Protocol (IP)

The Network layer protocol upon which the Internet is based. IP provides a simple connectionless packet exchange. Other protocols such as UDP or TCP use IP to perform their connection-oriented or guaranteed delivery services. See *TCP/IP, Internet*.

Internetwork Packet eXchange

The Network and Transport layer protocol developed by Novell for its NetWare product. IPX is a routable, connection-oriented protocol similar to TCP/IP but much easier to manage and with lower communication overhead. See *Internet Protocol*.

Internetworking

The process of connecting multiple local-area networks to form a wide-area network (WAN). Internetworking between different types of networks is handled by a *router*.

IP Address

A four-byte number that uniquely identifies a computer on an IP internetwork. InterNIC assigns the first bytes of Internet IP addresses and administers them in hierarchies. Huge organizations like the government or top-level Internet service providers (ISP) have Class A addresses, large organizations and most ISPs have Class B addresses, and small companies have Class C addresses. In a Class A address, InterNIC assigns the first byte, and the owning organization assigns the remaining three bytes. In a Class B address, InterNIC or the higher level ISP assigns the first two bytes, and the organization assigns the remaining two bytes. In a Class C address, InterNIC or the higher level ISP assigns the first three bytes, and the organization assigns the remaining byte. Organizations not attached to the Internet can assign IP addresses as they please. See *Internet Protocol, Internet*.

IPTUNNEL

A software driver that permits the encapsulation of IPX packets inside of IP packets for transmission over an IP network. This allows NetWare servers to communicate through links that support only TCP/IP, such as UNIX machines.

IPX External Network Number

A number that is used to represent an entire network. All servers on the network must use the same external network number.

IPX Internal Network Number

A number that uniquely identifies a server to the network. Each server must have a different internal network number.

IRTF (Internet Research Task Force)
One of the task forces of the IAB. The group responsible for research and development of the Internet protocol suite.

Local Area Network (LAN)
A network that is restricted to a local area—a single building, group of buildings, or even a single room. A LAN often has only one server, but can have many if desired.

Local Procedure Call (LPC)
A mechanism that loops remote procedure calls without the presence of a network so that the client and server portion of an application can reside on the same machine. Local procedure calls look like remote procedure calls (RPCs) to the client and server sides of a distributed application.

Mailslots
A connectionless messaging IPC mechanism that Windows NT uses for browse requests and logon authentication.

Management Information Base (MIB)
The entire set of objects that any service or protocol uses in SNMP. Because different network-management services are used for different types of devices or for different network-management protocols, each service has its own set of objects.

Map
To translate one value into another.

Master Browser
The computer on a network that maintains a list of computers and services available on the network and distributes the list to other browsers. The Master Browser may also promote potential browsers to be browsers. See *Browser, Browsing, Potential Browser.*

Media Access Control (MAC) Address
Hardware address burned into the Network Interface cards. Six bytes long, three given to the manufacturer from the IEEE, and three bytes designated by the manufacturer.

Message Switching

A type of network communication that sends an entire message, or block of data, rather than a simple packet.

Metropolitan Area Network (MAN)

A network spanning a single city or metropolitan area. A MAN is larger than local area networks (LANs), which are normally restricted to a single building or neighboring buildings, but smaller than wide area networks (WANs), which can span the entire globe.

MILNET (MILitary NETwork)

Originally part of the ARPANET, MILNET was partitioned in 1984 to make it possible for military installations to have reliable network service, while the ARPANET continued to be used for research.

Modem

A device used to convert the digital signals produced by a computer into the analog signals required by analog telephone lines, and vice-versa. This process of conversion allows computers to communicate across telephone lines.

Multihomed Host

A computer connected to more than one physical data link. The data links may or may not be attached to the same network.

Multilink

A capability of RAS to combine multiple data streams into one network connection for the purpose of using more than one modem or ISDN channel in a single connection. This feature is new to Windows NT 4.0.

Named Pipes

An interprocess communication mechanism that is implemented as a file system service, allowing programs to be modified to run on it without using a proprietary application programming interface. Named pipes were developed to support more robust client/server communications than those allowed by the simpler NetBIOS.

NetBEUI

Network Basic Input/Output System Extended User Interface. The primary local area network transport protocol in Windows NT. A simple Network layer transport developed to support NetBIOS installations. NetBEUI is not routable, and so it is not appropriate for larger networks. NetBEUI is the fastest transport protocol available for Windows NT.

NetBIOS

A client/server interprocess communication service developed by IBM in the early 1980s. NetBIOS presents a relatively primitive mechanism for communication in client/server applications, but its widespread acceptance and availability across most operating systems makes it a logical choice for simple network applications. Many Windows NT network IPC mechanisms are implemented over NetBIOS.

NetBIOS over TCP/IP (NetBT)

A network service that implements the NetBIOS IPC over the TCP/IP protocol stack. See *NetBEUI, Transmission Control Protocol/Internet Protocol.*

Network Address

A unique address that identifies each node, or device, on the network. The network address is generally hard-coded into the network card on both the workstation and server. Some network cards allow you to change this address, but there is seldom a reason to do so.

Network Information Center (NIC)

Originally there was only one, located at SRI International and tasked to serve the ARPANET (and later DDN) community. Today, there are many NICs operated by local, regional, and national networks all over the world. Such centers provide user assistance, document service, training, and much more.

Network Interface Card (NIC)

Physical devices that connect computers and other network equipment to the transmission medium used. When installed in a computer's expansion bus slot, a NIC allows the computer to become a workstation on the network.

Network Layer

The layer of the OSI model that creates a communication path between two computers via routed packets. Transport protocols implement both the Network layer and the Transport layer of the OSI stack. IP is a Network layer service.

Network Operating System (NOS)

The software that runs on a file server and offers file, print, and other services to client workstations. Windows NT Server 4 is an NOS. Other examples include NetWare, Banyan VINES, and IBM LAN Server.

NFS (Network File System)

A distributed file system developed by Sun Microsystems which allows a set of computers to cooperatively access each other's files in a transparent manner.

Node

In TCP/IP, an IP addressable computer system, such as workstations, servers, minicomputers, mainframes, and routers. In IPX networks, the term is usually applied to nonserver devices: workstations and printers.

Octets

A set of eight bits or one byte.

Open System Interconnection (OSI)

A model defined by the ISO to conceptually organize the process of communication between computers in terms of seven layers, called protocol stacks. The seven layers of the OSI model helps you to understand how communication across various protocols takes place.

OSI

See *Open System Interconnection*.

OSPF (Open Shortest Path First)

A proposed standard, IGP for the Internet.

Packet

The basic division of data sent over a network. Each packet contains a set amount of data along with a header, containing information about the type of packet and the network address to which it is being sent. The size and format of packets depends on the protocol and frame types used.

Packet Switching

A type of data transmission in which data is divided into packets, each of which has a destination address. Each packet is then routed across a network in an optimal fashion. An addressed packet may travel a different route than packets related to it. Packet sequence numbers are used at the destination node to reassemble related packets.

Packets

A unit of information transmitted as a whole from one device to another on a network.

Peer-to-Peer Communication

A networked computer that both shares resources with other computers and accesses the shared resources of other computers.

Peer-to-Peer Network

A local area network in which network resources are shared among workstations, without a file server.

Physical Layer

The cables, connectors, and connection ports of a network. These are the passive physical components required to create a network.

Ping (Packet Internet Groper)

A packet used to test reachability of destinations by sending them an ICMP echo request and waiting for a reply. The term is used as a verb: "Ping host A to see if it is up."

Polling

The process by which a computer periodically asks each terminal or device on a LAN if it has a message to send, and then allows each to send data in turn. On a multipoint connection or a point-to-point connection, polling is the process whereby data stations are invited one at a time to transmit.

Potential Browser

A computer on a network that may maintain a list of other computers and services on the network if requested to do so by a Master browser.

PPP

Point-to-Point Protocol. This protocol allows the sending of IP packets on a dial-up (serial) connection. Supports compression and IP address negotiation.

Presentation Layer

That layer of the OSI model that converts and translates (if necessary) information between the Session and Application layers.

Primary Domain Controller (PDC)

The domain server that contains the master copy of the security, computer, and user accounts databases and that can authenticate workstations. The primary domain controller can replicate its databases to one or more backup domain controllers and is usually also the Master browser for the domain.

Process/Application Layer

The upper layer in the DoD model that refers to the Application, Presentation, and Session layers of the OSI model.

Protocol Suite

A collection of protocols that are associated with and that implement a particular communication model (such as the DoD networking model, or the OSI reference model).

Public Switched Telephone Network (PSTN)

A global network of interconnected digital and analog communication links originally designed to support voice communication between any two points in the world. It was quickly adapted to handle digital data traffic when the computer revolution occurred. In addition to its traditional voice support role, the PSTN now functions as the Physical layer of the Internet by providing dial-up and leased lines for private and public use.

RARP

The TCP/IP protocol that allows a computer with a Physical layer address (such as an Ethernet address) but not an IP address to request a numeric IP address from another computer on the network.

Registry

Windows NT combined configuration database.

Request for Comments (RFCs)

The set of standards defining the Internet protocols as determined by the Internet Engineering Task Force and available in the public domain on the Internet. RFCs define the functions and services provided by each of the many Internet protocols. Compliance with the RFCs guarantees cross-vendor compatibility.

RIP

Routing Information Protocol. A distance-vector routing protocol used on many TCP/IP internetworks and IPX networks. The distance vector algorithm uses a "fewest-hops" routing calculation method.

Router

(A) A device that connects two dissimilar networks, and allows packets to be transmitted and received between them. (B) A connection between two networks that specifies message paths and may perform other functions, such as data compression.

Serial

A method of communication that transfers data across a medium one bit at a time, usually adding stop, start, and check bits to ensure quality transfer.

Session Layer

The layer of the OSI model dedicated to maintaining a bidirectional communication connection between two computers. The Session layer uses the services of the Transport layer to provide this service.

Simple Network Management Protocol (SNMP)

A management protocol used on many networks, particularly TCP/IP. It defines the type, format, and retrieval of node management information.

Simplex

Data transmission in one direction only.

SLIP (Serial Line Internet Protocol)

A protocol that permits the sending of IP packets on a dial-up (serial) connection. SLIP does not support compression or IP address negotiation by itself.

SMTP (Simple Mail Transport Protocol)

The Internet electronic mail protocol. Defined in RFC 821, with associated message format description in RFC 822.

Start Bit

A bit that is sent as part of a serial communication stream to signal the beginning of a byte or packet.

Stop Bit

A bit that is sent as part of a serial communication stream to signal the end of a byte or packet.

Subnet Mask

Under TCP/IP, 32-bit values that allow the recipient of IP packets to distinguish the network ID portion of the IP address from the host ID.

Switched Line

A communications link for which the physical path may vary with each usage, such as the public telephone network.

Synchronous

Pertaining to two or more processes that depend upon the occurrence of a specific event, such as a common timing signal.

TCP (Transport Layer Protocol)

Implements guaranteed packet delivery using the Internet Protocol (IP).

TCP/IP (Transmission Control Protocol/Internet Protocol)

Generally used as shorthand for the phrase "TCP/IP protocol suite."

Telnet

A TCP/IP terminal emulation protocol that permits a node, called the Telnet client, to log in to a remote node, called the Telnet server. The client simply acts as a dumb terminal, displaying output from the server. The processing is done at the server.

Terminal Emulation

The process of emulating a terminal, or allowing a PC to act as a terminal for a mainframe or UNIX system.

Token-Passing

See *Token Ring*.

Token Ring

The second most popular Data Link layer standard for local area networking. Token Ring implements the token passing method of arbitrating multiple-computer access to the same network. Token Ring operates at either 4 or 16Mbps. FDDI is similar to Token Ring and operates at 100Mbps. See *Data Link Layer*.

Transport Layer

The OSI model layer responsible for the guaranteed serial delivery of packets between two computers over an internetwork. TCP is the Transport Layer Protocol for the TCP/IP transport protocol.

Transport Protocol

A service that delivers discrete packets of information between any two computers in a network. Higher level connection-oriented services are built upon transport protocols.

UDP (User Datagram Protocol)

A non-guaranteed network packet protocol implemented on IP that is far faster than TCP because it doesn't have flow-control overhead. UDP can be implemented as a reliable transport when some higher-level protocol (such as NetBIOS) exists to make sure that required data eventually will be retransmitted in local area environments.

Universal Naming Convention (UNC)

A multivendor, multiplatform convention for identifying shared resources on a network.

UNIX

A multitasking operating system, created by AT&T's Bell Labs, that is used on a wide variety of computers including Internet servers.

UseNet

A massive distributed database of news feeds and special interest groups maintained on the Internet and accessible through most Web browsers.

Wide Area Network (WAN)

A network that extends across multiple locations. Each location typically has a local area network (LAN) and the LANs are connected together in a WAN. Typically used for enterprise networking.

Windows Internet Name Service (WINS)

A network service for Microsoft networks that provides Windows computers with Internet numbers for specified NetBIOS names, facilitating browsing and intercommunication over TCP/IP networks.

World Wide Web (WWW)

A term used for the collection of computers on the Internet running HTTP (Hypertext Transfer Protocol) servers. The WWW allows for text and graphics to have hyperlinks, which connect users to other servers. Using a Web *browser* such as Netscape or Mosaic, a user can cross-link from one server to another at the click of a button.

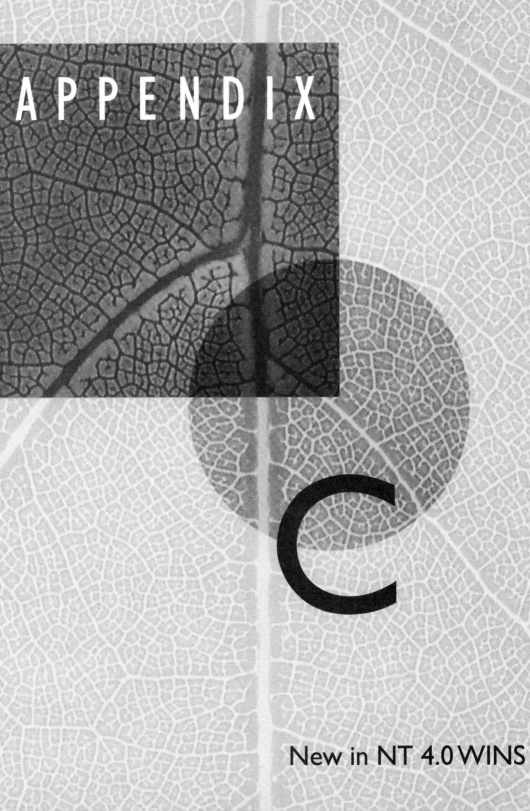

APPENDIX

C

New in NT 4.0 WINS

INS changed a bit in Microsoft NT Server 4.0, but not much. As you know from the DNS chapter, WINS will be going away in NT 5.0, but if you have older servers (3.5x,4.0), WINS will still be necessary. The text provided below is for informational purposes only, as none of it is included on the NT TCP/IP 4.0 test.

Burst Mode

Events, like many WINS clients coming online for the first time, are when the burst handling parameter comes in handy. The parameter is used to temporarily maintain a steady state in the WINS server. Why? Because these situations result in a large amount of name registration and name refresh traffic occurring en masse, and WINS servers currently store only 25,000 name registrations and refresh queries in their queue at maximum before they starts dropping queries. Here's where burst parameter comes in: with it, the WINS server can be configured to send success responses to those clients whose requests have been abandoned. The server's responses have TTLs that serve to slow down the refresh rate of the barrage of clients, and thereby regulate the burst of WINS client traffic. The elegant result is a steady state being reached a lot more quickly.

Great! But how do you configure the burst parameter? Well, it's enabled by creating the BurstHandling key under the HKEY_LOCAL_MACHINE\ SYSTEM\CurrentControlSet\Services\WINS\PARAMETERS key and setting the value to 1. You do this by setting the following parameters:

- Name: BurstHandling
- Type = REG_DWORD

- Value: 0 or 1
- Default = 0

Hitting the Wall and Working through It— Administering WINS through a Firewall

For remote WINS administration, set up an initial session to port 135, followed by another session to some random port above 1024. Why? Because the WINS administrator uses "dynamic endpoints" with a remote procedure call (RPC), and you can't make Internet firewalls pass this traffic when the port is not consistent. In Windows NT 4.0, system defaults for dynamic port appropriation are defined in the Registry.

A list of all ports available (or not available) from the Internet should be defined in the Registry in order to allow you to administrate WINS remotely through a firewall. You do this with the following keys, found under:

HKEY_LOCAL_MACHINE\SOFTWAREMICROSOFT\RPC\INTERNET

Ports: Delimits a set of IP port ranges comprised of either all the ports available from the Internet, or all the ports that aren't available. Each string either represents a solitary port or a set of ports, and will look like "1050-2000" or "1994." The RPC run time will regard the whole configuration invalid if any entries are outside the range of 0 to 65535, or if any string can't be interpreted. Type in **REG_MULTI_SZ - (set of IP port ranges)**.

PortsInternetAvailable The Y and N stand for (surprise) yes and no. If the ports listed in the Ports key enjoy a Y status, that means you're looking at all the Internet-available ports on that machine. If it's N, the ports listed in the Ports key equal unavailable Internet ports. Type in **REG_SZ - Y or N** (not case-sensitive).

UseInternetPorts Designates the system default policy. If it's Y, the processes that will be using the default are assigned ports from those in the Internet-available ports set. If it's N, they're only assigned ports out of the set of intranet-only ports. Type in **REG_SZ - Y or N** (again, not case-sensitive).

How Does WINS Check for Consistency?

Even though it's possible to periodically check the WINS database for consistency in Windows NT 4.0, consistency checking is a very network-intensive thing that consumes a lot of cycles on the WINS server. This is because WINS replicates all records for the owner whose records are being checked by another WINS machine so it can ascertain if its database is in synch with it. Good ol' common sense and discretion is the key when selecting the values for the different parameters below. The important thing to keep in mind and carefully consider here is your existing network configuration. How many WINS servers, WAN/LAN lines between them, and how many WINS clients are you working with, etc.? The answers will imply the best values for these parameters for your individual situation. You do this by creating the ConsistencyCheck key under:

HKEY_LOCAL_MACHINE\SYSTEM\CurrentControlSet\Services
WINS\PARAMETERS

The following values are options you can create under this key:

- **TimeInterval** Delimits the time interval when WINS will do a consistency check. Its default is 24 hours. Type in: **REG_DWORD -(Number of Seconds)**

- **SpTime** Pinpoints the exact time in *hh:mm:ss* format that the first consistency check will be done. Successive ones will be done periodically at TimeInterval seconds. Its default is: 2:00:00 (2:00 AM). To set it, you type in: **REG_SZ *hh:mm:ss***

- **MaxRecsAtATime** You guessed it—this limits the maximum number of records that'll be replicated in each consistency check cycle. WINS does consistency checks on each WINS owner's records. So, when it finishes checking one, it'll either go on to the next on its list, or stop depending on how the MaxRecsAtATime value is set. Its default is 30000. To set this one, type in: **REG_DWORD (Number of Recs)**

- **Name: UseRplPnrs** If this is set to anything but a zero value, WINS will only contact its pull partners when doing consistency checks. If the owner with records that need to be checked *is* a pull partner, then great—it'll be used. Otherwise, some random pull partner will be. To set it, type in: **DWORD 0 (or non-zero value)**

WINS never ever deletes records in its database if the partner with which it's verifying them isn't the owner. This isn't computer courtesy; it's because WINS has no idea which database is more current.

WINSCHK—Huh?

There's a new tool in the Windows NT 4.0 Resource Kit bag of tricks—WINSCHK. It's a command-line utility that checks name and version number inconsistencies that can creep up in WINS databases. It also monitors replication activity, plus authenticates replication topology in an enterprise network—a very cool, particularly useful tool indeed! With WINSCHK, you can not only check and resolve WINS database replication issues remotely, but also pinpoint some of the most common problems that cause database inconsistencies—and all by running this little gem in a central location! It supplements WINSCL with options geared towards flagging potential causes for database inconsistencies, including these likely demons:

- Asymmetric replication topologies

- High communication failures

WINSCHK recognizes both of these and responds by giving you a warning. It also helps monitor replication activity by allowing you to:

- Check for version number inconsistencies.

- Check up on the state of one or more names in various WINS databases in your network.

WINSCHK can be used in interactive or noninteractive mode, and when it's in the latter, it keeps a log of all its activities in the local directory (WINSTST.LOG). You can choose to monitor WINS activity in the background too. Doing this will cause all logs to be dumped into MONITOR.LOG. Here's a list of WINSCHK options:

> **0: Toggle the interactive switch** The default value is Interactive. All status messages will be logged into WINSTST.LOG, and if the Interactive switch is on, it permits you the option of having status messages printed on the command window.

1: Test for names (in NAMES.TXT) against WINS servers (in SERVERS .TXT) It tests for N names against M servers: A quick tool to check for consistency between various WINS servers, this utility is driven by two flat files that you can revise with your favorite text editor. The IP address of a starting WINS server from which a list of all the replicating WINS servers is built up to query is in the file SERVERS.TXT. The file NAMES.TXT holds a list of NetBIOS names to query, and may contain multiple NetBIOS names—one per line—that need to be checked. The names you'll see in this file follow this format: <name>*<16th byte>, for example, FOOBAR*20, and names must be in uppercase. This utility will run the list of NetBIOS names querying each WINS server, check for consistency of addresses, and report mismatched IP addresses, plus any instances of "name not found." It will also tattle on unresponsive WINS servers.

2: Check for version number consistencies This is how you get the owner address—version number maps (through an RPC function)— from different WINS servers so you can check how consistent their databases are. You do this by making sure a WINS server always has the highest version number for the records it owns—higher than all other WINS servers populating the network.

Here's what it'll look like:

```
A      A      B      C        <---list of owners

A      100    80     79       <---mapping table retrieved from A

B      95     75*    65       <---mapping table retrieved from B

C      78     45     110      <---mapping table retrieved from C
```

An intersection B with B is a problem that requires fixing.

3: Monitor WINS servers to detect communication failures between WINS servers This has two versions in which it can be run: once or continuous, with the latter running every three hours by default. Since it generates a lot of network activity, we recommend not running this option too often. It monitors WINS servers periodically to ensure that the primary and backup aren't down at the same time, and logs its activity in MONITOR.LOG. It also retrieves WINS statistics periodically, ensuring that replication failures aren't happening consistently. No matter what, the administrator is alerted to the situations it detects.

4: Verify replication configuration setup This option checks the registry of a WINS server to make sure each partner is pull and push, and that there's a defined pull interval. It'll check into this for each partner, covering the entire network (and therefore you), and flags any weird partner relationships it finds.

99: Exit this tool

Designing the WINS Infrastructure

It's important to understand the physical infrastructure of your network when designing your WINS environment. You also need to understand NetBIOS names and convergence time, which we'll explain below.

Design Pragmatism

For an enterprise network environment often spanning the globe via a routed network, you need NetBIOS connectivity. NetBIOS name spaces are flat, each of them has to be unique, and you need something to convert the NetBIOS name to an address. As described in RFC 1001 and RFC 1002, WINS is Microsoft's implementation of a NetBIOS name server, furnishing a distributed database for NetBIOS names and their corresponding addresses. Local WINS servers will replicate the entries (NetBIOS name/IP address pairs) that WINS clients have registered to them to other WINS servers, ensuring that NetBIOS names are unique, and making local name resolution possible.

What about WINS System Convergence Time?

An important consideration indeed! For your specific configuration, use the worst-case scenario—the longest it could possibly take to get a new entry in a WINS server database replicated to all the others. Since you've allowed a better than good chunk of time for your convergence to occur, you've guaranteed that name queries for a new name will be successful. If ample time isn't allowed, you'll run the risk that clients might be unable to find the new, or so recently modified, machine. To see how this works, take a look at Figure C.1.

FIGURE C.1

WINS convergence

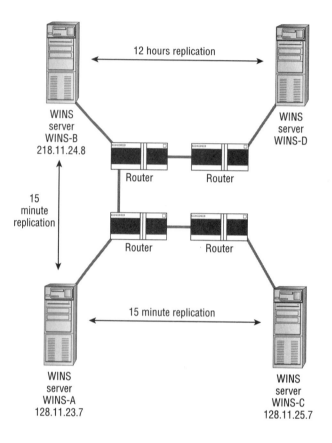

Assume a client is registering its name in WINS_C. Since other clients can query WINS_C for this name, they can get the IP address, but at this moment, if they query the *other* WINS servers (A, B, and D), they won't get a positive response—not until the entry is replicated to A, B, and D. When the push update count threshold (as configured on C) is exceeded, or when the pull replication interval (15 minutes, as configured on A) expires, replication from WINS_C to WINS_A will then take place. A guarantee that the entry will be replicated can only be had when the pull replication interval expires. And even then, name queries to WINS servers B and D may still be unsuccessful. However, after 15 minutes, it's guaranteed the entry will have been replicated to WINS server B, and after 12 hours, it's guaranteed to have been replicated to WINS server D. In this configuration, the convergence time is twice 15 minutes plus 12 hours, or 12.5 hours.

It's possible for name query requests to succeed before the convergence time has passed, but the entries would have to be replicated over some other path, if available. Also, if an update count threshold was passed before the replication interval expired, the result would be an earlier replication of the new entry. Remember, the longer the replication path, the longer the convergence time. Our example of 15 minutes between sites is pretty short by reality's standards, while 12 hours is actually rather long—even when hopping continents. The wisest choice in setting these intervals really depends on individual network requirements, and is mostly a result the design choices that created it.

And It All Comes Down to Fault Tolerance

We know it sounds cliché, but bear with us—there are basically two types of failures:

1. A WINS server crashing or being stopped for maintenance

2. Network failures where links go down or routers fail

In our example in Figure C.1, a WINS_A_or WINS_B failure would cause the network to become segmented, and entries would no longer be replicated between WINS_C to WINS_D. Other clients would be unable to connect to the updated machines because the IP address/name no longer matches for updated clients. But suppose you added replication between WINS_B and WINS_C—that would improve the configuration if WINS_A fails. The same goes for adding replication between WINS_D and WINS_C in the event WINS_B fails.

But why stop there? Why would you only add replication between those servers and not the rest? Because failures of the links between A, B, and C are already covered by the underlying router network which would reroute the traffic should that occur—that's why. Although not the most elegant, efficient scenario when compared to a healthy network, WINS replication will still continue uninterrupted. But any failure on the link between B and D would segment the WINS configuration. Additionally, failures on the B-D link would bring other network traffic to a grinding halt, so you'd want to have an on-demand backup link between D and C. Then, you're covered, and your WINS replication traffic would simply be rerouted by the underlying router infrastructure.

Okay, great—but what if the routers fail—what then? Yes, true—in our example, the routers are all single points of failure, and if one of them fails, it would segment the WINS configuration for sure. A good, generally accepted approach is to look at two simultaneous failures, analyze what their consequences would be, prioritize those, and proceed to come up with backup plans accordingly.

And don't panic—a segmented WINS configuration's not as catastrophic as it sounds. Most of the time, your clients can still resolve the names to addresses, and local WINS servers and/or broadcasts can take care of most of the name resolution. The only gimpy spot has to do with updated or new remote entries—they, of course, would be unknown. Remember, entries aren't dropped at scavenging time when the owning WINS cannot be reached, WINS service can be installed on some other machine, and the database backups can be restored on that new machine.

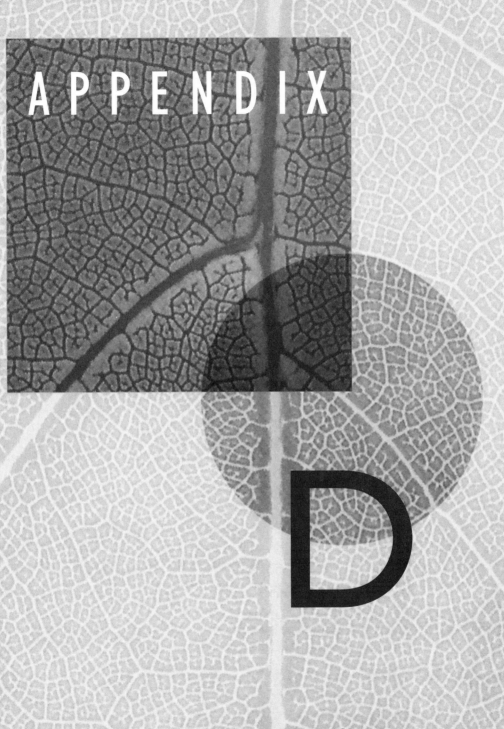

A P P E N D I X

D

NetBT Configuration Parameters

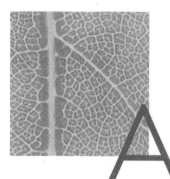

All of the NetBT (NetBIOS over TCP) parameters are Registry values located under one of two different subkeys of HKEY _LOCAL_MACHINE\SYSTEM\CurrentControlSet\Services:

- NETBT\PARAMETERS

- NETBT\ADAPTERS\<*Adapter Name*>, in which <*Adapter Name*> refers to the subkey for a network adapter that NetBT is bound to, such as Lance01.

Values under the latter key(s) are specific to each adapter. If the system is configured with DHCP, then a change in parameters will take affect if the command ipconfig /renew is issued in a command shell. Otherwise, rebooting the system is required for a change in any of these parameters to take affect.

Standard Parameters Configurable from the Registry Editor

The following parameters are installed with default values by the network control panel during the installation of the TCP/IP components. They may be modified using the Registry Editor (REGEDT32.EXE).

BcastNameQueryCount

Key: Netbt\Parameters

Value Type: REG_DWORD - Count

Valid Range: 1 to 0xFFFF

Default: 3

Description: This value determines the number of times NetBT broadcasts a query for a given name without receiving a response.

BcastQueryTimeout

Key: Netbt\Parameters

Value Type: REG_DWORD - Time in milliseconds

Valid Range: 100 to 0xFFFFFFFF

Default: 0x2ee (750 decimal)

Description: This value determines the time interval between successive broadcast name queries for the same name.

CacheTimeout

Key: Netbt\Parameters

Value Type: REG_DWORD - Time in milliseconds

Valid Range: 60000 to 0xFFFFFFFF

Default: 0x927c0 (600000 milliseconds = 10 minutes)

Description: This value determines the time interval that names are cached in the remote name table.

NameServerPort

Key: Netbt\Parameters

Value Type: REG_DWORD - UDP port number

Valid Range: 0 - 0xFFFF

Default: 0x89

Description: This parameter determines the destination port number to which NetBT will send name service–related packets, such as name queries and name registrations, to WINS. The Microsoft WINS listens on port 0x89. NetBIOS name servers from other vendors may listen on different ports.

NameSrvQueryCount

Key: Netbt\Parameters

Value Type: REG_DWORD - Count

Valid Range: 0 - 0xFFFF

Default: 3

Description: This value determines the number of times NetBT sends a query to a WINS server for a given name without receiving a response.

NameSrvQueryTimeout

Key: Netbt\Parameters

Value Type: REG_DWORD - Time in milliseconds

Valid Range: 100 - 0xFFFFFFFF

Default: 0x5DC (1500 milliseconds, 1.5 seconds)

Description: This value determines the time interval between successive name queries to WINS for a given name.

SessionKeepAlive

Key: Netbt\Parameters

Value Type: REG_DWORD - Time in milliseconds

Valid Range: 60,000 - 0xFFFFFFFF

Default: 0x36EE80 (3,600,000 milliseconds, 1 hour)

Description: This value determines the time interval between keepalive transmissions on a session. Setting the value to 0xFFFFFFFF disables keepalives.

Size/Small/Medium/Large

Key: Netbt\Parameters

Value Type: REG_DWORD

Valid Range: 1, 2, 3 (Small, Medium, Large)

Default: 1 (Small)

Description: This value determines the size of the name tables used to store local and remote names. In general, Small is adequate. If the system is acting as a proxy name server, the value is automatically set to Large to increase the size of the name cache hash table. Hash table buckets are sized as follows:

Large: 256

Medium: 128

Small: 16

Optional Parameters Configurable from the Registry Editor

These parameters normally do not exist in the Registry. They may be created to modify the default behavior of the NetBT protocol driver.

BroadcastAddress

Key: Netbt\Parameters

Value Type: REG_DWORD - Four byte, little-endian, encoded IP address

Valid Range: 0 - 0xFFFFFFFF

Default: The ones-broadcast address for each network

Description: This parameter can be used to force NetBT to use a specific address for all broadcast name related packets. By default, NetBT uses the ones-broadcast address appropriate for each network (that is, for a network of 11.101.0.0 with a subnet mask of 255.255.0.0, the subnet broadcast address would be 11.101.255.255). This parameter would be set, for example, if the network uses the zeros-broadcast address (set using the UseZeroBroadcast TCP/IP parameter). The appropriate subnet broadcast address would then be 11.101.0.0 in the example above. This parameter would then be set to 0x0b650000. Note that this parameter is global and will be used on all subnets that NetBT is bound to.

EnableProxyRegCheck

Key: Netbt\Parameters

Value Type: REG_DWORD - Boolean

Valid Range: 0 or 1 (False or True)

Default: 0 (False)

Description: If this parameter is set to 1 (True), the proxy name server will send a negative response to a broadcast name registration if the name is already registered with WINS or is in the proxy's local name cache with a different IP address. The hazard of enabling this feature is that it prevents a system from changing its IP address as long as WINS has a mapping for the name. For this reason, it is disabled by default.

InitialRefreshTimeout

Key: Netbt\Parameters

Value Type: REG_DWORD - Time in milliseconds

Valid Range: 960000 - 0xFFFFFFF

Default: 960000 (16 minutes)

Description: This parameter specifies the initial refresh timeout used by NetBT during name registration. NetBT tries to contact the WINS servers at 1/8th of this time interval when it is first registering names. When it receives a successful registration response, that response will contain the new refresh interval that should be used.

LmhostsTimeout

Key: Netbt\Parameters

Value Type: REG_DWORD - Time in milliseconds

Valid Range: 1000 - 0xFFFFFFFF

Default: 6000 (6 seconds)

Description: This parameter specifies the timeout value for LMHOSTS and DNS name queries. The timer has a granularity of the timeout value, so the actual timeout could be as much as twice the value.

MaxDgramBuffering

Key: Netbt\Parameters

Value Type: REG_DWORD - Count of bytes

Valid Range: 0 - 0xFFFFFFFF

Default: 0x20000 (128Kb)

Description: This parameter specifies the maximum amount of memory that NetBT will dynamically allocate for all outstanding datagram sends. Once this limit is reached, further sends will fail due to insufficient resources.

NodeType

Key: Netbt\Parameters

Value Type: REG_DWORD - Number

Valid Range: 1,2,4,8 (B-node, P-node, M-node, H-node)

Default: 1 or 8 based on the WINS server configuration

Description: This parameter determines what methods NetBT will use to register and resolve names. A B-node system uses broadcasts. A P-node system uses only point-to-point name queries to a name server (WINS). An M-node system broadcasts first, then queries the name server. An H-node system queries the name server first, then broadcasts. Resolution via LMHOSTS and/or DNS, if enabled, will follow these methods. If this key is present, it will override the DhcpNodeType key. If neither key is present, the system defaults to B-node if there are no WINS servers configured for the network. The system defaults to H-node if there is at least one WINS server configured.

RandomAdapter

Key: Netbt\Parameters

Value Type: REG_DWORD - Boolean

Valid Range: 0 or 1 (False or True)

Default: 0 (False)

Description: This parameter applies to a multihomed host only. If it is set to 1 (True), then NetBT will randomly choose the IP address to put in a name query response from all of its bound interfaces. Usually, the response contains the address of the interface that the query arrived on. This feature would be used by a server with two interfaces on the same network for load balancing.

RefreshOpCode

Key: Netbt\Parameters

Value Type: REG_DWORD - Number

Valid Range: 8, 9

Default: 8

Description: This parameter forces NetBT to use a specific opcode in name refresh packets. The specification for the NetBT protocol is somewhat ambiguous in this area. Although the default of 8 used by Microsoft implementations appears to be the intended value, some other implementations, such as those by Ungermann-Bass, use the value 9. Two implementations must use the same opcode to interoperate.

SingleResponse

Key: Netbt\Parameters

Value Type: REG_DWORD - Boolean

Valid Range: 0 or 1 (False or True)

Default: 0 (False)

Description: This parameter applies to a multihomed host only. If this parameter is set to 1 (True), NetBT will only supply an IP address from one of its bound interfaces in name query responses. By default, the addresses of all bound interfaces are included.

WinsDownTimeout

Key: Netbt\Parameters

Value Type: REG_DWORD - Time in milliseconds

Valid Range: 1000 - 0xFFFFFFFF

Default: 15,000 (15 seconds)

Description: This parameter determines the amount of time NetBT will wait before again trying to use WINS after it fails to contact any WINS server. This feature primarily allows computers that are temporarily disconnected from the network, such as laptops, to proceed through boot processing without waiting to timeout each WINS name registration or query individually.

Parameters Configurable from the Network Control Panel Applet

The following parameters can be set via the NCPA. There should be no need to configure them directly.

EnableDns

Key: Netbt\Parameters

Value Type: REG_DWORD - Boolean

Valid Range: 0 or 1 (False or True)

Default: 0 (False)

Description: If this value is set to 1 (True), NetBT will query the DNS for names that cannot be resolved by WINS, broadcast, or the LMHOSTS file.

EnableLmhosts

Key: Netbt\Parameters

Value Type: REG_DWORD - Boolean

Valid Range: 0 or 1 (False or True)

Default: 1 (True)

Description: If this value is set to 1 (True), NetBT will search the LMHOSTS file, if it exists, for names that cannot be resolved by WINS or broadcast. By default, there is no LMHOSTS file database directory (specified by TCPIP\PARAMETERS\DATABASEPATH), so no action will be taken. This value is written by the Advanced TCP/IP configuration dialog of the NCPA.

EnableProxy

Key: Netbt\Parameters

Value Type: REG_DWORD - Boolean

Valid Range: 0 or 1 (False or True)

Default: 0 (False)

Description: If this value is set to 1 (True), the system will act as a proxy name server for the networks to which NetBT is bound. A proxy name server answers broadcast queries for names that it has resolved through WINS. A proxy name server allows a network of B-node implementations to connect to servers on other subnets that are registered with WINS.

NameServer

Key: Netbt\Adapters\<*Adapter Name*>

Value Type: REG_SZ - Dotted decimal IP address (i.e., 11.101.1.200)

Valid Range: Any valid IP address

Default: Blank (no address)

Description: This parameter specifies the IP address of the primary WINS server. If this parameter contains a valid value, it overrides the DHCP parameter of the same name.

NameServerBackup

Key: Netbt\Adapters\<*Adapter Name*>

Value Type: REG_SZ - Dotted decimal IP address (i.e., 11.101.1.200)

Valid Range: Any valid IP address

Default: Blank (no address)

Description: This parameter specifies the IP address of the backup WINS server. If this parameter contains a valid value, it overrides the DHCP parameter of the same name.

ScopeId

Key: Netbt\Parameters

Value Type: REG_SZ - Character string

Valid Range: Any valid DNS domain name consisting of two dot-separated parts, or an asterisk (*)

Default: None

Description: This parameter specifies the NetBIOS name scope for the node. This value must not begin with a period. If this parameter contains a valid value, it will override the DHCP parameter of the same name. A blank value (empty string) will be ignored. Setting this parameter to the value "*" indicates a null scope and will override the DHCP parameter.

Nonconfigurable Parameters

The following parameters are created and used internally by the NetBT components. They should never be modified using the Registry Editor. They are listed here for reference only.

DhcpNameServer

Key: Netbt\Adapters\<Adapter Name>

Value Type: REG_SZ - Dotted decimal IP address (i.e., 11.101.1.200)

Valid Range: Any valid IP address

Default: None

Description: This parameter specifies the IP address of the primary WINS server. It is written by the DHCP client service, if enabled. A valid NameServer value will override this parameter.

DhcpNameServerBackup

Key: Netbt\Adapters\<Adapter Name>

Value Type: REG_SZ - Dotted decimal IP address (i.e., 11.101.1.200)

Valid Range: Any valid IP address

Default: None

Description: This parameter specifies the IP address of the backup WINS server. It is written by the DHCP client service, if enabled. A valid Backup-NameServer value will override this parameter.

DhcpNodeType

Key: Netbt\Parameters

Value Type: REG_DWORD - Number

Valid Range: 1 - 8

Default: 1

Description: This parameter specifies the NetBT node type. It is written by the DHCP client service, if enabled. A valid NodeType value will override this parameter. See the entry for NodeType for a complete description.

DhcpScopeId

Key: Netbt\Parameters

Value Type: REG_SZ - Character string

Valid Range: A dot-separated name string such as microsoft.com

Default: None

Description: This parameter specifies the NetBIOS name scope for the node. It is written by the DHCP client service, if enabled. This value must *not* begin with a period. See the entry for ScopeId for more information.

NbProvider

Key: Netbt\Parameters

Value Type: REG_SZ - Character string

Valid Range: _tcp

Default: _tcp

Description: This parameter is used internally by the RPC component. The default value should not be changed.

TransportBindName

Key: Netbt\Parameters

Value Type: REG_SZ - Character string

Valid Range: N/A

Default: \Device\

Description: This parameter is used internally during product development. The default value should not be changed.

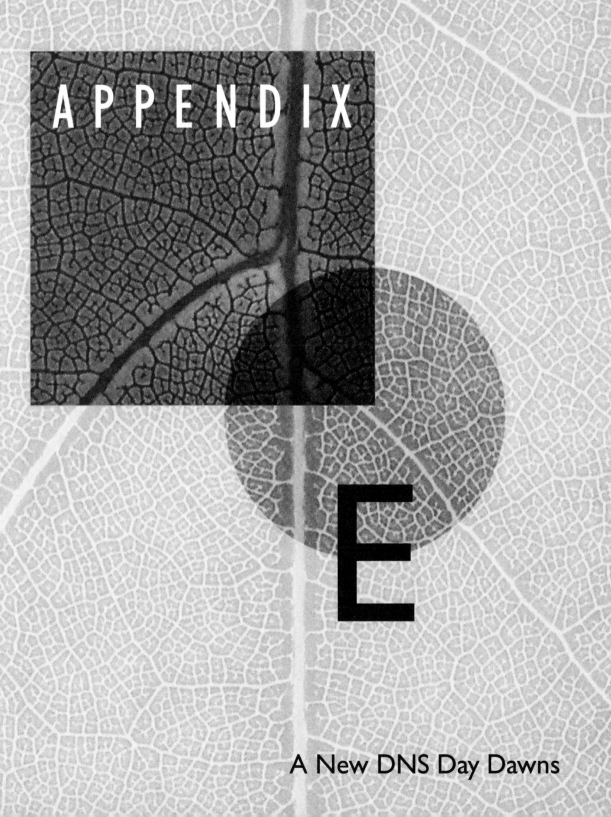

APPENDIX

E

A New DNS Day Dawns

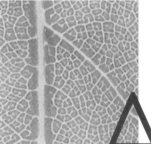

As said, soon Windows NT will come with an Enhanced Directory Services implementation, and a whole new way to deal with domains, users, groups, and trusts. In the brave new Windows NT world, Enhanced DS domains will directly map to DNS domains, and administration for groups and users will be the duty of Organizational Units in the directory. These glittering new Enhanced DS domains will predictably be a lot better than the dusty domains of today.

A major point is that in the Enhanced Directory Services network, DNS will be the primary locator service. To find other hosts on the network and servers running the DS service, Enhanced DS clients will use DNS similar to the way clients running Windows NT 4 use WINS today.

Let's canvass some future Enhanced Directory Services concepts and the new standards that'll soon change DNS, exploring first what a solid prospective DNS/DS design may look like. We hope this'll indicate how best to design your network now to be ready for future migration. (We actually know a guy who sits home on the weekend reading RFCs, so we've included some Web pages that list them, in case you're like him.)

Dynamic DNS

Windows NT 4 includes two name-to-IP address mapping services—WINS and DNS. One key difference between the two is that WINS accommodates *dynamic* registration of NetBIOS names and associated IP addresses, but DNS names and associated IP addresses must be *statically* entered into the DNS service database.

Static registration of name-to-IP address information is not a good thing in the Windows NT/Windows 95 operating systems. Why? Because in all but very small Microsoft network installations, machines don't have static IP address assignments. Machines generally use DHCP to obtain an IP address assignment each time they initialize.

A proposal for dynamic registration of DNS information is under consideration by the IETF (Internet Engineering Task Force). You can download the specification from `http://ds.internic.net/internet-drafts/draft-ietf-dnsind-dynDNS-09.txt`.

With DNS dynamic update, a client machine, having obtained its assigned IP address from DHCP, can use a standard protocol to dynamically register its DNS name and IP address in the DNS database. In the Windows NT 4 time frame, it was determined that dynamic update shouldn't be implemented because of the fluid status of the specification, and scalability concerns. The current dynamic DNS proposal is based on a "pull from single master" replication model and, consequently, if the single master is down or unreachable, dynamic updates just don't happen. Microsoft favors a multiple master arrangement similar to WINS that would allow registrations to continue without a single point of failure.

In the long run, using DNS dynamic update is better than using Windows NT 4 DNS-WINS integration for the following reasons:

- DNS-WINS integration doesn't enable efficient DNS reverse lookup (resolution of IP address to DNS name). Reverse lookup is used for security purposes by Internet, WWW (World Wide Web), and firewall services. Due to the recent proliferation of such services, the need for efficient DNS reverse lookup is significantly on the rise. If DNS dynamic update is used instead of WINS integration, the problem goes "poof."

- DNS-WINS integration doesn't enable a proper "primary-backup" relationship between Microsoft and non-Microsoft DNS name servers. This is due to the fact that non-Microsoft DNS name servers aren't capable of WINS lookup. For migration purposes, you should install Microsoft DNS servers as backups of non-Microsoft DNS primary servers. If DNS dynamic update is used instead of WINS integration, again, the problem vaporizes.

- Non-Microsoft hosts don't register in WINS, and therefore cannot "dynamically register" in DNS. DNS dynamic update is an IETF standard. If implemented (by Microsoft), non-Microsoft hosts (that support the DNS dynamic update standard) could dynamically register in the Microsoft DNS, and Microsoft hosts could dynamically register in a non-Microsoft DNS, as long as it supports the DNS dynamic update standard.

- WINS registration isn't secure, and has no reasonable means of becoming so. The IETF has worked to complete a standard for adding a security feature to DNS dynamic update. Some companies have already decided to forego a standard and have simply rolled out their own security implementation.

- Microsoft-based clients can't register with any of the current versions of dynamic DNS, and dynamic DNS servers can't replicate their dynamic data to other non-dynamic DNS servers.

- In current implementations of dynamic DNS, the primary is a single point of failure. All of the clients must register their names and IP addresses with this machine, so if it's down, then no updates to the DNS database can occur.

IPv6 (IPng)

IPv6 is defined in RFC 1883 (`http://ds2.internic.net/rfc/rfc1883.txt`). This protocol used to be referred to as "IP Next Generation" or "IPng." IP version 6 (IPv6) is a new version of the Internet Protocol designed as a successor to IP version 4 (Ipv4, RFC-791). The current header in IPv4 hasn't been changed or upgraded since the 1970s! The initial design, of course, failed to anticipate the growth of the Internet and eventual exhaustion of the Ipv4 address space. Ipv6 is an entirely new packet structure which is incompatible with IPv4 systems. The changes from IPv4 to IPv6 fall into the following categories:

- **Expanded addressing capabilities:** IPv6 has 128-bit source and destination IP addresses. With approximately 5 billion people in the world using a 128 bit address, there are 2^{128} addresses, or almost 2^{96} addresses per person! An IPv6 valid IP address will look something like this:

`3F3A:AE67:F240:56C4:3409:AE52:220E:3112`

IPv6 uses 16 octets; when written, it is divided into eight octet pairs, separated by colons and represented in hex.

- **Header format simplification:** The IPv6 headers are designed to keep the IP header overhead to a minimum by moving nonessential fields and option fields to extension headers that are placed after the IP header. Anything not included in the base IPv6 header can be added through IP extension headers placed after the base IPv6 header.

- **Improved support for extensions and options:** IPv6 can easily be extended for unforeseen features through the adding of extension headers and option fields after the IPv6 base header. Support for new hardware or application technologies is built in.

- **Flow labeling capability:** A new field in the IPv6 header allows the pre-allocation of network resources along a path so that time-dependent services such as voice and video are guaranteed a requested bandwidth with a fixed delay.

With the onset of this new standard, changes will need to be made to the DNS protocol. RFC 1886 (`http://ds2.internic.net/rfc/rfc1886.txt`) defines these changes, which include a new resource record type to store an IPv6 address, a new domain to support lookups based on an IPv6 address, and updated definitions of existing query types that return Internet addresses as part of additional section processing. The extensions are designed to be compatible with existing applications and, in particular, DNS implementations themselves.

Current support for the storage of Internet addresses in the DNS cannot easily be extended to support IPv6 addresses since applications assume that address queries return 32-bit IPv4 addresses.

Incremental Transfers—Multimaster Replication

Incremental Transfer serves to permit the propagation of changes to a DNS database quickly, and Windows NT 4 doesn't support it—not yet. This protocol's specialty is the reduction of latency and the quantity of data sent during a zone transfer. It accomplishes this in two ways.

- Notification is used to reveal changes in a zone file to servers and is achieved by the NOTIFY extension of DNS (Microsoft DNS support NOTIFY in Windows NT 4). To find out more about the NOTIFY specification, look up the Internet draft at `http://ds.internic.net/internet-drafts/draft-ietf-dnsind-notify-07.txt`.

- Zone propagation has been refined to send only changed information—a lot better than sending out the whole shebang as is currently the practice! To look into this further, check out the Internet draft at `http://ds.internic.net/internet-drafts/draft-ietf-dnsind-ixfr-06.txt`.

Dynamic data replication will work much like WINS works today, except instead of replicating a whole bunch of unnecessary data to each and every server like WINS does, the data will be kept within the zone itself.

Secure DNS

You might be thinking that as DNS becomes so critical to the operational part of Internet infrastructure, we'll all need a lot more in the way of security than is currently available. You're right—a defined method of security *will* need to be put in place to assure data integrity and authentication. Extensions to the DNS are described in the IETF-DRAFT *DNS Protocol Security Extensions—30 January 1996*. They provide these services to security-aware resolvers or applications through the use of *cryptographic digital signatures*—what? Well, these are included in secured zones as resource records, and in many cases, security can still be provided even through non-security-aware DNS servers.

Extensions also provide for storage of authenticated public keys in the DNS. This storage of keys can support general public key distribution service as well as DNS security. The stored keys enable security-aware resolvers to learn the authenticating key of zones in addition to those for which they are initially configured. And keys associated with DNS names can be retrieved to support other protocols. If that weren't enough, provision is even made for a variety of key types and algorithms. In addition, the security extensions provide for the optional authentication of DNS protocol transactions. For more on this, see `http://ds.internic.net/internet-drafts/draft-ietf-dnssec-secext-09.txt`.

In current implementations of dynamic DNS, the vendors had to come up with their own security protocol because of the lack of a defined standard. Be careful if you use one of these products, because it may become incompatible with future ones when a specification's finally defined!

Migration…from Where?

So, how's it all going to happen? To find out, let's first take a look at the migration process to Enhanced Directory Services. New Enhanced DS domains will be fully interoperable with Windows NT Server domains. This is to say that existing Windows NT Server domains will be able to trust Enhanced DS domains, just as they trust other Windows NT Server domains today. Enhanced DS servers will also be able to function as backup domain controllers. This interoperability will allow the upgrade to Enhanced DS server to occur in an orderly manner, while allowing existing Windows NT Server-based servers to work without modification—pretty clean!

And what's more, the Enhanced DS administration model won't be forced down the throats of administrators until they're ready to use it. What do we mean? Well, even with Enhanced DS servers on the network, you'll be able to maintain all account information in the Windows NT Server domain, using the current Windows NT Server administration tools. In other words, you'll be able to deploy Enhanced DS servers without righteously screwing up your network!

As Enhanced DS servers are deployed, you can begin to store user account information on them while simultaneously continuing to store and administer those accounts in and from the Windows NT Server domain. That means you'll be able to migrate account information to an Enhanced DS server in an incremental fashion as you gain confidence in their stability and capability—a feel-good feature for you and your company. Once your new Enhanced DS servers are well-established, you'll be able to maintain all account information on them, using the Enhanced DS tools. Furthermore, for non-Enhanced DS clients, the new kids on the block will continue to look and act just like Windows NT Server 4.*x*-based servers (even a feel-good feature for your machines, too—wow!).

Once all client and server transitions are complete, the Enhanced DS environment will be the everyday environment for both end users and system administrators. And, the transition enabled by the interoperability between, and integration of, Windows NT Server and Enhanced DS will allow you and your organization to make an easy transition to the unified and global namespace provided by Enhanced DS—as said, all without disrupting the day-to-day operations of the network.

What Happens to IPX and NetBEUI?

Even though the Microsoft direction is distinctly heading toward TCP/IP (true for most other networking vendors as well), there'll still be support for NetBEUI and IPX. Should you choose to use IPX and NetBEUI in the coming version of Windows NT, you'll have to use the NetBIOS interface; but if you choose TCP/IP instead, the NetBIOS interface won't be a required part of the picture.

Well, What about NetBIOS Names?

Obviously, you'll maintain the need to use NetBIOS name resolution on your network as long as you have applications that require NetBIOS names. When you begin the exodus to Enhanced DS, you'll need to find out all of the applications (services and so forth) that require NetBIOS, and come up with a host name migration plan for each.

Finding DCs in an Enhanced Directory Services Environment

Along the route to a genuine Windows NT Enhanced Directory Services environment—one devoid of NetBIOS—you'll follow a required migration path that embraces the use of all three standards for supporting backward compatibility with traditional NetBIOS systems.

When machines running the new Windows NT Enhanced Directory Services start up, they'll use a present WINS protocol for registering NetBIOS names with their WINS servers, and their "A" record (or records), with their DNS server. Thus, Windows NT NetBIOS and DNS name-to-IP-address mappings will be accessible to all machines using Windows NT Enhanced DS, plus those still using Windows for Workgroups, Windows 95, etc.

At startup, Windows NT Enhanced DS servers that contain the Directory Services Database will do the same, plus they'll also register an additional record with the DNS server delimiting location, the DS access protocols supported, and transport protocols, etc. Here's an example of what an Enhanced Directory Services Domain controller (DC) may register:

```
globalnet.nt.mmco.com               A    123.123.123.123

domain-controllers.nt.mmco.com      A    123.123.123.123
```

This provides other Enhanced Directory Services workstations with the information they need to find DCs and validate their security credentials.

Things You Can Count On for the Future

Microsoft will adopt a "secure" dynamic DNS solution, and the clients will automatically register with the DNS. There will also be a process for using DNS to locate the closest Directory Services DC.

The next revision of Directory Services will assume that DNS domains map to DS domains.

Where There Is No Vision...

Here are a few dos and don'ts for creating solid, future-oriented DNS solutions. Follow them, and thou shall not perish.

- If there are servers within a site, then there must be a DNS server within that site, too.

- Create a DNS zone for each Windows NT 4 domain.

- Every site DNS server should be a primary for the site-specific DNS domain and a secondary for the parent DNS domain.

- Windows-based clients should be registered in a site-specific DNS domain.

- Servers running Windows NT Server should be registered in a master DNS domain.

Index

Note to the Reader: Throughout this index **boldface** page numbers indicate primary discussions of a topic. *Italic* page numbers indicate illustrations.

D

O

S

MCSE ELECTIVE STUDY GUIDES FROM NETWORK PRESS®

Sybex's Network Press expands the definitive study guide series for MCSE candidates.

MCSE: TCP/IP FOR NT SERVER 4 STUDY GUIDE THIRD EDITION

EXAM 70-059

TODD LAMMLE
WITH MONICA LAMMLE
AND JAMES CHELLIS

ISBN: 0-7821-2224-8
688pp; 7½" x 9"; Hardcover
$49.99

MCSE: EXCHANGE 5.5 STUDY GUIDE

SECOND EDITION

EXAM 70-081

RICHARD EASLICK
WITH JAMES CHELLIS

ISBN: 0-7821-2261-2
848pp; 7½" x 9"; Hardcover
$49.99

MCSE: INTERNET INFORMATION SERVER 4 STUDY GUIDE

SECOND EDITION

EXAM 70-087

MATTHEW STREBE
CHARLES PERKINS

ISBN: 0-7821-2248-5
704pp; 7½" x 9"; Hardcover
$49.99

MCSE: SQL SERVER 6.5 ADMINISTRATION STUDY GUIDE

LANCE MORTENSEN
RICK SAWTELL
MICHAEL LEE

ISBN: 0-7821-2172-1
672pp; 7½" x 9"; Hardcover
$49.99

MCSE: PROXY SERVER 2 Study Guide

EXAM 70-088

ERIK ROZELL
AND TODD LAMMLE
WITH JAMES CHELLIS

ISBN: 0-7821-2194-2
576pp; 7½" x 9"; Hardcover
$49.99

MCSE: EXCHANGE 5 STUDY GUIDE

RICHARD EASLICK
WITH JAMES CHELLIS

ISBN: 0-7821-1967-0
656pp; 7½" x 9"; Hardcover
$49.99

Microsoft® Certified
Professional
Approved Study Guide

NETWORK PRESS®
SYBEX

STUDY GUIDES FOR THE MICROSOFT CERTIFIED SYSTEMS ENGINEER EXAMS

NETWORK PRESS® PRESENTS
MCSE TEST SUCCESS

THE PERFECT COMPANION BOOKS TO THE MCSE STUDY GUIDES

MCSE Test Success:
NETWORKING ESSENTIALS

EXAM 70-058

TODD LAMMLE

GET READY FOR THE EXAM—
OBJECTIVE BY OBJECTIVE

MASTER ALL THE MATERIAL
YOU NEED TO KNOW

PRACTICE ON 500 REVIEW
QUESTIONS AND SAMPLE
TEST QUESTIONS

Microsoft Certified
Professional
Approved Study Guide

ISBN: 0-7821-2146-2
352pp; 7¹/₂" x 9"; Softcover
$24.99

MCSE Test Success:
NT SERVER 4

EXAM 70-067

LISA DONALD

GET READY FOR THE EXAM—
OBJECTIVE BY OBJECTIVE

MASTER ALL THE MATERIAL
YOU NEED TO KNOW

PRACTICE ON 500 REVIEW
QUESTIONS AND SAMPLE
TEST QUESTIONS

Microsoft Certified
Professional
Approved Study Guide

ISBN: 0-7821-2148-9
352pp; 7¹/₂" x 9"; Softcover
$24.99

MCSE Test Success:
NT WORKSTATION 4

EXAM 70-073

TODD LAMMLE
LISA DONALD

GET READY FOR THE EXAM—
OBJECTIVE BY OBJECTIVE

MASTER ALL THE MATERIAL
YOU NEED TO KNOW

PRACTICE ON 500
REVIEW QUESTIONS AND
SAMPLE TEST QUESTIONS

Microsoft Certified
Professional
Approved Study Guide

ISBN: 0-7821-2149-7
400pp; 7¹/₂" x 9"; Softcover
$24.99

MCSE Test Success:
NT SERVER 4
IN THE ENTERPRISE

EXAM 70-068

LISA DONALD

GET READY FOR THE EXAM—
OBJECTIVE BY OBJECTIVE

MASTER ALL THE MATERIAL
YOU NEED TO KNOW

PRACTICE ON MORE THAN 500
REVIEW QUESTIONS AND SAMPLE
TEST QUESTIONS

Microsoft Certified
Professional
Approved Study Guide

ISBN: 0-7821-2147-0
442pp; 7¹/₂" x 9"; Softcover
$24.99

Here's what you need to know to pass the MCSE tests.

- Review concise summaries of key information

- Boost your knowledge with 400 review questions

- Get ready for the test with 200 tough practice test questions

Other MCSE Test Success titles:

- **Core Requirements Box Set**
  (4 books, 1 CD)
  [ISBN: 0-7821-2296-5] April 1998

- **Windows® 95**
  [ISBN: 0-7821-2252-3] May 1998

- **Exchange Server 5.5**
  [ISBN: 0-7821-2250-7] May 1998

- **TCP/IP for NT® 4**
  [ISBN: 0-7821-2251-5] May 1998

Microsoft Certified
Professional
Approved Study Guide

NETWORK PRESS®
SYBEX

NT® IN THE REAL WORLD

THE INFORMATION YOU NEED TO BUILD, SECURE, AND OPTIMIZE NT® NETWORKS

ISBN: 0-7821-2163-2
1,664 pp; 7^1/$_2$" x 9"; Hardcover
$59.99

ISBN: 0-7821-2123-3
544 pp; 7^1/$_2$" x 9"; Softcover
$44.99

ISBN: 0-7821-2006-7
929 pp; 7^1/$_2$" x 9"; Hardcover
$59.99

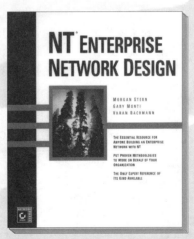

ISBN: 0-7821-2156-X
624 pp; 7^1/$_2$" x 9"; Hardcover
$54.99

NETWORK PRESS®
SYBEX

Take the
interactive
MULTIMEDIA COMPUTER-BASED TRAINING Challenge

Installation

Installation for Win95, NT 3.51 and NT 4.0

1. Start MS Windows 95, NT 3.51 or NT 4.0
2. Insert the CD into the CD-ROM drive
3. Choose "Run" from the Start button
4. Type D:\setup.exe (If necessary, substitute D with correct letter for your CD-ROM drive)
5. Follow the instructions that are found on the screen.
6. After the installation is complete, MS Video for Windows will launch. Installing the program is not necessary, simply select "Exit".

What's on this CD-ROM?

The complementary LearnKey training CD-ROM contained in this book is only the first course of a complete series. It is provided as a sample of what LearnKey's interactive training can do for you while you begin to learn topics relative to the content of this book. Each LearnKey CD-ROM combines expert instruction with interactive exercises. Our Microsoft Certified Trainers help perfect your MCSE skills, and our intuitive interface enables you to apply the techniques you've learned.

The Training Session begins with instruction from our Microsoft Certified experts in a digital movie window. Instructors demonstrate how to install and configure Microsoft networking software.

Each Challenge Session allows you to perform procedures learned in the Training Session through interactive task simulations. Two "Help" features are available to walk you through specific tasks.

Testing Sessions examine your network administration abilities. Each test concludes with a performance-based progress report that pinpoints your areas of strength and weakness. LearnKey's MCSE training program is an ideal way to enhance your networking skills and prepare to pass Microsoft certification exams.

In order for more than one user to use this CD, you must purchase additional site licenses. For more information regarding site licenses, or to purchase the remaining volumes in this set, call 800-865-0165.

Technical Support & FAQ

LearnKey provides comprehensive technical support online. Please refer any installation or troubleshooting questions to our technical support team at www.learnkey.com.

MCSE: TCP/IP for NT Server 4 Study Guide, Third Edition

Exam 70-059: Objectives